# REMAPPING
# COLD WAR MEDIA

# REMAPPING COLD WAR MEDIA

Institutions, Infrastructures, Translations

ALICE LOVEJOY and MARI PAJALA, *editors*

INDIANA UNIVERSITY PRESS

This book is a publication of

Indiana University Press
Office of Scholarly Publishing
Herman B Wells Library 350
1320 East 10th Street
Bloomington, Indiana 47405 USA

iupress.org

© 2022 by Indiana University Press

All rights reserved
No part of this book may be reproduced or utilized in any form or by any means, electronic or mechanical, including photocopying and recording, or by any information storage and retrieval system, without permission in writing from the publisher. The paper used in this publication meets the minimum requirements of the American National Standard for Information Sciences—Permanence of Paper for Printed Library Materials, ANSI Z39.48–1992.

Manufactured in the United States of America

First printing 2022

Cataloging information is available from the Library of Congress.

ISBN 978-0-253-06219-2 (hardcover)
ISBN 978-0-253-06220-8 (paperback)
ISBN 978-0-253-06221-5 (e-book)

# CONTENTS

Acknowledgments  vii
Note on Translation and Transliteration  ix

1. Introduction / *Alice Lovejoy and Mari Pajala*  1

PART I. MOBILE FORMS

2. Stalin Boulevard: Panoramic Vistas and Urban Planning in Eastern European Photobooks / *Katie Trumpener*  17
3. *The Peace Train:* Anticosmopolitanism, Internationalism, and Jazz on Czechoslovak Radio during Stalinism / *Rosamund Johnston*  43
4. Soviet Drama with Commercial Breaks: Living the Cold War in 1970s Finnish Television / *Anu Koivunen*  61

PART II. DISTRIBUTION, ADAPTATION, RECEPTION

5. Soviet Cinema in 1960s Cuba: Between Cold War Logics and Thirdworldist Affinities / *Masha Salazkina*  77
6. From the Antechamber to the International Stage: Early-Career Directors from Hungary at the Mannheim Film Festival in the Late 1970s / *Sonja Simonyi*  99
7. Manic Miners of the World, Unite!: How the British Hit Computer Game Got a Second Life in Czechoslovakia / *Jaroslav Švelch*  117
8. Between Scripts: Radio Berlin International (RBI) and Its Swedish Audience in November 1989 / *Marie Cronqvist*  139

## PART III. TRANSLATION

9. On Soviet Spoken Cinema / *Elena Razlogova*    157
10. A GDR Writer in America: Christa Wolf's Visit to Oberlin and the Circulation of Her Writing as World Literature / *Brangwen Stone*    176
11. Translating Cold War Internationalism: Allegoresis in Ryszard Kapuściński's Literary Reportage / *Marla Zubel*    193
12. Traveling with the President: Finnish-Soviet State Visits and 1970s Television Diplomacy / *Laura Saarenmaa*    211

## PART IV. INFRASTRUCTURE AND PRODUCTION

13. Hollywood Going East: State-Socialist Studios' Opportunistic Business with American Producers / *Petr Szczepanik*    227
14. Envisioning the Revolutionary South: The Soviet-Italian Coproduction *Life Is Beautiful* (1979) / *Stefano Pisu*    245
15. Dividing the Cosmos? INTELSAT, Intersputnik, and the Development of Transnational Satellite Communications Infrastructures during the Cold War / *Christine Evans and Lars Lundgren*    260
16. Spy from the Cloud: From Big Brother to Big Data / *Anikó Imre*    277

Index    297

# ACKNOWLEDGMENTS

THIS BOOK FIRST TOOK SHAPE during a conference, "Remapping European Media Cultures during the Cold War: Networks, Encounters, Exchanges," held at the University of Minnesota in spring 2017. We thank all of the conference's participants for the lively, generative dialogue at the event, which convinced us that the conversation should continue in print. We are particularly grateful to Tom Wolfe, who co-organized the conference with us and has remained an important interlocutor, as well as to Evelyn Davidheiser, Ruth Hodgins, Emily Janisch, Howard Louthan, Jim Parente, and Klaas van der Sanden for their collaboration in organizing the conference and its associated screening at the Walker Art Center.

The conference—and by extension the book—was made possible by the generous sponsorship of, at the University of Minnesota, the Government of Finland/David and Nancy Speer Visiting Professor in Finnish Studies, the Imagine Fund, the College of Liberal Arts, and the Dean's First-Year Research and Creative Scholars program, which supported the work of our talented editorial assistant, Ethan Voss.

We did not expect to complete the book in the midst of a pandemic, and we thank the contributors for their patience, cooperation, and enthusiasm in the face of the numerous difficulties Covid-19 posed to research and writing; we extend special thanks to Katie Trumpener for her tremendous efforts in sourcing images for chapter 2. We were fortunate to be able to workshop the introduction with the Cold War Media reading group at New York University, whose members offered helpful and inspiring feedback. And in the book's final stages, Erik McDonald generously helped us standardize its Russian transliterations.

At Indiana University Press, we have been supported by a wonderful team, including Janice Frisch, Allison Chaplin, Sophia Hebert, Nancy Lightfoot, and Pete Feely. We are grateful to Allison for her guidance; to the anonymous reviewers for their thoughtful, detailed readings of the manuscript; and to our indexer, Alexander Trotter.

# NOTE ON TRANSLATION AND TRANSLITERATION

UNLESS OTHERWISE INDICATED, ALL TRANSLATIONS in this book are the authors' own. The bibliography and notes use the simplified Library of Congress transliteration system for Russian names, words, and titles. In the text, the same system is used with a few modifications. In people's names, the final -ii has been replaced by -y, and the apostrophe representing the Russian soft sign (ь) has been omitted. Well-known names appear in their established English spellings (Mayakovsky). A few names that might have been misleading if transliterated in the usual way have been treated as special cases (Yuri, Yuli, and Vasiliev instead of Iury, Iuly, and Vasilev).

# REMAPPING COLD WAR MEDIA

CHAPTER 1

INTRODUCTION

Alice Lovejoy and Mari Pajala

ON A SEPTEMBER EVENING IN 1966, television viewers in Finland and the Estonian Soviet Socialist Republic gathered in front of their sets to watch a quiz show with the Finnish-Estonian title *Neighbor Quiz / Friendship Match* (*Naapurivisa / Sõprusvõistlus*, the first word in Finnish, the second in Estonian) (see fig. 1.1). The program, broadcast live from Helsinki, was a collaboration between Finland's sole commercial television company, Mainos-TV (MTV), and Estonian television (ETV). Before a jury of two elderly professors of Finno-Ugric linguistics, Estonian and Finnish teams answered questions about theater, music, space travel, and the history of ancient Greece and Rome. Musical performances by popular singers from both countries were interspersed throughout the competition.[1] Emphasizing its cultured, erudite tone, the program was bilingual, yet untranslated: the Estonian and Finnish hosts spoke their own languages, which viewers in both countries were encouraged to understand.[2] The initial round of *Neighbor Quiz / Friendship Match* was such a success that ETV and MTV each produced one show annually until 1970. Meanwhile, Estonian contestant Hardi Tiidus became a minor celebrity in Finland, starring in his own MTV-produced entertainment specials, *Neighbor's Son Hardi Tiidus* (*Naapurin poika, Hardi Tiidus*, 1968) and *Good Evening* (*Hyvää iltaa / Tere õhtust*, 1968).

With its staid—at times even boring—content and its companionable assembly of competitors, judges, audiences, and broadcasters from both

Figure 1.1. The Estonian *Neighbor Quiz / Friendship Match* team deliberates. Photograph courtesy of Eesti Rahvusringhääling.

sides of the Iron Curtain, *Neighbor Quiz / Friendship Match* offers a striking contrast to the common image of Cold War media as marked by conflict and propaganda. Indeed, although it mirrored the Soviet Union's relationship to its so-called friendly neighbor Finland (which pursued a policy of neutrality during the Cold War), the program was not primarily defined by the period's geopolitics.[3] Instead, it was the product of a range of other factors. These included media infrastructure such as the Tallinn–Helsinki connection—used to transmit news footage from the Soviet Union to Western Europe—which invited Estonian and Finnish viewers into a shared televisual experience. Institutionally, the program benefited MTV, which had been struggling within a Nordic political context that questioned the legitimacy of commercial television; a coproduction with ETV (which also carried commercials) signaled that the Finnish broadcaster was capable of pursuing its own "politics of neutrality."[4] History and language were also motivations: the prize for the winning team on *Neighbor Quiz / Friendship Match*, a statue dubbed *The Pondering Brothers*, figured Finns and Estonians as part of the same family—an idea whose origins lay in nineteenth-century nationalist thought.[5]

Factors like these are at the heart of this book, which considers the pragmatic, technological, economic, political, and aesthetic questions that linked media industries, cultures, professionals, and discourses in Europe's Cold War East to their counterparts in the West as well as the Global South. The interactions documented here occurred within and around media of various kinds (books, computer games, films, photography, radio, and television). They were often contingent and improvisatory; they had multiple, and at times conflicting, functions and meanings domestically and internationally. And while they helped shape the ways media circulates today—from film festivals, to satellite networks, to coproductions—they were also rooted in a longer history, one that extends beyond the Year Zero of 1945.[6]

## Encounters and Experiments

That year found European media industries at a crossroads. From the Atlantic coast to the Ural Mountains, and the Mediterranean and Black Seas to the Baltic, many were emerging from German occupation, and all were contending with the lack of materials, personnel, and space that World War II had made chronic. Yet the war had also made media's social import clearer and more pressing than ever before. Not only could images, words, and sounds help orient traumatized, deprived, and displaced populations in the transforming postwar world, they were an ideal means through which newly constituted governments could assert their identity and legitimacy. Moreover, these governments reasoned, local media industries could serve as a bulwark against American incursions into the European cultural sphere, a long-standing political and economic concern.[7] And so, between 1945 and 1948, most European states devoted considerable attention to these industries and their related infrastructures, in some cases even before reconstructing agricultural, transport, and banking systems. Across the continent, film and broadcasting industries were brought under partial or full state control, while international institutions such as the United Nations made media a foundational part of their nascent programs.

This postwar reconceptualization of media geopolitics had additional resonances in the countries assigned to the Soviet sphere of influence at the

1945 Yalta Conference. In Czechoslovakia, East Germany, Hungary, Poland, and elsewhere, media was not only discussed in national and international terms, it was also increasingly oriented toward the East, in the phrasing of the day. This shift was largely rhetorical, but it was also reflected in film import agreements that privileged Soviet cinema, in the presence of Soviet advisers in media industries, and in burgeoning translations of Soviet media theory and criticism and the like.

As the Cold War gathered force, so did this rhetoric and its Western counterparts, creating an apparent schism. Western Cold War–era criticism valorized banned books, films, writers, and artists from Eastern Europe while often sharply criticizing the region's nationalized media industries. In the East, readers and viewers were warned of so-called bourgeois nationalism lurking within some Western novels and films, of their tainted commercialism, and of the ideological threats posed by imported magazines or overheard radio programs. Yet such rhetoric overlooked the multiple factors beyond propaganda and political resistance that motivated postwar media's movement. It also obscured the fact that, both during and before the war, media in the East and West had been shaped by common historical, economic, social, and technological forces.[8] The notion that media could play an active role in constructing international polities and publics, for instance, drew on complex interwar legacies, from the numerous projects linked to the Comintern (Communist International), which sought to link Europe and the world to the Soviet Union, to the liberal media internationalism associated with the League of Nations.[9] To take just one example, televised Eurovision Song Contest (broadcast annually from 1956) was a postwar echo of the International Broadcasting Union's 1930s European Concerts, live international broadcasts that mirrored these interwar internationalist ideas.[10]

It is nevertheless true that the Cold War's ideological, economic, and political divisions spurred the development of distinct media cultures within Europe, as well as distinct ideas about media industries, form, and politics. This was especially the case in Eastern Europe before the mid-1950s thaws, when media discourse was marked not only by a desire for distinctiveness, but also by optimism about the aesthetic and institutional possibilities of a new kind of media for what was seen as a new world under construction—in a reflection of what Łukasz Stanek terms the Cold War's "worldmaking" projects.[11] Yet this newness was not epitomized solely by the Soviet model, nor did it imply an inward-looking nationalism or regionalism. Rather, as recent scholarship has argued, East European media engaged broadly with spaces beyond the Iron Curtain, and these very communications and connections helped give shape to the region's media cultures and practices, as well as to their counterparts elsewhere.[12] These connections were not just with Western Europe, but also with countries across Asia, North and South America, and Africa—especially from the mid-1950s onward, in the context of the Cold War's crucial Second–Third World relationships.[13]

Indeed, although transnational dynamics in East European media cultures have been best documented in the long 1960s—which saw loosened travel, censorship, and media import and export policies in much of the region—this book demonstrates their existence even during highly polarized moments such as the early 1950s, as well as during the relatively understudied decades of the 1970s and 1980s.[14] It documents these dynamics via a series of methods in media and literary history—among them, media industry and infrastructure studies, "entangled" and transnational media history, world literature studies, and the study of "useful," amateur, and ephemeral media—that have shifted attention away from texts and their content toward histories of media production and distribution.[15] These methods ask us to look beyond major works and figures to institutions, spaces, and practices historically seen as peripheral; to consider the interplay between forms and contexts; and to understand media within wider practical and discursive frameworks. All of this is part of the remapping at this book's core.

This is not to argue, however, that the interactions traced here were seamless or uncomplicated. Production plans collapsed, microphones cut out, interpreters mistranslated. And throughout the postwar years, border restrictions—jamming technologies, import and export controls, visa regimes—frustrated media's movement. Yet instead of confirming the binaries and easy answers that Cold War rhetoric attempted to offer, breakdowns and failures reflected a vibrant, dialogic process of experimentation and improvisation in the period's media, with translators and radio announcers going off script, computer amateurs tinkering with code, and the emergence of new forms of books and music and television programs. Failure, after all, can only result from an attempt to *do* something.

Such improvisation and experimentation reinforces the idea that failure plays an everyday and even generative role in infrastructure, helping illuminate the conditions of its functioning.[16] Paradoxically, perhaps, it also resonates with anthropologist Michał Murawski's call to consider socialism's *successes*.[17] However, experimentation was also rooted in broader postwar media dynamics, including a lack of consensus about the identity and function of particular technologies. This was the case in the 1950s, when the rise of television displaced cinema and radio socially and economically, forcing all media to adapt. Similarly, in the 1980s, computer games confounded existing frameworks governing media circulation and copyright.[18] Developments like these, as well as the period's shifting geopolitics, conditioned the encounters that this book documents—encounters that call our attention to the complex ways in which the Cold War shaped media.

## Chapters

Each of this book's four sections addresses a means through which these encounters occurred. The first section, "Mobile Forms," asks how media forms characteristic of the Cold War period moved across both space and time. It begins with Katie Trumpener's consideration of panoramic photobooks depicting urban space in postwar Eastern Europe. Trumpener locates the origins of this popular format both in interwar Soviet models and in panoramic photography's imbrication with modernization and colonization projects worldwide, beginning in the nineteenth century. In the early 1950s, panoramic photobooks were used to celebrate Stalinist urban reconstruction, but by the late 1950s, in the work of Czech photographer Josef Sudek, the medium had become a site for the critique of such projects. Rosamund Johnston's chapter on the 1950 Czechoslovak radio cantata *The Peace Train* offers another example of global influences on East European media at the height of the Stalinist period. The composition, Johnston demonstrates, represented a unique form of socialist-realist jazz—one that was simultaneously cosmopolitan and anticosmopolitan and that depended at once on Czechoslovak Radio's institutional culture and on radio's distinct technological and social dimensions. Finally, Anu Koivunen asks why Finnish television company MTV chose to broadcast Soviet drama in the 1970s. In scheduling classic Russian and contemporary Soviet plays, MTV did not merely show compliance with Finnish foreign policy; it also used the long tradition of repertory theater to seek cultural legitimacy for commercial television.

The encounters discussed in the second section, "Distribution, Adaptation, Reception," were marked by processes of interpretation, misinterpretation, and at times disagreement. Masha Salazkina's chapter examines the circulation of Soviet films and film discourse in postrevolutionary Cuba. Despite Cuba's extensive exhibition of Soviet films and intellectual engagement with Soviet film theory, Salazkina argues that Soviet cinema was less an influence on its Caribbean counterpart than a strategic tool through which Cuban institutions and individuals jostled for *local* political and cultural power. The interplay between the foreign and the local is also at the heart of Sonja Simonyi's chapter on two experimental Hungarian films that won prizes at West Germany's Mannheim Film Festival: Gábor Bódy's *American Postcard* (1976) and Béla Tarr's *Family Nest* (1977). Challenging the notion that for East European filmmakers, Western European film festivals served primarily as gateways to the West, Simonyi argues that the films' Mannheim prizes played an equally crucial role in shaping their directors' domestic careers.[19]

The section's last two chapters turn from cinema to computer games and shortwave (international) radio, respectively. Jaroslav Švelch chronicles the circulation of Western computer games in 1980s Czechoslovakia and details how the games were appropriated and adapted by Czechoslovak microcomputer hobbyists, most of them teenagers affiliated with the country's paramilitary computer clubs and cybernetics youth groups.[20] And in her study of Radio Berlin International's Swedish-language broadcasts from East Germany during late summer and autumn 1989, Marie Cronqvist analyzes a different form of adaptation and interpretation, as Swedish listeners came to terms with the fall of the Berlin Wall and Radio Berlin International hosts themselves improvised a new political and rhetorical script.

As this suggests, translation and translators, broadly understood, were crucial intermediaries in the encounters this book chronicles. The third section, "Translation," explores this in depth. Elena Razlogova's chapter, like Cronqvist's, addresses spoken and heard translation—here, through the simultaneous translation practices used, in Soviet cinemas, in place of subtitles for foreign films. While Soviet officials envisioned live translation as an ideological tool to promote the country's cinema at foreign film festivals, Razlogova shows how, within the Soviet Union itself, this imperfect and ephemeral practice shaped an alternative film distribution system in sites ranging from international film festivals to private and unofficial screenings. The section's following two chapters explore the institutions and politics of literary translation. Brangwen Stone turns to Cold War literary exchanges through the case of East German author Christa Wolf and her 1974 visit to Oberlin College as part of its writer-in-residence program. Wolf's visit, Stone argues, inaugurated a series of "recontextualizations" and "reframings" of her work in its English translation and publication, including feminist readings with which Wolf disagreed. Marla Zubel also explores the publishing dynamics that shaped the circulation and reception of Eastern European literature in the West, focusing on Polish author Ryszard Kapuściński's *Cesarz / The Emperor: Downfall of an Autocrat* (1978/1983), a magical-realist account of Haile Selassie I's dictatorship in Ethiopia. Kapuściński was known for his engaged reportage and his solidarity with anti-imperialist struggle, yet *The Emperor*'s style enabled US reviewers to frame the book as an allegory for the failures of both the Second and Third Worlds. In the section's fourth chapter, which explores television documentaries of Finnish-Soviet state visits in the 1970s, Laura Saarenmaa considers how

Finnish public broadcasting company YLE used television to interpret—and engage with—foreign policy. YLE's films did not merely document these visits and echo their well-known iconography; instead, television as a medium allowed journalists to present an intimate backstage view of politics and speak to Finland's unique geopolitical situation.

Cultural-diplomatic and political factors intersect economic and technological concerns in the book's final section, "Infrastructure and Production." Petr Szczepanik's chapter discusses American film producers who, from the 1960s to the 1980s, sought out East European shooting locations due to their relative cheapness and sophisticated production infrastructure (prefiguring the runaway productions that have characterized the East European media landscape since the 1990s). Via John Guillermin's 1969 *Bridge at Remagen*—whose shooting was interrupted by the 1968 Warsaw Pact invasion of Czechoslovakia—Szczepanik illuminates the negotiations between Hollywood and East European production cultures that characterized cross-bloc coproductions. Like the Americans Szczepanik discusses, the Italian producers in Stefano Pisu's chapter on the Italian-Soviet coproduction *Life Is Beautiful* (1979) were not primarily driven by ideological commitments. Instead, their collaboration with the USSR represented a business opportunity at a moment of crisis for the Italian film industry. Nevertheless, the film's subject—resistance to a southern European authoritarian regime waging war against an anti-colonial movement in Africa—brought politics to the foreground. The mutual benefits that parties on both sides of the Iron Curtain sought from cross-bloc collaborations are central, finally, to Christine Evans's and Lars Lundgren's history of Soviet and US efforts to create global satellite communications infrastructure in the 1960s. While scholarship on satellites has emphasized a narrative of US economic and technological domination, Evans and Lundgren argue that this obscures the common objectives and extensive interactions between the US and USSR that defined attempts to develop this infrastructure.

Satellites have enabled international television transmissions since the 1960s. Today, however, television content travels largely via the internet—and above all via companies like Netflix and Amazon Prime. The book ends with Anikó Imre's consideration of the resurgence of Cold War spies on these platforms, bringing the book's remapping into the present. These agents' proliferation, in series and films ranging from *Deutschland '83* to *The Americans* to *Red Sparrow*, is not simply a symptom of nostalgia, or *Ostalgie*. It also calls into question post–Cold War discourses of freedom, as viewers' seemingly endless choices are coupled with digital media companies' unprecedented capacity to surveil their users. In other words, if traces of

Cold War media institutions, infrastructures, and cultures remain visible in today's global media landscape, the same is true for the period's conceptual frameworks. It is for this reason, among others, that they demand our attention.

## Notes

1. Singers performing in this episode were Hendrik Krumm, Helgi Sallo, and Heli Lääts from Estonia and Ritva Mustonen and the Hootenanny Trio from Finland. The final part of the program has been lost, but the first forty-three minutes can be viewed in the online archive of Eesti Rahvusringhääling (ERR), https://arhiiv.err.ee/vaata/55588.
2. Estonian and Finnish are distinct languages, but some of the vocabulary is understandable for speakers of both languages. Transborder television broadcasts have long played a role in familiarizing people in both countries with the language of the neighboring country. In Estonia in particular, many people learned Finnish from watching Finnish television channels that reached across the Baltic Sea to northern Estonia. From 1956, Estonian television, for its part, broadcast weekly programs in Finnish, targeting audiences in Finland. See Keinonen, "Early Commercial Television in Finland"; Lepp and Pantti, "Window to the West."
3. In the 1960s, Finland was officially neutral. It had signed an Agreement of Friendship, Cooperation, and Mutual Assistance with the USSR in 1948.
4. Pajala, "A Forgotten Spirit of Commercial Television?" See also Koivunen, "Soviet Drama with Commercial Breaks," in this volume.
5. Immonen and Onnela, *Suomi ja Viro*.
6. For more in this volume on connections between Cold War media cultures and institutions and their present-day counterparts, see, on film festivals, Razlogova, "On Soviet Spoken Cinema," and Simonyi, "From the Antechamber to the International Stage"; on satellite networks, Evans and Lundgren, "Dividing the Cosmos?"; on coproductions, Pisu, "Envisioning the Revolutionary South," and Szczepanik, "Hollywood Going East." See also Szczepanik, *Screen Industries in East-Central Europe*.
7. See, for example, de Grazia, *Irresistible Empire*, and Jarvie, *Hollywood's Overseas Campaign*.
8. Such Cold War binaries have been thoroughly challenged, especially in the social sciences, since the revisionist historical scholarship of the 1970s. See, for instance, Fitzpatrick, "Revisionism in Retrospect," and Jarausch, "Beyond Uniformity." Recent engagements with Cold War culture and history include Autio-Sarasmo and Miklóssy, *Reassessing Cold War Europe*; Babiracki and Zimmer, *Cold War Crossings*; Bazin, Glatigny, and Piotrowski, *Art beyond Borders*; Mikkonen and Koivunen, *Beyond the Divide*; Mikkonen, Scott-Smith, and Parkkinen, *Entangled East and West*; Kacandes and Komska, *Eastern Europe Unmapped*; Komska, *The Icon Curtain*; Péteri, *Imagining the West*; Vowinkel, Payk, and Lindenberger, *Cold War Cultures*.
9. On such interwar projects, see, for example, Glaser and Lee, *Comintern Aesthetics*; Clark, *Moscow*; Salazkina, "Moscow-Rome-Havana"; and Druick, "'Reaching the Multimillions'" and "Visualising the World." On their postwar resonances, see Hogenkamp, *Film, Television and the Left*.
10. Fickers and Lommers, "Eventing Europe;" Pajala, "Intervision Song Contests."
11. Stanek, *Architecture in Global Socialism*. On media's postwar newness, see Česálková, "Socialism for Sale," and Lovejoy, *Army Film*.
12. See, for example, Badenoch, Fickers, and Henrich-Franke, *Airy Curtains in the European Ether*; Hilaire-Pérez and Zakharova, *Les techniques de la globalisation*; Evans, *Between Truth and Time*; Imre, *TV Socialism*; Mihelj and Huxtable, *From Media Systems to Media Cultures*; and Cronqvist, "From Socialist Hero to Capitalist Icon." On print culture and literature, see, for example, Blum, "Circulation, Transfers, Isolation"; Kind-Kovács, *Written Here*; Labov, *Transatlantic Central Europe*; and Popa, "Un transfert littéraire politisé."

13. On these relationships, see Djagalov, *From Internationalism to Postcolonialism*; Djagalov and Salazkina, "Tashkent '68"; Popescu, *At Penpoint*; Stanek, *Architecture in Global Socialism*; and Stejskalová, *Filmmakers of the World*.

14. On the 1960s, see Gorsuch and Koenker, *The Socialist Sixties*. On the supposedly stagnant 1970s and early 1980s, see Bren, *The Greengrocer and His TV*, and Evans, *Between Truth and Time*. In examining these decades, this book is in dialogue with works such as Badenoch, Fickers, and Henrich-Franke's *Airy Curtains in the European Ether* and Kind-Kovács and Labov's *Samizdat, Tamizdat, and Beyond*, as well as recent work on coproductions, such as Skopal, "Barrandov's Co-Productions"; Shaw, "Nightmare on Nevsky Prospekt"; Siefert, "Co-Producing Cold War Culture" and "Meeting at a Far Meridian"; Silberman, "Learning from the Enemy"; and Michaels, "Mikhail Kalatozov's *The Red Tent*."

15. On media industry studies, see Szczepanik and Vonderau, *Behind the Screen*. On media infrastructure studies, see Parks and Starosielski, *Signal Traffic*; Starosielski, *The Undersea Network*; and Larkin, *Signal and Noise*. On useful cinema, see Acland and Wasson, *Useful Cinema*; on amateur cinema, see Salazkina and Fibla, *Global Perspectives*. On world literature, see Apter, *Against World Literature*; Casanova, *The World Republic*; and Damrosch, *What Is World Literature?* On entangled media and literary histories (*histoires croisées*), see Blum, "Circulation, Transfers, Isolation"; Cronqvist and Hilgert, "Entangled Media Histories"; Fickers and Johnson, "Transnational Television History"; and Salazkina, "Moscow-Rome-Havana."

16. On failure and breakdown in critical infrastructure studies, see Parks and Starosielski, *Signal Traffic*, 13; and Larkin, "Politics and Poetics."

17. Murawski notes how the discussion of socialist architecture and urban planning has tended to emphasize unsuccessful and abandoned projects, constructing a narrative of socialist failure. Failure-centric post–Cold War narratives have obscured "still-existing achievements and enduring legacies of built socialism," such as the "diversity, conceptual sophistication and global reach of built socialist modernity." See Murawski, "Actually-Existing Success," 910, 922.

18. For debates about the uses of television, see Roth-Ey, *Moscow Prime Time*; and Cramer, *Utopian Television*.

19. On Cold War film festivals, see, among others, Fehrenbach, *Cinema in Democratizing Germany*; Moine, *Screened Encounters*; Bláhová, *Filmové festivaly*; Djagalov and Salazkina, "Tashkent '68"; and Lovejoy, "Moving Images."

20. For an extended discussion of microcomputing in socialist Czechoslovakia, see Švelch, *Gaming the Iron Curtain*.

## Bibliography

Acland, Charles R., and Haidee Wasson, eds. *Useful Cinema*. Durham, NC: Duke University Press, 2011.

Apter, Emily. *Against World Literature: On the Politics of Untranslatability*. London: Verso, 2013.

Autio-Sarasmo, Sari, and Katalin Miklóssy, eds. *Reassessing Cold War Europe*. New York: Routledge, 2011.

Babiracki, Patryk, and Kenyon Zimmer, eds. *Cold War Crossings: International Travel and Exchange across the Soviet Bloc, 1940s–1960s*. Arlington: Texas A&M University Press, 2014.

Badenoch, Alexander, Andreas Fickers, and Christian Henrich-Franke, eds. *Airy Curtains in the European Ether: Broadcasting and the Cold War*. Baden-Baden: Nomos, 2013.

Bazin, Jérôme, Pascal Dubourg Glatigny, and Piotr Piotrowski, eds. *Art beyond Borders: Artistic Exchange in Communist Europe (1945–1989)*. New York: Central European University Press, 2016.

Bláhová, Jindřiška, ed. *Filmové festivaly*. Special issue of *Iluminace* 26, no. 1 (2014).

Blum, Alain. "Circulation, Transfers, Isolation." *Kritika: Explorations in Russian and Eurasian History* 9, no. 1 (2008): 231–242.

Bren, Paulina. *The Greengrocer and His TV: The Culture of Communism after the 1968 Prague Spring*. Ithaca, NY: Cornell University Press, 2010.

Casanova, Pascale. *The World Republic of Letters*. Translated by M. B. DeBevoise. Cambridge, MA: Harvard University Press, 2004.

Česálková, Lucie. "Socialism for Sale: Czechoslovak *Krátký* film, Custom-Made Film Production, and the Promotion of Consumer Culture in the 1950s." In Karl and Skopal, 166–195.

Clark, Katerina. *Moscow, the Fourth Rome: Stalinism, Cosmopolitanism, and the Evolution of Soviet Culture, 1931–1941*. Cambridge, MA: Harvard University Press, 2011.

Cramer, Michael. *Utopian Television: Rossellini, Watkins, and Godard beyond Cinema*. Minneapolis: University of Minnesota Press, 2017.

Cronqvist, Marie. "From Socialist Hero to Capitalist Icon: The Cultural Transfer of the East German Children's Television Programme *Unser Sandmännchen* to Sweden in the Early 1970s." *Historical Journal of Film, Radio and Television* 41, no. 2 (2021): 378–393.

Cronqvist, Marie, and Christoph Hilgert. "Entangled Media Histories." *Media History* 23, no. 1 (2017): 130–141.

Damrosch, David. *What Is World Literature?* Princeton, NJ: Princeton University Press, 2003.

de Grazia, Victoria. *Irresistible Empire: America's Advance through 20th Century Europe*. Cambridge, MA: Belknap Press, 2005.

Djagalov, Rossen. *From Internationalism to Postcolonialism: Literature and Cinema between the Second and the Third Worlds*. Montreal: McGill-Queen's University Press, 2020.

Djagalov, Rossen, and Masha Salazkina. "Tashkent '68: A Cinematic Contact Zone." *Slavic Review* 75, no. 2 (2016): 279–298.

Druick, Zoë. "'Reaching the Multimillions': Liberal Internationalism and the Establishment of Documentary Film." In *Inventing Film Studies*, edited by Lee Grieveson and Haidee Wasson, 66–92. Durham, NC: Duke University Press, 2008.

———. "Visualising the World: The British Documentary at UNESCO." In *The Projection of Britain: A History of the GPO Film Unit*, edited by Scott Anthony and James G. Mansell, 272–280. New York: Palgrave Macmillan, 2011.

Evans, Christine. *Between Truth and Time: A History of Soviet Central Television*. New Haven: Yale University Press, 2016.

Fehrenbach, Heide. *Cinema in Democratizing Germany: Reconstructing National Identity after Hitler*. Chapel Hill: University of North Carolina Press, 1995.

Fickers, Andreas, and Catherine Johnson. "Transnational Television History: A Comparative Approach." *Media History* 16, no. 1 (2010): 1–11.

Fickers, Andreas, and Suzanne Lommers. "Eventing Europe: Broadcasting and the Mediated Performances of Europe." In *Materializing Europe: Transnational Infrastructures and the Project of Europe*, edited by Alexander Badenoch and Andreas Fickers, 225–251. Basingstoke: Palgrave Macmillan, 2010.

Fitzpatrick, Sheila. "Revisionism in Retrospect: A Personal View." *Slavic Review* 67, no. 3 (2008): 682–704.

Gilburd, Eleonory. *To See Paris and Die: The Soviet Lives of Western Culture*. Cambridge, MA: Harvard University Press, 2018.

Glaser, Amelia, and Steven S. Lee. *Comintern Aesthetics*. Toronto: University of Toronto Press, 2020.

Gorsuch, Anne E., and Diane P. Koenker, eds. *The Socialist Sixties: Crossing Borders in the Second World*. Bloomington: Indiana University Press, 2013.

Hilaire-Pérez, Liliane, and Larissa Zakharova. *Les techniques de la globalisation au XXe siècle*. Rennes: Presses Universitaires de Rennes, 2016.

Hogenkamp, Bert. *Film, Television and the Left in Britain, 1950–1970*. London: Lawrence & Wishart, 2000.

Immonen, Kari, and Tapio Onnela, eds. *Suomi ja Viro: yhdessä ja erikseen*. Turku: Turun yliopisto, 1998.

Imre, Anikó. *TV Socialism*. Durham, NC: Duke University Press, 2016.

Jarausch, Konrad. "Beyond Uniformity: The Challenge of Historicizing the GDR." In *Dictatorship as Experience: Towards a Socio-Cultural History of the GDR*, edited by Konrad Jarausch, 3–16. New York: Berghahn, 1999.

Jarvie, Ian. *Hollywood's Overseas Campaign: The North Atlantic Movie Trade, 1920–1950*. Cambridge: Cambridge University Press, 1992.

Kacandes, Irene, and Yuliya Komska, eds. *Eastern Europe Unmapped: Beyond Borders and Peripheries*. New York: Berghahn, 2017.

Karl, Lars, and Pavel Skopal, eds. *Cinema in Service of the State: Perspectives on Film Culture in the GDR and Czechoslovakia, 1945–1960*. New York: Berghahn, 2017.

Keinonen, Heidi. "Early Commercial Television in Finland." *Media History* 18, no. 2 (2012): 177–189.

Kind-Kovács, Friederike. *Written Here, Published There: How Underground Literature Crossed the Iron Curtain*. New York: CEU Press, 2014.

Kind-Kovács, Friederike, and Jessie Labov, eds. *Samizdat, Tamizdat, and Beyond: Transnational Media During and After Socialism*. New York: Berghahn, 2013.

Komska, Yuliya. *The Icon Curtain: The Cold War's Quiet Border*. Chicago: University of Chicago Press, 2015.

Labov, Jessie. *Transatlantic Central Europe: Contesting Geography and Redefining Culture beyond the Nation*. New York: CEU Press, 2019.

Larkin, Brian. "The Politics and Poetics of Infrastructure." *Annual Review of Anthropology* 42 (2013): 327–43.

———. *Signal and Noise: Media, Infrastructure, and Urban Culture in Nigeria*. Durham, NC: Duke University Press, 2008.

Lepp, Annika, and Mervi Pantti. "Window to the West: Memories of Watching Finnish Television in Estonia during the Soviet Period." *View: Journal of European Television History and Culture* 2, no. 3 (2013): 77–87.

Lovejoy, Alice. *Army Film and the Avant Garde: Cinema and Experiment in the Czechoslovak Military*. Bloomington: Indiana University Press, 2015.

———. "Moving Images: On Institutions, Geography, and History." *East European Politics and Societies and Cultures* 28, no. 4 (November 2014): 709–714.

Lundgren, Lars. "Live from Moscow: The Celebration of Yuri Gagarin and Transnational Television in Europe." *View: Journal of European Television History and Culture* 1, no. 2 (2012): 45–55.

Michaels, Paula A. "Mikhail Kalatozov's *The Red Tent*: A Case Study in International Coproduction across the Iron Curtain." *Historical Journal of Film, Radio and Television* 26, no. 3 (2006): 311–325.

Mihelj, Sabina, and Simon Huxtable. *From Media Systems to Media Cultures: Understanding Socialist Television*. Cambridge: Cambridge University Press, 2018.

Mikkonen, Simo, and Pia Koivunen, eds. *Beyond the Divide: Entangled Histories of Cold War Europe*. New York: Berghahn, 2015.

Mikkonen, Simo, Giles Scott-Smith, and Jari Parkkinen, eds. *Entangled East and West: Cultural Diplomacy and Artistic Interaction during the Cold War*. Oldenburg: De Gruyter, 2019.

Moine, Caroline. *Screened Encounters: The Leipzig Documentary Film Festival, 1955–1990*. Oxford: Berghahn Books, 2018.

Murawski, Michał. "Actually-Existing Success: Economics, Aesthetics, and the Specificity of (Still-)Socialist Urbanism." *Comparative Studies in Society and History* 60, no. 4 (2018): 907–937.

Pajala, Mari. "A Forgotten Spirit of Commercial Television? Co-productions between Finnish Commercial Television Company Mainos-TV and Socialist Television." *Historical Journal of Film, Radio and Television* 39, no. 2 (2018): 366–383.

———. "Intervision Song Contests and Finnish Television between East and West." In Badenoch, Fickers, and Henrich-Franke, 215–239.

Parks, Lisa, and Nicole Starosielski, eds. *Signal Traffic: Critical Studies of Media Infrastructures*. Urbana: University of Illinois Press, 2015.

Péteri, György, ed. *Imagining the West in Eastern Europe and the Soviet Union*. Pittsburgh: University of Pittsburgh Press, 2010.

Popa, Ioana. "Un transfert littéraire politisé: Circuits de traduction des littératures d'Europe de l'Est en France, 1947–1989." *Actes de la recherche en sciences sociales* 144, no. 1 (2002): 55–69.

Popescu, Monica. *At Penpoint: African Literatures, Postcolonial Studies, and the Cold War*. Durham, NC: Duke University Press, 2020.

Roth-Ey, Kristin. *Moscow Prime Time: How the Soviet Union Built the Media Empire That Lost the Cultural Cold War*. Ithaca, NY: Cornell University Press, 2011.

Salazkina, Masha. "Moscow-Rome-Havana: A Film Theory Road Map." *October* 139 (2012): 97–116.

Salazkina, Masha, and Enrique Fibla, eds. *Global Perspectives on Amateur Film Histories and Cultures*. Bloomington: Indiana University Press, 2021.

Shaw, Tony. "Nightmare on Nevsky Prospekt: *The Blue Bird* as a Curious Instance of U.S.-Soviet Film Collaboration during the Cold War." *Journal of Cold War Studies* 14, no. 1 (2012): 3–33.

Siefert, Marsha. "Co-producing Cold War Culture. East-West Film-Making and Cultural Diplomacy." In *Divided Dreamworlds? The Cultural Cold War in East and West*, edited by Peter Romijn, Giles Scott-Smith, and Joes Segal, 73–94. Amsterdam: Amsterdam University Press, 2012.

———. "Meeting at a Far Meridian: US–Soviet Cultural Diplomacy in the Early Cold War." In *Cold War Crossings: International Travel and Exchange across the Soviet Bloc, 1940s–1960s*, edited by Patryk Babiracki and Kenyon Zimmer, 166–209. Arlington: Texas A&M University Press, 2014.

Silberman, Marc. "Learning from the Enemy: DEFA-French Co-Productions of the 1950s." *Film History* 18, no. 1 (2006): 21–45.

Skopal, Pavel. "Barrandov's Co-productions: The Clumsy Way to Ideological Control, International Competitiveness and Technological Improvement." In Karl and Skopal, 89–106.

Stanek, Łukasz. *Architecture in Global Socialism: Eastern Europe, West Africa, and the Middle East in the Cold War.* Princeton, NJ: Princeton University Press, 2020.

Starosielski, Nicole. *The Undersea Network: Sign, Storage, Transmission.* Durham, NC: Duke University Press, 2015.

Stejskalová, Tereza, ed. *Filmáři všech zemí, spojte se!/Filmmakers of the World, Unite!* Prague: Tranzit, 2017.

Švelch, Jaroslav. *Gaming the Iron Curtain: How Teenagers and Amateurs in Communist Czechoslovakia Claimed the Medium of Computer Games.* Cambridge, MA: MIT Press, 2018.

Szczepanik, Petr. *Screen Industries in East-Central Europe.* International Screen Industries. New York: Bloomsbury, 2021.

Szczepanik, Petr, and Patrick Vonderau, eds. *Behind the Screen: Inside European Production Cultures.* New York: Palgrave Macmillan, 2013.

Vowinkel, Annette, Marcus M. Payk, and Thomas Lindenberger, eds. *Cold War Cultures: Perspectives on Eastern and Western European Societies.* New York and Oxford: Berghahn Books, 2012.

ALICE LOVEJOY is Associate Professor of Cultural Studies and Comparative Literature and Moving Image Studies at the University of Minnesota. She is author of *Army Film and the Avant Garde: Cinema and Experiment in the Czechoslovak Military* (IUP, 2014).

MARI PAJALA is Senior Lecturer of Media Studies at the University of Turku. Her work is published in *Media History, Television & New Media,* and *International Journal of Cultural Studies.*

# PART I. MOBILE FORMS

CHAPTER 2

## STALIN BOULEVARD
## *Panoramic Vistas and Urban Planning in Eastern European Photobooks*

Katie Trumpener

> Wipe everything old from your heart.
> Streets are our brushes.
> Squares, our palettes.
> The days of the Revolution have yet to be sung by the thousand-paged book of time.
>     Vladimir Mayakovsky, "An Order to the Army of Art" (1918)[1]

BETWEEN 1952 AND 1960, A two-kilometer-long boulevard of continuous apartment buildings, the Stalinallee, was erected as the architectural centerpiece of East Berlin, capital of the new German Democratic Republic, or GDR (see fig. 2.1). Equally monumental building projects were being constructed across the postwar—especially the socialist—world; these were the subject of the 1958 Moscow conference of the International Union of Architects and its two-volume commemorative photobook. The first volume was dedicated not only to post-bombardment rebuilding in Coventry and Rotterdam, but also to the reconstruction of Pyongyang (leveled during the Korean War, now rebuilt as a Soviet-style planned city) and the erection of new industrial cities in Bulgaria (Dimitrovgrad), Hungary (Stálinváros), and the GDR (Stalinstadt, in 1961 renamed Eisenhüttenstadt), while the second volume documented a range of major projects across the Soviet Union.

Like this photobook's sections on new buildings in the Soviet Union, Gerhard Puhlmann's 1953 photobook, *Stalinallee: National Reconstruction Program* (*Die Stalinallee: Nationales Aufbauprogramm*), had made heavy use of panoramic photography. In both cases, the projects being documented were frequently organized around grand boulevards, which are particularly well suited to panoramic depictions. This chapter explores the unexpected postwar revival and conjuncture of these two quintessential nineteenth-century forms: the photopanorama and the boulevard.

Figure 2.1. V is for vista. Gerhard Puhlmann, *Stalin Boulevard: National Reconstruction Program* (*Die Stalinallee: nationales Aufbauprogramm*, 1953). Photograph courtesy of Beinecke Rare Book Library, Yale University.

## BOULEVARD/PHOTOPANORAMA:
## NINETEENTH-CENTURY RESURRECTIONS

From its nineteenth-century origins, the medium of photography was often used to document urban space. The first photograph to show a visible human figure, Louis Daguerre's very early *Boulevard du Temple* (1838 or 1839), was taken on a seventeenth-century Parisian thoroughfare. Over the course of its ten-minute exposure, all human and vehicular traffic disappeared from the image (save one man standing still while his boots were blacked). The photograph's main subject, however, arguably became the street's apparently deserted and melancholy air.

Within a few years of photography's 1830s invention, photographers began experimenting with panoramic formats; the first dedicated panoramic camera was invented in 1845. Soon thereafter, the Paris that Daguerre had photographed began to change dramatically. From 1853 to 1870, Baron Haussmann oversaw the razing of the city's labyrinthine medieval quarters to construct new bourgeois neighborhoods anchored by vast, wide boulevards and fronted by architecturally standardized apartment houses.[2]

Although the transformation was presented as an attempt to improve public health and beautify the urban environment, Friedrich Engels noted in his 1872 article "The Housing Question" that this "Bonapartist" urban renewal actually involved "breaking long, straight and broad streets right through the closely built workers' quarters and lining them on both sides with big luxurious buildings." In the wake of the 1848 revolution, Engels underscored, Haussmann's "strategic aim" was to make "barricade fighting more difficult," to develop a "building trades' proletariat dependent on the government and to turn Paris into a luxury city."[3] Marx, too, lamented "the vandalism of Hausmann, razing historic Paris to make place [room] for the Paris of the sightseer!"[4]

Hausmann's use of boulevards and radials indeed created new urban sight lines. And as Walter Benjamin would later argue in his unfinished *Arcades Project*, Hausmannization thus spurred new practices of urban strolling or *flânerie*, while the city itself became a major subject for new art forms and a source of political, economic, and psychic self-understanding.[5] Haussmann's tactics for urban rebuilding were rapidly echoed across Europe (in Berlin's Kurfürstendamm, Vienna's Ringstrasse, Prague's Pařížká street, Budapest's Grand Boulevard, and Barcelona's Eixample District) and across the nineteenth-century colonial world (including Hanoi, Phnom Penh, Calcutta, Bombay, Buenos Aires, Mexico City, Jakarta, and Tel Aviv). Wherever such Haussmannesque boulevards were built, a distinctive new urban visual culture and self-understanding soon followed.

This key trend in nineteenth-century architecture and urban planning overlapped with an efflorescence of panoramic photography. Indeed, the dramatic sight lines created by diagonally planned streets, boulevards, and intersections lent themselves to panoramic photography, with its innate tendency toward an anamorphic bend in the center of the image. Whether in European metropolises or across the colonial world, the process of boulevard building often served to destroy traditional, potentially rebellious neighborhoods, replacing them with architectural forms designed to sustain upper-class hegemony or proclaim Western colonial domination.[6] Over the course of the nineteenth century, as this essay's second section will argue, panoramic photography itself was frequently deployed in tandem with related processes of colonization and modernization.

From a Marxist perspective, both the boulevard-centered city plan and the panoramic photograph might thus seem forms with a deeply compromised political history. Nonetheless, each was revived—indeed, they became conjoined—in Communist Eastern Europe, ostensibly to serve radically different political goals than in their nineteenth-century incarnations. In postwar East Germany and Eastern Europe, paradoxically enough, newly erected boulevards thus became icons of a new socialist urbanism alongside a renewed panoramic architectural photography eager to capture the monumental scale, solidity, and permanence of socialism's achievements.

In the GDR, the still-recent legacies of Nazism heightened the significance of such reconstruction projects. Yet even before it was built, the Stalinallee became a flash point for heated internal debates between architects and party functionaries over Germany's modernist architectural legacy. Although postwar architects repeatedly proposed reviving modernist styles, Paul Stangl has shown, party officials rejected these as capitalist, citing Soviet precedents and physically transporting Soviet city planners to East Berlin to offer in-person critiques.[7] This fight between modernist and Soviet approaches to urban planning extended even to the window shapes in buildings along the boulevard. After repeated redesigns, Stalinallee, in its final form, featured much bigger, more heavily ornamented, luxurious, and expensive buildings than originally planned. Its showpiece apartments thus excited not only admiration but envy from East Berliners still living in squalid, half-ruined tenements. Meanwhile, the prefabricated materials and assembly processes adopted on the Stalinallee—and the pace of scheduled completion—fed growing discontent among thousands of construction workers employed on the project.[8]

From its title onward, Puhlmann's *Stalinallee: National Reconstruction Program* nonetheless signals Stalinallee's aspirational, indeed utopian potential.[9] The *Aufbau* in the title is particularly significant. During World War II, David Blackbourn has argued, Nazi strategists frequently used the term to describe the project of colonizing their newly conquered Eastern European territories (from physical land reclamation to clearing local populations so that their lands could be resettled by ethnic Germans).[10] The Communist reuse of the word *Aufbau*, ubiquitous in the 1940s, in turn suggests a very different political, moral, and institutional reclamation of Germany's east (and Eastern Europe). In its postwar use, *Aufbau* evoked not only architectural but also political and cultural new beginnings, a rebuilding from the ashes of Nazism toward a fully Communist society. The GDR's most important literary press, founded in 1945, was thus the Aufbau Verlag—the Press of Rebuilding—while the title and opening line of the GDR's rousing new 1949 national anthem evokes a society "Auferstanden aus Ruinen," risen or resurrected from ruins.[11]

Stefan Heym's 1963 GDR novel *The Architects* (*Die Architekten*) captures the emphatically utopian rhetoric surrounding Stalinallee: "This is the street on which Peace first came to this city in the person of Comrade [Joseph]

Stalin, on his way to Potsdam. That's why we chose it to be the first to be cleared of rubble, the first to rise from the ruins, wider, airier, more beautiful and splendid than any street this city has ever had, the first street of socialism." The use of volunteer labor itself becomes legendary. "And we called on the people to help ... And the people came, voluntarily, after work. By the thousands ... like black ants crawling over the ruins, working away with pickaxe and chisel, passing the salvaged bricks from hand to hand, cleaning them." As Heym asks rhetorically, "Where have there ever been architects building on such a foundation?"[12]

In 1814, Karl Friedrich Schinkel had designed a nationalist monument for Berlin, a cathedral to commemorate the War of Liberation (1813–1814) from Napoleonic rule. The monument was to be erected of exposed brick, a building material with a storied national tradition (given northern Germany's Brick Gothic cathedrals). Schinkel even envisioned the entire population carrying bricks to the site, symbolically representing the collective nature of the (national) project while reviving the medieval building guilds and workshops so central to Germany's early cities.[13] Schinkel's project remained unrealized, but its spirit was unexpectedly reanimated in the late 1940s. Widely disseminated photographs and newsreels showcased volunteer bucket brigades—often foregrounding elderly women—as they painstakingly dismantled Berlin's ruined buildings, brick by brick, conserving them for reuse in new buildings (see fig. 2.2). In Kurt Maetzig's 1952 GDR feature film *Story of a Young Marriage* (*Roman einer jungen Ehe*), the protagonist, a rising young East Berlin theater star, spends her leisure time participating joyfully in collective ruin clearance.

During Stalinallee's building, in fact, volunteers who logged a hundred hours on the construction site could enter a lottery, with favorable odds, to rent one of its new apartments. Hence the Stalinallee could represent itself quite literally as a building complex by the people, for the people.[14] It was to be the outward epitome of the collective will, of life in a new political and architectural order. Puhlmann's *Stalinallee* goes even further; it evokes the entire socialist world's symbolic participation in Stalinallee's construction, banishing the specters of World War II and fascist occupation. In its photographs and expository texts, the photobook thus showcases the activist construction process developed by a Soviet engineer and the volunteer construction shifts worked by a record-breaking Polish activist brigade, Chinese and North Korean foreign students, a GDR socialist realist novelist, and even a vacationing Czech opera singer.

Puhlmann's photobook made extensive use of panoramic photography—from the 1930s through the 1960s, the privileged medium and default choice,

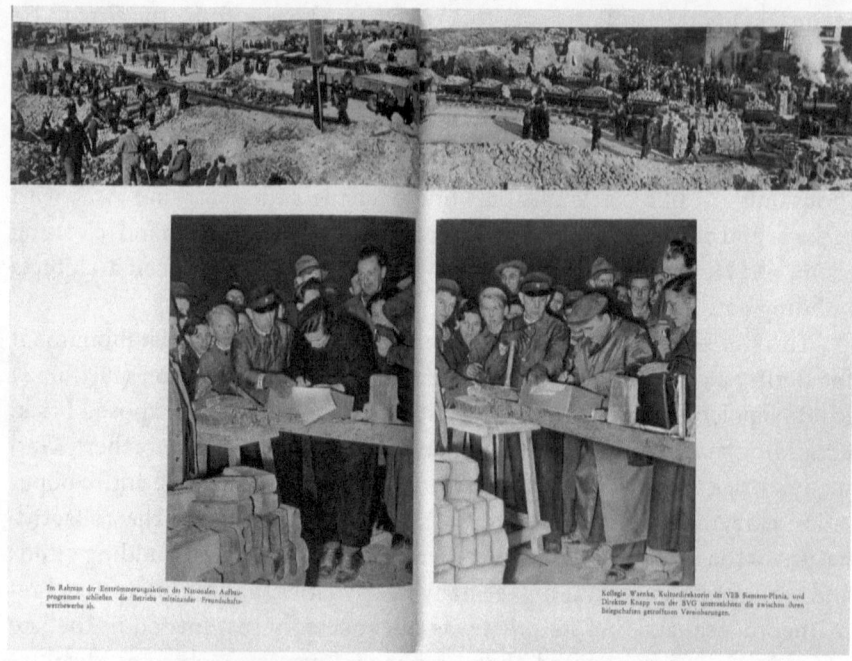

Figure 2.2. Risen from the ruins. Puhlmann, *Stalin Boulevard*. Photograph courtesy of Beinecke Rare Book Library, Yale University.

across the socialist world, for documenting urban renewal. Yet at least a few contemporaneous Eastern European panoramic photographers offered more differentiated, critical accounts. This chapter thus ends with Josef Sudek's celebrated photobook *Panoramic Prague* (*Praha panoramatická*, 1959). In Czechoslovakia, Sudek's images suggest, socialist urbanization efforts accelerated nineteenth-century industrial transformation, destroying, degrading, or eroding the natural and built environment in the name of progress. Such critique seems particularly profound given panoramic photography's historical imbrication with the projects of modernization and colonialism. Yet for maverick photographers like Sudek, the panoramic photograph's innate peculiarities of form—particularly its anamorphic distortion toward the center—offered the means to challenge Stalinist efforts at urban recentering and architectural, photographic, and political gigantism.[15]

## The Architects: Modernism, Utopia, and the Photobook

In its modernist origins, the socialist photobook understood itself as an experimental, revolutionary form. In *Moscow Under Reconstruction* (USSR, 1938), Alexander Rodchenko and Varvara Stepanova documented Moscow's

 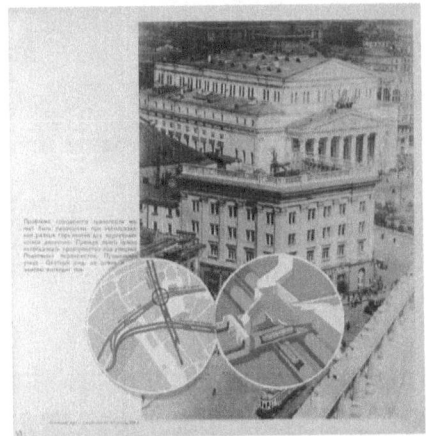

Figures 2.3 and 2.4. Alexander Rodchenko and Varvara Stepanova, "Untitled," from *Moscow Under Reconstruction* (1938) © 2021 Estate of Alexander Rodchenko / UPRAVIS, Moscow / ARS, NY © 2021 Estate of Varvara Stepanova / UPRAVIS, Moscow / ARS, NY. Photograph courtesy of Beinecke Rare Book Library, Yale University.

Soviet efflorescence through a mixture of photographs, maps, graphs, and cartoons contrasted with historical engravings.¹⁶ That book opens with a large photograph of Stalin, and photography remains a privileged medium throughout, yet pictures *per se* are not sacrosanct. In the middle of several black-and-white cityscape photographs, rounded flaps open to reveal colored maps or diagrams (see fig. 2.3 and fig. 2.4). The apparently objective view provided by the photograph is thus put into dialogue, perhaps even conflict, with other objective, more abstract representations. Diagrams and maps are arguably this photobook's most striking, defining features—and some have photographs literally stapled in and overlaid on top of them. Rodchenko and Stepanova likewise put into perspective Moscow's architectural rebuilding by focusing simultaneously on subterranean and infrastructural reconstruction: the city's new subway, its bridge and tunnel systems, its piping and waterworks, and even (most invisibly of all) its public health network.

The design for East Berlin's Stalinallee owed much to Soviet precedents, particularly the 1930s plans for the "linear city."¹⁷ Puhlmann's *Stalinallee*, in parallel, evokes the precedents of 1930s Soviet photobooks like *Moscow Under Reconstruction*. Yet in Rodchenko and Stepanova's photobook, even the four gatefold photopanoramas (taken from different elevations and stretching up to four pages) seem as interested in traffic flows and the visual collage of street signage, tram wires, and pedestrian movement as in Moscow's new centerpiece buildings. Puhlmann, in contrast, focuses far more

Figure 2.5. Building the avenue. Puhlmann, *Stalin Boulevard*. Photograph courtesy of Beinecke Rare Book Library, Yale University.

single-mindedly on architecture—and on photopanoramas. His book's panoramas generally extend over two pages and depict ruin-clearing brigades, construction, and cranes as the new buildings go up—and (mirroring the angle of the opened double-spread page itself) the final, wide V formed by the new facades, converging from both ends, stretching to the horizon.

Puhlmann's panoramic shots of buildings under scaffolding function almost like time-lapse footage, capturing the speed, skill, and uniformity with which particular Stalinallee blocks are constructed. One particularly heroic spread captures several building stages simultaneously; on the right page, a builder on a ladder affixes a beam held by girders onto a partially built wall, while down the left (across the cavernous building site soon to become the boulevard itself) stretches a significant line of buildings in progress (see fig. 2.5). The construction worker looks modestly away from the camera. Like Lewis Hine's influential Empire State Building photobook *Men at Work* (US, 1932), such images showcase the matter-of-fact head for heights strong, brave men bring to fashioning tall new buildings. Yet the camera positioning also echoes Yevgeny Khaldei's iconic panoramic photograph of Red Army soldiers hoisting the Soviet flag atop the Brandenburg Gate on May 2, 1945, the day they liberated Berlin.[18] The altitude of such men working above the city heroicizes, indeed mythologizes, their labor and vigilance; they become demi-gods, harbingers and guardians of a lofty new world order.

Between such panoramas, Puhlmann intersperses close-ups of the Stalinallee's new apartments, whose spacious rooms, central heating, interior toilets, and bathtubs represented huge improvements over the ruins or slums many Berliners still inhabited. And as Puhlmann's photographs demonstrate, stores along the boulevard offered a wide range of goods, although its layout—long buildings running almost continuously for two kilometers—cut off surrounding neighborhoods and forced residents to walk long distances to shop. Merely crossing the busy boulevard was possible only at long intervals and was hazardous even then.

In most respects, nonetheless, the buildings were received as bold, successful new experiments in apartment living. They were inhabited by a mixture of party officials, GDR intelligentsia, working-class labor activists, and ordinary citizens who earned/won apartments through the volunteer-labor lottery—a residential mix itself intended to herald a newly egalitarian society. Yet on June 17, 1953, increased construction norms ignited spontaneous protests by Stalinallee's construction crews and, as West Berlin radio spread news of the insurrection, scattered protests across the country. As Stalinallee became the epicenter of the GDR's only major workers' uprising, its new inhabitants unexpectedly found themselves not only witnesses to history but in some cases under physical attack as putative party "functionaries."[19] Soviet tanks and troops deployed rapidly to suppress the protests, killing 125 civilians. As bystanders threw rocks at the tanks, West Berlin media broadcast the Soviet military action around the world, catalyzing something of the international shock and revulsion later felt during the 1956 Hungarian Uprising, the 1968 Warsaw Pact invasion of Czechoslovakia, or Beijing's 1989 Tiananmen Square massacre.

The Stalinallee uprising occurred only a few months after Stalin's death. Caught off guard by the workers' protests, the GDR government thereafter remained deeply distrustful of its own citizenry, effectively forestalling further de-Stalinization, lest that catalyze the toppling of the government itself. Thus, the GDR, unlike its neighbors, never publicly disavowed its Stalinist past. The enormous statue of Stalin anchoring Stalinallee, erected in 1951, was removed only in 1961, and even then surreptitiously. This was fully five years after Nikita Khruschev's 1956 "secret speech" to the Twentieth Congress of the Communist Party of the Soviet Union ("On the Cult of Personality and Its Consequences") had roiled the socialist world, triggering more rapid removals of Stalin statues across much of the Eastern Bloc. The renaming of Stalinallee as Karl-Marx-Allee likewise occurred quietly in 1961, unaccompanied by public discussion and overshadowed by the far more radical transformation, on August 13, of Berlin's urban geography, as the GDR government suddenly sealed the city's borders and rapidly erected the Berlin Wall (known by GDR officials as the Anti-Fascist Protection Wall).

In a succession of controversial novels and films, GDR intellectuals nonetheless returned repeatedly to architecture and construction sites as metaphors for the malformation of the socialist state. Such texts followed the officially sanctioned Soviet precedent of *Cement*, Fyodor Gladkov's bittersweet 1925 socialist-realist novel, as of Andrei Platonov's long-suppressed 1930 Soviet novel, *The Foundation Pit* (*Kotlovan*). Unsurprisingly, many of the GDR texts were likewise deemed defeatist or subversive, bowdlerized, or banned.[20] Stefan Heym's *Five Days in June* (1959) described the 1953 Workers' Uprising from the vantage point of Stalinallee's striking construction workers—and hence, until 1989, remained publishable only in West Germany.

Heym's long-unpublished novel *The Architects* focused centrally on Stalinallee itself, its inflated scale and grandiosity a troubling metaphor for Stalinist Party culture. The novel's architect protagonist, the wife of East Berlin's head urban planner, extols his monumental boulevard plans. But she belatedly learns that long ago, during their shared Soviet exile, he betrayed her parents, who then died in the Stalinist purges. She thus became his ward, later his wife. This fundamental, if long-buried, political and familial betrayal becomes linked to aesthetic betrayal as well. As the architect eventually realizes, her husband's design for the Stalinallee is borrowed stylistically from Albrecht Speer's Third Reich plans to reconfigure Berlin as a Nazi world capital. As she is repeatedly forced to reexamine her previously naive faith in paternalistic, monumental forms of political and architectural power, GDR readers were clearly meant to undergo a parallel process of disillusionment and rethinking. Yet like *Five Days*, *The Architects* never reached its intended readers. Before Heym had even talked to editors, the renewed 1965 government clampdown on artistic expression left him unable to publish anything for several years. Thus his novel completely missed its moment, and, like other attempts by German intellectuals and writers to interrogate Stalinallee and Stalinist urban planning, it failed to reach the GDR public. It was published only in 2000, a full decade after the GDR had legally ceased to exist.

### Urban Vistas: Panoramic Photography Between Modernization and Colonialism

Throughout the 1950s and '60s, as architectural photobooks made extensive use of panoramic photography, they also reactivated, however inadvertently, the form's long and politically charged history. Across the nineteenth-century world, ordinance surveyors and photographers commissioned by colonial armies and governments had deployed panoramic photography as a way of mapping terrain, whether for military purposes or to site new industrial or transportation infrastructure. Although utilitarian in origin, such panoramic photography often yielded images of surprising power and beauty.[21] Early panoramic photographers also self-consciously documented places and cultures in transition, at times engaging in "salvage photography."[22] And as a new breed of European war photographers made photopanoramas of colonial expeditions into Ethiopia and Afghanistan or of the Opium Wars,

Figure 2.6. "The Church of the Holy Body—Recife District" ("Igreja do Corpo Santo—Bairro do Recife," c. 1913), Francisco Du Bocage / Instituto Moreiro Salles Collection.

they also chronicled the erection of European-style infrastructure—new districts, plazas, and boulevards—in new colonial capitals.

In many locations, indeed, panoramic photography had accompanied, documented, and established the sight lines for nineteenth-century colonial and modernization projects. In the Americas, panoramic photographers like Carleton Watkins, Eadweard Muybridge, and Marc Ferrez documented not only remaining wilderness, but also genocidal campaigns against surviving Indian tribes, and not only frontier and gold-rush boomtowns, but also the partial destruction of urban fabric, whether by natural causes (the San Francisco earthquake) or to enable their industrial reorganization. In Brazil, Francisco Du Bocage's extraordinary 1913 photopanoramas document the dismantling of colonial Recife—and the enormous voids that preceded its rebuilding (see fig. 2.6). Du Bocage uses his panoramas' bending middle to suggest a continually empty center: the apparently depopulated old colonial city, its monumental buildings too spaced out to produce a coherent urban fabric; the cityscape in ruins, its historic buildings razed to build the railway; the station's skeletal interior; the empty plaza fronting the new center.[23]

It might be argued, á la Benjamin, that in creating broad vistas and a new, reality-saturated sublime, most nineteenth-century panoramic photography implicitly countenanced large-scale clearance and modernization efforts. Panoramic photographers lived in and promulgated a world of expanded and expansive perspectives at the expense of what was visually or experientially familiar. In concrete ways, panoramic photography enabled colonial and city officials to imagine forms of urban renewal and cultural transformation far beyond the scale of individual needs and attachments.[24]

Across Eastern Europe and Asia, the 1950s likewise saw the rebuilding of war-destroyed cities and the imperative to create new socialist public and industrial space. In postwar Czechoslovakia, as Kimberly Elman Zarecor has detailed, newly planned housing projects and new uses of prefabricated construction adapted interwar modernist architecture, as well as experimental models and methods.[25] Elsewhere in Eastern Europe, postwar socialist urban planning belatedly realized aspects of 1930s Soviet constructivism, Le Corbusier's Ville Radieuse, Red Vienna, and Weimar Republic social housing.[26] Yet in the process, large-scale rebuilding also reactivated the principles of Haussmann's transformative boulevardization. And as once before, in the nineteenth century, the erection of the (socialist) boulevard was accompanied by a resurgence of officially commissioned architectural photography, often in panoramic format.[27]

As Engels had insisted already in the 1870s, the boulevard remained a vehicle for mobilizing, expressing, and visualizing political power. In postrevolutionary Paris, Haussmann's partial razing, rebuilding, boulevard creation, and road paving were motivated not least by the desire to avoid future political unrest and to end communards' ability to dismantle cobblestone streets to throw stones or erect barricades across narrow streets. Similarly, after World War II, newly built boulevards across the socialist world worked both to dwarf spontaneous crowds and to enable shows of state power. Boulevards like Leningrad's Moskovsky Prospect, Minsk's Sovetskaia Street, and Warsaw's Marszałkowska Street became standard routes for military parades. And such parades often originated or ended in vast plazas (from Moscow's Red Square to Pyongyang's Kim Il-sung Square) lined with reviewing stands. In East Berlin, as I myself witnessed in October 1979, in the hours preceding a military parade commemorating the GDR's fortieth anniversary, plainclothes Stasi agents had already stationed themselves at regular intervals along major arteries to mingle with the crowd as it assembled, listening for critical remarks and arresting offenders. Under such political conditions, the socialist boulevard served not merely as an elegant, Parisian-style avenue down which to drive, promenade, or window-shop, but a place of active social control.

## SOCIAL DISTANCE: FROM AGORA TO MONUMENT

Early Soviet photobooks frequently used panoramic spreads to evoke the urban crowd, the political force of the mass rally.[28] Photobooks from Benito Mussolini's Italy and Third Reich Germany followed suit. In Italy, Jeffrey Schnapp has shown, magazines featured adulatory spreads of rallies filling Renaissance or Roman piazzas. Like many nineteenth-century panoramic photographs, such images were often photo collages pasted together from adjacent photographic plates, subtly distorting the contours of the public space to show a fuller, tighter, more cohesive crowd, rapt as fascist oratory reanimated Italy's historic city centers.[29] Karl Hermann Frank's *Sudeten Germanhood in Struggle and Crisis* (*Sudetendeutschtum in Kampf und Not: Ein Bildbericht*), published in Nazi Germany in 1936, showcases nationalist orators addressing huge open-air political rallies of ethnic Germans in Czechoslovakia's western borderland.

Yet during the early Stalinist period, Soviet architectural photobooks also began cultivating the opposite extreme: panoramic photographs of empty or almost-empty boulevards, plazas, or other architectural ensembles.[30] By the 1950s, this more monumental aesthetic had become the norm across Eastern Europe, matching the renewed emphasis on the abstract geometry of the boulevard and the mega-square. Photopanoramas taken during the planning or execution of urban projects were now often shot at hours with few bystanders, the better to showcase the built spaces themselves or perhaps to emulate architectural models.[31]

Ostensibly, the period's vast plazas were still created for the benefit of the masses. The GDR delegation to the 1958 Moscow International Architects Union conference thus underscored the political significance of the agora: "Political demonstrations, meetings, and public gatherings are held on its central squares. In this way, the civic center dominates the town from a planning and architectural point of view."[32] Yet in practice, socialist governments worried about crowds—and during the 1950s and '60s, convoked them mainly in tightly choreographed pageants of state.

In East Berlin, the postwar rebuilding of Alexanderplatz (Alexander Square) occurred on such a massive scale that its vast central plaza dwarfed all human presence. During the Weimar Republic, Alexanderplatz had been one of the city's most crowded business and traffic hubs—hence the setting and implicit protagonist of Alfred Döblin's 1929 modernist city novel, *Berlin Alexanderplatz*. Thereafter, however, Alexanderplatz was architecturally compromised, first by World War II enemy airstrikes, then in 1945, as the Red Army fought its way into the city center. In the postwar period, as Heinz Lieber's early-'60s architectural photopanoramas showcase, Alexanderplatz underwent a monumental transformation, its enormous new buildings implicitly representing a political fresh start.

One of Lieber's photopanoramas, *The Alexanderplatz around 1970*, framed on one side by a building crane, showcases 1960s office and apartment buildings, the block-long, ten-story House of the Electric Industry (1967–1969) inaugurating Alexanderstraße's broad boulevard of new prefabs stretching into the distance. Twelve lanes of traffic separated Alexanderstraße's two sides, making it wider even than Paris's ten-lane, shop- and tree-lined Champs Elysées, and it was flanked by more uniform, higher (eight-story, vs. Haussmannian Paris's five- or six-story) buildings.[33] Despite then-low car ownership rates, moreover, Alexanderstraße's sidewalk and street-level orientation were entirely determined by cars and parking, not pedestrian safety, comfort, or sight lines. Lieber's photograph, a bird's-eye view probably taken from a neighboring building or crane, focuses not on the grounded concerns of daily use, but on an architectural sublime.

This implicit vision of the postwar city as an idealized, futuristic surface or shell departs crucially from Rodchenko and Stepanova's modernist precedent. *Moscow in Reconstruction* presented itself not only as a collection of views and facts, but as a constructivist collage capturing the city's busy chaos, as well as its underlying planned infrastructural order.[34] Even streets or plazas newly anchored by resplendent construction, *Moscow*'s photopanoramas underscored, remained living, dynamic spaces in which unruly lines of traffic and pedestrians enlivened and disrupted intended architectural symmetries. By 1953, in contrast, Puhlmann's very different *Stalinallee* photopanoramas reflected Stalinism's development into a far more thorough, authoritarian mode in which a monumental top-down architectural order not only choreographed daily life but narrowed axes of vision.

Following Stalin's death and Khrushchev's secret speech, Soviet—and hence also GDR—architects were freer to abandon ornamental facades in favor of "better, cheaper and quicker building."[35] Yet key aspects of urban planning and its documentation remained unchanged. The 1958 Soviet photobook commemorating Moscow's International Union of Architects conference thus retains photographic and editorial practices very similar to Puhlmann's photobook. Volume II, devoted to rebuilt or newly constructed Soviet cities, is presumably (like Puhlmann's?) the work of many different photographers, yet its uncredited views share a recognizable aesthetic: taken from at least medium distance, they minimize human figures, and most cityscapes feature very few cars, buses, or trams. The overwhelming majority of panoramic views present built spaces completed and inhabited but not (as yet) looking particularly lived in, let alone landscaped.[36]

Volume II's photographers also tended to select semi-aerial vantage points that reduce architectural details and distinctiveness.[37] Instead, they focused on the stark architectural ensemble created by large, newly finished civic squares (Lenin Square, Yerevan) or on the relationship between wide boulevards (Kutuzov Prospect, Moscow) and the symmetrical rows of high, wide buildings (colonnaded in some cases, large-paneled pre-fab in others) that bisect them or line them on either side.[38] In riverfront cities like Rostov-on-Don or Kaliningrad, indeed, elevated views from one embankment of the other give the intervening river itself the effect of an

Figure 2.7. "Metallurgists' Boulevard, Magnitogorsk," 1954–1955, International Union of Architects, Fifth Congress, *Construction and Reconstruction of Towns 1945–1957 / Construction et Reconstruction des Villes*, Vol. II (1958), 338–339. Photograph courtesy of Sterling Memorial Library, Yale University.

unusually spacious boulevard.³⁹ The combination of emptied cityscape and elaborate grillwork on Magnitogorsk's Metallurgists' Prospect lends the boulevard the melancholy elegance of Versailles (see fig. 2.7). In sum, these 1950s photographs are preoccupied with linearity, with defining axes of vision, access, and architectural organization. Panoramic photography, with its orientation toward vistas and soaring scale, thereby became a natural fit with Stalinist (re)construction projects—an ideal medium to capture the grandeur, massive size, and transformational ambition of postwar socialist building.

## The Empty Center: Panoramic Photography and Its Discontents

In Sudek's *Panoramic Prague* (1959), in contrast, panoramic photography's formal qualities are used to critique the hollowness and grandiosity of postwar reconstruction. Sudek's photobook is overwhelmingly elegiac, although unlike most other European capitals, Prague's famously elegant architecture survived the war (and a long, brutal German occupation) virtually intact. The photobook's 284 panoramic photographs celebrate a capital as beautiful as ever. Yet Prague is photographed largely without its population. Benjamin saw Eugène Atget's nineteenth-century photographs of Paris (often taken at dawn in uncharacteristically empty streets) as evoking a surrealist ghost city, a "crime scene"; Sudek's Prague, likewise, appears architecturally intact at its people's expense.⁴⁰

Figure 2.8. "Pankrác," Josef Sudek, *Panoramic Prague* (1959). © I & G Fárová Heirs. Photograph courtesy of the Museum of Decorative Arts, Prague.

During World War I, as a soldier on the Italian front, Sudek was hit by a grenade and had one arm amputated to the shoulder. From 1922 to 1927, he thus lived in the renowned Baroque veterans hospital, Invalidovna, in Prague's Karlín district, where his rehabilitation included training to become a professional photographer and where his fellow veterans and the architecture of the hospital itself were among his earliest photographic subjects. During the 1950s, carrying his heavy tripod one-armed through Prague, Sudek shot hundreds of panoramic photographs of the city, even though his 1899 Panoram camera could not capture a particularly crisp view, his viewfinder only allowed him to preview the middle of each image, and the camera's inherent anamorphism required particular legerdemain, especially when producing vertical panoramas.[41] Whether for such technical reasons or because of Sudek's own surrealist, atmospheric proclivities, his images often convey a dreamlike atmosphere of heightened attention, blurred around the edges.[42]

Many of Sudek's views—verdant formal gardens, views from the statuary-lined Charles Bridge—echo the formal beauty of Atget's photographs of Saint-Cloud or Versailles. Some images remain conventionally centered, often by old forms of architecture planning and symmetry—the view through an archway or balanced by towers on the skyline. Yet when Sudek reaches Prague's outskirts (and then, in a subsequent, long-unpublished panorama series, plunges into northern Bohemia's industrial wastelands), that formal sense of composition gives way to something looser, more improvisatory. Such terrain itself has a troublingly uncared-for look, a sense of built-in decay, obsolescence, and erosion.[43]

Several particularly disturbing images indict Prague's current urban planning. *Pankrác* was taken in the southeastern neighborhood best known for its prison, notorious during the Nazi occupation as Prague's Gestapo headquarters (see fig. 2.8). Here only one building seems to remain of a formerly built landscape. What is left is a large, empty gap in the urban fabric—a stop or turnaround for trams, crisscrossed above by their wires. Otherwise the space appears desolate and thoroughly denatured. More than in any other *Panoramic Prague* image, the camera gives this scene a slight fish-eye distortion, elongating and bending its almost empty middle. On the picture's left edge are houses and a distant water tower, signs of human settlement. To the right is an almost empty horizon; a featureless, vehicle-free road stretches flatly into the distance, marked as a vista by its tram-pole supports on either side of the road but framing nothing at all. This panorama of nothingness evokes a way station of quotidian desolation centered on blankness and stretching into emptiness. The bend of this image and its ominous vacuity might productively be read against surrealists' long-standing interest in distortion, distention, and the ominous (as against Sudek's other surrealist-tinged landscapes and still lifes produced during this period).

*Near Invalidovna in the Karlín District* returns to the neighborhood where Sudek lived during his long post–World War I convalescence. Stretched along one axis of the current streetscape are a row of functionalist buildings, the closest topped with a Communist star. Yet this image remains centered (anamorphically) on a tilting modernist fixture (likely a gas pump, if not a bus stop). Together they evoke Czechoslovakia's ambitious modernist architectural heritage—now apparently in a state of dilapidation (see fig. 2.9).

Sudek's own animus was not against modernism. In the mid-1930s, as an early exponent of the New Photography, he spent years producing crisply functional advertising images in the mode of the New Objectivity.[44] Even in *Near Invalidovna*, the modernist structure continues to center the image, still projecting its cool symmetry against the general backdrop of decrepitude and neglect. But Sudek was also a surrealist interested in processes of ruin and decay both for their own sake and as counterparts to Communism's official rhetoric of rebuilding, industrialization, and progress. In the late 1950s, Eastern Europe's nascent cinematic New Waves were likewise beginning to make visible, sometimes in a neorealist mode, many areas' continuing poverty and neglect long after the advent of state socialism.[45]

Sudek's unpublished 1959–1962 series on northern Bohemia, now known as *Sad Landscape* (*Smutná krajina*), proffered a similar critique. Among its subjects were the medieval center of the city of Most, soon to be demolished to enable the expansion of lignite mining, and the newly built settlements of prefabricated concrete *panelák* apartment buildings to which Most's population was to be moved.[46] (In 1968, as chap. 12 here recounts at length, key scenes for John Guillermin's 1969 Hollywood World War II drama, *The Bridge at Remagen*, were thus filmed in Most's old city center, its deliberately razed buildings standing in for war ruins.) In post-1989 retrospect, Most's

Figure 2.9. "Near Invalidovna in the Karlin District," Josef Sudek, *Panoramic Prague* (1959). © I & G Fárová Heirs. Photograph courtesy of the Museum of Decorative Arts, Prague.

Figure 2.10. Panorama of Podžatecká neighborhood, Most, Josef Sudek, *Sad Landscape*. © I & G Fárová Heirs. Photograph courtesy of the Museum of Decorative Arts, Prague.

demolition and redevelopment is widely understood as a key postwar planning failure.[47]

As Sudek suggests in his panorama of the Podžatecká neighborhood, Most's new satellite district, the paneláks stretching to the horizon are also clearly planned to form a miniature boulevard or prospect, making them ideal fodder for the heroic panoramic vista (see fig. 2.10). As yet, however, the wide central road is only a dirt access route; its dusty, crumbling surface, stretching diagonally across the photograph, takes up most of the foreground. Most prominent is a long, muddy ditch, perhaps a shallow trench where pipes are being laid. Although the new buildings' paneled walls look clean and crisp, they are shadowed by cranes and surrounded by construction residue—cement mixers, building material, dirt piles, a listing pole, and a tilting, already dilapidated building shed. A late modernist housing project intended to embody utopian promise appears here already as a scene of preemptive desolation.

During the 1950s, as we have seen, Eastern Bloc panoramic architectural photographs laid huge emphasis on the triumphal vertical canyon effect created by long lines of prefabricated buildings. Such photographs used their wide view to show the proliferation and symmetrical uniformity of facades

Figure 2.11. "Brooklyn Bridge," Ben Rose (ca. 1953). Courtesy of Peter Rose.

stretching on ahead, sometimes as far as the eye could see. But those panoramas were typically taken from an elevated vantage point, key to an aesthetic of sublimity. Sudek's photograph remains resolutely at ground—indeed mud—level.[48]

The relative pessimism of Sudek's Podžatecká photograph is particularly clear when compared to Ben Rose's more playful experimental photopanoramas taken in New York City just a few years earlier. A distinguished professional commercial and advertising photographer, Rose experimented with panoramic photography in his spare time. In *Brooklyn Bridge* (ca. 1953), the angling of his panoramic lens creates elongating distortion, and an almost fish-eye bend emanates from the center of the image (see fig. 2.11). New York's cityscape, as a result, becomes oddly fragmented, its iconic buildings virtually unrecognizable and the built environment rendered scattershot, as if it were gravitationally impossible for anyone to move from one cluster to another. In a decade when American moviegoers packed cinemas for wide-screen Westerns and musicals, Rose's photographs suggest a more skeptical, whimsical relationship to the American dream as to panoramic photography as medium.

Benjamin, indeed, might have read Rose's anamorphically distorted, potentially disturbing cityscape as emblematic of urban alienation under capitalism, the odd separation of people from one another, as from civic institutions and landmarks. Yet Rose plays with an accreted and intact urban environment still (in the pre-Robert Moses era) full of nineteenth-century buildings. Sudek in 1960s Most, in contrast, much like Du Bocage in 1910s Recife, photographs an impending, apparently inevitable future. For Sudek, the socialist dream has failed already before the model suburb is inhabited, its sight lines and scale so impersonal that the eye must take refuge in the ditch and the dirt. And here, paradoxically, only the panoramic form, the photopanorama's bend and distortions, can still deliver a belated riposte to postwar urban planners and their geometric socialist sublime.

## Notes

This essay is rooted, perhaps, in my childhood fascination with A. J. M. and F. Goico Aguirre's Franco-era urbanist picture book, *A First Look at a City in Spain*, with its geometric rendering of streets and blocks. My thinking was further spurred by long-term interlocutors, dead and alive:

my late father, Ulrich Trumpener, raconteur of East Berlin life under Stalinism (including June 17, 1953); my late husband, Richard Maxwell, student of the nineteenth-century city and panoramic form; my colleague Katerina Clark, with whom a 2002 walk down the former Stalinallee inaugurated two decades of friendship; and my son Alexander Maxwell, in whose company, on a 2018 bus ride down Parisian boulevards, this essay began to take shape. Many thanks also to Tim Barringer, Craig Buckley, Oksana Chefranova, Loren Kruger, Alice Lovejoy, Fatima Naqvi, John Peters, Anke Pinkert, Benjamine Toussaint, participants at Rough Cut (Yale Film and Media Studies Program), the Topographical Views workshop (Walpole Library), and the 30th IPC Conference.

1. Mayakovsky, "An Order to the Army of Art." English translation copyright © 2013 by James H. MacGavran. Published in 2013 by Northwestern University Press. All rights reserved.
2. See Le Corbusier, *Precisions on the Present State*; and Giedion, Sert, and Léger, "Nine Points on Monumentality."
3. All quotations from Engels, *The Housing Question*, 69.
4. Marx, "The Civil War in France," 571.
5. Benjamin, *Arcades Project*; see also Buck-Morss, *Dialectics of Seeing*.
6. See, for instance, Wright, *Politics of Design*.
7. As Paperny traces in his provocative *Architecture in the Age of Stalin*, the Soviet Union had previously undergone its own transition from modernist to Stalinist conceptions of urban architecture. See especially his "Horizontal-Vertical," 44–70.
8. Stangl, *Risen from Ruins* (chap. 6, "Stalinallee"); and Schätzke, *Zwischen Bauhaus*, 57–63.
9. Puhlmann, *Die Stalinallee*.
10. Blackbourn, *Conquest of Nature*, 262.
11. Matching Johannes R. Becher's lyrics ("Resurrected from ruins, and turned towards the future"), Hanns Eisler's music proceeds up the tone row to enact this resurrectional process.
12. Heym, *The Architects*, 21, 53.
13. Bergdoll, *European Architecture*, 148.
14. From the 1930s onward, Paperny argues, Soviet Stalinist architecture aimed for similar political fusion, "trying to blend the designer with the builder and the user ... [with] concrete workers, welders and bricklayers" seen as "fully legitimate authors of the building." Paperny, *Architecture*, 206.
15. Some East Germans were equally (if silently) critical of Stalinallee itself. As nineteen-year-old East German schoolboy Einar Schleef (later an important writer and dramaturg) noted in an April 27, 1963, diary entry on his first visit to East Berlin:
    Stalin Boulevard, what assholes built this?
    We looked at
    a. The stores, the size of the doors and show windows
    b. The balconies and balustrades ...
    d. The buildings from front and back, what a difference ...
    f. Use of materials ... what a waste of work and material (Schleef, *Tagebuch*, 304.)
16. Rodchenko and Stepanova collaborated on a long series of experimental photobooks and magazine issues (see Tupitsyn, "Exiting the Avant-Garde," esp. 154–155). On Rodchenko's 1932 collaboration with caricaturists Kukryniksy on a (never published) photobook, *Two Moscows*, contrasting Moscow as early modern "merchant city" with Soviet-era Moscow, see Tupitsyn, *Alexander Rodchenko*; on his place in early Soviet photography, see Tupitsyn, *The Soviet Photograph*.
17. See, for instance, May, "City Building."
18. Yevgeny Khaldei, "Panorama Pariser Platz, May 2, 1945," rpt. in *So weit*, 138.
19. Queisser, *Leben hinter der Zuckerbäckerfassade*.
20. In East Germany, Volker Braun's construction-site novella *The Mud* (*Der Schlamm*, 1959), Erik Neutsch's construction-site novel *Trace of Stones* (*Spur der Steine*, 1964, filmed 1965 by Frank Beyer), Brigitte Reimann's unfinished urban planning novel *Franziska Linkerhand* (1964–1974, published posthumously 1974, filmed 1981 by Lothar Warnecke as *Unser kurzes Leben/Our Short Life*),

Benno Pludra's children's novel *Island of Swans* (*Insel der Schwäne*, 1980, filmed 1983 by Hermann Zschoche), and Peter Kahane's film *The Architects* (*Die Architekten*, 1990) explored the project of GDR socialism as prefabricated or still emerging and potentially amenable to redesign from beneath (as workers discovered meaning in work, as planners learned to anticipate inhabitants' needs, as residents agitated for more humane housing). Beyer's film was banned (rereleased only in 1990); Reimann's text was bowdlerized before publication (an uncensored version appeared only in 1998); Zschoche and Kahane's films met sustained official resistance. *Island of Swans* detailed the blighted architectural and social atmosphere of East Berlin's new satellite city (Marzahn, built beginning in 1977, on the site of a Nazi concentration camp); even young residents' attempt to build themselves an unofficial playground is condemned and paved over. Kahane's *The Architects* sharpened such critique: young architects' attempts to build a social center for a satellite district lay bare East Germany's increasingly untenable political, social, and generational contradictions. On the corresponding literary texts, see Swope, *Building Socialism*; and Bivens, "Neustadt."

21. Many such photographic groups, forgotten or lost for decades in the archives, have recently been exhumed and displayed, offering detailed records of past industrial worlds. See Williams and Cahan, *Lost Panoramas*.

22. British India's Madras government commissioned Linnaeus Tripe to document endangered historical structures; Augustus Le Plongeon and Alice Dixon Le Plongeon self-financed expeditions to record Mexican temple ruins. Pelizzari, *Traces of India*; and Desmond, *Dreams of Maya*.

23. For Du Bocage's full image series, see "Francisco Du Bocage," IMS, accessed August 28, 2021, https://ims.com.br/titular-colecao/francisco-du-bocage/.

24. Trumpener, "Panoramic Journeys."

25. Zarecor, *Manufacturing a Socialist Modernity*.

26. See, for instance, Hatherley, *Landscapes of Communism*, especially chapter 1, "Magistrale," detailing the 1930s Stalinist rebuilding of Moscow's Tverskaya and Red Vienna's uses of huge, monumental, symmetrical apartment buildings on the Gürtel as a socialist riposte to the famous Ringstrasse.

27. From 1949 to 1951, surveyor Fritz Tiedemann was commissioned to inventory East Berlin's ruined and surviving buildings. During the war's final years, hundreds of bombardments reduced to rubble Berlin buildings, blocks, and plazas. Newly exposed exterior walls sometimes unexpectedly sported still-fresh-looking Wilhelmine business names and advertisements. Shot largely from street level, Tiedemann's architecturally and sociologically grounded photographic series—posthumously pasted together in *So weit kein Auge reicht* to form continuous panoramas—find a beauty in depth, detail, and sharpness of focus. Formally his series encompasses long swathes of urban fabric, yet also reveals the city's architectural skeleton and historical depth, the palimpsestic nature and contrasts of urban development. See Gröschner, Messmer, and Tiedemann, *Berlin, Fruchtstraße*, for a reconstruction of Tiedemann's further series of a Berlin street intersecting with the new Stalinallee project. Because he had shared his photographs of now-razed historical buildings with Western occupation authorities, Tiedemann was imprisoned in East Berlin in 1953 and later fled to West Germany.

28. The photobooks showcased in Karasik's *Soviet Photobook* feature decontextualized crowds (*From the Masses to the People*, 1934), Union Proletarian Brothers supporters filling an arena in Republican Barcelona (Ilya Ehrenburg's *Spain, Vol. I: V.H.P.*, 1937), and enormous, evenly spaced rows of Red Army soldiers filling Red Square (Rodchenko and Stepanova's *USSR, The Red Army and Navy*, 1939; *Moscow*, 1939; and Lev Kassil, *Parade on Red Square*, 1937).

29. Schnapp, "The Mass Panorama."

30. Examples from Karasik's *Soviet Photobook* include *Kharkov in Building* (1931); *Dneprostroi and the new Zaporozhye* (1932); *Ten Years of Soviet Tiflis* (1931); and *The Mechanization of Agriculture* (1940).

31. In *Soviet Photobook*, see *Kharkov in Building* (1931); *Dneprostroi and the New Zaporozhye* (1932); *Ten Years of Soviet Tiflis* (1931); and *The Mechanization of Agriculture* (1940).

32. International Union of Architects, *Construction and Reconstruction of Towns 1945–1957*, vol. I, "German Democratic Republic," 4.

33. Lieber, Galerie Berinson, accessed August 27, 2021, http://berinson.de/exhibitions/lieber/.

34. Svidel's 1934 essay, "Volume and Line: Notes on Panoramic Shooting," likewise seems committed to faceted perspective, discussing the possibility of building almost cubist perspectivism into a single panoramic shot—instanced in Svidel's photopanorama of a Crimean palace; the angle was shifted partway through shooting to capture visiting tourists alongside what they were seeing.

35. von Byme, "Leitbilder," 13.

36. Only a few *Construction and Reconstruction II* images show grids of cranes and scaffolding behind the lines of massive buildings arising in Leningrad (p. 95) or Zaporizhia (pp. 404–405), with trees lining an avenue (Mira Avenue, Moscow) or softening a square (Victory Square, Minsk; Square of the Fallen Fighters, Stalingrad; Komsomol Square, Magnitogorsk).

37. On aerial perspective in socialist aesthetics, see Widdis, *Visions* (chap. 5); and Lovejoy, *Army Film* (chap. 3).

38. See International Union of Architects, *Construction II*, Koutouzov Prospect, Moscow, 1956–1957, 37; Metallurgists' Prospect, Magnitogorsk, 338–339; and Lenin Square, Yerevan, 137.

39. International Union of Architects, *Construction II*, Rostov-on-Don, 258–259; and Kaliningrad, 288–289.

40. Benjamin, "Little History," 294. Like Atget, Čermanová's "Landscapes of Disaster" argues, Sudek radically de-auraticizes urban (and rural) landscapes, exploring their emptiness. Czech photographic theorists already in the 1920s and '30s had debated the question of how to represent modern urban space. See Witkovsky, *Foto*.

41. James, "Josef Sudek and the Panorama."

42. In another now-famous *longue durée* photographic series, taken inside the window of his Prague studio before, during, and after the German occupation, Sudek had experimented with the effects of rain, fog, snow, condensation, and ice on the window's surface and what became visible or invisible through and beyond it. See Sudek, *The Window of My Studio*. A similar compositional mixture of precision and imprecision informs the framing and execution of his Prague panoramas.

43. Parr and Badger, conversely, read Sudek's composition and affect as expressing his love for Prague, down to "the most slovenly industrial suburbs, and the scrofulous fringes where the city meets the country... Sudek's democratic eye... disregards nothing. He treats cathedral and castle in exactly the same way he treats a factory or a garage. The great public spaces of Prague... are here rendered intimate, while the humblest house or industrial building in a far-flung suburb is monumentalized, graced with Sudek's poetry... [*Praha panoramatická*] is a veritable encyclopedia of how to plot, construct and unify a panoramic photograph." See Parr and Badger, *The Photobook*, vol. I, 211.

44. Dufek, "Sudek the Outsider."

45. See, for instance, *Shadow* (*Cień*, Jerzy Kawalerowicz, Poland, 1956); *Berlin, Schönhauser Corner* (*Berlin, Ecke Schönhauser*, Gerhard Klein, GDR, 1957); *Sun Seekers* (*Sonnensucher*, Konrad Wolf, GDR, 1958/released 1972); and *The Noose* (*Pętla*, Wojciech Has, Poland, 1958).

46. Sudek, *Smutná krajina* and *Nordböhmen*. On Sudek's northern Bohemian photographs, see Lovejoy and Trumpener, "Sad and Bitter Landscapes."

47. Spurný, *Making the Most of Tomorrow*; and Glassheim, *Cleansing the Czechoslovak Borderlands*.

48. Filmed in Prague's Jižní Město neighborhood, then under construction, Věra Chytilová's *Prefab Story* (*Panelstory*, Czechoslovakia, 1979) memorably explores the aesthetics of such developments—the building materials' dreary grey uniformity, the Wild West of concrete and mud their first inhabitants find themselves in, but also the constructivist beauty as cranes lift to place mirrored panels, flashing, twinkling, obscurely signaling. On this and contemporary Czechoslovak films documenting paneláks and housing estate construction, see Lovejoy, "'A World Eternally under Construction.'"

# Bibliography

A. J. M. *A First Look at a City in Spain.* Illustrated by F. Goico Aguirre. Translation of *La Ciudad*, 1957. New York: Franklin Watts, 1960.

Benjamin, Walter. *The Arcades Project.* Translated by Howard Eiland and Kevin McLaughlin. Cambridge: Belknap Press, 1999.

———. "Little History of Photography." In *The Work of Art in the Age of Mechanical Reproduction and Other Writings about Media*, edited by Michael Jennings, 274–298. Cambridge, MA: Harvard University Press, 2008.

Bergdoll, Barry. *European Architecture, 1750–1890.* Oxford: Oxford University Press, 2000.

Bivens, Hunter. "Neustadt: Affect and Architecture in Brigitte Reimann's novel *Franziska Linkerhand*." *Germanic Review* 83, no. 2 (2008), 139–166.

Blackbourn, David. *The Conquest of Nature: Water, Landscape and the Making of Modern Germany.* New York: Norton, 2006.

Braun, Volker. "Der Schlamm." In *Das ungezwungene Leben Kasts.* Berlin: Aufbau-Verlag, 1979.

Buck-Morss, Susan. *The Dialectics of Seeing: Walter Benjamin and the Arcades Project.* Cambridge, MA: MIT Press, 1989.

Čermanová, Eva. "Landscapes of Disaster: Sudek, Tarkovsky, Tarr." In *Film Landscapes: Cinema, Environment and Visual Culture*, edited by Jonathan Rayner and Graham Harper, 88–104. Cambridge: Cambridge Scholars Publishing, 2013.

Desmond, Lawrence. *Dream of Maya: Augustus and Alice Le Plongeon in Nineteenth-Century Yucatan.* Albuquerque: University of New Mexico Press, 1988.

Dufek, Antonín. "Sudek the Outsider." In *Josef Sudek: Legacy of a Deeper Vision*, edited by Maia-Mari Sutnik, 240–249. Munich: Hirner, 2021.

Engels, Friedrich. *The Housing Question.* Moscow: Progress Publishers, 1970.

Frank, Karl Hermann. *Sudetendeutschtum in Kampf und Not.* Kassel: Bärenreiter-Verlag, 1936.

Giedion, Siegfried, José Luis Sert, and Fernand Léger. "Nine Points on Monumentality." In *Architecture Culture, 1943–1968: A Documentary Anthology*, edited by Joan Ockman, 27–30. New York: Columbia University Press, 1993.

Gladkov, Fedor. *Cement.* Translated by A. S. Arthur and C. Ashleigh. Evanston, IL: Northwestern University Press, 1994.

Glassheim, Eagle. *Cleansing the Czechoslovak Borderlands: Migration, Environment, and Health in the Former Sudetenland.* Pittsburgh: University of Pittsburgh Press, 2015.

Gröschner, Annett, Arwed Messmer, and Fritz Tiedemann. *Berlin, Fruchtstraße on March 27, 1952.* Ostfilern: Hatje Cantz, 2012.

Hatherley, Owen. *Landscapes of Communism: A History Through Buildings.* New York: New Press, 2015.

Heym, Stefan. *The Architects.* London: Daunt Books, 2012.

———. *Five Days in June.* Buffalo, NY: Prometheus Books, 1978.

International Union of Architects, Fifth Congress. *Construction and Reconstruction of Towns/Construction et Reconstruction des Villes 1945–1957*, 2 vols. Moscow: State Architecture and Building Publishing House, 1958.

James, Geoffrey. "Josef Sudek and the Panorama." In *Josef Sudek: Legacy of a Deeper Vision*, edited by Maia-Mari Sutnik, 251–258. Munich: Hirner, 2021.

Karasik, Mikhail. *The Soviet Photobook*, edited by Manfred Heiting. Göttingen: Steidl, 2015.

Le Corbusier. *Precisions on the Present State of Architecture and City Planning.* Translated by Edith Schreiber Aujame. Cambridge, MA: MIT Press, 1991.

Lieber, Heinz. "Der Alexanderplatz um 1970—Photographische Panoramen Teil 2." Galerie Berinson. Accessed August 27, 2021. http://berinson.de/exhibitions/lieber/.
Lovejoy, Alice. *Army Film and the Avant Garde: Cinema and Experiment in the Czechoslovak Military*. Bloomington: Indiana University Press, 2015.
———. "'A World Eternally under Construction': Věra Chytilová and Late-Socialist Prague." *Studies in Eastern European Cinema* 9, no. 3 (2018): 250–264.
Lovejoy, Alice, and Katie Trumpener. "Sad and Bitter Landscapes: Ecology and the Built Environment in Czech and East German Photography and Film." To be published in *Cinema and the Environment in Eastern Europe*, edited by Masha Shpolberg and Lucas Brasikis. New York: Berghahn, under contract.
Marx, Karl. "The Civil War in France." In *The Marx Engels Reader*, edited by Robert C. Tucker, 526–576. New York: Norton, 1972.
May, Ernst. "City Building in the USSR." In *Russia: An Architecture for World Revolution*, edited by El Lissitzky, 188–203. Translated by Eric Dluhosch. Cambridge, MA: MIT Press, 1972.
Mayakovsky, Vladimir. *Selected Poems*. Translated by James H. McGavran. Evanston, IL: Northwestern University Press, 2013.
Neutsch, Eric. *Spur der Steine*. Leipzig: Faber & Faber, 1996.
Paperny, Vladimir. *Architecture in the Age of Stalin: Culture Two*. Translated by John Hill and Roann Barris. Cambridge: Cambridge University Press, 2002.
Parr, Martin, and Gerry Badger. *The Photobook: A History*, vol. I. London: Phaidon, 2004.
Pelizzari, Maria Antonella. *Traces of India: Photography, Architecture and the Politics of Representation*. Montreal: Canadian Center for Architecture/New Haven: Yale Center for British Art, 2003.
Platonov, Andrei. *The Foundation Pit*. Translated by Robert Chandler, Elizabeth Chandler, and Olga Meerson. New York: New York Review Books, 2009.
Pludra, Benno. *Insel der Schwäne*. Berlin: Kinderbuchverlag, 1989.
Puhlmann, Gerhard. *Die Stalinallee: Nationales Aufbauprogramm*. [East] Berlin: Verlag der Nation, 1953.
Queissar, Ylva, ed. *Leben hinter der Zuckerbäckerfassade: Erstbewohner der Karl-Marx-Strasse erzählen*. Leipzig: form+zweck, 2004.
Reimann, Brigitte. *Franziska Linkerhand*. Edited by Angela Drescher. Berlin: Aufbau-Verlag, 1998.
Rodchenko, Alexander, and Varvara Stepanova. *Moscow Under Reconstruction* (*Moskva rekonstruiruetsia: alb'om diagramm, toposkhem i fotografii po rekonstruktsii gor. Moskvy*). Text by Viktor Shklovskii. Edited by V. M. Gorfunkel. Moscow: In-t izobrazitel'noĭ statistiki sov. stroitel'stva i khoziaistva TSUNKhU gosplana SSSR, 1938.
Schätzke, Andreas. *Zwischen Bauhaus und Stalinallee. Architekturdiskussion im östlichen Deutschland 1945–1955*. Braunschweig: Vieweg, 1991.
Schleef, Einar. *Tagebuch 1953–1963. Sangerhausen*. Edited by Winifried Menninghaus, Wolfgang Rath and Johannes Windrich. Frankfurt: Suhrkamp, 2004
Schnapp, Jeffrey. "The Mass Panorama." *Modernism/Modernity* 9, no. 2 (2002): 243–281.
Skřivánková, Lucie, Rostislav Švácha, and Irena Lehkoživová. *The Paneláks: Twenty-Five Housing Estates in the Czech Republic*. Prague: Museum of Decorative Arts, 2017.
Spurný, Matěj. *Making the Most of Tomorrow: A Laboratory of Socialist Modernity*. Prague: Karolinum, 2019.
Stangl, Paul. *Risen from Ruins: The Cultural Politics of Rebuilding East Berlin*. Stanford: Stanford University Press, 2018.

Sudek, Josef. *Nordböhmen*. Munich: W. Storms, 1988.
———. *Prague Panoramic*. Prague: Odeon, 1992.
———. *Smutná krajina: Severozápadní Čechy 1957–1962*. Litoměřice: Galerie výtvarného umění v Litoměřicích, 1999.
———. *The Window of My Studio*. Edited by Anna Fárová. Prague: Torst, 2015.
Svidel, S. "Volume and Line: Notes on Panoramic Shooting" ("Ob"em i linii: Zametki o panoramnoi s"emke"). *Sovetskoe foto* 2 (1934): 32–33.
Swope, Curtis. *Building Socialism: Architecture and Urbanism in East German Literature, 1955–73*. New York: Bloomsbury Academic, 2018.
Tiedemann, Fritz. *So weit kein Auge reicht: Berliner Panoramafotographien aus den Jahren 1949–1952*. Reconstructed and interpreted by Arwed Messmer. Berlin: Berlinische Galerie, 2009.
Trumpener, Katie. "Panoramic Journeys, 1900/2000: Documentary Survey in Panoramic Photography, Early Cinema, and Contemporary Installations." In *On the Viewing Platform: The Panorama Between Canvas and Screen*, edited by Katie Trumpener and Tim Barringer, 205–228. New Haven: Yale University Press, 2020.
Tupitsyn, Margarita. *Alexander Rodchenko: The New Moscow*. Munich: Schirmer Art Books, 1998.
———. "Exiting the Avant-Garde: Soviet Imagery under Stalin." In *Glaube Hoffnung Anpassung: Sowjetische Bilder 1928–1945*, edited by Margarita Tupitsyn, 144–161. Essen: Museum Folkswang, 1995.
———. *The Soviet Photograph*. New Haven: Yale University Press, 1996.
von Beyme, Klaus. "Leitbilder der Wiederaufbau in Deutschland." In *Neue Städte aus Ruinen: Deutscher Städtebau der Nachkriegszeit*, edited by Klaus von Beyme, Werner Durth, Niels Gutschow, and Winfried Nerdinger, 9–31. Munich: Prestel-Verlag, 1992.
Widdis, Emma. *Visions of a New Land: Soviet Film from the Revolution to the Second World War*. New Haven: Yale University Press, 2013.
Williams, Michael, and Richard Cahan. *The Lost Panoramas: When Chicago Changed Its River and the Land Beyond*. Chicago: CityFiles, 2011.
Wright, Gwendolyn. *The Politics of Design in French Colonial Urbanism*. Chicago: University of Chicago Press, 1991.
Zarecor, Kimberly Elman. *Manufacturing a Socialist Modernity: Housing in Czechoslovakia, 1945–1960*. Pittsburgh: University of Pittsburgh Press, 2011.

## Filmography

*The Architects* (*Die Architekten*, Peter Kahane, GDR, 1990)

*Berlin, Schönhauser Corner* (*Berlin, Ecke Schönhauser*, Gerhard Klein, GDR, 1957)

*The Bridge at Remagen* (John Guillermin, USA, 1969)

*Island of Swans* (*Insel der Schwäne*, Hermann Zschochke, GDR, 1983)

*The Noose* (*Pętla*, Wojciech Has, Poland, 1958)

*Our Short Life* (*Unser kurzes Leben*, Lothar Warneke, GDR, 1981)

*Prefab Story* (*Panelstory*, Věra Chytilová, Czechoslovakia, 1979)

*Shadow* (*Cień*, Jerzy Kawalerowicz, Poland, 1956)

*Story of a Young Couple* (*Roman einer jungen Ehe*, Kurt Maetzig, GDR, 1951)

*Sun Seekers* (*Sonnensucher*, Konrad Wolf, GDR, made 1958, released 1972)

*Trace of Stones* (*Spur der Steine*, Frank Beyer, GDR, 1965)

KATIE TRUMPENER is Emily Sanford Professor of Comparative Literature and English at Yale University. She is author of *Bardic Nationalism: The Romantic Novel and the British Empire* and editor (with Tim Barringer) of *On the Viewing Platform: The Panorama between Canvas and Screen*.

CHAPTER 3

*THE PEACE TRAIN*
## Anticosmopolitanism, Internationalism, and Jazz on Czechoslovak Radio during Stalinism

Rosamund Johnston

AIRED ON CZECHOSLOVAK RADIO IN 1950, the radio cantata *Vlak míru* (*The Peace Train*) has resonated with historians less than other elements of the broadcaster's output that year.[1] But the piece tells us as much about Stalinism in Czechoslovakia as the sound archive's more famous contemporaneous holdings: the recordings of Czechoslovakia's notorious show trials. While this chapter argues that both the trial recordings and the cantata responded to the same anticosmopolitan directives, *The Peace Train* allows us to trace an alternative to totalitarian understandings of radio and its function in Stalinist Czechoslovakia, which tend to overstate the amount of control exercised by Communist Party officials and law enforcement over the state broadcaster's daily programming.[2] An evaluation of *The Peace Train* reveals, moreover, that while radio was a key site of Sovietization in Stalinist Eastern Europe, this initiative only ever partially inflected the work of radio professionals and the programs they made.

Examining *The Peace Train*'s structure, sound, and influences, this chapter focuses on the three themes outlined in its title: jazz, anticosmopolitanism, and internationalism. My arguments are threefold: First, *The Peace Train* demonstrates how state radio became an incubator for a socialist-realist form of jazz during Stalinism—a period during which this musical genre was highly restricted in Czechoslovakia. Second, it embodies radio's paradoxical status as both an anticosmopolitan *and* a cosmopolitan medium at the peak of the Soviet-instigated (and eagerly Czechoslovak-championed) anticosmopolitan campaign. Third, *The Peace Train*'s internationalism situates it within a relatively large body of radio programming that introduced Czechs and Slovaks to foreign people and places during Stalinism.[3] This, in turn, makes clear that the isolationism propounded by the show trials was only one among several responses to the connected world that technologies such as radio continued to promote well into the Cold War in Eastern Europe.

## The Peace Train's Structure and Sound

*The Peace Train* was a thirty-seven-minute-long light entertainment program written specifically for radio. Its narration was largely spoken by the prominent radio announcer Antonín Zíb, with choral interludes and moments in which its characters burst into song. Its musical score was eclectic, sounding classical and symphonic in turns and employing a folksy and big-band sound at others.

The piece's premise was that a locomotive full of passengers from around the globe raced through Czechoslovakia, welcomed by citizens across the country. "Two hundred young people born in 30 countries . . . waved from the train's ten wagons," recounted Zíb, who then outlined the seating arrangements as proof of the locomotive's ability to foster accord (Englishmen sat with Spaniards, Germans with Palestinians; Zíb also noted the presence of Americans, Hungarians, Albanians, Arabs, Vietnamese, and Nigerians on the train).[4] Reprising this international list of passengers in the final minutes of the piece, the production was bookended with a roll call of all the foreigners onboard.

In between, the microphone was given to actors playing the Czech workers who witnessed the train. They spoke of how the locomotive had provided them with a newfound empathy for foreign workers.[5] Their testimonials were contrasted with the soliloquies of unhappy proletarians in the capitalist world (an unemployed Frenchman, a hungry Italian, and a homesick Scottish woman displaced to London for work). The first group's tone was one of joy, the second's one of sorrow, but both constituencies were presented favorably. In the very middle of the production, radio audiences were encouraged to listen to what the train itself had to say. On cue, the locomotive burst into song, personified by a choir chanting repeatedly in the rhythm of a shunting engine *"Chceme mír!"* ("We want peace!").

*The Peace Train*'s soundtrack likewise evoked foreign lands. Oldřich Letfus's score was performed by the Prague Symphony Orchestra, and both the Czechoslovak Radio and Julius Fučík choirs sang the chorus.[6] It opened with a pastiche of Antonín Dvořák's *New World Symphony*, which reappeared toward the end, when a variation on the Largo underlay one character's description of the hardships faced by anti-colonial activists around the world.[7] Letfus further gestured toward the United States when he retooled Irving Berlin's recent hit "The Freedom Train." At other moments, *The Peace Train* took a brassy, big-band turn reminiscent of "Chattanooga Choo Choo." Choral singing in Russian and English, suggestive of the Alexandrov Ensemble and "Battle Hymn of the Republic," marked the first few minutes of the piece. But despite this brief foray into Soviet-style singing, if the listener was encouraged to imagine one place through the choice of musical idiom, it was the United States.

Embedded in *The Peace Train*'s classical-sounding introduction was also an allusion to the Czech national anthem, "Kde domov můj?" ("Where is my home?"). This motif and the exclusive use of Czech throughout (despite the narrator's frequent reference to an undefined, utopic world language) were designed to evoke national sentiment in Czech listeners, while mention of Czech place names in the onlookers' testimonials anchored the production spatially in the listener's own backyard (Slovaks were merely along for the ride). Indeed, if Dvořák's *New World Symphony* thematically gestured toward the United States, it also equally belonged firmly to the Czech national canon and was championed as a template for the composers of the early 1950s who were developing a homegrown socialist-realist musical style.[8]

*The Peace Train* belonged to this moment and project. Yet listeners knew its main contributors from an earlier era. Librettist František Kožík and director Josef Bezdíček had been pioneers of radio drama during the interwar years—the medium's first "golden age."[9] In 1934, they had collaborated on the radio play *Cristobal Colón (Christopher Columbus)*, considered a "milestone" in Czechoslovak Radio history.[10] Kožík became a theorist of the medium, presenting his views on radio's unexhausted potential in *Rozhlasové umění (Radio Art)* in 1940.[11] Following the Communist Party's rise to power in May 1948, he and Bezdíček reprised *Christopher Columbus*. Reassembling important cast members and returning to a theme of world travel and discovery for *The Peace Train*, Kožík and Bezdíček redeployed in the latter what had made them famous in the former.[12] As such, in its creators, cast, and themes, *The Peace Train* was indicative of continuities (or institutional inertia) at Czechoslovak Radio between the interwar period and Stalinism.

## Acknowledged and Unacknowledged Influences

*The Peace Train* took inspiration from an actual locomotive. In 1950, as Melissa Feinberg explains, "Czechoslovak activists created a 'Peace Train' which journeyed to seven towns across the country. In each town, a peace congress was held and on the train, 'sketches, songs and dances' illustrated 'the fight against the warmongers of the world.'"[13] The entertainment-packed locomotive was a product of the peace movement, an initiative officially founded under Soviet auspices in Wrocław in 1948.[14] The movement brought artists, intellectuals, and scientists together from both sides of the Iron Curtain. When, in 1949, it was Prague's turn to stage a congress, the event attracted delegates from around the world, including American actor and musician Paul Robeson, who addressed the assembled crowd about civil rights in the United States and sang. Having had his passport confiscated by American authorities upon his return, he was singled out for special mention in Zíb's narration.[15]

Building on these real-life events, *The Peace Train* premiered on October 17, 1950, winning the inaugural Peace Prize awarded by the Czechoslovak Association for the Defenders of Peace (Československý výbor obránců míru); it was therefore reprised the following month.[16] This second airing coincided with the Second World Peace Conference in Warsaw, which ran from November 16 to November 22—a point at which "the main aim [of Soviet policy]," as Geoffrey Roberts suggests, "was to ensure the movement involved as many people as possible, irrespective of national, political and religious differences."[17] In the following years, as the peace movement adopted a more partisan position of support for the Soviet Union's isolationist foreign policy, its popularity waned.[18] Nevertheless, Roberts argues that through its diverse membership and international activities, "the peace movement chipped away at Soviet isolationism, even at the peak of Stalinist xenophobia."[19] It left a rhetoric "of 'world society' as well as of world capitalism, of 'international public opinion' as well as of international class struggle" as a lasting legacy in the Soviet Union.[20] And, around the Eastern Bloc, the rhetoric of the peace movement was omnipresent in the early 1950s and was found, as Feinberg writes, "in posters on factory walls, in newspaper articles, on radio programs, and in the speeches of officials on all levels, from the workplace to the highest reaches of government."[21] As in the *Peace Train*, this rhetoric often contrasted a peace-loving world citizenry with a small number of warmongers in the capitalist West who stood to gain financially through a continuous string of conflicts.

Despite their anti-Western tendencies, however, the locomotive and broadcast of *The Peace Train* also bore an uncanny—and unacknowledged—resemblance to "The Freedom Train," an American, Hollywood-sponsored initiative spanning from 1947 to 1949. In those years, "The Freedom Train" had toured the United States, "selling America to Americans."[22] This locomotive had likewise inspired its own soundtrack: a three-and-a-half-minute hit composed by Irving Berlin and performed by Bing Crosby and the Andrews Sisters. Berlin's "Freedom Train" had championed the ways in which Americans could exercise their democratic rights and demand accountability from their elected representatives.

Beyond these thematic similarities, *The Peace Train* at times mirrors Berlin's "Freedom Train." For instance, the American hit opens with instrumentation mimicking a shunting locomotive and the Andrews Sisters singing in harmony; after this, Crosby sings in recitative: "This song is a train song—a song about a train."[23] Then, alternating with the Andrews Sisters, he lists all the songs (and trains) that this was not: "Not the Atchison, Topeka—Not the Chattanooga Choo Choo."[24] In a similar-sounding passage of *The Peace Train*, narrator Antonín Zíb bursts into song, hypothesizing that "maybe the other [*druhý*] world can hear. The train song resounds far and wide."[25] Zíb's recitative similarly references a "train song" and similarly overlays an orchestra and choir mimicking the movement of a chugging engine. While this reference remains indirect, then, *The Peace Train* was clearly an answer to "The Freedom Train" (with *freedom* and *peace* the respective rallying cries for American and Soviet platforms in the early Cold War). And with this, *The Peace Train* made reference to both the Iron Curtain and sound's ability to transcend it. For as Zíb's recitative suggested, not only could the Czechoslovaks "hear" the West, but those in the West might also take note of *The Peace Train*'s sound.

If *The Peace Train* found some of its musical influence in the West, it also adhered to musical directives from the East. While one can debate the extent, Soviet Minister of Culture Andrei Zhdanov's thoughts on socialist realism in music—his tirades against "formalism" and art for art's sake—certainly influenced music policy in the Eastern Bloc after 1948.[26] His edicts "in the name of the Central Committee, on literature, music, art, theatre, and film" came to be known as the *Zhdanovshchina*, a term that also incorporated, as David Caute suggests, "the shrill ideological crusades, violent purges, outbursts of Russian chauvinism, and strident cold-war rhetoric that marked the period from 1946 to 1949."[27]

However, the resonances of these ideas in Czechoslovakia were not straightforward: Kimberly Elman Zarecor has argued that Czechoslovak socialist realism (implemented in the country after the war and with increased intensity after the Communist takeover) should not merely be seen as a Soviet import. Instead, debates took place in Czechoslovakia about how this style might work locally, with Information Minister Václav Kopecký tending toward a straight adoption of "the Soviet model" and Culture Minister

Zdeněk Nejedlý advocating a variant incorporating national and vernacular elements.[28] At a speech to the Union of Composers in 1951, for instance, Nejedlý exhorted those present to embrace programmatic music, as their Soviet peers had done, as a rejection of the pointless, "pure" music produced in Czechoslovakia in prerevolutionary times.[29] Zhdanov had elevated nineteenth-century Russian composers such as Pyotr Tchaikovsky and Mikhail Glinka as musical examples; here, Nejedlý evoked their Czech contemporaries Bedřich Smetana and Dvořák as suitable templates.[30] "In practice," Zarecor concludes, "Nejedlý was more important to the formulation of [socialist realism] than Kopecký was," a fact that she attributes to "deep-seated feelings of national pride and a sense of Czechoslovak regional exceptionalism that remained throughout the socialist period."[31]

Czechoslovak Radio demonstrates both ministers' influence: it fell under the purview of Václav Kopecký's Ministry of Information, and it was restructured according to the Soviet model in 1952.[32] The broadcaster was rearranged into four different sections, following the example of Radio Moscow.[33] But the Soviet model that shaped the institution's structure was not always all that audible. The music it played, for example, was composed by those who answered to Nejedlý's directives and often, as in *The Peace Train*, incorporated Czech and Slovak folk elements and borrowed from a nineteenth-century national canon.

Neighboring Poland offers a similar example. By the late 1940s, Patryk Babiracki argues, radio became one of the first venues where Soviet influence upon local culture became clear. This influence chiefly took the form of music programming, as well as discussions of Soviet topics, Russian language lessons, and news about the Soviet Union.[34] But even then, the effects of radio's Sovietization remained partial, with Moscow officials fuming that the medium continued to broadcast Western-style content.[35] By shifting the lens away from dissatisfied cultural functionaries and toward radio staff, an even clearer picture emerges of how such directives only ever partially inflected cultural producers' work.[36] This was particularly the case when professionals like Kožík and Bezdíček had the institutional clout of a high-profile interwar radio career behind them.

## Socialist Realist Jazz at Czechoslovak Radio

Overlapping with the *Zhdanovshchina* was the anticosmopolitan campaign.[37] As Kiril Tomoff writes, this was marked in the Soviet Union by a broad "fear of foreign influence," with antisemitism forming another "essential component."[38] The Soviet campaign targeted popular music alongside other forms of culture; its proponents expressed a "preference for . . . music based on folk song rather than jazz."[39] It was taken up with gusto in Czechoslovakia, where jazz also became a particular casualty.[40] As Lubomir Dorůžka and Miloslav Ducháč explain, "any drum solo, the baritone saxophone (a bourgeois instrument), vocal harmonies (an American paradigm), and unnecessary improvisation" were prohibited from the radio as part of the campaign to rein in jazz.[41] Big bands such as that of preeminent Czechoslovak jazzman Karel Vlach were also banned from recorded performances at Czechoslovak Radio from 1949 until 1951.[42] Jazz, however, did not disappear altogether from Czechoslovak Radio's frequencies. Instead, *The Peace Train* shows how the broadcaster became an incubator for a socialist-realist form of jazz during Stalinism—a form that found mainstream popularity and lived on in Czech and Slovak film scores and record collections for decades to come.

Author Josef Škvorecký documents this, albeit sardonically. While arguing that jazz musicians in Stalinist Czechoslovakia had inherent resistance credentials (in his words, "the ideological guns and sometimes even the police guns of all dictatorships are aimed at the men with horns"), Škvorecký notes the simultaneous, *sanctioned* existence of less highbrow forms of jazz.[43] At the heart of his criticism of Czechoslovak music policy in the period was the idea that Communist functionaries were guilty of crimes against good taste. "Uncle Tom [Dixieland] music was really the only form of jazz suffered at the depressing congregations called youth entertainments," he complained, "where urban girls in pseudo-national costumes got up and sang bombastic odes to Stalin in the style of rural yodeling."[44] One might somewhat more charitably reclassify the yodeling that Škvorecký "suffered" as Czechoslovak middlebrow culture of the early 1950s.

If *The Peace Train* struck a balance between Dixieland and cosmopolitan jazz music, doing so constituted less of an act of wily resistance (as Škvorecký would have it) and more of an act of vibrant creativity within particular boundaries. In addition to the piece's *Freedom Train* allusions, jazz is folded into the production through use of tonality; jazz scales appear at copious intervals throughout.[45] The work's instrumentation, which relies heavily on brass but eschews the saxophone, creates a big-band sound. And one of the characters, Milan Mach—starring, according to the piece's credits, as "černoch" ("Black man")—embodied a form of minstrelsy when detailing the predicament of the world's colonized poor.[46]

It would be absurd, of course, to suggest that Czechoslovak Radio was listeners' go-to broadcaster for jazz during Stalinism. As Dorůžka and

Ducháč relate, musicians tuned in to American Forces Network and Voice of America for such music instead, in some instances making recordings to circulate among peers.⁴⁷ And according to her mother, Jo Langer, future jazz singer Zuzka Lonská listened "late into the night, patiently, over and over, to the same songs transmitted by foreign radio stations, until she had learnt them and could write down the English texts. Ella Fitzgerald was her God; and she got down a lot of Gershwin, Cole Porter and some of the latest hits. As this sort of music was unobtainable on records or otherwise, it was all the more loved by the young."⁴⁸

But to conclude from such recollections that domestic jazz production ground to an ignominious halt in Stalinist Czechoslovakia would be to overlook how the state broadcaster provided resources for a reinvention of the genre. In an environment where a choice remained between Czechoslovak Radio and Western stations, Czechoslovak Radio embarked on initiatives such as *The Peace Train*, in which composers sought to develop a socialist sort of jazz that could draw listeners away from Western broadcasts. Such output borrowed from and ideologically defanged the contemporary American works that Czechs and Slovaks might hear elsewhere.⁴⁹

This story thus nuances the Cold War history of jazz offered in histories of American-sponsored stations such as Voice of America and Radio Free Europe.⁵⁰ Stalinist Czechoslovakia, in short, cultivated its own distinct form of jazz that served specific social, political, and aesthetic roles. As scholars of the Soviet Union have pointed out, such a reworking of the generic boundaries of jazz was not distinct to Czechoslovakia, but state radio's preeminent role in fostering such innovation is remarkable in the Czechoslovak case.⁵¹ Moreover, this new form of jazz had staying power; the sound that composers such as Letfus came up with entered into the repertoires of jazz singers such as Lonská, alongside the Fitzgerald and Gershwin that returned to official favor by the mid-1950s.⁵² Indeed, when Karel Vlach's orchestra was again able to release records with state label Supraphon, it had adopted something of this middlebrow sound. Jan Friedlaender, an unimpressed student, complained to newspaper *Literární noviny* that Vlach's 1954 release of jazz composer Jaroslav Ježek's music sounded "no different from regular pop songs [*šlágrů*]—perhaps only slightly better."⁵³ Any radical elements of interwar leftist Ježek's music are drowned in a sea of large-scale choral harmonies and punctilious 4/4 beats.⁵⁴ Responding to Friedlaender, *Literární noviny*'s editors agreed that the "progressive" nature of Ježek's music had been lost by Vlach's orchestra and apportioned some of the blame to Czechoslovak Radio.⁵⁵ The part jazz, part oompah Czech "national" sound that made its way into Vlach's orchestra would go on to be heralded and marketed abroad for valuable Western currency by the early 1970s in albums such as *Ze země polek (From the Land of Polkas)*.[56]

## Radio as an (Anti)Cosmopolitan Medium

When historians analyze anticosmopolitanism on Czechoslovak Radio's frequencies, they do not often focus on music. The term is most frequently evoked in relation to the antisemitic show trials of alleged "cosmopolitans" Rudolf Slánský and his codefendants, prominent Communist Party members who were arrested in 1950 and indicted for serving foreign powers two years later.[57] Slánský's was "the classic Communist show trial" for Tony Judt, who stresses the role Czechoslovak Radio played in disseminating the proceedings.[58] Similarly, Melissa Feinberg and Kevin MacDermott have demonstrated how the trial constituted a means through which the nascent Communist dictatorship sought to communicate with citizens. Both chart how such communication was two-directional: listeners were expected to engage with what they heard in particular, prescribed ways—something they did not always do.[59]

Memoirs likewise characterize Czechoslovak Radio of the period as anticosmopolitan. "Those were the days of the Cold War," recalls Heda Margolius Kovály, whose husband was executed in the Slánský trials. "The Iron Curtain had come down and had cut us off from the rest of the world."[60] Radio was partially responsible for this severance. With a few tantalizing exceptions, when the state broadcaster did air foreign news, it was from the Soviet Union: "Once I was listening to the news on the radio and caught the word 'Netherlands,'" Kovály noted. "I pricked up my ears but the news item was only that the Soviet Folk Dance Collective had enjoyed a great success in Amsterdam. That was the only bit of news we had from the West in months."[61] In her memoir, Kovály describes foreign stations as being blocked out by jamming, but this practice took a great deal of infrastructural preparation and only came into full effect in 1952.[62] Regardless, for Kovály in the early 1950s, the radio primarily served as a means of following her husband's "odd monotonous voice" during his trial.[63]

Czechoslovak Radio was most certainly the mouthpiece for an officially articulated anticosmopolitanism in Stalinist-era Czechoslovakia—but this was only part of the story. I have thus far discussed *The Peace Train* as a creative outcome of the anticosmopolitan campaign and the regulations that the campaign placed on jazz composition. But in its content, *The Peace Train* should also be read as a cosmopolitan piece and specifically as a comment on radio's potential as a medium to transcend national and cultural boundaries and foster world understanding.

In fact, broadcast on the same frequencies and during the same years as xenophobic programming like the Slánský trials, *The Peace Train* is representative of a considerable and wildly popular (yet largely overlooked) body of work that brought foreign people and places into Czechoslovak homes.[64] Such inward- and outward-looking programming formulated two different responses to the question of where Czechs and Slovaks might fit in the emergent Cold War geopolitical order—and in a world made smaller by technological advances, among them radio. While the medium had existed for decades already, its international potential was increasingly realized in the postwar period with a host of new foreign stations targeting Czechs and Slovaks with world news in their languages and Czechoslovak Radio dispatching its own correspondents overseas for the first time. Considering *The Peace Train* as an example of programming that sought to position Czech and Slovak listeners within a larger, global community unpicks lingering Cold War frameworks that posit a closed East against an open West during Stalinism.[65]

The notion that radio might be an inherently cosmopolitan medium was, in fact, discussed by Czechoslovak functionaries and broadcasters at the time. In tandem with Canadian media scholar Harold Innis but in somewhat more bombastic tones, Information Minister Václav Kopecký reflected on the medium's capacity to reconfigure perceptions of time and space.[66] In his 1952 speech "Proti kosmopolitismu jako ideologii amerického imperialismu" ("Against Cosmopolitanism as an American Imperial Ideology"), Kopecký issued a stream of invective against both Zionism and world citizens—linking the presence of both of these constituencies in Czechoslovakia to radio.[67] The minister dedicated much of the speech to excoriating the head of Radio Free Europe's Czechoslovak section, Ferdinand Peroutka, as well as the émigrés who announced a cosmopolitan American program from Munich, RFE's base.[68] If cosmopolitanism had a sound, it was, for Kopecký, Radio Free Europe. If this sound had a vehicle, it was the radio set residing in the Czechoslovak home. Kopecký's haranguing tone and overt antisemitism make his speech disturbing reading, but in his larger set of ideas, the minister may have been onto something: radio was indeed a medium reconfiguring contemporary Czechoslovak society's (the polity's) image of the wider world (the cosmos).

Kožík, Bezdíček, and Letfus explored this idea in *The Peace Train*, in which the eponymous train served as a metaphor for radio and other technology that standardized time and compressed distance.[69] Czechs and Slovaks had become accustomed to train timetables and radio listings structuring their day by the interwar period, with schedules for both providing a temporal framework that held true across a large geographic territory.[70] As Felix Jeschke writes of railways in interwar Czechoslovakia, radio, too, had tiptoed into "the routines of everyday life and ... structured it to an ever-greater extent both in terms of senses and in terms of space."[71] Just as railways had brought "visible symbols of nationhood" and a "cosmopolitan consciousness" to the towns through which they passed, radio conveyed both an explicitly national and deeply cosmopolitan message to listeners in *The Peace Train*.[72] Through Kožík's libretto, both train carriage and wireless set introduced Czechs and Slovaks to fellow workers from around the globe.

### THE PEACE TRAIN'S SOCIALIST INTERNATIONALISM

If the train was a metaphor for the radio, then it was also a symbol of the Bolshevik Revolution. In the Soviet Union, a number of agit-trains had traveled around the country in the interwar period, bringing the revolution to the masses. At first glance, then, the Soviet Union provided the straightforward model for *The Peace Train* bringing revolution to the Czechoslovak provinces in 1950. But the socialist revolutionary symbol of the train in fact proved fertile ground for authors seeking to articulate their state's relationship to the Soviet Union, as Rossen Djagalov has shown.[73]

Djagalov, alongside Rachel Applebaum and Patryk Babiracki, characterizes the late 1940s and early 1950s as the peak of the Soviet Union's role as international arbiter of contacts between socialist states—despite a simultaneous drive on the part of the Soviet Union to limit the presence of foreigners on Soviet soil.[74] For Balázs Apor, the image of Stalin himself was the prime vehicle for internationalism within the Eastern Bloc in the early Cold War years. In such interpretations, internationalism is a concept that radiated out from and pointed back to Moscow—with the Soviet Union the go-between and agenda-setter in such configurations.[75] By contrast, *The Peace Train* presented a rather chaotic, multidirectional image of international relations (all supported nevertheless on railway tracks constructed according to the Soviet model).[76] Mention of the generalissimo and the ultimate destination of Moscow were missing from the piece (in fact, unlike the radio to which it was likened, this train crossed no borders at all). Yet in decentering the role of the Soviet Union in *The Peace Train*, Kožík and Bezdíček were not making an anti-Soviet statement. Instead, their work reflected the limited information available about the Soviet Union in Czechoslovakia at the time. As Applebaum notes, in the absence of firsthand contact with Soviet art or indeed the country itself, Czechoslovak-made propaganda about the Soviet Union in the early Cold War routinely "reduced the USSR to a series of tropes: the defender of peace, the builder of the radiant future, the caretaker of women and children."[77]

The crux of *The Peace Train*'s socialist internationalism derived instead from the older notion of the workers of the world uniting. Laborers from the West were afforded the same amount of airtime as joyful Czechoslovak workers. Czech children were described as maintaining regular, direct contact with their Chinese peers (although one would assume that Russian was the *lingua franca* of the letters they sent). Representatives of diplomatically recognized countries sang alongside those from territories lacking formal statehood.[78] And a parity of sorts was suggested between the Soviet Union and the United States by the choral singing at the beginning (with the US then gaining the musical edge in the piece). In *The Peace Train*, the diverse range of characters represented a shared set of values rather than their own states or even their blocs.

Frantisek Kožík's script emphasized this, opening with the assertion that "the world is not big ... the whole world is our homeland [*vlast*]," before claiming that workers from Europe, Asia, and Africa all "speak the same language."[79] The idea of mutual, utopic world understanding was broached repeatedly; at one point it was prophesized that children of the world would all come to speak the same language (though what this language would be was left uninvestigated). Elsewhere, understanding was posited as translinguistic, with the narrator claiming, "We understand your words—the goal is peace!" And the listener was assured that understanding came through the practice of listening itself when the peace train was personified and heard to sing *"Chceme mír!"* ("We want peace!"). Kožík was an avid Esperantist, and he had directed an Esperanto program, *Verda Stacio* (*The Green Station*), with Josef Bezdíček on Czechoslovak Radio between 1933 and 1940.[80] His text suggested that mutual understanding was possible when the topic of discussion was universally comprehensible and that peace provided one such subject. *The Peace Train* additionally presented workers from around the world as biologically and spiritually the same. This was underscored by casting Czechs in each of the foreign roles: foreign culture was located in Czech voices, pointing to the interchangeability of us all.[81]

## Conclusion

*The Peace Train* incorporated influences from East and West at a moment when the Iron Curtain was at its most seemingly impermeable. It utilized jazz and recent American composition, not as a sign of anticommunist resistance but instead to convey a Soviet-sponsored message of peace—with the program's creators judging socialist activism and American-sounding music compatible. Through the analysis of the piece, then, a counterpoint to totalitarian understandings of radio in Stalinist Czechoslovakia emerges: rather than merely serving as a mouthpiece for an authoritarian state, radio programming bears traces of its contributors' creative processes and ideas. It also reveals the strict limits placed on both. Czechoslovak Radio did become an important site of Sovietization in Stalinist-era Czechoslovakia, but a close reading of *The Peace Train* shows that the effects of this drive were only ever partially audible—particularly when radio staff brought a sound associated with their earlier broadcasts to their work.

Through programming such as *The Peace Train*, Czechoslovak Radio cultivated a unique socialist-realist sound that left an enduring mark on Czechoslovak jazz music. Using the eponymous *Peace Train* as a metaphor for radio, Kožík, Bezdíček, and Letfus contemplated how innately cosmopolitan the medium might be at a moment when, as Pauline Fairclough writes, "'cosmopolitanism' was either a term of abuse or a description of someone at risk of arrest."[82] The forms of internationalism they propounded show how Czechs and Slovaks attempted to define and understand their place in a reconfiguring Cold War world. Isolationism and xenophobia were two expressions of this project, to be sure, but it is not enough to take this part for the whole. In 1950, radio brought the cosmos, as well as the courtroom, into the Czechoslovak home.

## NOTES

Thank you to Sujit Thomas, Alice Lovejoy, Mari Pajala, Michael Beckerman, and Joanna Curtis for their edits and comments and the Collegium Carolinum in Munich for providing a stimulating and supportive environment in which to develop this chapter.

 1. A "radio cantata" is how librettist František Kožík described the piece in *Kapitoly z dějin Československého Rozhlasu*, č. 3: 259 in Box "Pozůstalost František Kožík, 1934–1993." Czech Radio Archive, Prague.

 2. Scholars arguing that Communist Czechoslovakia was a totalitarian state have invoked its radio network as proof, suggesting the medium fell under a "near-complete monopoly of [party and government] control." Such control was used to implement a "system of terror ... [exploiting] modern science, and more especially scientific psychology" (Friedrich and Brzezinski, *Totalitarian Dictatorship and Autocracy*, 22). More recent works espousing this view include Anne Applebaum's *Iron Curtain* and contributions to A. Ross Johnson and Eugene Parta's edited volume *Cold War Broadcasting*. This totalitarian model has come under criticism, however, for overstating the power and monolithic nature of Eastern Europe's Communist Parties. For such critiques, see Geyer and Fitzpatrick, *Beyond Totalitarianism*; and Jarausch, "Beyond Uniformity."

 3. See the vast output of traveler-journalists Jiří Hanzelka and Miloslav Zikmund on Czechoslovak Radio between 1947 and 1952, alongside the several spin-offs their tremendously popular programming spurred—the foreign dispatches, for example, of *Namořník Lesný* (Sailor Lesný) and, for children, "*Pohledy do světa*" (Views of the World). For more on the latter, see Franc and Knapík, *Volný čas v Českých zemích 1957–1967*, 49.

 4. Czech Radio Archive, Prague, AF02251_2_AF9158: *Vlak míru*, November 19, 1950.

 5. Ibid.

6. The Julius Fučík choir was comprised of around 120 young people who both sang and danced. It was founded in 1950. The choir "focused on light music in particular," according to its web pages. For more details, see Pěvecký sbor ČVUT Praha, "Historie Sboru."

7. Czech Radio Archive, *Vlak míru*.

8. See Nejedlý, "O programovosti v hudbě." This point, and this text, will be discussed in more depth later.

9. See Ladislav Daneš, "František Kožík a Objevení Ameriky," in Box "Pozůstalost František Kožík, 1934–1993." Czech Radio Archive, Prague. Czechoslovak Radio is often said to have enjoyed a second golden age in the 1960s. See, for example, Kotalová, "Redakce mezinárodního života Československého rozhlasu."

10. Velíšek, "František Kožík: Cristobal Colón."

11. Kožík, *Rozhlasové umění*.

12. For example, narrator Antonín Zíb and actor Artuš Kalous starred prominently in both. See Panáček v říši mluveného slova, "Vlak míru (1950)" and "Cristobal Colón (1948, 1989)."

13. Feinberg, *Curtain of Lies*, 51. The source she cites therein is called *In Defense of Peace* 2, no. 8.

14. For an analysis of the peace movement's origins and outcomes, see Roberts, "Averting Armageddon."

15. Czech Radio Archive, *Vlak míru*. See circa 33:30.

16. Kožík, *Kapitoly z dějin Československého Rozhlasu*, 259.

17. For details of this conference and why it ended up in Warsaw (as opposed to Sheffield, where it was to have been held), see Roberts, "Averting Armageddon," 327. For more on the early inclusivity of the peace movement, see Ibid., 324.

18. Ibid., 330.

19. Ibid., 325.

20. Ibid., 333.

21. Feinberg, *Curtain of Lies*, 33.

22. Brophy, *Cold War in a Cold Land*.

23. See Devine, "Victrola Phonograph."

24. Ibid.

25. Ibid.

26. Fairclough stresses this point in *Classics for the Masses*, 208.

27. Caute, *The Dancer Defects*, 7.

28. Zarecor, *Manufacturing a Socialist Modernity*, 131.

29. For Communists such as Nejedlý, the revolution took place in Czechoslovakia at the end of World War II on May 5, 1945. See Nejedlý, "O programovosti v hudbě," 44.

30. Ibid., 41–48. Parallel to Nejedlý and Zhdanov's appeals to composers to return to their "national" roots, Leonard Bernstein and Aaron Copland were espousing American motifs in their compositions, and English composers like Benjamin Britten were turning back in their work to Elizabethan themes. It is in the international context of such apparent turns inward and backward that we should understand Letfus's incorporation of allusions to both Dvořák and the Czech national anthem.

31. Zarecor, *Manufacturing a Socialist Modernity*, 134.

32. Kotalová, "Redakce mezinárodního života Československého rozhlasu," 10.

33. For more details, see Běhal, "Rozhlas po nástupu totality," 246.

34. Babiracki, *Soviet Soft Power in Poland*, 111.

35. Ibid., 121.

36. That such directives were intended to apply to Czechoslovak as well as Polish radio is indicated by Babiracki in *Soviet Soft Power in Poland*, 112.

37. See Tomoff, *Creative Union*, 152. He dates the anticosmopolitan campaign from 1949 to Stalin's death in 1953 and argues that it has largely been overlooked in comparison to the *Zhdanovshchina*.

38. Ibid., 152.
39. Ibid., 153.
40. Culture Minister Zdeněk Nejedlý denounced jazz as an "expression of cosmopolitanism" during this period. See Dorůžka and Ducháč, *Karel Vlach*, 114.
41. Ibid., 112.
42. Ibid., 118.
43. Škvorecký, "Red Music," 5. Throughout the essay, Škvorecký plays up the bravery of himself and former fellow band members who performed jazz during the late 1940s and early 1950s, equating the metaphorical "slavery" of citizens of the "captive nations" behind the Iron Curtain with the actual slavery experienced by African Americans in the United States.
44. Ibid., 20.
45. See Caute, *The Dancer Defects*, 444.
46. See Panáček v říši mluveného slova, "Vlak míru (1950)."
47. Dorůžka and Ducháč, citing Jaroslav Kopáček, *Karel Vlach*, 120.
48. Langer, *Convictions*, 116.
49. I have written about the effects of choice on radio policy in early socialist Czechoslovakia; see Johnston, "Secret Agents," 15–32.
50. See von Eschen, *Satchmo Blows Up the World*; and Pospíšil, "Inspiration, Subversion, and Appropriation."
51. On the work that composers and musicians undertook to reinvent jazz in the Soviet Union at this moment, see Starr, *Red and Hot*; and Tsipursky, "Jazz, Power and Soviet Youth in the Early Cold War."
52. For more on the rehabilitation of jazz in Czechoslovakia, see Vidomus, "'Američan—a musí emigrovat do Československa!'"
53. Friedlaender, letter published in *Literární noviny*.
54. See, for example, Prague Municipal Theatre Choir, "Svítá," 1954; and Cortés, "O Španělsku si zpívám," 1954.
55. Response to Jan Friedlaender.
56. This is essentially an album of brass band favorites (such as *The Beer Barrel Polka* or *Škoda lásky*), rendered jazzy largely through their syncopated rhythm, released on three separate occasions with a German market in mind. See Vlach, "Karel Vlach Und Sein Orchester—Vom Land Der Polkas."
57. See, for example, MacDermott, "A 'Polyphony of Voices'?"; and Feinberg, "Fantastic Truths, Compelling Lies," 107–125. In addition, Czechoslovak Radio aired the prosecutions of foreign nationals such as Johannes Louwers, likewise charged with working for foreign governments hostile to socialist Czechoslovakia. This has also received scholarly analysis; see Sklenářová, "Nizozemská špionážní aféra."
58. Judt, *Postwar*, 185.
59. Feinberg, *Curtain of Lies*, 51; and MacDermott, "A 'Polyphony of Voices'?"
60. Kovály, *Under a Cruel Star*, 93.
61. Ibid., 94.
62. For details, see Barta, "Přestaňte okamžitě rušit modré."
63. Kovály, *Under a Cruel Star*, 141.
64. For more details, see footnote 4.
65. Such ideas have been helpfully challenged, for example, by Susan Carruthers, who has examined the limits to American mobility at the period. See Carruthers, *Cold War Captives*.
66. For Innis's views on this point, see Innis, *The Bias of Communication*.
67. Kopecký, *Proti kosmopolitismu*, 6.
68. As well as foreign stations that spilled over into Czech and Slovak receivers, Radio Free Europe began broadcasting in 1950 from West Germany, intentionally setting out to reach Czech and Slovak audiences. Along with Czechoslovakia's position near German radio transmitters installed

expressly to relay broadcasts East, the ubiquity of radio sets in Czechoslovakia during the period ensured that most households had the technological capacity to receive broadcasts originating in the West. For the Munich reference, see Kopecký, *Proti kosmopolitismu*, 17.

69. That infrastructure should be understood as media is a point stressed by Marshall McLuhan, who reminds readers that roads and the written word have long been "closely interrelated," as betrayed by the title "communications" conferred on both. Before the telegraph, written communications could not travel any faster than a messenger, and physical infrastructure thus facilitated and expedited access to information. Both railroads and radio had served to accelerate the transfer of news, leading space, rather than time, to become the main factor in social differentiation in an increasingly instant age. But while wireless and locomotives both diminished the time it took to transport information, the impact both media came to have on space was not identical—railroads left their physical mark on a city; by contrast, "electric forms" of media, such as the telegraph and radio, were indifferent to the layout of urban space. See McLuhan, *Understanding Media*, 89.

70. As Gordon Allport and Hadley Cantril note in their 1935 work on radio, "one of the outstanding characteristics of broadcasting is its punctuality. Like train dispatching, it is on time." Allport and Cantril, *The Psychology of Radio*, 23–24.

71. van Laak, cited in Jeschke, "Iron Landscapes," 17.

72. Ibid., 25.

73. Djagalov, *From Internationalism to Postcolonialism*, 125.

74. See Djagalov, "The Zone of Freedom?"; Applebaum, *Empire of Friends*; and Babiracki, *Soviet Soft Power in Poland*.

75. Apor, "The Stalin Cult and the Construction of the Second World," 49–76.

76. Czech Radio Archive, *Vlak míru*.

77. Applebaum, *Empire of Friends*, 45

78. For example, Palestine and Scotland.

79. Czech Radio Archive, *Vlak míru*.

80. See Esperanto.cz, "Historie."

81. This is something that Alice Lovejoy finds in Czechoslovak Army documentary films of the period. See Lovejoy, *Army Film*, 82.

82. Fairclough, *Classics for the Masses*, 221.

## Bibliography

Allport, Gordon, and Hadley Cantril. *The Psychology of Radio*. New York & London: Harper, 1935.

Apor, Balázs. "The Stalin Cult and the Construction of the Second World in Hungary in the Early Cold War Years." In *Socialist Internationalism in the Cold War*, edited by Patryk Babiracki and Austin Jersild, 49–76. London: Palgrave MacMillan, 2016.

Applebaum, Anne. *Iron Curtain: The Crushing of Eastern Europe, 1944–1956*. New York: Anchor, 2013.

Applebaum, Rachel. *Empire of Friends: Soviet Power and Socialist Internationalism in Cold War Czechoslovakia*. Ithaca, NY: Cornell University Press, 2019.

Babiracki, Patryk. *Soviet Soft Power in Poland: Culture and the Making of Stalin's New Empire, 1943–1957*. Chapel Hill: University of North Carolina Press, 2015.

Barta, Milan. "Přestaňte okamžitě rušit modré." *Paměť a dějiny*, no. 3 (2012).

Běhal, Rostislav. "Rozhlas po nástupu totality, 1949–1958." In *Od mikrofonu k posluchačům*, edited by Eva Ješutová, 246. Prague: Radioservis, 2003.

Brophy, Thomas D'Arcy. *Cold War in a Cold Land: Fighting Communism on the Northern Plains*. Norman: University of Oklahoma Press, 2015.

Carruthers, Susan. *Cold War Captives*. Berkeley: University of California Press, 2009.
Caute, David. *The Dancer Defects: The Struggle for Cultural Supremacy during the Cold War*. Oxford: Oxford University Press, 2005.
Cortés, Rudolf. "O Španělsku si zpívám." *Karel Vlach hraje písně Jaroslava Ježka* (Supraphon 1954).
Devine, Mitch. "Victrola Phonograph—Bing Crosby and the Andrews Sisters 'The Freedom Train.'" YouTube. July 16, 2011. Accessed April 21, 2019. https://www.youtube.com/watch?v=m-PayWAG9XY.
Djagalov, Rossen. *From Internationalism to Postcolonialism: Literature and Cinema between the Second and Third Worlds*. Montreal: McGill-Queens University Press, 2020.
———. "The Zone of Freedom? Differential Censorship in the Post-Stalin-Era People's Republic of Letters." *The Slavonic and East European Review* 98, no. 4 (2020): 601–631.
Dorůžka, Lubomir, and Miloslav Ducháč. *Karel Vlach: 50 let s hudbou*. Prague: Ekopress, 2003.
Esperanto.cz. "Historie." Accessed July 10, 2018. http://www.esperanto.cz/cs/co-to-je-esperanto/kultura/rozhlas.
Fairclough, Pauline. *Classics for the Masses: Shaping Soviet Musical Identity under Lenin and Stalin*. New Haven, CT: Yale University Press, 2016.
Feinberg, Melissa. *Curtain of Lies: The Battle over Truth in Stalinist Eastern Europe*. New York: Oxford University Press, 2017.
———. "Fantastic Truths, Compelling Lies: Radio Free Europe and the Response to the Slánský Trial in Czechoslovakia." *Contemporary European History* 22, no. 1 (2013): 107–125.
Franc, Martin, and Jiří Knapík. *Volný čas v Českých zemích 1957–1967*. Prague: Academia, 2013.
Friedlaender, Jan. Letter published in *Literární noviny*, no. 3 (1955): 9.
Friedrich, Carl, and Zbigniew Brzezinski. *Totalitarian Dictatorship and Autocracy*, 2nd ed. New York: Praeger, 1963.
Geyer, Michael, and Sheila Fitzpatrick, eds. *Beyond Totalitarianism: Stalinism and Nazism Compared*. Cambridge: Cambridge University Press, 2012.
Innis, Harold. *The Bias of Communication*. Toronto: University of Toronto Press, 1951.
Jarausch, Konrad. "Beyond Uniformity: The Challenge of Historicizing the GDR." In *Dictatorship as Experience: Towards a Socio-Cultural History of the GDR*, edited by Konrad Jarausch, 3–15. New York: Berghahn, 1999.
Jeschke, Felix. "Iron Landscapes: Nation-Building and the Railways in Czechoslovakia, 1918–1938." PhD diss., University College London, 2016.
Johnson, A. Ross, and Eugene Parta, eds. *Cold War Broadcasting: Impact on the Soviet Union and Eastern Europe*. Budapest: Central European University Press, 2012.
Johnston, Rosamund. "Secret Agents: Reassessing the Agency of Radio Listeners in Czechoslovakia, 1945–1953." In *Perceptions of Society in Communist Europe: Regime Archives and Popular Opinion*, edited by Muriel Blaive, 15–32. London: Bloomsbury Academic, 2019.
Judt, Tony. *Postwar*. New York: Penguin, 2005.
Kopecký, Václav. *Proti kosmopolitismu jako ideologii amerického imperialismu*. Prague: Orbis, 1952.
Kotalová, Zdenka. "Redakce mezinárodního života Československého rozhlasu v 60. letech." Unpublished diss., Faculty of Social Sciences, Charles University, 2012.
Kovály, Heda Margolius. *Under a Cruel Star: A Life in Prague, 1941–1968*. London: Granta, 2012.
Kožík, František. *Rozhlasové umění*. Prague: Českomoravský Kompas, 1940.

Langer, Jo. *Convictions: My Life with a Good Communist*. London: Granta, 2011.
Lovejoy, Alice. *Army Film and the Avant Garde: Cinema and Experiment in the Czechoslovak Military*. Bloomington: Indiana University Press, 2015.
MacDermott, Kevin. "A 'Polyphony of Voices'? Czech Popular Opinion and the Slánský Affair." *Slavic Review* 67, no. 4 (2008): 840–865.
McLuhan, Marshall. *Understanding Media: The Extensions of Man*. Cambridge, MA: MIT Press, 1964.
Nejedlý, Zdeněk. "O programovosti v hudbě." *O výtvarnictví, hudbě a poesii*. Prague: Československý spisovatel, 1952.
Panáček v říši mluveného slova. "Cristobal Colón (1948, 1989)." Accessed January 17, 2018. http://mluveny.panacek.com/rozhlasove-hry/4218-cristobal-colon-1948.html.
———. "Vlak míru (1950)." Accessed January 17, 2018. http://mluveny.panacek.com/rozhlasove-hry/69759-vlak-miru-1950.html.
Pěvecký sbor ČVUT Praha. "Historie Sboru." Accessed March 13, 2019. http://sbor.cvut.cz/historie/.
Pospíšil, Filip. "Inspiration, Subversion, and Appropriation: The Effects of Radio Free Europe Music Broadcasting." *Journal of Cold War Studies* 21, no. 4 (2019): 124–149.
Prague Municipal Theatre Choir. "Svítá." *Karel Vlach hraje písně Jaroslava Ježka* (Supraphon 1954).
Response to Jan Friedlaender. *Literární noviny*, no. 3 (1955): 9.
Roberts, Geoffrey. "Averting Armageddon: The Communist Peace Movement, 1948–1956." In *The Oxford Handbook of the History of Communism*, edited by Stephen A. Smith, 322–338. Oxford: Oxford University Press, 2014.
Sklenářová, Sylva. "Nizozemská špionážní aféra: Proces s Janem A. Louwersem v březnu 1950." *Soudobé dějiny* 15, no. 1 (2008): 62–84.
Škvorecký, Josef. "Red Music." *The Bass Saxophone*. Hopewell, NJ: Ecco.
Starr, Frederick. *Red and Hot: The Fate of Jazz in the Soviet Union, 1917–1980*. New York: Oxford University Press, 1983.
Tomoff, Kiril. *Creative Union: The Professional Organization of Soviet Composers, 1939–1953*. Ithaca, NY: Cornell University Press, 2006.
Tsipursky, Gleb. "Jazz, Power, and Soviet Youth in the Early Cold War, 1948–1953." *The Journal of Musicology* 33, no. 3 (2016): 332–361.
Velíšek, Martin. "František Kožík: Cristobal Colón." *Český rozhlas Vltava*. February 9, 2013. Accessed December 18, 2017. https://vltava.rozhlas.cz/frantisek-kozik-cristobal-colon-5047095.
Vidomus, Petr. "'Američan—a musí emigrovat do Československa!'—Škvoreckého jazzman Herbert Ward optikou zpráv FBI." *Soudobé dějiny* 1–2 (2017).
Vlach, Karel. "Karel Vlach Und Sein Orchester—Vom Land Der Polkas." Composed by Karel Vlach, Supraphon, 1972, Vinyl. Accessed January 17, 2018. https://www.discogs.com/Karel-Vlach-Und-Sein-Orchester-Vom-Land-Der-Polkas/release/11387819.
von Eschen, Penny. *Satchmo Blows Up the World: Jazz Ambassadors Play the Cold War*. Cambridge, MA: Harvard University Press, 2004.
Zarecor, Kimberly Elman. *Manufacturing a Socialist Modernity: Housing in Czechoslovakia, 1945–1960*. Pittsburgh, PA: University of Pittsburgh Press, 2011.

ROSAMUND JOHNSTON is a REWIRE Postdoctoral Fellow at the University of Vienna. She is author (with Lenka Kabrhelová) of *Havel in America: Interviews with American Intellectuals, Politicians, and Artists* (in Czech).

CHAPTER 4

SOVIET DRAMA WITH COMMERCIAL BREAKS
*Living the Cold War in 1970s Finnish Television*

Anu Koivunen

WHEN THE UPCOMING SEASON OF TV programs was presented in the main Finnish TV magazine, *Katso*, in August 1977, commemoration was described as a prominent theme: TV programs in different genres of fact and fiction would celebrate sixty years of Finnish independence. In addition, the preview article contended, "the jubilee of Finnish independence is closely related to the 60th anniversary of the Soviet Union." In honor of this, the upcoming winter season would celebrate Soviet drama, not only in Finnish theaters, but also in TV theater programming.[1] Both the public service television company, Finnish Broadcasting Company (Yleisradio, YLE), and the privately owned Mainos-TV (MTV) contributed to this celebration with new theater productions—YLE with three and MTV with two. YLE Television Theater (Channel 1) staged *Birds of Our Youth* (1972) by Ion Drutse (a recording of the Finnish Theater in Petroskoi, Russia), *The Dragon* (1944) by Evgeny Shvarts, and *Minutes of a Meeting* (1974) by Aleksandr Gelman, whereas MTV Theater broadcast Maksim Gorky's 1908 play *The Last Ones* and Viktor Rozov's contemporary drama *From Evening to Midday* (1970).

While it was, of course, factually correct to link Finnish independence and the October Revolution—both of which occurred in 1917, the one (according to common scholarly understanding) enabled by the other—the magazine's matter-of-fact tone in introducing the two as equally worthy of celebration seems odd from a post–Cold War perspective. It reads as a

61

flagrant example of *Finlandization*, a term that German political scientist Richard Löwenthal coined around 1966 to describe the domination of a small state by a larger one. Disputed and much criticized, Finlandization depicts Finland's relationship to the USSR as a paradigmatic example of how a small state bargains ideologically with its neighboring superpower, accepting a significant measure of influence over its domestic governance and foreign policy and, through pressure and self-censorship, compromising its freedom of speech.[2] How else to explain for contemporary audiences the fact that, in the 1970s, commercial MTV—literally "television with advertisements" and a broadcaster specializing in entertainment and imported TV series from the US—also produced and televised Soviet dramas? In 1977, the MTV Theater produced ten new stand-alone plays, two of them Soviet and framed in popular TV magazines as contributions to the anniversary. MTV's annual report depicted the company's acquisitions that year as focusing on the anniversary of the October Revolution in the Soviet Union, commemorating it with documentaries, televised concerts, and feature films.[3]

This chapter approaches these 1977 commemorations, and commercial television's role in enacting them, from a different perspective. It reads them as symptomatic of how the Cold War was lived in Finland through everyday TV programming, rather than as a case of scandalous Finlandization. While there is ample research on how foreign policy and domestic politics interacted in Finland in the 1970s, affecting news production and journalistic integrity, understandings of Finnish cultural and television history still suffer from political reductionism.[4] In this framework, Soviet drama in commercial TV programming—and any other cooperation across the Iron Curtain—is read primarily as a sign of moral corruption. The 1967 framework agreement and annual plans between YLE and the Television and Radio Committee of the USSR are discussed as "bridling" YLE, promoting "official liturgy," and leaving Finland "on its knees" (*rähmällään*).[5] Inspired by recent attempts to go beyond such reductionism, this chapter unpacks the various contexts in which the commercial television company produced Soviet drama, suggesting three concurrent and overlapping frames: the Cold War frame of TV as a site of foreign policy, the intricacies of domestic media policy, and the legacy of repertory theater.[6] Instead of close-reading the drama productions themselves, analyzing their themes and styles or their critical reception, the chapter argues for a de-dramatized reading of the sticky object of Soviet TV drama, suggesting its many meanings in 1970s Finland.[7] While MTV's programming of Soviet drama is symptomatic of how the nation's foreign policy of official friendship made its way to TV schedules beyond those of public service company YLE, it was also a strategic move for domestic media policy and an undramatic continuation of the repertory theater tradition.

## TV LISTINGS AS FOREIGN POLICY

The fact that MTV produced Soviet dramas in the 1970s and helped celebrate the anniversary of the October Revolution indicates its accommodation of existing broadcasting policies. The 1970s has been described as the decade when Finland was at its most Finlandized, in the sense that both YLE and the independent press practiced heavy self-censorship to promote "national interests" and conformed their news journalism to support the country's foreign policy agenda.[8] During the Cold War, YLE was under strict political control and steered by the Finnish Parliament via its governing body, the Administrative Council, which featured politicians and representatives of political parties.[9] In this administrative structure, political pressures were intensely reflected in YLE—as well as in MTV, which did not have its own broadcasting license or channel, but instead operated within YLE's license, renting airtime and cooperating in scheduling. Official foreign policy trickled down to broadcasting policies through the YLE administration, as the Administrative Council stipulated "Guidelines for the Production of Programs" that also constrained MTV. Besides approving program charts, the YLE Television Program Council—a body consisting of members appointed by political parties and thus reflecting political power relations in the current parliament—intensely monitored compliance to the guidelines.

When, in 1973, the Finnish government granted YLE a two-year broadcasting license, it stipulated that "the company consider Finland's endeavors to maintain good relations with all countries, especially with neighboring countries."[10] The same year, Finland and the Soviet Union signed a communiqué in which the press was given "a special responsibility to uphold friendly relations."[11] While these formulations did not entail state censorship of TV and radio, they intensified self-censorship in media, which was defined, more explicitly than before, as a site and instrument of foreign policy. In addition, they brought to media policy the language of the Treaty of Friendship, Cooperation, and Mutual Assistance (signed in 1948 and renewed in 1970), a pact that regulated relations between Finland and the Soviet Union until its dissolution in 1992. The pact enabled Finland to maintain an official policy of neutrality in the Cold War—a national identity centered on the idea of building bridges between the East and the West—but it also allowed Soviet influence in domestic political power games such as forming governments and electing high offices, as well as in determining Finland's degree of cooperation with the West.

In the 1970s, then, Finnish media was explicitly given the role of bridge builder, charged with mirroring and imitating the practices of contemporary politicians.[12] This—as well as media's role in the doctrine of neutrality—was emphasized in a 1973 consensus statement by YLE's Program Council: "The Program Council requires that, in the future, both current affairs programs and other programming emphasize and sufficiently, correctly, and convincingly present positions on foreign policy that are based on the Paasikivi-Kekkonen policy of neutrality, the essence of which is uncompromising compliance to the YYA pact and the Paris peace treaty."[13]

While a representative of the Finnish Communist Party initiated this statement, which emphasized journalism and other media's role in foreign policy, it was a representative of the right-wing Coalition Party who, in 1973, intervened in YLE's film programming and demanded that three Soviet films be added to the spring film schedule (one to the summer program and two to the autumn list of films). As this example suggests, the surveillance of TV listings was at times highly detailed; in this case, the Program Council required that "three further Soviet films, with the contemporary Soviet Union as their subject... be included in the spring programming."[14] Support for Soviet programming, in other words, came from across the entire political spectrum.

In 1973, MTV further supported the twenty-fifth anniversary of the Treaty of Friendship, Cooperation, and Mutual Assistance by calling for informative programs whose "particular objective is to widen Finns' knowledge of the everyday life of the citizens of the Soviet Union."[15] And when, in 1974, the commercial broadcaster screened *Silk Stockings*, Ruben Mamoulian's 1957 remake of *Ninotchka* as a spy musical, it was reprimanded by the Program Council. The film was deemed "not consistent with the limits of The Guidelines for the Production of Programs and Content or with the role of a country that relates to other states in a neutral and balanced way."[16]

In this context, producing Soviet drama in television theater brought bridge-building policy to everyday TV programming. The policy was literalized in the TV listings, which articulated the Finnish self-narrative of neutrality as the idea of being between two blocs and belonging to both. Yet this also reflected an industrial reality: as Anikó Imre has underlined, the Cold War did not place an Iron Curtain between television networks, but rather resulted in an extensive television diplomacy program between the blocs. YLE, for instance, was a member of both the European Broadcasting Union (EBU) and its socialist counterpart, the Organisation Internationale de Radiodiffusion et de Télévision (OIRT), and exercised program exchanges with both.[17] In TV charts of the 1970s, the doublespeak of Finnish foreign policy was clear: the friendship policy with the Soviet Union was practiced and voiced, but simultaneously, Finland was integrated into Western structures.[18] In this doublespeak and in its televisual politics of neutrality, commercial television served as "a balancing act," symbolizing Finland's role in the Cold War.[19]

### Media Policy: MTV Strives for Legitimacy

While it accommodated the existing understanding of TV policy as foreign policy, the MTV production of Soviet dramas was also a strategic move by the channel. In the 1970s, a moment when leftist politicians, media critics, and cultural conservatives alike criticized commercial TV, it was in MTV's interest to seek increased cultural legitimacy. Indeed, MTV's advertisements, as well as its large number of US imports and focus on entertainment, were controversial in Finland. In 1972, for instance, the Program Council criticized "the overrepresentation of English language in TV programs" and, in the name of diversity and offering "alternatives" to viewers, urged YLE and MTV to increase programming from non-English-speaking countries.[20] The same year, the council stated that MTV's plans for the holiday season focused "excessively" on foreign, especially American, entertainment and demanded that MTV, in the future, include "more domestic and internationally varied productions in its programming and pay special attention to increasing factual programs on social issues."[21]

In this context, MTV's emphasis on responsibility and cultural worth supported its claim to legitimacy.[22] This was important for maintaining existing airtime in a strictly coordinated schedule and, especially from 1977, as an argument in MTV's campaign for a license to produce news programming (a goal realized in 1980). In MTV's annual reports, the company spoke of itself as a full-service broadcasting company, although its airtime was restricted and its main programming consisted of US and other entertainment. Exercising performative politics, MTV sought to match YLE in order to attain an equivalent status in the media landscape, even if—for the time being—it was de facto subordinate to it.

Original quality programming was a key ingredient in striving for cultural legitimacy, and having a television theater of its own was a particularly important element. In television's "era of scarcity," before the advent, in the 1980s, of competing multichannel systems, drama productions organized as "television theaters" not only served as entertainment, but also, in John Tulloch's words, legitimized the institution of TV by signaling "quality."[23]

In Finland, as in many other countries, the presence of theater brought an aura of prestige and quality to a mass medium: "TV's 'balance' between informing ('leading' society) and entertaining ('serving' it) ... [was] seen as a balance between 'art' ('dealing with ideas') and commerce."[24] To this end, following YLE's 1961 establishment of a television theater, MTV launched its own in 1965.

This made the 1960s and 1970s the golden era of television theater in Finland. In 1966, Finnish television audiences were offered more than five theater productions each week. Four drama units produced stand-alone plays, series and serials, TV movies, and recordings of live stage performances for two channels. YLE alone housed three units: Television Theater (Channel 1), Swedish-language Television Theater, and the Drama Department (Channel 2), while MTV had a permanent theater ensemble, MTV-Theater. In the late 1960s, all had fixed slots in the program chart, and as in countries like Britain, television drama held an important position within Finnish television for a long time; this structure was preserved until the 1980s, despite the fact that stand-alone plays became fewer and their share of prime time smaller.[25]

In MTV's annual reports, the drama unit is described not in the language of business, but in that of art and cultural significance. The annual outputs were characterized as "multifaceted mapping of the atmosphere, conditions, and problems of our country," and the MTV Theater was described "as an interpreter of Finnish way of life and mediator of foreign plays."[26] Yet in the words of a sardonic theater critic in the monthly magazine *Teatteri*, the picture was less enthusiastic: "Harmless. Not hurting anybody. Without risk. Colorless. Unenthusiastic. Schematic. Gutless. Sticking to the old. What is this? Not television, but a MTV-like making of plays. It reflects MTV's production more generally."[27] Nevertheless, in the 1970s, prestigious TV drama productions were assessed as theater on cultural pages and by professional critics.

Moreover, for MTV, the 1977 celebration of Soviet drama and the anniversary of the October Revolution was not an exceptional occurrence, but rather a logical step in a long-term strategy of establishing independent relations with the Soviet Union. In 1970, MTV's CEO and programming director were invited to the Soviet Union by the Soviet State Committee for Television and Radio Broadcasting.[28] In 1976, MTV coproduced a documentary on *Pravda*, "the world's biggest newspaper," with this committee and made six programs with the Soviet public information agency APN (Novosti Press Agency).[29] By 1978, MTV concluded that its strength lay in such coproductions.[30] To these and program exchanges with socialist countries, the production of Soviet and other Eastern European plays a signal of political responsibility, loyalty to the national politics of friendship, and commitment to high cultural value. All this promised prestige for MTV, strengthening its position in the domestic media market.

## The Legacy of Repertory Theater

To the early broadcasting companies, the notion of theater brought with it professional structures borrowed from existing municipal theaters, which had unionized professionals and the habit of thinking about programming as repertory: something for all, drawn from the canon of world drama.[31] The ambition to offer a broad repertory was evident in 1985, when MTV Theater celebrated its twentieth anniversary and narrated its own history with a small booklet.[32] In addition to highlighting its adaptations of Finnish literature for TV plays and movies, the booklet also mentioned six productions of plays by Federico García Lorca, six August Strindberg plays, four Anton Chekhov productions, four adaptations of D. H. Lawrence, three William Shakespeare plays, three by George Bernard Shaw, and three by Jean Anouilh. Within this framework, the production of both Russian classics and contemporary Soviet dramas (including those in the late 1970s) seems unexceptional, even ordinary. Between 1965 and 1985, MTV Theater broadcast twelve stand-alone Russian or Soviet plays, with two Soviet productions featured in the early 1980s, as follows:

> 1965: *The Gamblers* (*Huijarit*, dir. Pauli Virtanen), based on the 1836 play by Nikolai Gogol.
> 1967: *The Emperor's New Clothes* (*Alaston kuningas*, dir. Pauli Virtanen), based on the 1934 play by Evgeny Schwartz.
> 1970: *Pontius Pilate* (*Pilatus*, dir. Seppo Wallin), based on the 1966 play by Mikhail Bulgakov.
> 1973: *An Unpleasant Incident* (*Nolo tapaus*, dir. Risto Aaltonen), based on the 1888 play by Anton Chekhov.
> 1975: *Another Man's Wife* (*Vieras rouva*, dir. Esko Elstelä), based on the 1848 play by Fyodor Dostoyevsky.
> 1975: *Anjuta* (*Anjuta*, dir. Pauli Virtanen), based on the 1886 play by Anton Chekhov.
> 1977: *The Last Ones* (*Viimeiset*, dir. Sakari Puurunen), based on the 1908 play by Maksim Gorky.
> 1977: *From Evening to Midday* (*Illansuusta puoleenpäivään*, dir. Jyrki Lehtinen) based on the 1970 play by Viktor Rozov.

1978: *Short Story from Autumn in the Oak Woods* (*Jonninjoutavaa*, dir. Pauli Virtanen), based on 1956–1959 short stories by Yuri Kazakov.
1980: *French Lessons* (*Ranskantunnit*, dir. Evgeny Tashkov; Soviet production), based on the 1973 novel by Valentin Rasputin.
1983: *A Dangerous Age* (*Vaarallinen ikä*, dir. Aleksandr Proshkin; Soviet production), based on the 1981 play by Roman Furman.
1984: *We, the Undersigned* (*Me allekirjoittaneet*, dir. Raimo O. Niemi), based on the 1979 play by Aleksandr Gelman.

When presented and reviewed in *Katso*, these plays were discussed neither as realistic representations of life in the Soviet Union nor as propagandistic works. Instead, following the tradition of the Russian classics performed in Finnish repertory theaters beyond television, they were viewed in general humanist terms as plays about people and their issues, moral or otherwise. In 1977, *From Evening to Midday* was characterized as a depiction of a family in "a state of alienation and meaninglessness" and a young person "who matures into making independent decisions."[33] In the TV listings, it was advertised as "a play by an author representing the new Soviet generation of playwrights on the importance of close relationships and about critical questions within both family and society." The broadcast of *The Last Ones*, "a family drama from the turn-of-the-century Russia," was introduced as MTV Theater's contribution to introducing new works to the national theater audience: "Maksim Gorky's plays have, during the past couple of years, had a renaissance in many parts of Europe. With this wave, plays not previously staged in Finland have been brought to light. One of these is from Gorky's early work, *The Last Ones*, a family drama in which the author presents his view of how old and new values clash in turn-of-the-century Russia."[34]

For MTV, then, the discourse of art and the frame of classic drama repertory enabled both Russian drama classics and contemporary Soviet drama to be distinguished from politicized actualities and current affairs programming—even when they were scheduled, as in 1977, as celebrations of the October Revolution. A similar rhetorical strategy was used in the Finnish yearbook *What, Where, When 1979* (*Mitä-missä-milloin 1979*) to characterize how theaters in Finland celebrated 1977's thematic year of Soviet drama by producing an unprecedented number of Soviet plays, especially contemporary dramas by Viktor Rozov, Aleksei Arbuzov, Aleksandr Vampilov, and Chinghiz Aitmatov. Their plays were described as combining "a kind of propaganda about the new humanism with a warm sense of humor": "People are depicted in their typical everyday situations, onto which questions of social responsibility are projected."[35] Questions of working life were said to characterize plays by Boris Vasiliev, Gennady Bokarev, and Vladimir Tendriakov, as well as those by Aleksandr Gelman and Vasily Shukshin.[36]

Even if, in 1977, Finnish theaters celebrated the year of Soviet drama, an overview of Finnish theater in that year diagnosed a generally very slow dissemination of Soviet plays in the country. According to critic Maija Savutie, "Brecht arrived slowly on the scene, and so did socialism."[37] Alongside Russian classics (Gogol, Ostrovsky, and Chekhov), Finnish theaters—also on television—occasionally produced early Soviet plays by Bulgakov, Babel, Kataev, Erdman, Shvarts, and Gorky, but new Soviet drama was mostly absent. This was also lamented by Soviet guests visiting a symposium organized by the Finland-Soviet Society and the Association for Amateur and Professional Theatres in Finland (Työväen Näyttämöiden Liitto) to celebrate the year of Soviet drama. According to the report in *Teatteri* magazine, the Soviet representatives (high-ranking officials in and the chair of the Soviet Writers' Union) regretted that Soviet theater was poorly known in Finland and lamented the rudimentary knowledge of the theories of Stanislavsky, Vakhtangov, and Meyerhold. The organizers, moreover, were disappointed at the symposium's few Finnish participants, none of whom were at the rank of the Soviet guests. In the symposium, socialist realism was highlighted as a "belief in the transformative power of art and the mutual interaction of art and society," and the notion of the production play (*tuotantonäytelmä*) was introduced as an aesthetic and political ideal for Finnish theater as well. Depicting workplaces and human beings at work was envisioned as a way to demonstrate "the unbreakable unity of social, production, and ethical problems." An ideal play, it was suggested, promotes the socialist system not as a rational but as an ethical choice made by individuals.[38]

Notably, such discourse did not make its way to the TV pages or television theater repertory, in which Soviet plays instead symbolized highbrow art, diversity, international programming, and contemporaneity.[39] The overall context of theater in Finland contributed to this. Since the early twentieth century and the Civil War of 1918, Finnish theater had been defined by the dual legacies of bourgeois and workers' theaters, and it remained highly politicized in the 1970s, when many writers, directors, and actors saw their work as contesting or defending worldviews. Yet even if producing Soviet drama may have been a political gesture for directors and actors in MTV Theater and elsewhere, it also signaled up-to-dateness, showing peers that one followed trends.[40] In this decade, furthermore, theater politics did not focus on the choice of foreign plays, but instead on how Finnish history, especially the Civil War and the Second World War, were depicted and how contemporary Finnish society was portrayed.

In the context of the Cold War, then, art operated as an enabling discourse. It offered a frame that, in a subdued manner, combined foreign policy, cultural diplomacy, and cultural legitimacy, and served as an arena for soft power and friendship politics. A prime example of this was the Finnish "Soviet Literature" ("Neuvostokirjallisuutta") publishing series, which was launched in 1975 as a joint venture coordinated by the Finnish Publishers Association. The series' publishers released almost a hundred titles by 1985, but notably (unlike other Western countries), they did not feature émigré or dissident literature.[41] The choice of titles, purportedly a nonpolitical selection based on artistic criteria, indicated an obvious loyalty to official Soviet cultural politics.

## Conclusion

Interpreting the presence of Soviet drama in Finnish commercial television in the 1970s requires one to take into account several contexts and frames. First, Soviet dramas read as a continuation of decades-long programming traditions in Finnish repertory theaters, which played Russian dramas alongside other classic plays. This was true of both bourgeois and working-class theaters. Second, including both domestic and foreign dramas in television theater repertoires was an important part of the public service model of television, in which information and education were key values. In Finland, for instance, a so-called "informational programme policy" was introduced in 1965 to activate audiences intellectually, broaden their worldview, and call for socially active citizenship.[42] While this policy was quickly discarded as too radical, a general ethos of information and education permeated Finnish TV programming throughout the 1970s. Given MTV's subordinate position to YLE's broadcasting license and its desire for cultural and political legitimacy, the informational ethos was also adopted by commercial television, as were the ideals of reaching beyond the anglophone world and promoting international understanding through program exchange as well as drama productions and documentaries. Third, and most intensely, Finnish TV programming was a site of foreign policy in the 1970s, and both public service and commercial television practiced the doctrine of friendship politics. The high degree of MTV's loyalty to this policy was indicated by Keijo Korhonen, Minister of Foreign Affairs (1976–1977), who, in an MTV seminar on Finnish identity, defined the national mentality as an embodiment of the Cold War and confirmed MTV as a site for its practice: "The Finnish man (*ihminen*) survived defeat, and learned to accommodate the inevitable and really turn it into a virtue. War reparations evolved into a flourishing eastern trade, and the compulsory acceptance of the heavy conditions of peacemaking has resulted in a new Finnish way of life in the family of nations: a new and distinctively Finnish policy of neutrality enabled by good and developing relations with the Soviet Union."[43]

Living the Cold War entailed practicing a politics of friendship that was highly performative, necessitating gestures and doublespeak and asserting and promoting friendship while using this performance to other strategic political and economic ends. In the 1970s, MTV skillfully practiced this doublespeak. It produced both Russian classics and contemporary Soviet dramas, playing with a distinction that offered a productive ambivalence while also coproducing documentaries and entertainment with Soviet television institutions, thereby supporting the Finnish "building bridges" policy.[44] The company's US-dominated entertainment programming and the advertising industry provided a solid economic basis, but MTV also spoke the language of realpolitik—as did Finnish industry and trade overall. Despite the communiqué between the Soviet Union and Finland, which gave the press "a special responsibility to uphold friendly relations," MTV's mastery of the friendship policy was undoubtedly less important in relation to the Soviet Union itself than as a domestic media-political strategy.[45] Drama productions, including of Soviet/Russian literature, gave the broadcaster an instrument of cultural—and by implication also political—legitimacy in a context where fierce political debates were fought over MTV's future and the question of allowing it to establish a newsroom. At the same time, the languages of art and cultural legitimacy offered tools to depoliticize the gesture and to negotiate the demands of Finlandization.

## NOTES

1. All quotations from Wiik, "Suomi-neidon juhlahumua," 11.
2. Salminen, *The Silenced Media*; Salokangas, "The Shadow of the Bear"; and Lounasmeri, "A Careful Balancing Act."
3. Mainos-TV, *Toimintakertomus 1977*, 53.
4. Salokangas, *Aikansa oloinen*; Salminen, *The Silenced Media*; Pernaa, *Uutisista, hyvää iltaa*; Salokangas, "The Shadow of the Bear"; and Lounasmeri, "A Careful Balancing Act."
5. Sharma, *Ikuiset ystävät*, 148–50.
6. Pajala, "Long Live the Friendship"; and Pajala, "Pictures from Beyond the Eastern Border."
7. For an approach to Cold War cultures as plural and contingent, see Vowinckel, Payk, and Lindenberger, "European Cold War Culture(s)?"
8. Salokangas, "The Shadow of the Bear," 77–79; and Lounasmeri, "A Careful Balancing Act," 88–90.
9. For a discussion of parliamentary control in the 1970s, see Virmavirta, "Yleisradion perussuunnan ratkaisee"; and Salokangas, *Aikansa oloinen*.
10. Salokangas, "The Shadow of the Bear," 78.
11. Lounasmeri, "A Careful Balancing Act," 88.
12. Lounasmeri, "A Careful Balancing Act," 88–90.

13. Quote of minutes from television's Programming Council, January 12, 1973. Salokangas, *Aikansa oloinen*, 78.
14. Mainos-TV, *Toimintakertomus 1972*, 14.
15. Mainos-TV, *Toimintakertomus 1973*, 19.
16. Mainos-TV, *Toimintakertomus 1974*, 22.
17. Imre, *TV Socialism*, 17. For a discussion of socialist television in Finland, see Pajala, "Images from Beyond."
18. Salokangas, "The Shadow of the Bear," 79. On the "friendship policy," see Pernaa, *Tehtävänä Neuvostoliitto*; Pajala, "Long Live the Friendship"; and Sharma, *Ikuiset ystävät*.
19. Keinonen, "Early Commercial Television"; and Lounasmeri, "A Careful Balancing Act," 85.
20. Mainos-TV, *Toimintakertomus 1972*, 12.
21. Ibid., 14.
22. For a discussion of this strategy, see Pajala, "A Forgotten Spirit of Commercial Television."
23. On the "era of scarcity," see Ellis, *Seeing Things*, 49–50.
24. Tulloch, *Television Drama*, 120.
25. Caughie, *Television Drama*; and Cooke, *British Television Drama*.
26. Mainos-TV, *Toimintakertomus 1970*, 33; Mainos-TV, *Toimintakertomus 1973*, 34; and Mainos-TV, *Toimintakertomus 1975*, 39.
27. Haikara, "Tuotteet," 12.
28. Mainos-TV, *Toimintakertomus 1970*, 40.
29. APN was founded in 1961 to "to contribute to mutual understanding, trust, and friendship among peoples in every possible way by broadly publishing accurate information about the USSR abroad and familiarizing the Soviet public with the life of the peoples of foreign countries." Its motto was "Information for Peace, for the Friendship of Nations." Wikipedia, s.v. "RIA Novosti," last modified May 7, 2021, 23:35, https://en.wikipedia.org/wiki/RIA_Novosti.
30. Mainos-TV, *Toimintakertomus 1972*, 17; Mainos-TV, *Toimintakertomus 1975*, 51; and Mainos-TV, *Toimintakertomus 1978*, 30. On MTV coproductions with socialist countries, see Pajala, "A Forgotten Spirit of Commercial Television."
31. Cooke, *British Television Drama*, 37–42; and Caughie, *Television Drama*.
32. Wallin, "20 vuotta MTV-teatteria."
33. Perttola-Flinck, "Illansuusta puoleenpäivään," 21.
34. "Viimeiset," 20–21.
35. Kyrö, "Näyttämötaide," 359.
36. Ibid.
37. Savutie, "Ulkomaisen ohjelmiston virtoja," 42–43.
38. All quotations from Markkula, "Suomalais-neuvostoliittolainen teatterisymposium," 8.
39. Ibid.
40. Suutela, "Joukkojen aika"; Seppälä, "Teatteri ja politiikka"; and Niemi, *Nykyteatterin juuret*.
41. Jänis and Pesonen, "Venäläinen kirjallisuus," 203.
42. Salokangas, *Aikansa oloinen*.
43. Korhonen, "Suomalainen identiteetti," 7–10.
44. Pajala, "A Forgotten Spirit of Commercial Television."
45. Lounasmeri, "A Careful Balancing Act," 88.

## Bibliography

Caughie, John. *Television Drama: Realism, Modernism, and British Culture*. Oxford: Oxford University Press, 2000.

Cooke, Lez. *British Television Drama: A History*. London: BFI, 2003.

Ellis, John. *Seeing Things: Television in the Age of Uncertainty*. London: I. B. Tauris, 2000.

Haikara, Kalevi. "Tuotteet." *Teatteri* 34, no. 11–12 (1978): 12–13.
Imre, Anikó. *TV Socialism*. Durham, NC: Duke University Press, 2016.
Jänis, Marja, and Pekka Pesonen. "Venäläinen kirjallisuus." In *Suomennoskirjallisuuden historia 2*, edited by H. K. Riikonen, Urpo Kovala, Pekka Kujamäki, and Outi Paloposki, 189–202. Helsinki: Suomalaisen Kirjallisuuden Seura, 2007.
Keinonen, Heidi. "Early Commercial Television in Finland." *Media History* 18, no. 2 (2012): 177–189.
Korhonen, Keijo. "Suomalainen identiteetti." In *Televisio vaikuttajana suomalaisessa yhteiskunnassa*, edited by Mirja Lappi-Seppälä. *MTV-julkaisuja* 5 (1977): 7–10.
Kyrö, Pekka. "Näyttämötaide." In *Mitä-missä-milloin – kansalaisen vuosikirja 1979*, edited by Pauli Kojo, 359–367. Helsinki: Otava, 1978.
Lounasmeri, Lotta. "A Careful Balancing Act: Finnish Culture of Self-Censorship in the Cold War." In *The Nordic Media and the Cold War*, edited by Henrik Bastiansen and Rolf Werenskjold, 83–100. Göteborg: Nordicom, 2015.
Mainos-TV, *Toimintakertomus 1970*. Helsinki: Mainos-TV, 1970.
Mainos-TV, *Toimintakertomus 1972*. Helsinki: Mainos-TV, 1972.
Mainos-TV, *Toimintakertomus 1973*. Helsinki: Mainos-TV, 1973.
Mainos-TV, *Toimintakertomus 1974*. Helsinki: Mainos-TV, 1974.
Mainos-TV, *Toimintakertomus 1975*. Helsinki: Mainos-TV, 1975.
Mainos-TV, *Toimintakertomus 1977*. Helsinki: Mainos-TV, 1977.
Mainos-TV, *Toimintakertmus 1978*. Helsinki: Mainos-TV, 1978.
Markkula, Jorma. "Suomalais-neuvostoliittolainen teatterisymposium aukoi tietä yhteistyöhön." *Teatteri* 9 (October 25, 1977): 6–9.
Maude, George. "The Further Shores of Finlandization." *Cooperation and Conflict* 10, no. 7 (1982): 3–16.
Niemi, Irmeli. *Nykyteatterin juuret*. Helsinki: Tammi, 1975.
Pajala, Mari. "A Forgotten Spirit of Commercial Television? Co-Productions Between Finnish Commercial Television Company Mainos-TV and Socialist Television." *Historical Journal of Film, Radio and Television* 39, no. 2 (2018): 366–383.
———. "'Long Live the Friendship between the Soviet Union and Finland!' Irony, Nostalgia, and Melodrama in Finnish Historical Television Drama and Documentaries." *European Journal of Cultural Studies* 20, no. 3 (2017): 271–284.
———. "'Pictures from Beyond the Eastern Border': Socialist Television in Finland, 1963 to 1988." *Television & New Media* 19, no. 5 (2018): 448–466.
Pernaa, Ville. *Tehtävänä Neuvostoliitto: Opetusministeriön Neuvostoliittoinstituutin roolit suomalaisessa politiikassa 1944–1992*. Helsinki: Venäjän ja Itä-Euroopan instituutti, 2002.
———. *Uutisista, hyvää iltaa: Ylen tv-uutiset ja yhteiskunta 1959–2009*. Helsinki: Karttakeskus, 2009.
Perttola-Flinck, Aikki. "Illansuusta puoleenpäivään." *Katso* 39 (September 26, 1977): 21.
Salminen, Esko. *The Silenced Media: The Propaganda War between Russia and the West in Northern Europe*. Basingstoke: Macmillan, 1999.
Salokangas, Raimo. *Aikansa oloinen: Yleisradion historia 2, 1949–1996*. Helsinki: Yleisradio, 1996.
———. "The Shadow of the Bear: Finnish Broadcasting, National Interest and Self-Censorship during the Cold War." In *The Nordic Media and the Cold War*, edited by Henrik Bastiansen and Rolf Werenskjold, 67–82. Göteborg: Nordicom, 2015.
Savutie, Maija. "Ulkomaisen ohjelmiston virtoja teatterissamme 60- ja 70-luvuilla." In *Monikasvoinen teatteri: 50. teatteripäivien juhlajulkaisu*, edited by Pekka Kyrö, 27–49. Helsinki: Teatterijärjestöjen Keskusliitto, 1977.

Seppälä, Mikko-Olavi. "Teatteri ja politiikka." In *Suomen teatteri ja draama*, edited by Mikko-Olavi Seppälä and Katri Tanskanen, 303–329. Helsinki: Like, 2010.

Sharma, Leena. *Ikuiset ystävät: Suomen ja Neuvostoliiton kulttuurisuhteet sotien jälkeen*. Helsinki: Suomalaisen Kirjallisuuden Seura, 2018.

Suutela, Hanna. "Joukkojen aika." In *Seiskytluvun teatterin moninaiset äänet*, edited by Hanna Suutela and Misa Palander, 194–214. Helsinki: Like, 2005.

Tulloch, John. *Television Drama: Agency, Audience and Myth*. London and New York: Routledge, 1990.

"Viimeiset." *Katso* 7 (February 14, 1977), 21.

Virmavirta, Jarmo. "Yleisradion perussuunnan ratkaisee poliittinen päätöksentekijä." *Parnasso* 3 (1978), 166–168.

Vowinckel, Annette, Marcus Payk, and Thomas Lindenberger. "European Cold War Culture(s)? An Introduction." In *Cold War Cultures: Perspectives on Eastern and Western European Societies*, edited by Annette Vowinckel, Marcus Payk, and Thomas Lindenberger, 1–20. New York: Berghahn Books, 2012.

Wallin, Seppo. "20 vuotta MTV-teatteria." *MTV-teatteri 1965–1985*. Helsinki: MTV, 1985.

Wiik, Anna-Kerttu. "Suomi-neidon juhlahumua ja pitkiä sarjoja." *Katso* 33, (August 15, 1977), 11.

> ANU KOIVUNEN is Professor of Gender Studies at University of Turku and Professor of Cinema Studies at Stockholm University. She is author of *Performative Histories, Foundational Fictions*. She is editor (with Jari Ojala and Janne Holmén) of *The Nordic Economic, Social and Political Model: Challenges in the 21st Century* and (with Katariina Kyrölä and Ingrid Ryberg) of *The Power of Vulnerability: Mobilising Affect in Feminist, Queer and Anti-Racist Media Cultures*.

# PART II. DISTRIBUTION, ADAPTATION, RECEPTION

CHAPTER 5

SOVIET CINEMA IN 1960S CUBA
## Between Cold War Logics and Thirdworldist Affinities

Masha Salazkina

THE RELATIONSHIP BETWEEN THE SOVIET and Cuban cultural spheres resists easy geopolitical identification: it does not fit neatly either within the postcolonial paradigm recently used to account for the historical power dynamics within the former Soviet Bloc or that of neocolonialism, traditionally used to describe Latin American countries' economic and political dependency on the US or Europe.[1] When, in April 1961, Fidel Castro declared the revolution to be a socialist one and turned to the Kremlin for support, there had been little history of extensive cultural contact or shared experience (positive or negative) between Cuba and the Soviet Union.[2] The lack of any significant cultural relationship between the two countries prior to Castro's rise to power heightened the perception of Russian culture as alien to and incompatible with the spirit of the Caribbean. Moreover, not only did the island's precarious status—suspended in political space between two superpowers—become painfully apparent to every Cuban during the Missile Crisis, but many artists and intellectuals who were familiar with both the theory and practice of national liberation struggle were quick to raise concerns about the influence of a (quasi) European nation seeking to impose a socialist version of modernization onto a Caribbean island.

Indeed, Soviet revolutionary culture, which held sway for so many leftists around the world in the 1920s and '30s, had had relatively little impact in Cuba prior to the 1960s; the Soviet avant-garde's machine ethos and constructivist spirit, which had parallel movements, significant resonances, and continuities all across Europe, were perceived in Cuba as largely foreign to its artistic spheres.[3] Yet Cuban film culture was an exception to this overall tendency: here, Soviet cinema did have a significant cultural presence leading up to the revolution. As early as the 1930s, the early Soviet models of a new art for the new world resonated with the dreams of Cuban cinephiles, many of whom would later shape postrevolutionary Cuban cultural institutions. This familiarity, however, did not imply artistic or theoretical influence or even particular affinities between the two socialist film industries. Rather, from the earliest days of the revolution and throughout the 1960s, Soviet cinema provided less inspiration than notes of caution for Cuba's search for a model of a genuinely socialist culture, and the leaders of Cuban cultural institutions engaged with Soviet cinema in a highly selective and strategic way in their bids for power and political and artistic autonomy. The goal of this essay, then, is to unpack some of the dynamics behind the reception of Soviet cinema in Cuba in the 1960s, placing them in the context of the global Cold War's transnational socialist cultures.[4]

The downplaying of the impact of Soviet cinematic models on Cuban film culture has been, at least in part, historically self-determined. From the overthrow of the Batista government onward, Cuban cinema showcased the successes of the country's new revolutionary culture to the rest of the progressive world, explicitly positing itself as an alternative to the Eastern Bloc model. Postrevolutionary Cuban cinema emphasized the island's unique national culture and historical trajectory as well as its links with the rest of Latin America. And over the course of the 1960s, Cuba—and its postrevolutionary film institutions, particularly the Cuban Institute of Cinematic Art and Industry (hereafter, ICAIC)—increasingly positioned itself as an important player in the Non-Aligned and Thirdworldist movements, which culminated in the Tricontinental Conference in 1966 and the 1968 Havana Cultural Congress.[5] The confluence of these frameworks further mediated and complicated Cuba's relationship to the Eastern Bloc, since an important declarative aspect of these geopolitical formations was their independence from the Soviet Union's political and cultural influences.

Moreover, throughout the 1960s, Cuban cultural policies—and their refractions in film and media practices and discourses—were characterized by a multiplicity of positions, competing and often contradictory models, internal struggles, and complex political negotiations irreducible to any one monolithic policy vis-à-vis the relationship between the Soviet and Cuban cultural spheres.[6] In the midst of these cultural and political struggles,

Soviet (film) culture became an important referent, both positive and negative, within many of the cultural debates taking place in Cuba throughout the 1960s, largely through allusions to the possible imposition of Soviet-style policies on the island. As such, Soviet cinema in general, and the notion of socialist realism in particular, played an important role in the articulation and negotiation of postrevolutionary Cuban film culture's new aesthetic norms and cultural policies.

## SOVIET CINEMA ON CUBAN SCREENS

It is worth recalling that the Cuban revolution was not in any way directed by the Soviets. Its leaders had had no significant prior contact with the Soviet Bloc, and the Soviet Union itself took a cautious attitude in the first months after the revolution. Official diplomatic relations were not established until a year later, after the Soviet Exposition held in Havana in February 1960, which included an official visit by First Deputy Premier Anastas Mikoyan to discuss trade prospects.[7] The exposition played an important role in establishing the image of the Soviet Union (and by extension the Soviet Bloc) as a model of successful alternative modernity. Importantly, this model foregrounded Soviet production and consumption of mass media. Thus, as part of the exposition, Soviet movies were screened in two major Havana theaters for two weeks, among them classics like Sergei Eisenstein's *Battleship Potemkin* (*Bronenosets Potemkin*, 1925) and recent films like Ivan Pyryev's *The Idiot* (*Idiot*, 1958) and Sergei Yutkevich's *Othello* (*Otello*, 1956).[8] Subsequently, the same shift and orientation towards the East that took place in East European media and entertainment industries in the early postwar period was reflected in Cuba over the course of the 1960s by way of its film import and programming practices, translations and uses of Soviet film theory and criticism, festival participation, and early attempts at coproductions. The shift was gradual: In 1958, 57 percent of the films distributed in Cuba came from the United States, 14 percent from Mexico, 10 percent from Great Britain, and 6 percent from Italy. In 1960, despite the introduction of films from the USSR and Czechoslovakia, 44 percent of the movies shown in Cuba still came from the United States.[9] In December 1960, however, a new movie theater operated by ICAIC, La Rampa, showcased the first retrospective of socialist cinema in Cuba, a weeklong series that included seven recent Soviet films, as well as a number of other Socialist Bloc productions. The retrospective coincided with a visit by Soviet documentarian Roman Karmen, who would subsequently make two films in Cuba, and by other directors and actors.[10] Six thousand people attended the event, and La Semana (The Week), as it became known, would be a regular occurrence in Cuba until 1990.[11]

Along with the exposition, this event marked a further decisive association between Cuba and the Socialist Bloc.

A year later, in December 1961, Castro made his famous speech declaring a Marxist-Leninist orientation for the new Cuban state. That year saw a dramatic change in film programming, with only 4.7 percent of new films shown in Cuba originating in the United States, versus 25.8 percent from the Soviet Union and 29 percent from six other socialist nations.[12] That same year, ICAIC's cultural department was officially reformed as the Cinemateca de Cuba, whose inaugural event was the retrospective Three Decades of Soviet Cinema, comprising twenty-four Soviet films made before 1948. In the thirty years that followed, until 1991, about eight hundred new Soviet films were screened in Cuban commercial movie theaters (usually a year or two after their initial release), and the Cinemateca programmed over fifteen hundred different events dedicated to Soviet cinema.[13] Similarly, Soviet and Eastern European film festivals (Moscow, Karlovy Vary, Leipzig, and, to a lesser degree, Tashkent) provided reliable opportunities to exhibit Cuban films, greatly contributing to their international circulation.

Cuban official discourse on cinema—as expressed in particular on the pages of the ICAIC-run journal *Cine Cubano*—reflected this shift in Cuban postrevolutionary film culture's point of reference from American cinema to Soviet (and other socialist) cinemas. Throughout the 1960s and early 1970s, *Cine Cubano* represented not only Cuban film culture, but also, to a large extent, the entire critical apparatus of the emerging New Latin American Cinema, whose political and aesthetic positions it both shaped and reflected. In the opening pages of the very first issue, ICAIC director Alfredo Guevara gave the following account of the new Cuban cinema in relation to its Soviet counterpart: "One cannot make films without having studied Soviet cinema, without knowing or reflecting on the images of *October* or *Strike*, without knowing *Potemkin, Mother, Storm over Asia, The End of Saint Petersburg, Alexander Nevsky*, or *Arsenal*. These films, and many others, as well as the theoretical movement initiated by their directors, belong to the best film heritage."[14]

Guevara's references to films by Eisenstein and Vsevolod Pudovkin, coinciding with the Cinemateca's programming choices, are anything but surprising: 1920s Soviet montage has been widely seen as an aesthetic signature and ideological inspiration for the more radical manifestations of the New Cinemas of the 1960s and in particular of the New Latin American Cinema, of which Cuba came to be the self-appointed but largely undisputed center. Not only did it serve as a model for a state-supported film production that could be as experimental in its form as it was revolutionary in its content, but early Soviet cinema formed part of the alternative canon that had emerged in noncommercial film institutions in Cuba (and elsewhere in Latin America and most of the world), especially in the 1940s and 1950s. Given the absence of a strong film industry and/or established art cinema, film clubs, societies, and courses were foundational for the New Latin American Cinemas and Cuban cinema in particular.[15] They became the major sphere for film as an artistic and cultural practice, creating generations of film amateurs and cinephiles shaped by a notion of cinema different from the dominant commercial canon and often engaged in political activism. In the same decades, film criticism in Cuba, as in many other Latin American countries (Brazil, Argentina, Mexico), also grew more culturally prominent, developing links with other, better established educational and cultural institutions, which in turn endowed film education in its largest sense with social value.[16] Both the films and the writings of the early Soviet avant-garde (Lev Kuleshov, Pudovkin, and Eisenstein in particular) played an important part of this broader transnational process, which after the revolution became fully institutionalized in the ICAIC, the first cultural institution created by Castro's new government.

And yet, for powerful geopolitical reasons, in the 1960s, Cuban artists and critics were reluctant to admit any influences from Soviet cinema. Thus, Santiago Álvarez famously disputed the notion that he was in any way influenced by Dziga Vertov or had seen any of his films, a claim whose accuracy is highly dubious. Vertov was very likely screened in Cuba in the 1950s (by the film section of the society Nuestro Tiempo, to which Álvarez belonged) and most certainly in 1961, as part of the Cinemateca's retrospective of Soviet cinema—an event that it is unlikely that Álvarez, one of the earliest participants in Cuban cinema's institutional development, missed.[17] One of the key reasons for Álvarez's discomfort was the unavoidable association of Soviet cinema with socialist realism and Stalinism (an association from which Vertov was certainly not exempt). The European New Left, defined among other things by its opposition to the Soviet Union and its Stalinist legacy, was an important ally for Cuban (and radical Latin American) cineastes.

Moreover, throughout much of the 1960s and until 1968 (when Castro reluctantly sided with the Soviet Union over the invasion of Czechoslovakia), Cuba's relationship with the Soviet Union was quite tense. Further exacerbated by the conflicts brought about by the Missile Crisis, Cuba openly opposed the Soviet stance on peaceful coexistence, which rejected the guerilla principles of armed struggle—principles that were embraced by many of the radical national liberation movements actively supported by Castro and especially Che Guevara.[18] As an expression of solidarity, ICAIC and Álvarez in particular, alongside other radical Latin American filmmakers, were eager to develop ties with Algeria, Vietnam, and the Lusophone African anticolonial liberation movements. Ironically, many of these initial cinematic connections took place via festivals in the Socialist Bloc—first at Karlovy Vary and Moscow and subsequently at the Leipzig documentary film festival, where, starting in the 1960s, Vietnamese, African, Cuban, and, eventually, Palestinian documentarians were regular guests and where Álvarez's films won numerous awards.[19] And yet, despite the strategic importance of these encounters, the production and exhibition practices of the Soviet cinematic establishment were antithetical to the kind of Thirdworldist guerilla filmmaking advanced by Álvarez (and most famously articulated in 1969 in Fernando Solanas and Octavio Getino's manifesto, "Towards a Third Cinema," which came out in the official publication of Tricontinental).[20] Indeed, whether within international film circles or among Cuban intellectuals and artists, references to Soviet cinema served as a proxy for Cuba's engagement and relationship with the Soviet Union, reflecting the public perception of the constant threat of the loss of political and cultural autonomy and inevitable Sovietization of the island.

Despite these perceptions, throughout the 1960s, ICAIC (at least in part as a benefit of director Alfredo Guevara's friendship with Castro) was largely able to set and follow an agenda based on its own understanding of socialist cinema and culture—an understanding that at times differed drastically from that formulated and executed in other Cuban cultural spheres. This independence extended to its relationship with the Socialist Bloc, with the ICAIC fully able to control its exhibition choices and production practices and openly voice disagreement with its Socialist Bloc colleagues. These tensions were particularly evident in the case of coproductions, of which Cuban filmmakers and critics were often skeptical. Such coproductions as Vladimír Čech's *For Whom Havana Dances* (*Para quién baila La Habana*, Czechoslovakia, 1962), Mikhail Kalatozov's *I Am Cuba* (*Ia Kuba/Soy Cuba*, USSR, 1964), and Kurt Maetzig's *Preludio 11* (GDR, 1964) provided ICAIC with infrastructural help and professional training (which were some of the main objectives, from the Cuban perspective, of hosting foreign film crews in Cuba) and increased Cuba's visibility abroad. And yet their reception in Cuba was mostly negative, and ICAIC overtly considered them to be failures. Thus, in 1969, in an interview by the journal *Romances*, when Alfredo Guevara was asked about the possibility of reembarking on coproductions, he responded negatively and explained that Cuba could only benefit from "genuine collaboration on equal terms," which would imply "handing over the direction, cinematography, editing, soundtrack ... to the *artists of the developing country,*" clearly implying that this hadn't happened with films such as *I Am Cuba*.[21] In the same interview, Guevara further discussed ICAIC's difficulties in finding international films to include in its programs. While foreign commercial cinema, according to Guevara, was "dominated by sadism and pornography," the productions of socialist countries did not meet ICAIC's criteria either, since "many films from socialist countries [were] tangled up in artistic rhetoric, neo-conventionalism, or an almost total lack of rhythm."[22] While it may be difficult to accept such an assessment of the state of cinema in 1969 on either side of the Iron Curtain in good faith, this list of specific failings of Soviet and Eastern European films perhaps speaks more to the broad Cuban cultural perception of its aesthetic superiority as the flip side of the need to continuously assert autonomy from the Soviet Union.

### Soviet Cinema in Prerevolutionary Cuba

One way to understand ICAIC's seemingly contradictory stance vis-à-vis Soviet Bloc cinema is to analyze the dual context of the geopolitical pressures postrevolutionary Cuba faced and the legacy of Soviet cinema's reception in prerevolutionary Cuba. This legacy was particularly important, as it came to mark ideological differences between the major political factions competing for power over cultural production in Cuba throughout the 1960s.

Soviet cinema—and the 1920s avant-garde in particular—had a long reception history in Cuba (as elsewhere in Latin America). The most important figure in this respect was Cuban film historian and educator José Manuel Valdés-Rodríguez (1896–1971), who did more to disseminate Soviet cinema, and Eisenstein's ideas in particular, than any other comparable Latin American figure. In the late 1920s, Valdés-Rodríguez began working as a newspaper film critic, running a cine-club from his home and looking for films that did not have commercial exhibition. This was how he originally encountered Soviet films. In 1932, Valdés-Rodríguez began to contribute regularly to the US journal *Experimental Cinema*, and he subsequently became actively involved in the journal's campaign to save Eisenstein's Mexican film. Two years later, he traveled to the Soviet Union as a correspondent for *Bohemia* and *Ahora* (*Now*) to cover the 1934 Soviet Writers' Congress, where he met with Eisenstein on several occasions and had an opportunity to discuss the latter's plans for the curriculum at the Moscow film school, GIK (later VGIK).[23]

Starting in 1942, Valdés-Rodríguez implemented what he learned from Eisenstein and others when he began teaching Cinema: The Industry and Art of Our Times at the University of Havana's Summer School; this insistence on both a materialist (as in *industry*) and aesthetic (*art*) understanding of the medium was later reprised in the name of the film institute, ICAIC.[24] The first film Valdés-Rodríguez acquired for the collection was Eisenstein's *Alexander Nevsky* (1938). This and several other Soviet films became the cornerstone of his teachings in his university summer course and were used as the foundation of the newly created university film archive. After the revolution, he donated the prints to ICAIC for its archive.[25] Valdés-Rodríguez's influence extended well beyond the university, since it was a group of his students who ran the film section of the cultural society Nuestro Tiempo, an organization considered foundational for postrevolutionary Cuban culture. And although Valdés-Rodríguez himself did not come to occupy any official position at ICAIC (he resumed his teaching position at the University of Havana), he collaborated with the institution in its film publications and educational initiatives (including his own 1963 book on Soviet cinema, which begins with quotes from Vladimir Lenin and Anatoly Lunacharsky).[26]

While the impact of Valdés-Rodríguez's efforts at disseminating Soviet cinema in Latin America was indeed exceptional, such appreciation of early Soviet film masters was not particular to Cuba. Instead, it was emblematic of Latin American film cultures, whose admiration for Soviet cinema could fit just as well within the liberal rhetoric of authentic artistic expression and high modernism (as opposed to commercial cinema) or within a drive to develop a strong national film industry (in opposition to the dominance of Hollywood or hegemonic European cinemas) as within a more explicitly politically radical revolutionary platform.[27] And in fact, among Valdés-Rodríguez's disciples were some of the key figures of Cuban culture's liberal wing, who would very quickly emerge as the antagonists to the leaders of ICAIC and end up in exile—while ICAIC itself never came to carry Valdés-Rodríguez's mantle as the promoter of Soviet cinema to the rest of the world.

Overall, the impressive range of Soviet-centered cinematic activities in Cuba were not unique within the region; the 1961 retrospective of Soviet cinema in Cuba was outshone by one held in Brazil the same year.[28] And despite Alfredo Guevara's programmatic statements in *Cine Cubano*, the legacy of Soviet theory within Cuban critical writings is comparatively thin: one rarely finds in the copious writings of Tomás Gutiérrez Alea or Julio García Espinosa on revolutionary aesthetics any direct references to Kuleshov, Eisenstein, or Pudovkin (it is often Bertolt Brecht who, for them, signifies the political avant-garde). Although ICAIC published some works by Eisenstein and Pudovkin over the course of the 1960s, considerably more translations of Soviet theory had been made in the 1950s in Argentina and Uruguay.[29] An important reason for this lack of enthusiasm, in addition to those already discussed, is that by the early 1960s, the promotion of Soviet cinema in Cuba was associated not only with the kind of alternative film culture represented by Valdés-Rodríguez's students, but mostly with their direct competitors for power: the culturally conservative party hard-liners who had historically formed the Socialist Party of Cuba (PSP).

## Dogmatists, Revolutionaries, and Liberals

In the period leading up to 1959, the PSP was the main disseminator of Soviet culture in Cuba, organizing a wide range of cultural activities, including film and cultural criticism and cine-club repertoire. As early as the 1940s, one PSP militant in particular, Mirta Aguirre, became a model for a certain kind of politically engaged pro-Soviet (and pro-socialist realist, pro-Stalinist) film criticism. As one of the leaders of the National Council of Culture (hereafter CNC), the main governmental organization charged with matters of culture and education (in the 1960s, specifically plastic and performing arts), she would continue to argue for this position, explicitly positing socialist realism against all other artistic manifestations as the only authentically revolutionary style for all arts.[30]

In contrast, the future leaders of ICAIC all belonged to the film section of the cultural society Nuestro Tiempo, which was affiliated with PSP but stood at a certain distance from it. Run by a younger generation of radicals, Nuestro Tiempo in the 1950s advanced Italian neorealism as the privileged model for cinema in Cuba, and it is this group that formed the core of ICAIC after the revolution. The more liberal wing of Nuestro Tiempo, in contrast, favored British direct cinema and subsequently the French New Wave while defending Hollywood and evincing open hostility toward Soviet cinema.

These three clusters, corresponding to the three dominant cultural/political camps (often referred to in ICAIC discourse as *dogmaticos*, or dogmatists, *revolucionarios*, or revolutionaries, and *liberales*, liberals), competed for power in the cultural sphere in the 1960s and were distinguishable in particular by their attitude toward the Soviet Union and its cultural policies.[31] Thus Guevara originally belonged to the PSP militants but split from them in the 1950s over his criticism of the 1956 Soviet invasion of Hungary and his open opposition to socialist realism, stances that were both broadly supported by PSP.

The battle between these three camps constituted the core of the cultural debates throughout the 1960s. As the liberals were gradually removed from all positions of influence early in the decade (and most of the key figures were eventually exiled), the old-guard PSP dogmatists increasingly gained power over the cultural field. ICAIC's revolutionaries, however, managed to retain almost full control over the cinematic sphere and a great degree of aesthetic and political independence at least until the mid-1970s. Just as in the prerevolutionary days, the attitude of each faction toward Soviet culture more generally and Soviet cinema in particular remained an important marker of difference within their competing programs.

## Cultural Polemics of the 1960s and Soviet Cinema

After the 1959 revolution, attitudes toward Soviet cinema in Cuba continued to be ideologically charged and rife with potential political consequences. As early as 1960, the first Semana of Soviet and Eastern European cinema triggered a series of reviews by the critic (and famous writer) Guillermo Cabrera Infante in the journal *Carteles* and in the February 1961 special issue of *Lunes de Revolución* (aka *Lunes*), a journal directly associated with the liberal wing. His reviews made visible his well-known preferences for American cinema while openly critiquing Stalinism and socialist realism, and they celebrated post-Stalinist Soviet cinema for what Cabrera Infante saw as its return to the theme of "the triumph of love over ideology."[32] While generally asserting the view that films from the East were "primitive" in their poetics, Cabrera Infante makes some unexpected claims—for instance, that he prefers *Chapayev* (dir. Georgy and Sergei Vasiliev, 1934) over *Ivan the Terrible* (*Ivan Grozny*, dir. Sergei Eisenstein, 1944) because "between a bombastic Western and a simple one this critic always prefers simplicity, which always makes for better cinema."[33] Referring to Grigory Kozintsev as "another old Stalinist," Cabrera Infante calls his version of *Don Quijote* (*Don Kikhot*, 1957) "the longest, heaviest, and most boring film ever made" and dismisses *The Cranes Are Flying* (*Letiat zhuravli*, dir. Mikhail Kalatozov, 1957) as an exercise in formalism and a poor imitation of Orson Wells, G. W. Pabst, and Walter Ruttmann—or even of "the worst of the British 'psychological' melodramas."[34] The film's positive reception, he claims, can only be the result of "either well-managed propaganda or the desire to witness a resurrection: for Soviet cinema to return to what it was thirty years ago."[35]

Cabrera Infante's lack of recognition of Kozintsev and Kalatozov's role in the 1920s avant-garde is not surprising (after all, neither filmmaker's early experimental work was known outside of the Soviet Union). More remarkable is his skepticism about the possibility of Soviet cinema's resurrection, which was clearly an open challenge to the pro-Soviet dogmatists. Such a position came with increasingly risky political consequences. This was the case with Nestor Almendros's 1961 review of the Czechoslovak film *The White Dove* (*Bílá holubice*, dir. František Vláčil, 1960), also published in *Lunes*. Almendros's review praised Vláčil's film as the best in a recent showing of Eastern European cinema for its poetic vision and "neoexpressionist avant-gardism."[36] This triggered an attack on Almendros in a series of articles in the Communist Youth newspaper *Mella* accusing Vláčil's film (in recognizably Stalinist terms) of "excessive formalism" and claiming the need for cinema with a direct message and less symbolism.[37] The articles concluded with an open defense of Stalin and an unveiled threat to Almendros. And indeed, like the rest of the critics associated with *Lunes*, Almendros would soon lose his position and be forced into exile.[38]

The reference to cinema with a direct message and less symbolism was clearly legible as a reference to *socialist realism*, a term widely used and discussed in Cuba. And yet it is worth pausing to acknowledge that a precise understanding of socialist realism, despite its explicit development as an artistic method and official imposition by the Soviet Communist Party in 1932, eluded its contemporary practitioners as much as it does cultural historians. Originally linked to abstract concepts (*partiinost'*, or adherence to the party; *klassovost'*, or emphasis on class; *ideinost'*, or commitment to ideological content; and *pravdivost'*, or truthfulness), in its initial application to cinema it could be summarized as an expectation that a film would address a clear political theme through easily accessible formal means and feature a positive hero and a successful resolution of the narrative conflict, usually enabled by a representative of the Communist Party. The imposition of socialist realism coincided with the so-called "campaign against formalism," which targeted the avant-garde and, more broadly, creative expression that was stylistically challenging and insufficiently ideologically clear.[39] The correct application of socialist realism was a mysterious and confusing process, especially in cinema, and its interpretation and application were further destabilized after the mid-1950s Thaw. And thus, while in transnational contexts it came to be associated with Stalinist epics or any glorification of the socialist regime, internally, beyond an emphasis on ideological and political themes and a general push for formal accessibility, the doctrine never cohered into a prescription that could be easily followed or recognized. As such, it could conveniently serve as an arbitrary and unstable justification for censorship.[40] Overall, both in the Soviet Union and in Cuba in the 1960s, references to socialist realism were largely deictic, pointing to a cluster of meaning that, while presumed to be stable, in fact was entirely dependent on the context and position of the speaker. In postrevolutionary Cuba, such deictic references to socialist realism served particularly effectively as rhetorical strategies for ideological jostling.

ICAIC's own 1961 attack on a documentary entitled *PM* (*Pasado meridiano*, Orlando Jiménez Leal and Sabá Cabrera Infante, 1961) was one of the first such instances. Made and exhibited outside of ICAIC by two young aspiring filmmakers with the direct support of ICAIC's then-primary cultural rival, *Lunes* (Sabá was the younger brother of Guillermo Cabrera Infante, whose film reviews I discuss earlier), the film was barred from public exhibition on the grounds that it gave a supposedly partial picture of life in Havana and therefore potentially misrepresented the advances of postrevolutionary Cuba—a critique that to all parties sounded like the imposition of a socialist realist formula.[41] This led to a series of public debates that concluded with Castro's famous "Words to the Intellectuals" address, which coined the famous formula "Within the Revolution, everything; against the Revolution, nothing." While seemingly leaving issues of artistic form to artists, freeing matters of aesthetic style from interventions by the state, and placing all ideological weight on the content, this dictum ultimately created ambivalence and paranoia much in the way socialist realism did in the Soviet context.[42]

In these debates, despite ICAIC's strong stance against socialist realism, Alfredo Guevara sided with the hard-liners by accusing the filmmakers of "playing a dangerous game" and the group around *Lunes* of being "enemies of the Soviet Union," taking the opportunity to get rid of his opponents in a highly successful bid for the consolidation of ICAIC's power over the cinematic cultural sphere.[43] Soviet poet Evgeny Evtushenko, who was present at these debates, immediately likened them to Stalinist trials, apparently warning his new friend Heberto Padilla, another regular contributor to *Lunes*, of an impending clampdown and evoking the fate of Boris Pasternak in the Soviet Union and the Petöfi Circle in Hungary.[44]

Indeed, the debates led to the further centralization of control over the artistic sphere. *Lunes* was closed, and the Union of Writers, UNEAC, was founded, coming to occupy a repressive position (fully realized by the end of the decade in Padilla's own infamous case). The outcome of the debates also affirmed ICAIC's control not merely over their definition of *revolutionary cinema*, but also over all film production and exhibition on the island. Having achieved this victory by resorting to an essentially socialist-realist critique of Leal and Cabrera Infante's documentary, however, ICAIC immediately took the opportunity to publicly reiterate its rejection of socialist realism. Thus, in 1962, in an article in *Cine Cubano*, Alfredo Guevara would differentiate between ICAIC's fiction filmmaking and its documentary production, which was intended to fulfill specific political or didactic functions (such as the documentary newsreels *Noticiero ICAIC Latinoamericano*, led by Álvarez, or the series of scientific and cultural documentaries that formed part of the Popular Encyclopedia project). These different criteria, according to the head of ICAIC, allowed the institution to "reserve for the feature films and artistic documentaries the possibility, and the right, to forget all didactic intention."[45]

In the same year, at a roundtable at ICAIC entitled "What is Modern in Art?" that included Alea, García Espinosa, and Jorge Fraga, as well as invited guests Andrzej Wajda and Kalatozov, Alea declared, in an obvious allusion to socialist realism, that "an artist cannot rely on pre-established rhetorical formulas with the purpose of gaining approval of [his] artistic creation."[46] And in 1963, García Espinosa published an article entitled "Living Under the Rain," in which he played on the metaphors of frost and rain in an allusion to the Soviet Thaw in order to emphasize his—and by extension, Cuban cinema's—explicit rejection of Stalinism and the imposition of any artistic method as the correct one by the party: "In a meeting held not long ago, the positive role of the hero in Socialist films was discussed. We were thinking about the damage that most of these films have done to the truly positive heroes.... We shouldn't overlook the fact that the triumph of the Cuban revolution coincides with the beginning of the Socialist thaw ... Moreover, we cannot forget that the Cuban revolution itself emerged [already] thawed."[47]

This last sentence should perhaps be understood, however, as a programmatic statement rather than a reflection of reality, as 1963 witnessed three public attacks on ICAIC by the dogmatists. First, in response to an ICAIC statement that attempted to provide a broad and heterogeneous definition of culture under socialism, former PSP militant Edith Garcia Buchaca unleashed a thorough critique of ICAIC's ideological position. In addition to her attack on ICAIC's proclamation of cultural pluralism within a socialist society, referring to the seemingly innocuous statement that "in a socialist society the promotion and development of culture is the right and duty of the Party and the State," she retorted that "in a socialist society the Government and the Party have the duty not only to 'promote the development of culture' but also to orient and direct it, according to [its] goals."[48] This sounded less like a theoretical disagreement than an open threat.

At the same time, a series of public debates (subsequently published in the newspaper *La Gaceta de Cuba*, the official publication of the UNEAC) took place between ICAIC representatives who signed the proclamation and professors of the Department of Letters of the University of Havana, Juan J. Flo and Sergio Benvenuto, who similarly accused the ICAIC filmmakers of taking an anti-Marxist and therefore anti-revolutionary position. One of the most vocal responses was by Alea, Cuba's most famous filmmaker, who explicitly linked Flo's rhetoric with the language of Eisenstein's infamous autocritique of *Ivan the Terrible*, part two, which was attacked for its decadence and old ideas, deemed incompatible with socialist culture, with

Eisenstein acknowledging his mistakes. After an extended quotation from Eisenstein's well-known (and widely translated) 1946 *mea culpa*, Alea goes on to say that it was precisely the kind of "witch hunt" that Eisenstein fell victim to—directly mirrored in Flo's declarations—that was responsible for the way "Soviet cinema, which in the first years of the revolution surprised audiences all over the world with its vitality and drive, sadly decayed to the point of becoming one of the blandest cinemas in the world. And this was done in the name of the Revolution."[49]

As this reference perfectly illustrates, Cuban cineastes' considerable knowledge of Soviet cinema was used as a weapon—in this case, against the prospect of adopting socialist realism and thus losing artistic autonomy. Indeed, by the 1960s, associations between Eisenstein's *Ivan the Terrible* and Stalinism were common among liberal anticommunist intellectuals both in the Eastern Bloc (including the Soviet Union) and the West.[50] This argument was immortalized in Aleksandr Solzhenitsyn's "One Day in the Life of Ivan Denisovich," which came out in the Soviet Union just two years before Alea's essay and became an important point of cultural reference in Cuba throughout the 1960s, clearly associated with "dissident" forms of socialist culture.[51] But ultimately, unlike Solzhenitsyn's protagonist, Alea defends Eisenstein, affirming that "the analogies between Eisenstein and Professor Flo do not go much further: Eisenstein was a great artist and without a doubt (and we appreciate this now, with the years' passing) an authentic representative of the Soviet Revolution. A sincere man who was sentenced to sterility by the representatives of a bureaucracy who believed they had the right to play the role of mediators between the artist and the people."[52] Despite this affirmation, Alea's reference to Eisenstein remained considerably different from the copious praise of the Soviet director on the pages of *Cine Cubano* (such as Guevara's statement cited above)—a cautionary tale of the pitfalls of socialist culture rather than a celebration.

Also in 1963, *Hoy* (*Today*) took issue with ICAIC's programming practices. The newspaper was edited by Blas Roca Calderio, another PSP militant and a frequent visitor to the Soviet Union (having traveled there as early as the Seventh Congress of the Communist International in Moscow in 1935 and presented Khrushchev with the Cuban flag as the leader of the Cuban delegation to a meeting of the Communist Party of the Soviet Union in 1961). Its editorial accused ICAIC of anti-revolutionary actions for screening Lautaro Murúa's *Alias Gardelito* (1961), Luis Buñuel's *Exterminating Angel* (1962) and *Viridiana* (1961), Federico Fellini's *La dolce vita* (1960), and Pier Paolo Pasolini's *Accattone* (1961), deeming these films "decadent and harmful to the public" and accusing them of "weakening the spirit of combat, the sacrifice and the fight of our people." This triggered a series of exchanges on the pages of *Hoy* between Blas and Guevara. In defense of ICAIC, Guevara explicitly framed Blas's attacks as advocating for socialist realism: "We know what it's about, and it's not the first time that we listen to these siren songs: the positive hero, the need for a happy ending, the constructive moral, the creation of archetypes, so-called socialist realism." The stakes of the polemic were high, as it was clear that Blas was expressing the official position of the CNC and seeking to articulate a unified cultural policy for the Revolutionary Government that appeared perfectly aligned with the most dogmatic Soviet articulations. Guevara categorically rejected these demands, arguing, "If, as expected or recommended, we were to limit ourselves to exhibiting works of agitation that calm or reassure, the artistic work (and the multiple paths it opens to consciousness and perception) would be replaced by a propaganda sweetened by aestheticized formulas. The public would be reduced to a mass of babies fed with a perfectly prepared and sterilized 'ideological mush' by wet-nurses, in this way guaranteeing their best and most complete assimilation."[53]

In this standoff, Guevara and ICAIC again achieved a political victory, successfully defending the independence of their programming policies and broader cultural position against CNC's. ICAIC's explicit stance against socialist realism would be further strengthened by the publication in 1965 of Che Guevara's highly influential "Socialism and Man in Cuba," which widened the ideological stance between progressive Cuban cultural practitioners and the Soviet Union. In it, Che explicitly asked, "Why should we pretend to look in the frozen forms of socialist realism for the only valid recipe [for socialist cultural policies]?"[54]

And yet, after Che's death and Castro's support of the Soviet invasion of Czechoslovakia, ICAIC would once again have to side with its former enemies—this time during the infamous Padilla affair. Heberto Padilla's collection of poetry *Fuera del juego* (*Out of the Game*), which in 1968 had initially been given a prize by the Writer's Union, was soon pronounced counterrevolutionary because of its critique of Stalinism and Soviet foreign policy, landing the author in prison by 1971. This was apparently triggered by Castro's fear that the poetry collection would serve as a "primer on dissidence for Cubans."[55] Padilla, a devoted Communist himself, saw self-critique as an extension of his revolutionary duty and was inspired by the Soviet intelligentsia's sense of the artist's social and political responsibility (Padilla had gotten to know Soviet intellectuals well during his stay in Moscow as a correspondent for the Latin American News Agency *Prensa Latina*, and most of the poems in the collection were written there).[56] Padilla's arrest had a wide international response: several European thinkers, writers, and artists who had initially supported the revolution signed two open letters to Castro linking Padilla's public session of self-criticism to the Stalinist trials and cautioning against the country's move toward the Soviet model of communism. Initially published in the French newspaper *Le Monde*, these letters promptly circulated in other languages and publications, marking a definitive rift between Castro and a great number of Western European and American leftists.

In response to these events, ICAIC's so-called Declaration of the Cuban Filmmakers of 1971 sided with the government, using the same rhetoric Guevara used in his 1961 attack against *Lunes* and claiming that Padilla's liberal critique of the Soviet Union, while not problematic in absolute terms, could under the present conditions be dangerous to the revolution and should therefore not be tolerated: "The characteristics of the practices and debates that have been shaping the Cuban cultural reality since the triumph of the revolution are in crisis. . . . The task of the revolutionaries is to take action in this ideological struggle, attempting to analyze the extreme that, today, is critical: the liberal trend. We know that the dogmatists, as liberals do on other occasions, will call themselves our allies. It is a risk we consciously take. They don't confuse us, and they won't deceive anyone."[57]

Here, Guevara (who authored most official statements on behalf of ICAIC, unless they were explicitly signed by others) takes pains to rhetorically distance himself from his old enemies, the dogmatists from the PSP and UNEAC—who were, after all, directly responsible for Padilla's incrimination—while by default siding with them. This was, then, yet another attempt to keep ICAIC away from similar attacks while maintaining some degree of control in the face of the obvious changes in the political climate.

The Padilla affair marked the beginning of a series of new cultural policies in Cuba. Starting in 1971, the Congress on Culture and Education made artists into wage laborers and instituted Soviet-style intellectual property laws. In 1972, Cuba became a member of the Council for Mutual Economic Assistance (COMECON). It was in this context that Leonid Brezhnev visited Cuba in 1974 (the first visit by a head of the Soviet Communist Party to Latin America), heralding the signing of a great number of commercial, cultural, athletic, educational, and scientific agreements between the two countries. This was followed by Cuba's First Communist Party Congress in 1975 and the Constitution of 1976, which was modeled on the Soviet one. This period has become known in Cuba as the Quinquenio Gris (the Gray Five Years, an ironic reference to Soviet five-year plans) or, alternatively, La Decada Negra (the Dark Decade) or the Trinquenio Amargo (the Bitter Fifteen Years).

Here, Sovietization meant intense cultural and political repression in all spheres of life, including cinema.

## Conclusion

Throughout the debates that marked the 1960s and '70s, Guevara and his colleagues at ICAIC explicitly defended their ambiguous or contradictory position as an example of a dialectical approach that foregrounds concrete historical reality and its needs rather than a general or absolute set of principles (aesthetic, cultural, or political). They were further enabled by Castro's "Within the Revolution, everything; against the Revolution, nothing." The specific needs and pressures Cuba experienced at that moment "dialectically" justified the swift redefinition of aesthetic or ideological criteria and institutional allegiances as necessitated by the specific historical and geopolitical conditions.[58] This theoretical position supported ICAIC's highly strategic approach to engaging with Soviet cinema and its role within the institution, which was intended to provide internal advantages in the moment. As easy as it may be to accuse ICAIC of acting out of sheer political opportunism, this highly pragmatic approach nonetheless reflects the larger cultural logic governing many similar relationships between the Soviet Bloc and the countries of Africa, Asia, and Latin America, especially as seen through cinematic history. While the Soviet Union was pursuing its own geopolitical interests, local actors (such as the Cuban cineastes, in this case) often built shifting alliances guided less by ideological motivations than by pragmatic short-term goals. Working with their Soviet supporters often presented them with opportunities that would otherwise be denied by politically and economically weaker (Thirdworldist) allies or by more explicitly neo-imperialist (capitalist) hegemonies. Indeed, collaboration with the Soviet Bloc through film festivals and broader exhibition strategies contributed, often successfully, to these cineastes' continuing efforts to create a lively and heterogeneous cultural sphere, however unstable, on their own terms. And the way that Cuban film institutions strategically employed highly self-conscious polemics on socialist realism (and, by extension, on Soviet cinema) allowed them to navigate inescapable and overwhelming (geo)political pressures, both locally and internationally. This highly pragmatic strategy was certainly successful for ICAIC throughout the 1960s, when the institute managed to produce and exhibit some of the greatest works of Cuban and world cinematography, projecting internationally an image of political engagement coupled with artistic freedom and independence, of democratization of the media with the full support of the state, and of a proud national culture combined with internationalist solidarity and sophisticated cosmopolitanism. This image resonated throughout the world, speaking to the hopes and dreams of the "long 1960s" on both sides of the Iron Curtain and around the world.

The history of these complex and seemingly self-contradictory dynamics, in turn, demonstrates how Cold War media ecologies served as sites for the negotiation of multiple ideologies and motivations. Understanding these complexities allows us to reconstruct the Soviet, Eastern European, and Cuban cultural and media space of the period as a shared one with overlapping influences and struggles, while also preventing us from making simplistic assumptions about the political and artistic agency of its actors, their allegiances, and the transnational networks to which they contributed.

## NOTES

I would like to thank the editors of this volume and Laura-Zoe Humphreys for their generous and formative feedback and suggestions for revision.

1. See Imre, "Postcolonial Media Studies in Postsocialist Europe," 113–134.
2. For detailed accounts of this, see Lévesque, *The USSR and the Cuban Revolution*; and Duncan, *The Soviet Union and Cuba*.
3. See Hernández-Reguant, "The Inventor, the Machine, and the New Man."
4. This research builds on similar work by such as scholars as Malitsky, Gorsuch, Gonçalves, and Loss.
5. Gallardo Saborido, *El martillo y el espejo*, 149. For more on the pan–Latin American and Third Worldist contexts for Cuban cinema in English, see Pick, *The New Latin American Cinema*; Mahler, *From the Tricontinental to the Global South*; and Mestman, "Algiers-Buenos Aires-Montréal," 41–51.
6. See Pedemonte, "Birches Too Difficult to Cut Down."
7. Gonçalves, "Sputnik Premiers in Havana," 92.
8. Ibid., 93.
9. Paranagua and Cobas, *Le Cinéma cubain*, 32–33.
10. Garcia Borrero, *Cine Cubano de los Sesenta*, 59.
11. Muguiro Altuna, "Kinofikatsia cubana y sus fantasmas," 267.
12. Gonçalves, "Sputnik Premiers in Havana," 112.
13. Muguiro Altuna, "Kinofikatsia cubana y sus fantasmas," 264.
14. Guevara, "Realidades y perspectivas de un nuevo cine," 8.
15. López, "Cine-clubs," in *Encyclopedia*, 349.
16. See Xavier, *Sétima arte*, 125–130, 207.
17. Del Valle Dávila, *Cámaras en trance*. For more on Álvarez in relation to Vertov, see Malitsky, *Post-Revolution Nonfiction Film*.
18. On the broader context for this, see Pedemonte, "Birches Too Difficult to Cut Down."
19. See Razlogova, "World Cinema at Soviet Festivals"; and Moine, *Screened Encounters*.
20. Solanas and Getino, "Towards a Third Cinema."
21. Guevara, "Reconocer en el cine la imagen," in *Tiempo de fundación*, 180–181.
22. On this sense of superiority, see Loss, *Dreaming in Russian*, 81–86.
23. Valdés-Rodríguez, "El hombre, el creador, el técnico," 24–26.
24. Rozsa, "Film Culture and Education in Republican Cuba"; and Feeney, *Hollywood in Havana*.
25. Rozsa, "Film Culture and Education in Republican Cuba," 309, 312–133; and Valdés-Rodríguez, *El cine en la Universidad de La Habana*, vii–xii, 372–380, 393–429, 456–485.
26. Valdés-Rodríguez, *Cursillos de cinematografía Cine Por Paises*, 1.
27. See Wells, "Parallel Modernities?"; and Salazkina, "Eisenstein in Latin America."

28. Notari, *A recepção do cinema de Serguei M. Eisenstein no Brasil*.

29. Comintern-founded publisher Ediciones Pueblos Unidos and university film journal *Cine Universitario del Uruguay* in Montevideo together published at least six translated works by Eisenstein, Pudovkin, and Alexander Dovzhenko in the 1950s. Publishers such as Futuro, Losange, and La Reja in Argentina also published several works by Kuleshov, Pudovkin, Eisenstein, Dovzhenko, and Semyon Timoshenko in the 1950s. In comparison, the ICAIC publications of Soviet film theory were made in the late 1960s and were considerably fewer, and none contained previously untranslated material.

30. Most famously Mirta Aguirre, "Notes of Literature and Art," originally published in the newspaper *Cuba Socialista* in 1963. Pogolotti, *Polémicas culturales de los 60*, 43–71.

31. See Gordon-Nesbitt, *To Defend the Revolution Is to Defend Culture*.

32. Cabrera Infante, *Un Oficio*, 387.

33. Ibid., 391–392.

34. Ibid.

35. Ibid., 423.

36. "La paloma blanca," 88.

37. "Cine: Debate en torno a *La paloma blanca*," 39.

38. Luis, *Lunes de Revolución: literatura y cultura en los primeros años de la Revolución Cubana*, 39.

39. For historical explorations of socialist realism, see Lahusen and Dobrenko, *Socialist Realism Without Shores*; and Tihanov and Dobrenko, *A History of Russian Literary Theory and Criticism*.

40. For a thorough recent investigation of the relationship between ideology and practice in Stalinist-era cinema, see Belodubrovskaya, *Not According to Plan*.

41. For a detailed account see Vincenot, "Censure et cinéma à cuba."

42. For a discussion of how this dictum triggered a regime of (auto)censorship, see Humphreys, *Fidel Between the Lines*.

43. Garcia Borrero, *Cine Cubano de los Sesenta*, 78–83.

44. Padilla, *La mala memoria*, 59–61.

45. Guevara, "Creemos un deber ser modernos," in *Revolución es Lucidez*, 369.

46. Fornet, *Alea, una retrospectiva crítica*, 286.

47. Quoted in Pogolotti, *Polémicas culturales de los 60*, 12–13.

48. Ibid., 17, 26–27.

49. Tomás Gutiérrez Alea, "Donde menos se piensa salta el cazador ... de brujas," *La Gaceta de Cuba*, March 20, 1964, in Pogolotti, *Polémicas culturales de los 60*, 111–124.

50. In fact, the Eisenstein text that Alea quotes was immediately translated and published in full in the US socialist anticommunist journal *New Leader* in December 1946. See Caute, *The Dancer Defects*, 122.

51. Rojas, "Souvenirs de un Caribe soviético," 24.

52. Pogolotti, *Polémicas culturales de los 60*, 119.

53. Ibid., 145–148.

54. Quoted in Guanche Zaldívar, "Tensiones históricas del campo político-cultural," 7.

55. Prieto, "Heberto Padilla, the First Dissident."

56. Manuel Díaz Martínez, *El Caso Padilla*, quoted in Ibid., 124.

57. Guevara, "Declaración de los cineastas cubanos."

58. For another instance of this, see Rozsa and Salazkina, "Dissonances in 1970s European and Latin American Political Film Discourse."

## Bibliography

Balderston, Daniel, Mike Gonzalez, and Ana M. López, eds. *Encyclopedia of Contemporary Latin American and Caribbean Cultures*. New York: Routledge, 2000.

Belodubrovskaya, Maria. *Not According to Plan: Filmmaking under Stalin*. Ithaca, NY: Cornell University Press, 2017.

Cabrera Infante, Guillermo. *Un Oficio del Siglo 20 G. Cain 1954–60*. Mexico: Alfaguara, 2005.
Caute, David. *The Dancer Defects: The Struggle for Cultural Supremacy during the Cold War*. Oxford: Oxford University Press, 2003.
"Cine: Debate en torno a La paloma blanca." *Mella*, July 4, 1961, n.p.
Del Valle Dávila, Ignacio. *Cámaras en trance: el Nuevo Cine Latinoamericano, un proyecto cinematográfico subcontinental*. Santiago, CL: Editorial Cuarto Propio, 2014.
Duncan, Raymond W. *The Soviet Union and Cuba: Interests and Influence*. New York: Praeger, 1985.
Espinosa, Julio García. "For an Imperfect Cinema." In *New Latin American Cinema Volume One: Theory Practices and Transcontinental Articulations*, edited by Michael T. Martin, 71–82. Detroit: Wayne State University Press, 1997.
Feeney, Megan. *Hollywood in Havana: US Cinema and Revolutionary Nationalism in Cuba before 1959*. Chicago: University of Chicago Press, 2019.
Fornet, Ambrosio. *Alea, una retrospectiva crítica*. La Habana: Editorial Letras Cubanas, 1998.
Gallardo Saborido, Emilio José, *El martillo y el espejo: Directrices de la politica cultural cubana, 1959–1976*. Madrid: Consejo Superior de Investigaciones Científicas, 2009.
Garcia Borrero, Juan Antonio. *Cine Cubano de los Sesenta: Mito y Realidad*. Cuba: Ocho y Medio, 2007.
Gonçalves, João Felipe. "Sputnik Premiers in Havana: A Historical Ethnography of the 1960 Soviet Exposition." In *The Socialist Sixties: Crossing Borders in the Second World*, edited by Anne E. Gorsuch and Diane Koenker, 84–120. Bloomington: Indiana University Press, 2013.
Gordon-Nesbitt, Rebecca. *To Defend the Revolution Is to Defend Culture: The Cultural Policy of the Cuban Revolution*. Oakland, CA: PM Press, 2015.
Gorsuch, Anne E. "'Cuba, My Love,' The Romance of Revolutionary Cuba in the Soviet Sixties." *The American Historical Review* 120, no. 2 (2015): 497–526.
Guanche Zaldívar, Julio César. "Tensiones históricas del campo político-cultural: la polémica Alfredo Guevara-Blas Roca." *Perfiles de la Cultura Cubana* (May–August 2003), 1–8.
Guevara, Alfredo. "Declaración de los cineastas cubanos." In *Tiempo de fundación*, 173–177. Madrid: Iberautor, 2003.
———. "Realidades y perspectivas de un nuevo cine." *Cine Cubano* 1, no.1 (1960): 1–11.
———. *Revolución es lucidez*. Havana: Ediciones ICAIC, 1998.
———. *Tiempo de fundación*. Madrid: Iberautor, 2003.
Hernández-Reguant, Ariana. "The Inventor, the Machine, and the New Man." In *Caviar with Rum: Cuba-USSR and the Post-Soviet Experience*, edited by Jacqueline Loss and José Manuel Prieto, 199–211. New York: Palgrave MacMillan, 2012.
Humphreys, Laura-Zoe. *Fidel Between the Lines*. Durham, NC: Duke University Press, 2019.
Imre, Anikó. "Postcolonial Media Studies in Postsocialist Europe." *boundary 2* 41, no. 1 (2014): 113–134.
Lahusen, Thomas, and Evgeny Dobrenko, eds. *Socialist Realism without Shores*. Durham, NC: Duke University Press, 1997.
"La paloma blanca," *Bohemia*, June 18, 1961, 88.
Lévesque, Jacques. *The USSR and the Cuban Revolution: Soviet Ideological and Strategical Perspectives, 1969–1977*. New York: Praeger, 1978.
Loss, Jacqueline. *Dreaming in Russian: The Cuban Soviet Imaginary*. Austin: University of Texas Press, 2013.
Luis, William. *Lunes de Revolución: literatura y cultura en los primeros años de la Revolución Cubana*. Madrid: Editorial Verbum, 2003.

Mahler, Anne Garland. *From the Tricontinental to the Global South*. Durham, NC: Duke University Press, 2017.

Malitsky, Joshua. *Post-Revolution Nonfiction Film: Building Soviet and Cuban Nations*. Bloomington: Indiana University Press, 2013.

Mestman, Mariano. "Algiers-Buenos Aires-Montréal: Thirdworldist Links in the Creation of the Latin American Filmmakers Committee (1974)." *Canadian Journal of Film Studies* 24, no. 2 (2015): 41–51.

Moine, Caroline. *Screened Encounters: The Leipzig Documentary Film Festival, 1955–1990*. New York: Berghahn, 2018.

Muguiro Altuna, Carlos. "Kinofikatsia cubana y sus fantasmas: Inventario de la presencia (y de la ausencia) del cine soviético en las pantallas de Cuba (1961–1991)." *Kamchatka: revista de análisis cultural* 5 (2015): 1–10.

Notari, Fabiola Bastos. *A recepção do cinema de Serguei M. Eisenstein no Brasil: um estudo de caso, a VI Bienal de São Paulo (1961)*. São Paulo: VII Simpósio Nacional de História Cultural, 2014.

Padilla, Heberto. *La mala memoria*. Barcelona: Plaza & Janés, 1989.

Paranagua, Paulo Antonio, and Roberto Cobas. *Le Cinéma cubain*. Paris: Centre Georges Pompidou, 1990.

Pedemonte, Rafael. "Birches Too Difficult to Cut Down: The Rejection and Assimilation of the Soviet Reference in Cuban Culture." *International Journal of Cuban Studies* 9, no. 1 (2017): 127–141.

Pick, Zuzana M. *The New Latin American Cinema: A Continental Project*. Austin: University of Texas Press, 1993.

Pogolotti, Graziella. *Polémicas culturales de los 60*. La Habana: Editorial Letras Cubanas, 2006.

Prieto, Jose Manuel. "Heberto Padilla, the First Dissident (of the Cuban Revolution)." In *Caviar with Rum: Cuba-USSR and the Post-Soviet Experience*, edited by Jacqueline Loss and Jose Manuel Prieto, 119–132. New York: Palgrave, 2012.

Razlogova, Elena. "World Cinema at Soviet Festivals: From Cultural Diplomacy to Personal Ties." *Studies in European Cinema* 17, no. 2 (2020): 140–154.

Rojas, Rafael. "Souvenirs de un Caribe soviético." *Encuentro de la cultura cubana* no. 48–49 (2008): 18–33.

Rozsa, Irene. "Film Culture and Education in Republican Cuba: The Legacy of José Manuel Valdés-Rodríguez." In *Cosmopolitan Film Cultures*, edited by Rielle Navitski and Nicolas Poppe, 298–323. Bloomington: Indiana University Press, 2017.

———. "The Institutionalization of Film Exhibition in Cuba (1959–64)." *Studies in Spanish & Latin American Cinemas* 14, no. 2 (2017): 153–170

Rozsa, Irene, and Masha Salazkina. "Dissonances in 1970s European and Latin American Political Film Discourse: The Aristarco–García Espinosa Debate." *Canadian Journal of Film Studies* 24, no. 2 (2015): 66–81.

Salazkina, Masha. "Eisenstein in Latin America." In *The Flying Carpet: Studies on Eisenstein and Russian Cinema*, edited by Joan Neuberger and Antonio Somaini, 343–367. Paris: Éditions Mimésis, 2018.

———. "Transnational Genealogies of the Institutional Film Cultures in Cuba, 1960s–1970s." In *The Routledge Companion to Latin American Cinema*, edited by Marvin D'Lugo, Ana M. López, and Laura Podalsky, 192–203. London: Routledge, 2017.

Solanas, Fernando, and Octavio Getino. "Towards a Third Cinema: Notes and Experiences for the Development of a Cinema of Liberation in the Third World." In *Film Manifestos and Global Cinema Cultures*, edited by Scott McKenzie, 230–250. Berkeley: University of California Press, 2014.

Tihanov, Galin, and Evgeny Dobrenko. *A History of Russian Literary Theory and Criticism: The Soviet Age and Beyond*. Pittsburgh: University of Pittsburgh Press, 2011.

Valdés-Rodríguez, José Manuel. *El cine en la Universidad de La Habana (1942–1965)*. La Habana: Empresa de Publicaciones Mined, 1966.

———. *Cursillos de cinematografía Cine Por Paises: Union Sovietica*. Havana: Consejo Nacional de Cultura, 1962.

———. "El hombre, el creador, el técnico: Sergei Mijailovich Eisenstein." *Lunes de Revolución*, February 6, 1961, 24–26.

———. "Letras: Rusia a los doce años." *Revista de Avance*, January 15, 1929.

Vincenot, Emmanuel. "Censure et cinéma à cuba: l'affaire P.M." *L'Âge d'or* [online] 2, 2009. http://journals.openedition.org/agedor/ 2750 ; DOI : 10.4000/agedor.2750

Wells, Sarah Ann. "Parallel Modernities? The First Reception of Soviet Cinema in Latin America." In *Cosmopolitan Film Cultures in Latin America*, edited by Rielle Navitsky and Nicolas Poppe, 151–175. Bloomington: Indiana University Press, 2017.

Xavier, Ismael. *Sétima arte: Um culto modern*. Rio de Janeiro: Editora Perspectiva, 1978.

MASHA SALAZKINA is Professor of Film Studies and Research Chair in Transnational Media Arts and Cultures at Concordia University. She is author of *In Excess: Sergei Eisenstein's Mexico* and editor (with Lilya Kaganovksy) of *Sound, Speech, Music in Soviet and Post-Soviet Cinema* (IUP, 2014) and (with Enrique Fibla) of *Global Perspectives on Amateur Film Histories and Cultures* (IUP, 2021).

CHAPTER 6

FROM THE ANTECHAMBER TO THE
INTERNATIONAL STAGE
*Early-Career Directors from Hungary at the
Mannheim Film Festival in the Late 1970s*

Sonja Simonyi

IN THE 1970S, HUNGARIAN DIRECTORS produced a series of notable wins at West Germany's Mannheim film festival. Several of them, such as István Dárday, Judit Elek, and Gyula Maár, had worked at the Balázs Béla Stúdió (BBS), the socialist country's state-owned institution for filmmaking, which operated as a crucial site for experimentation in cinema until the fall of communism. By the time most of these directors received their prizes abroad, they had left behind the minor production sphere of the BBS for Hungary's well-developed—and also state-owned—studio system for fiction and documentary film. As such, their careers underscored the state's control over virtually all areas of cultural production while also exemplifying a common, linear trajectory for motion-picture professionals under socialism. This led filmmakers from studies at the film academy (Színház- és Filmművészeti Főiskola [Academy of Theater and Film Arts]) to the BBS, where they made short films, and on to industry positions where they could craft their first feature-length projects.

Yet two Hungarian wins of the decade at Mannheim markedly counter this established linearity. Gábor Bódy's *American Postcard* (*Amerikai anzix*, 1975)—a rare BBS-produced experimental feature film—won the Grand Prize in 1976. *American Postcard* had functioned as Bódy's controversial graduation project at the film academy, and the award it received abroad eventually positively shaped its domestic reception and Bódy's status within the industry. Béla Tarr's *Family Nest* (*Családi tűzfészek*, 1977), a socially engaged docu-fiction, in turn received a prize at Mannheim in 1979. Tarr also directed it at the BBS as an amateur outsider, and his legitimacy as a professional was similarly enhanced due to Mannheim and the international exposure it provided.

Bódy's and Tarr's careers radiate an aura of exceptionality, reinforced by their colorful personal histories and the idiosyncratic formal styles of their films.[1] Beyond positing their powerful personalities and strong determination as catalysts for their journeys toward professionalization and recognition, this chapter connects their early international successes to significant institutional shifts at the BBS during the 1970s and to Hungarian cinema's wider distribution networks domestically and abroad. It rejects the primacy often given to Western exposure—frequently understood as the final or only aim of Eastern European filmmakers—and instead frames these festival wins as part of a multidirectional, transnational system of cultural influence and exchange. Indeed, the wins were at the core of the films' legitimacy, not only in Western Europe, but also back home. As such, this chapter also exposes intersecting networks of interaction and often contradictory opportunities and limitations in socialist film culture, which hinged on individual negotiations, shifting organizational structures, and the formal categorizations of films. It illustrates that Western film festivals primarily served the purpose of validating marginal film productions back home, a process fundamentally attached to the negotiation, ambiguity, and ambivalence that defined cultural policy under state socialism.

## Shifting Membership Structures at the BBS

The BBS's significant restructuring in the 1970s frames this history. The studio was established in 1959, and through much of the 1960s, it was reserved for graduates of the film academy. Its establishment was the result of a countrywide overhaul and decentralization of cultural life in Hungary in the late 1950s, following the consensus-driven aftermath of the failed 1956 uprising.[2] The BBS offered young filmmakers an unprecedented degree of creative freedom within a state-controlled environment, partially in order to contain and control voices of subversion and dissent. In the studio, aspiring directors and other motion-picture professionals could hone their craft after exiting film school—receiving hands-on training with celluloid, still rare in Hungarian film education in the 1950s—before entering the state studio system. The studio's annual budget was overseen through an exceptionally democratic system: each proposed project was internally debated and voted on before it was allowed to go into production. Although an outside state entity (the Filmfőigazgatóság, or General Directorate of Film) was to approve the public circulation of films, production was largely overseen by an internal directorate that consisted of select studio members.[3] Given the BBS's unique status at the periphery of formal film production, it had no obligation to publicly screen the films it produced and thus bypassed the more stringent censorship to which works from the central film studios were subjected. This decision yielded an opaque and uncoordinated—rather than fully restricted—system for distributing the studio's films both domestically and internationally throughout the late socialist period.

In the early 1960s, as Bódy dismissively noted in an influential text from 1977, the BBS could be seen as the "antechamber" of the film industry proper.[4] Yet this structure was soon challenged. The opening up of Hungarian society in the late 1960s inspired a new generation of BBS members to call for the studio's democratization and the abandonment of restrictive professionalization trajectories. This resulted in a restructuring that eventually produced two distinct branches of the BBS. In 1973, Bódy launched the Film Language Series (Filmnyelvi sorozat), a project that brought together a series of avant-garde experiments on film. With the series as an umbrella, key figures of the Hungarian experimental art scene with little to no formal training in film and no interest in a career in cinema were able to produce films at the studio. This experimental section split from another, more socially committed documentary group that, from the late 1960s through the 1970s, developed a well-organized system for producing and distributing its films.[5] Tarr's film career matured within the latter section. Both models vied for primacy and funding within the BBS through the 1970s, as the institution grew increasingly detached from its initial function as a space for professionalization.

*American Postcard* and *Family Nest* represent this institutional bifurcation within the BBS between experimental and documentary modes, respectively, which in turn also shaped the films' foreign exposure. Throughout the 1970s, the studio highlighted the need to better organize and develop BBS projects' circulation abroad, yet this did not yield systematic results.[6] While its documentary output became a mainstay within certain festivals (such as Kraków), experimental films' position remained fluid. These films' categorization thus informed virtually all aspects of their production, circulation, and reception. Although the Mannheim festival provided domestic visibility and legitimacy for both Bódy and Tarr, the fact that their films came from different sections of the BBS affected their international trajectories.

## Cold War Film Festivals: Mannheim and Eastern European Cinemas

Beyond the perspective of the individual filmmakers, these films' festival wins were also part of a media-geopolitical system within which Western European, and specifically West German, festivals regularly showcased films from the socialist sphere as part of their political commitment to leftist thought. Bódy's and Tarr's wins thus also generated reflections back home about how Western European festival appearances negotiated issues of aesthetics and politics. The leftist ideology espoused by key West German festivals was a point of connection for the films from socialist Eastern Europe that featured heavily in their programs. Yet at times, Hungarians reporting on these foreign events de-emphasized or outright dismissed this ideological closeness in order to instead foreground a film's formal merits or its reflection of *really existing socialism*, as the discussions of the Mannheim victories illustrate.

In this sense, the films' West German awards underscore the complexity of the East/West relationship demonstrated in the growing literature on Cold War film festival culture. This revisionist scholarship includes a thorough rethinking of the idea of the West as a consistently desired cultural, economic, and political final destination.[7] Moving away from such a Eurocentric framing of Cold War histories, for instance, Rossen Djagalov and Masha Salazkina examine the Tashkent Film festival as a "geopoetical" milieu that from 1968 onward provided an alternative "contact zone" for the interaction between the Soviet Bloc and the Third World and as such allowed for wide-ranging discussions of cultural, economic, and geopolitical alternatives to the East-West dynamic, which primarily served Western interests.[8] But even studies that trace more familiar geopolitical patterns have produced new insights into how exhibiting films from socialist countries at Western (European) film festivals had repercussions beyond their mere exposure abroad. Dunja Jelenković compares press reports on Yugoslav Black Wave films—productions that were vocally critical of the failings of Josip Broz Tito's regime—screened at the Internationale Kurzfilmtage Oberhausen and domestically at the film festival in Belgrade between 1967 and 1973.[9] Her comparative approach highlights more than the familiar tropes about state censorship and Western exposure. Instead, she argues that Yugoslavia's desire to make its unique implementation of state socialism internationally visible through these films' circulation coexisted with attempts to decrease their cultural or indeed ideological weight both at home and abroad.

My analysis aligns with Jelenković's, redirecting our focus from the Western European festival as a mere showcase for films produced under repressive regimes and instead highlighting the effects of these foreign victories within a local film-cultural milieu. Such studies decenter the role of the festival site as a coveted "window to the West," a term used in one publication to describe the Mannheim film festival during the Cold War, which implies that without this visibility, Soviet Bloc film culture lacked perspective.[10] Nevertheless, while focusing on the repercussions of Mannheim wins in Hungary, it is important to also outline the particularities of this festival and the culture within which it developed. Bódy's and Tarr's films, while negotiating precarious production and distribution cultures at the BBS, were particularly well suited to reflect Mannheim's commitment to Eastern European cinema and its interest in presenting first feature films. Tracing these relations also allows us to position the BBS's output in the 1970s and the domestic conflicts surrounding it within wider Cold War culture as simultaneously exceptional and representative of complicated transnational film-cultural negotiations.

Mannheim, founded in 1952, was one of several West German film festivals that appeared during the decade, alongside the Berlinale (1951) and Oberhausen (1954). Leipzig, in East Germany, was established in 1955.[11] Heide Fehrenbach, in narrating the history of West German film festival culture, describes how Mannheim initially operated as a city-funded showcase for Kulturfilme (educational short films covering a wide range of subjects), conceiving of this as a form of resistance to the popularity and influx of commercial films, notably from Hollywood.[12] The narrow focus was expanded in 1960 to first feature films (initially those by documentarists); this eventually became the festival's specialization.

Competition from Oberhausen was one reason for this forced reinvention; indeed, Oberhausen was central to the opening up of cultural exchange between Western and Eastern Europe from the late 1950s onward.[13] Like Mannheim, its origins lay in a citywide initiative focused on Kulturfilme, yet by the late 1950s, its refashioning under the motto *Weg zum Nachbarn* (the path to neighbors) signaled a focus on bringing films from Czechoslovakia, Poland, Hungary, and even East Germany to West German audiences. In this way, Oberhausen preceded the official revision of East-West relations that Ostpolitik (Eastern policy) would produce in the mid-1960s, becoming "the gateway to the East in both cultural and economic terms."[14]

Mannheim in this period appears to have defined itself largely in relation to this better-known festival, whose similarly leftist political agenda drove its programming; the focus on debut feature films represented an attempt to carve out a unique identity. As the influential film critic and historian Enno Patalas disparagingly noted in 1964, Mannheim sat "between two stools: that of a feature film festival, and that of a short film festival. Berlin sits on one of these, Oberhausen on the other."[15] These events' programming indeed had several overlaps, significant among them the discovery of Eastern European New Waves in the early 1960s; the films of Věra Chytilová, Krzysztof Zanussi, and István Szabó were championed in this period as exciting new voices in the region's film culture. By the 1970s, the festivals increasingly featured films from the Global South. Yet film critic Vince Zalán, who traveled to Mannheim with Bódy and Tarr in 1979, maintains that the early popularity of Eastern European New Waves at Western festivals was still felt well into this decade, which is why Bódy's film was "welcomed with open arms" at Mannheim.[16] Nevertheless, the particular opposition *American Postcard* encountered during its production and the domestic structures that controlled distribution of BBS films at the time complicate this story, particularly when compared to the relatively straightforward circulation of BBS films a few years prior.

## Hungarofilm, Hungarian Distribution Contexts, and the BBS

Hungarofilm was the state entity responsible for the international circulation of films under socialism and thus also oversaw festival participation. It was founded in 1956 as part of the general postwar reorganization of the film industry, and its activities soon encompassed virtually all aspects of international film relations; its staff handled the circulation of prints and all publicity pertaining to recent productions and maintained ties with foreign film-cultural bodies, both on an organizational and a personal level. Additionally, it managed the list of foreign invitees to the Magyar Filmszemle (Hungarian film review), an event known internationally as Hungarian Film Week, which presented the annual output of domestic film production. Held in February, this pre-curated selection had considerable influence on the films selected for foreign markets and film festivals.[17]

Film historian Balázs Varga explains that the establishment of Hungarofilm demonstrates the growing importance, both economic and political, of foreign film distribution from the late 1950s onward.[18] Showcasing the dynamism of Hungarian film culture became a tool for legitimizing the state-socialist regime in the West, and the film industry mobilized BBS films to this end.[19] Early BBS films often bypassed the explicit social criticism or formal experimentation that typified much of the output of the 1970s. Instead, they foregrounded a lyrical, poetic film language and frequently centered on universal themes and private emotions, as reflected, for instance, in Szabó's early work. This playful, accessible, and inoffensive aesthetic was thus ideally suited for foreign circulation for official purposes. The charismatic director of

Hungarofilm, István Dósai, confirmed this in 1966, writing that "a few years ago, we were once again able to draw attention to ourselves with short films, those of the Balázs Béla Stúdió, which was the first sign of a boom that is demonstrated across all of our filmmaking today."[20] In line with the studio's original function, the Hungarian state instrumentalized young filmmakers and their work through a symbiotic process of international exposure that also benefited their nascent careers.

In contrast to the mutually beneficial process that marked the 1960s, Bódy perceived a dramatic generational schism in the 1970s, leading to the BBS's increased marginalization within the Hungarian film ecosystem by the middle of the decade. He noted that the General Directorate of Film organized "veritable *press conferences*" in Budapest's cinemas for the earlier generation, who as a result, almost without exception, "brought home their medals from Oberhausen." Bódy dramatically juxtaposed this with a characterization of his own generation as "walled in," claiming it had, time and again, been isolated from wider opportunities and (foreign) visibility.[21] These shifts were primarily related to the studio's changing focus and status, as sketched above; as the BBS grew more detached from the film industry at large, producing work that was increasingly politically and aesthetically probing, its films' purpose as exports or legitimizing cultural capital drastically diminished. The early 1970s also saw the first cases of BBS films being censored.

Yet rather than presenting a novel system of control that hinged on increasingly severe rules and regulations, the new decade brought with it an increased lack of transparency regarding distribution, both domestic and foreign. A 1973 letter by György Aczél, the notorious head of cultural affairs in Hungary, highlights this succinctly. In the letter, Aczél voices concern that more and more BBS films were finding their way to the broader public, for example through (domestic) festivals, countering the foundational identity of the studio as a testing ground. As he notes, when the studio was established "we—along with the filmmakers—envisioned the films produced there to be not made for the public. If state, societal, or professional organizations nevertheless deem that some of the films—due to their high standards—should be presented to the public—as an exception—we will do so."[22] Aczél thus suggested that the state reserved the right to continue to use BBS films for its own ideological or political purposes, as it had done in the previous decade, without being compelled to systematically distribute them. Corroborating this lack of a systematic approach to distribution, István B. Szabó, the former head of the General Directorate of Film (no relation to the accomplished filmmaker István Szabó), recalled that even those BBS films that were banned during this period were screened with some regularity in "college dorms, film clubs, and youth clubs" and thus at times amassed "at least a hundred thousand viewers" without ever becoming part of official film distribution platforms.[23]

This unfixed domestic film distribution context undoubtedly informed the way BBS films traveled to foreign film festivals. That is, the films' trajectories were driven by individually negotiated decisions and interpersonal exchanges that were entwined with processes of official supervision and control. The status of the film festivals in question also affected these trajectories. While prestige feature-film projects were shown in Cannes and short films were screened at Oberhausen, Mannheim provided a comfortable middle ground; focused on first feature films, it offered a path toward commercial film distribution and international visibility. Yet, as Zalán notes, "Mannheim was evidently different from Cannes," and as a more minor international cinematic outpost, it was undoubtedly less stringently policed by Hungarian officials.[24] Its relative marginalization within the Western (European) festival circuit thus ultimately also benefited Bódy's and Tarr's films.

### American Postcard in Mannheim and Back Again

*American Postcard*, set in North America during the Civil War, concerns a group of Hungarian émigrés who battle on the US military frontier. While questions of (national) identity and displacement surface throughout the film, it is primarily concerned with the cinematic representation of history. Bódy engaged with the materiality of film through a faux-archival aesthetic (applied to the black-and-white film stock via a range of postproduction techniques) that made it seem as though *American Postcard* was a time-worn, anachronistic, pre-cinematic artifact of the nineteenth century (see fig. 6.1).

Bódy had already made several experimental shorts at the studio when he started working on *American Postcard*, which was to simultaneously function as his graduation project at the film academy. The BBS rarely produced feature films, and the format was even more exceptional for graduation projects, largely due to financial restrictions. This made Bódy's successful appropriation of BBS funds for his diploma film remarkable. Beyond creatively funding an ambitious film experiment, the BBS's involvement also meant that the film academy no longer controlled the fate of the final project, which allowed Bódy to campaign for its wider international release.[25] The aura of legitimacy BBS films enjoyed abroad undoubtedly helped this process. Additionally, the feature format made *American Postcard* available to be screened beyond short-film festivals, expediting Bódy's maturation into a commercial-mainstream film circuit both domestically and abroad.

Figure 6.1. Bódy's historical fiction *American Postcard* presented as a timeworn, anachronistic artifact of the nineteenth century (frame grab, DVD, BBS Archive).

Upon its completion, Bódy's film immediately encountered opposition. This came, first and foremost, from the film academy itself, which rejected the work's experimental tone and formal language as inaccessible and indecipherable. In response, Bódy wrote a long letter to a senior official of the General Directorate of Film, dated January 5, 1976.[26] The letter, at once imploring and hyperbolic, not only revealed the filmmaker's attempts to mitigate resistance to the film's formal language, but keenly mapped this resistance onto larger questions about its (international) circulation. Bódy pleaded for *American Postcard*, despite its challenging formal style, to be allowed to be screened at Hungarian Film Week. It can be assumed that Bódy understood the international exposure inclusion in the Film Week implied, given its status as a meeting point for foreign festival scouts.[27] In his plea, Bódy also noted that the film's primary audience was ideally what he termed the "Art-Kino" network. This foreign term radiated both a subtle sense of arrogance and, more importantly, an acute understanding of the film's place within the foreign art-cinema distribution system, something that socialist Hungary lacked.

Bódy ultimately achieved the desired effect through a striking transnational trajectory: *American Postcard* was programmed at Mannheim in 1976, where it received the Großer Preis der Stadt Mannheim in October. Several months later, in February 1977, it was included in the program of Hungarian Film Week. Although certain reports note that the film had already been screened at the 1976 Film Week as part of a showcase of recent BBS projects, the following year it was lauded as a stand-alone feature film, receiving the Filmkritikusok Díja (Film Critics' Award) special prize for best directorial debut at the event.[28] Ulrich Gregor, an eminent figure in West German film culture who worked at Mannheim and later at the Berlinale, was invited to the 1977 edition, and he was interviewed about his experiences alongside his "Soviet" and "English" colleagues in the Hungarian film journal *Filmkultúra*.[29] The fact that Gregor, together with the other foreign invitees, highlighted *American Postcard* as one of the Film Week's notable films after it had already won at Mannheim obscured somewhat the complicated trajectory Bódy's project took to reach visibility and acceptance in Hungary.

In short, the foreign appearance of *American Postcard* legitimized it domestically. Remarkably, the film academy only awarded Bódy a degree after his graduation film proved successful on the (international) film festival circuit.[30] In addition, the film's Mannheim win seemed to validate its experimental aesthetic. Yet these formal issues also sparked a domestic conversation about how the foreign showcasing of Hungarian films served political and cultural interests back home. One reviewer saw its innovative filmic language as more significant than its importance as an ideological win for a socialist country. As he concluded, "The focus of Western film festivals on a particular film can often be explained by political motivations," yet in Bódy's case, it was predominantly the formal experimentation that mattered.[31] *American Postcard*'s success indeed deviated from previous wins by Hungarian films at festivals in the West, which were at least partially ideologically, rather than exclusively aesthetically, driven. This win thus appeared to be a victory for Hungarian experimental film, even if it did not yield immediate acceptance of the alternative branch of the BBS within the country's wider film-cultural milieu.

In light of Bódy's determined negotiation of domestic power structures, his assessment of his film's trajectory as accidental, in an interview for a Hungarian magazine following its Mannheim success, appears almost comical. Bódy's self-deprecating comments emphasized that *American Postcard* "was made at the Balázs Béla Stúdió entirely without the aim of bringing it to the wider public."[32] This statement notably revealed a slippage between the film's status as a personal triumph, orchestrated largely behind the scenes, and the role state officials had envisioned for the BBS, in which its experimental films were to have limited exposure, entirely within government control.

The Mannheim win undoubtedly marked Bódy as an exciting new voice within film culture, both domestically and internationally. Toward the end of the 1970s, having aged out of the BBS's membership system, he continued to experiment with film and media in a range of interdisciplinary contexts.[33] These spanned television films and theatrical adaptations, experimental work on video, and his kaleidoscopic magnum opus, the feature film *Narcissus and Psyche* (*Nárcisz és Psyché*, 1980).[34] Bódy was invited to Mannheim as a jury member in 1979, the year that *Family Nest* received its award. This invitation further solidified his status as an internationally recognized Hungarian filmmaker.

## Family Nest and Widening Opportunities for Docu-Fiction Films

*Family Nest* is emblematic of Hungarian docu-fiction of the mid to late 1970s—films grouped under the moniker of the Budapest School (Budapesti Iskola), whose key figures emerged from BBS's documentary branch. Shot with a shoestring budget and an amateur cast on location in Budapest, the film concerns the abysmal housing conditions of a young couple forced to live with the husband's family and the wife's desperate attempts at relocation (see fig. 6.2). Tarr's early interest in depicting social issues first emerged within an amateur/documentary context. Already as a teen, he had made an amateur film that critiqued the living and labor conditions of workers; Tarr screened the finished project to the same workers, a gesture that did not sit well with Communist Party officials, who refused to grant him acceptance to several postsecondary educational institutions, including the film academy.[35] Tarr entered the BBS in 1977 under the tutelage of Dárday, a seminal figure in the studio's documentary section and originator of the Budapest School aesthetic. The fact that Tarr was allowed to make *Family Nest* at the BBS without any formal professional training or relevant educational background illustrates the studio's openness during this period but also suggests the primacy documentaries enjoyed. And while Tarr's individual trajectory in some ways echoes Bódy's exceptional early career as a rebellious marginal filmmaker, the BBS had changed considerably since Bódy started there.

The documentary section in particular was by now more firmly organized, as it approximated an official sphere of socialist cultural production tasked with undertaking ideologically suitable educational, cultural, and leisure activities, particularly for youth and workers. Initially, in the postwar period, these activities took place under the label of people's education (*népművelés*); among other things, this encompassed the programs of so-called Houses of Culture as well as the activities of amateur cultural groups. But as Anne White

Figure 6.2. *Family Nest*, an emblematic work of docu-fiction laying bare the crises of really existing socialism (frame grab, DVD).

explains, in the 1970s, népművelés "was replaced by közművelődés, which means public (not popular) participation in culture... suggesting that cultural enlightenment is voluntary, not imposed, and that the system is a democratic one."[36] From 1974 onward, the concept of *közművelődés* entered public debates, and film production and distribution were foregrounded as tools for ideological education in socialist society. One recurring phrase underlined the medium's role in forging a "community out of an audience" ("*közönségből közösséget*"), which at the same time suggested the less didactic goal of giving a social purpose to film projects.[37] While this renewed system was hardly democratic, it did yield opportunities for the BBS.[38] The studio's documentary branch established the Community Culture Group (*Közművelődési Csoport*) in 1975.[39]

The Community Culture Group's distribution efforts focused on so-called social distribution (*társadalmi forgalmazás*), echoing state-socialist cultural priorities by bringing cinematic works to social groups that were most directly affected by a film's subject matter; as such, it was supported by authorities. Yet in reality, these films often exposed the shortcomings and absurdities of really existing socialism through a perceptive cinema vérité style. Furthermore, systematic post-screening debates allowed for discussions of a range of (controversial) subjects that rarely surfaced in mainstream media and thus functioned as a form of resistance to official authority.[40]

The Budapest School was shaped within the BBS's documentary branch. Although the new docu-fictional mode continued to critique contemporary society, the conventional narrative and stylistic elements that filmmakers appropriated from fiction film aligned with accessible aesthetic forms that were acceptable and intelligible to state authorities. At the same time, the fictional component was useful in negotiating the limits of social critique: by fictionalizing shocking revelations on the living conditions of average Hungarians and the dysfunction of socialist society more generally, the filmmakers distanced themselves from claims about this reality, stating instead, in the clever formulation of *Family Nest*'s opening titles, that "the true events did not happen to the people in the story, but could have happened to them."[41]

## *Family Nest* and Negotiating Hungarian Victories at Mannheim

Dárday received an award at Mannheim in 1975 for his docu-fiction *Holiday in Britain* (*Jutalomutazás*, 1974). He was among the originators of the Budapest School, and he also set the stage for Tarr's subsequent debut feature at the festival, a process that was undoubtedly aided by Bódy's presence as a jury member. *Family Nest*'s win in 1979 had important repercussions for its filmmaker; while Tarr was attending the film academy in the years following his award, in reality he had simultaneously entered the ranks of the professional film community, finishing the feature *The Outsider* (*Szabadgyalog*) in 1980. In the words of András Bálint Kovács, *Family Nest*'s successes meant that Tarr was "allowed to do whatever he liked, and he was not required to live a regular film student's life."[42]

Despite the challenges Tarr's outsider status posed to his early career, in comparison to Bódy's marginal avant-garde experiment, *Family Nest* displayed the relatively popular and accessible (aesthetic, formal, and thematic) cinematic tropes that by 1979 had become the studio's most broadly acknowledged contribution to nonmainstream Hungarian film culture. Unlike *American Postcard*, which to some extent needed foreign success to be legitimized back home, Tarr's work was already acceptable in film-cultural terms before its foreign run. One regional daily's review of the film even argued that the docu-fictional form was the BBS's only valid contribution to Hungarian cinema, stating that with *Family Nest*, the studio finally also "denoted quality" (implying that its earlier efforts had not been up to standard).[43]

Yet despite the overall praise it garnered in Hungary, *Family Nest*'s win at Mannheim was met with some reservation at home. The festival report from *Filmkultúra* contrasts markedly with the way Bódy's victory was framed two years prior—as a win on formal, rather than ideological, terms. The report paid an ambiguous compliment to Hungarian film exporters, who in the author's view expertly negotiated Mannheim's expectations by sending works that were "documentary-like, unpolished, rough and skillfully masked [their] professionalism."[44] *Family Nest*'s success was highlighted as the epitome of this strategy. Yet the report's somewhat cynical assessment of Tarr's victory ultimately reflected not on the film's quality, but on what the reviewer understood to be Mannheim's ideological naiveté and ignorance about the world that its international programming displayed. This criticism also extended to the outspokenly leftist West German festivalgoers (facetiously described in the report as "lovers of exoticism" and "jeans-wearing messiahs"), who desperately required post-screening discussions and contextualization to understand the issues at stake in films from non-Western countries—increasingly not just from the Soviet Bloc, but from the Global South as well.

Vince Zalán recalls how he and Tarr, who attended the festival together, knowingly negotiated this reality; during the film's press conference, they vocally publicized that "the entire budget of *Family Nest* was 'merely' the sum with which one could buy a modest apartment in Hungary," a statement that, as he notes, "had a big impact in the West."[45] This declaration perceptively brought the low-budget film's unique production context to bear on the actually existing housing crisis that it depicted. It did this with a view to a Western audience that was undoubtedly uninitiated in either aspect of life under socialism. As such, the Hungarian envoys used Mannheim as a platform to self-consciously mediate between the cultural and sociopolitical realities of socialist Hungary on one hand and the international film-cultural stage on the other.

## Conclusion

Bypassing an understanding of state-socialist cultural policy as a rigid system of state control wherein individual actors had little influence, this chapter has highlighted the imbrication of institutional, political, aesthetic, and interpersonal negotiations and exchanges that drove two marginal Hungarian film productions to the mainstream. In this regard, it is important to understand the Western European film festival experience in a state-socialist context not merely as a way out, but also as a way to renegotiate a given production's domestic reception and reshape a filmmaker's own position within the cultural landscape of her or his country. Tracing these films' trajectories side by side, the chapter has shown how their aesthetic-thematic modes—Bódy's deconstructed experimental narrative versus Tarr's docu-fictional work—informed their production and distribution context before and after Mannheim. Beyond innovative and striking aesthetic and narrative tools, this required a keen understanding of the expectations of the West German festival milieu, within which both filmmakers expertly maneuvered in their own ways. Finally, this chapter serves as an invitation to study the impact of international film festivals beyond top-tier events such as Cannes. As the Mannheim case illustrates, understanding the trajectories of films to and from such supposedly less prestigious film events allows us to map the issues at stake in transnational film cultural flows beyond questions of prestige and (Western) visibility.

## Notes

The author would like to thank Vince Zalán for providing invaluable insights on his experiences at the Mannheim Film Festival, which fundamentally shaped the direction of this research.

1. Tarr's vocally announced retirement from filmmaking in 2011 has furthered his image as an elusive figure of international art cinema. Bódy, on the other hand, was an *enfant terrible* of latesocialist artistic life, inspiring everyone from Tarr himself to media artists such as Péter Forgács. His untimely, unresolved death in 1985 and alleged entanglement with the secret police as an informant have only added to his status as an infinitely complex character. On Bódy's complicated posthumous image, see Simonyi, "The Man Behind the Curtain."

2. For more on the early period of the BBS, see Udvarnoky and Varga, "Variációk egy stúdióra."

3. The Filmfőigazgatóság was established in 1955 as part of the Ministry of Culture. It served as the ministerial body controlling production and distribution matters within the film industry, including the BBS.

4. Bódy, "A fiatal magyar film útjai," 114. Bódy and others critiqued the studio's role as an "antechamber," advocating instead for its status as a distinct experimental "workshop" to function independently from the industry at large. On the workshop model in the context of Czechoslovak Army films in the 1960s, see Lovejoy, *Army Film*, 139–143.

5. An early declaration outlining this socially attuned direction for the BBS appeared in the film journal *Filmkultúra* in 1969. Although Bódy spearheaded the studio's experimental movement, he co-signed this published statement in support of the documentarists. See Grunwalsky et al., "Szociológiai filmcsoportot!," 95.

6. Directorate of the Balázs Béla Stúdió, *A Balázs Béla Stúdió programja 1978–79*. Annual report. Budapest: BBS, 1978, March 22, Lsz.11829 / D 2459, p. 10, Magyar Nemzeti Filmarchívum / Hungarian National Film Archive.

7. See, for example, Kötzing and Moine, "Introduction."

8. Djagalov and Salazkina, "Tashkent '68."

9. Jelenković, "The Film Festival as an Arena for Political Debate."

10. Kötz and Minas, *Zeitgeist mit Eigensinn*, 117.

11. For a recent study on the Leipzig film festival, see Moine, *Screened Encounters*.

12. Fehrenbach, *Cinema in Democratizing Germany*, 214–215.

13. For a comparative reading of Oberhausen and Leipzig and the ways in which festival culture entwined with broader Cold War policy and geopolitics in the two Germanys, see Kötzing, "Cultural and Film Policy in the Cold War."

14. Fehrenbach, *Cinema in Democratizing Germany*, 223; see also Kötzing, "Cultural and Film Policy in the Cold War."
15. Enno Patalas quoted without citation in Kötz and Minas, *Zeitgeist mit Eigensinn*, 114.
16. Zalán, email correspondence, May 20, 2018.
17. Hungarofilm launched the yearly *Filmévkönyv* in 1979, which listed not just the foreign festival runs of Hungarian films but the names of foreign visitors to Film Week, demonstrating their importance. For an extended reflection on Hungarofilm's history by a former employee, see Somogyi, "Egy filmkereskedelmi vállalat."
18. Varga, "Filmirányítás, gyártástörténet és politika Magyarországon 1957–63," 86.
19. Ibid., 89.
20. Dósai, "Magyar filmek külföldön," 29.
21. Bódy to Bogács, "Tisztelt Bogács elvtárs!" 362. BBS member Szabó's 1962 film *Koncert*, for instance, won in Oberhausen in 1963.
22. Aczél to Simó.
23. Gervai, "Én vittem el a balhét."
24. Zalán, email.
25. Ibid.
26. Bódy to Bogács, 365.
27. Ibid.
28. *American Postcard* was to be screened alongside András Lányi's historical narrative film *Segesvár* (1974). "A VIII magyar játékfilm-szemle pécsett."
29. Berkes, "Beszélgetések a IX. Filmszemle vendégeivel," 16–20.
30. In a 2008 reflection, writer András Forgách suggested that Bódy's Mannheim win prompted the academy to revise its earlier rejection, while Bódy's 1981 curriculum vitae mentions that the film's presentation at the Film Week led to his successful graduation. Forgách, "Sötét angyal," 25; Bódy, "Önéletrajz," 20.
31. Gönczi, "El kell indulni minden úton...," 80.
32. "Amerikai anzix," *Tükör*, 31.
33. Bódy describes his departure from the BBS as prompted by having "reached the age limit." Bódy, "Önéletrajz," 20.
34. In 1980, Bódy established the path-breaking international "magazine" *INFERMENTAL*, consisting of a series of videocassettes. Released annually, each issue had a different geographic focus and featured work by contemporary video artists, curated by guest editors. See *INFERMENTAL*, accessed September 7, 2021, http://www.infermental.de/.
35. Kovács, *The Cinema of Béla Tarr*, 8.
36. White, *De-Stalinization and the House of Culture*, 27.
37. For one such discussion, see Pozsgay, "A film és közművelődés," 80–81.
38. For a short overview on the subject, see Földiák, "A magyar művelődési intézet ötven évének öt korszakáról."
39. Bódy established the *K/3 Group* (*K/3 csoport*) in 1976 in direct response to this documentary group. As his earlier Film Language Series, it was an important platform for experimentation within the studio.
40. Győri, "Discourse, Power and Resistance," 108. The program of the Közművelődési filmhét, held in the Hungarian city of Pécs in 1977, illustrates the types of thematic screenings that were organized under the banner of social distribution (for instance, showing the five-part *Educational Series / Nevelésügyi sorozat* (1973–1975) for teachers in the Pécs area). It also exemplifies the appropriation of social distribution to screen virtually all of the studio's output, remarkably including Judit Ember and Gyula Gazdag's banned documentary *The Resolution* (*A határozat*, 1972), which focused on the controversial resignation of the chairman of a rural collective farm, as well as a selection of avant-garde shorts, including those of the Film Language Series that were screened for

"visual artists and museologists" at the Ethnographic Museum of Pécs. For the full program, see the booklet published on the occasion of the film week. Balázs Béla Stúdió, *BBS '77 Közművelődési filmhét*. Pamphlet. Pécs-Baranya, March 21–26, 1977, D111/1, Magyar Nemzeti Filmarchívum / Hungarian National Film Archive.

41. For more on the Budapest School, see Zalán, *Budapesti Iskola*.
42. Kovács, *The Cinema of Béla Tarr*, 9.
43. "Filmjegyzet: Családi tűzfészek," *Somogy Megyei Hírlap*.
44. Zöldi, "Divatok, előítéletek," 76.
45. Zalán, email.

## Bibliography

Aczél, György, to Dr. Jenő Simó. May 15, 1973. In *A tanúk*, edited by András Gervai. Accessed May 2018. http://gervaiandras.hu/koenyvekm/a-tanuk/36-a-balazs- bela-studio- filmjei -es- a-nyilvanossag.html.

"Amerikai anzix." *Tükör*, June 15, 1977.

"A VIII magyar játékfilm-szemle pécsett: sajtótájékoztató Budapesten." *Dunántúli Napló*, January 7, 1976.

Berkes, Ildikó. "Beszélgetések a IX. Filmszemle vendégeivel." *Filmkultúra* 13, no. 2 (1977): 16–20.

Bódy, Gábor. "A fiatal magyar film útjai." In *Bódy Gábor egybegyűjtött filmművészeti írások 1*, edited by Vince Zalán, 111–116. Budapest: Akadémiai kiadó, 2006.

———. "Önéletrajz." In *Bódy Gábor*, edited by Vince Zalán, 18–21.

———, to Antal Bogács. "Tisztelt Bogács elvtárs!" January 5, 1976. In *Végtelen kép: Bódy Gábor írásai*, edited by Miklós Peternák and László Beke, 361–369. Budapest: Pesti Szalon kiadó, 1996.

Djagalov, Rossen, and Masha Salazkina. "Tashkent '68: A Cinematic Contact Zone." *Slavic Review* 75, no. 2 (2016): 279–298.

Dósai, István. "Magyar filmek külföldön." *Filmkultúra*, no. 2 (1966): 26–32.

Fehrenbach, Heide. *Cinema in Democratizing Germany: Reconstructing National Identity After Hitler*. Chapel Hill: University of North Carolina Press, 1995.

"Filmjegyzet: Családi tűzfészek." *Somogy Megyei Hírlap*, April 10, 1979.

Földiák, András. "A magyar művelődési intézet ötven évének öt korszakáról." *Szín* 1, no. 2 (1996): 2–7. Accessed April 2018. http://dla.epitesz.bme.hu/appendfiles/1464 -EPA01306_Szin_1996_01_02_002-007,%20magyar%20m%C5%B1vel%C5%91d%C3% A9si%20int%C3%A9zet.pdf.

Forgách, András. "Sötét angyal. Kerekasztal-beszélgetés Bódy Gáborról–2. rész." *Filmvilág* 51, no. 7 (2008): 24–28.

Gervai, András. "Én vittem el a balhét: beszélgetés Szabó B. Istvánnal." *A tanúk*. Accessed February 2017. http://gervaiandras.hu/koenyvekm/a-tanuk/22-en-vittem-el-a-balhet .html.

Gönczi, László. "El kell indulni minden úton. . . ." *Filmkultúra* 13, no. 4 (1977): 78–80.

Grunwalsky, Ferenc, Dezső Magyar, László Mihály, György Pintér, István Sipos, Árpád Ajtony, Gábor Bódy, Péter Dobai, and Csaba Kardos. "Szociológiai filmcsoportot!" *Filmkultúra* 3 (1969): 95.

Győri, Zsolt. "Discourse, Power and Resistance in Sociographic Documentaries of the Late Kádár-Era." *Studies in Eastern European Cinema* 5, no. 2 (2014): 103–123.

Jelenković, Dunja. "The Film Festival as an Arena for Political Debate. The Yugoslav Black Wave in Belgrade and Oberhausen (1967–1973)." In *Cultural Transfer and Political*

Conflicts: Film Festivals in the Cold War, edited by Andreas Kötzing and Caroline Moine, 47–62.

Kötz, Michael, and Günter Minas. *Zeitgeist mit Eigensinn / Eine filmfestival-geschichte Internationales Filmfestival Mannheim-Heidelberg*. Mannheim: Internationales Filmfestival Mannheim-Heidelberg, 2001.

Kötzing, Andreas. "Cultural and Film Policy in the Cold War: The Film Festivals of Oberhausen and Leipzig and German-German Relations." In *Cultural Transfer*, edited by Kötzing and Moine, 31–46. Göttingen: Vandenhoeck & Ruprecht, 2016.

Kötzing, Andreas, and Caroline Moine. "Introduction." In *Cultural Transfer*, edited by Kötzing and Moine, 7–12. Göttingen: Vandenhoeck & Ruprecht, 2016.

Kovács, András Bálint. *The Cinema of Béla Tarr: The Circle Closes*. London: Wallflower Press, 2013.

Lovejoy, Alice. *Army Film and the Avant Garde: Cinema and Experiment in the Czechoslovak Military*. Bloomington: Indiana University Press, 2015.

Moine, Caroline. *Screened Encounters: The Leipzig Documentary Film Festival, 1955–1990*. Oxford: Berghahn Books, 2018.

Pozsgay, Imre. "A film és közművelődés." *Filmkultúra* 10, no. 3 (1974): 80–81.

Simonyi, Sonja. "The Man Behind the Curtain. Gábor Bódy, Experimental Film Culture and Networks of State Control in Late Socialist Hungary." *Third Text* 32, no. 4 (2018): 519–529.

Somogyi, Lia. "Egy filmkereskedelmi vállalat: a Hungarofilm története (1956–2001)." *Filmkultúra* (2005). Accessed July 2018. https://filmkultura.hu/regi/2005/articles/essays/hungarofilm.hu.html.

Udvarnoky, Virág, and Balázs Varga. "Variációk egy stúdióra: A BBS megalakulásai és a kora-kádári kultúrpolitika." In *BBS 50: A Balázs Béla Studio 50 éve*, edited by Gábor Gelencsér, 61–79. Budapest: Műcsarnok, 2009.

Varga, Balázs. "Filmirányítás, gyártástörténet és politika Magyarországon 1957–63." PhD diss., ELTE Budapest, 2008.

White, Anne. *De-Stalinization and the House of Culture: Declining State Control Over Leisure in the USSR, Poland and Hungary, 1953–89*. London: Routledge, 1990.

Zalán, Vince. Email correspondence. May 20, 2018.

———, ed. *Budapesti Iskola: magyar dokumentum-játékfilmek 1973–1984*. Budapest: Magyar Dokumentumfilm Rendezők Egyesülete, 2005.

Zöldi, László. "Divatok, előítéletek– világmegváltók– Mannheimi jegyzetek." *Filmkultúra* 16, no. 1 (1980): 72–76.

SONJA SIMONYI is an independent scholar of Eastern European audiovisual culture. She is the editor of *Experimental Cinema in State-Socialist Eastern Europe*, and a special issue of *Studies in Eastern European Cinema* on this subject, both with Ksenya Gurshtein.

CHAPTER 7

MANIC MINERS OF THE WORLD, UNITE!
*How the British Hit Computer Game Got a Second Life in Czechoslovakia*

Jaroslav Švelch

IN 1988—THE PENULTIMATE YEAR of Communist Party rule in Czechoslovakia—the country's first book-length treatise on computer games was published. Written by leading Czechoslovak game programmer and collector František Fuka, it starts with a chapter on British programmer Matthew Smith, his hit game, *Manic Miner*, and its sequel, *Jet Set Willy*.[1] "You can hardly find a Spectrum user who doesn't know *Manic Miner*," it reads.[2]

At the time, the UK-manufactured Sinclair ZX Spectrum computer was the most popular home computer platform in the country, but *Manic Miner's* fame reached even beyond the Spectrum community. Smith's status among Czechoslovak computer enthusiasts was comparable to the Beatles's among rock fans. Not only did Smith also hail from Liverpool, but his work was likewise considered groundbreaking and foundational.[3] The similarities do not stop there. As was the case with the Beatles (and much of Western popular culture in general), most Eastern European fans knew his work from bootlegs rather than original copies.

The circulation of Western film and music behind the Iron Curtain is relatively well documented. In many Eastern European countries, some Hollywood films were shown in theaters and some Western popular music was issued by local publishers; this official distribution—usually limited and censored—was supplemented by unofficial means, including bootlegging

117

and piracy.⁴ In comparison to TV, film, or pop music, computer games reached significantly fewer people. In the Soviet Bloc, they were niche entertainment, enjoyed by small but enthusiastic hobby communities. Nevertheless, games deserve more attention in research on transnational media flows in the Cold War era. They were among the first digital artifacts to travel across national borders and into the homes of ordinary people. Computer games belonged to both technology *and* culture, and their history offers a unique view of the intersection between technology policies, consumer electronics, technical hobbies, and popular culture. In one rare case, a computer game even triggered a diplomatic row. When the unapologetically anti-Soviet US action title *Raid Over Moscow* was launched on the Finnish market, the Soviet embassy considered it enemy propaganda and requested that it be banned. However, Finnish laws only allowed import restrictions when a product posed a health hazard. Consequently, the game was never banned, and instead—thanks to the free publicity—became the country's top-selling game of the year 1985.⁵

This chapter will use the example of *Manic Miner* (and, to a lesser extent, *Jet Set Willy*) to document the improvised (and often outright illicit) flow of software from the West to the Soviet Bloc and its appropriation by Czechoslovak players. It develops ideas presented in my monograph on the history of gaming in Czechoslovakia, *Gaming the Iron Curtain*.⁶ It builds on oral history interviews with local players and programmers, archival material (mainly computer club newsletters), and the preserved games themselves. The analysis has a number of theoretical and methodological inspirations, among them work on informal distribution of media content by authors such as Brian Larkin and Ramon Lobato, who agree that there is no pure distribution, as distribution is often inseparable from modification, translation, or localization. As Lobato puts it, "the act of distribution also materially shapes the text itself."⁷ In the vein of Riccardo Fassone's media archeology of bootleg games in 1980s Italy, I will explore the *variantology* of *Manic Miner*, using the analysis of differences between individual versions of the game to capture the multiplicity of meanings and pleasures with which it was associated in Czechoslovakia.⁸ Finally, when discussing the practice of local users, I will draw from Claude Lévi-Strauss's classic account of *bricolage*. In Lévi-Strauss's view, a bricoleur's "universe of instruments is closed, and the rules of his game are always to make do with 'whatever is at hand.'"⁹ Hobby-computing practices were often built on improvisation and on making the most out of the available resources. When *Manic Miner* fans happened to use a machine that did not run a version of *Manic Miner*, they programmed their own.

In the following sections, I will reconstruct and compare the contexts in which *Manic Miner* was received in the UK and Czechoslovakia and show how the game's framing changed when it was removed from the context of the UK's booming commercial industry and installed in Czechoslovak computer clubs, whose primary mission was programming education. Along the way, I will explain how Smith became an unlikely role model for Czechoslovak teens. The second half of the article will map the Czechoslovak conversions, mash-ups, and imitations of *Manic Miner* and highlight the ways in which they reflected the values and practices of the local home-computing communities.

## Merchant of Mayhem

In its country of origin, *Manic Miner* was one of the first software blockbusters, and its history is inextricably connected to the boom in the UK microcomputer hardware and software industries. While the country had initially lagged behind the US and Japan, a series of late-1970s and early-1980s government initiatives and educational programs sparked the interest in—and demand for—home computers. US machines by Tandy/RadioShack and Commodore had some early impact, but it was the domestic models that kick-started the UK market.[10] Most famous of these was the diminutive ZX Spectrum, released in 1982 by Sinclair Research. Although its audiovisual capabilities were limited compared to those of its American contemporaries, the bargain price of 175 British pounds made the machine an enormous success. While not designed as a gaming device, it soon became one, opening the door for a homegrown game industry that combined a youthful everything-goes attitude with the neoliberal dream of entrepreneurial success.[11] This industry was built on the labor of (mostly) young enthusiasts programming in their bedrooms.

Matthew Smith (born 1966) was one of those so-called bedroom coders. He was about thirteen when he got his first microcomputer, a Tandy TRS-80, for Christmas 1979. Soon he was frequenting Liverpool's Tandy shop, a hub for the local computer-hobby scene. In an interview, he remembers that "Tandy were really quite accommodating to the hordes of children lurking around the shop all day playing on their machines. And we'd often pick up light work doing software for businesses who were buying machines there."[12] While the shop provided the kids with a place to gather, it also introduced them to the idea of coding as paid labor. Smith's programming talent was soon noticed by the local company Bug-Byte Software, which loaned him the brand new ZX Spectrum so that he could write games for it. With a soldering iron, Smith connected the Spectrum to his Tandy machine, creating an improvised but efficient development system that enabled him to build the game on the Tandy and immediately test it on the Spectrum.[13] His first Spectrum game, *Styx* (1983), was a modest success, but it was *Manic Miner*, the first game featuring the miner Willy, that made him a star.[14]

Like many early British games, *Manic Miner* built on existing trends in game design, originating mostly in Japan and the US.[15] Its core gameplay consists of jumping between platforms, avoiding monsters, and collecting treasure (see fig. 7.1). The two most immediate inspirations were Nintendo's 1981 arcade game *Donkey Kong* and the 1982 American computer game *Miner 2049er*.[16] However, Smith's creation added an idiosyncratic personal touch. The game takes place in twenty screen-sized caverns—a staggering number for the time—each designed around a distinct theme or gameplay challenge. Each features a set of grotesque *nasties*, such as mutant telephones and killer toilets, and each has a name, many of them containing cultural references and in-jokes.[17] When Willy dies, he is crushed by a Monty Python–esque foot in a noninteractive animated scene. All of the above make *Manic Miner* a prototypical example of a design aesthetic retrospectively labeled "British surrealism."[18]

Released in July 1983 for the Spectrum (and later for other platforms), *Manic Miner* was considered an outstanding achievement. Contemporary reviews praised its "impressive graphics" and "highly original scenarios," described it as "original, amusing and habit-forming," and pointed out its "humor, horror and wholesome addiction."[19] Although the gaming press was still in its infancy, it had already developed a discourse for evaluating games as entertainment products.[20] In this discourse, *addictiveness* was seen as a positive quality—a measure of the game's value for money. Additionally, one of the reviews refers to Smith as the designer (and not, for example, the programmer), highlighting his unique creative input.[21]

Sensing that *Manic Miner* would become a blockbuster, Smith gave up his freelancer status and cofounded the company Software Projects, which rereleased the game in a slightly altered version. *Manic Miner* made extraordinary profits, helped transform the bedroom scene into a formidable industry, and spawned numerous copycats. By the mid-1980s, Liverpool was likened to the Silicon Valley of Britain, and some British game industry executives drove sports cars.[22] At the same time, UK companies made significant inroads into mainland Europe. Original or licensed copies of British games were sold in many Western European cities, as were British computers.

Smith was under considerable pressure from his business partners, the gaming press, and fans to finish the sequel, *Jet Set Willy*. In this game, miner Willy, now wealthy thanks to the treasures he collected in the previous game,

Figure 7.1. Opening screen of the original *Manic Miner* (frame grab).

has to clean up his mansion after throwing an opulent party. This time, Willy can walk between sixty-one screens of the house in a nonlinear fashion. Despite being rushed and buggy, *Jet Set Willy* was also a massive hit—but it turned out to be Smith's last. A 1984 magazine report from the Software Projects headquarters painted Smith, then seventeen or eighteen, as a "merchant of mayhem" and a rock-star game designer: "He is now the most famous programmer in the country, the embodiment of the otherwise spurious myth of the school millionaire." However, Smith did not care much for fame and squandered his money on an "experimental lifestyle," which—in Smith's own words—included "partying, getting drunk and falling over a lot."[23] He never managed to finish another game and quit in 1988, leaving behind a legacy as a hero and a victim of the game industry. He was likely an inspiration for the character of the eccentric British programmer Colin Ritman in "Bandersnatch," a 2018 interactive episode of the *Black Mirror* TV series.[24] But he also became an unlikely role model for Czechoslovak teenagers.

## Willy's Eastward Journey

The home-computing scene was markedly different behind the Iron Curtain. In the 1980s, the Czechoslovak Socialist Republic was ruled by one of the region's most dogmatic Communist parties. Censorship and secret police surveillance stunted public and cultural life; private enterprise was only partially legalized in 1988. Party leadership was preoccupied with maintaining the political status quo instead of modernizing the economy. According to an implicit social contract, the government maintained an acceptable living standard for its citizens in exchange for their acquiescence. This strategy seemed to work, at least in the short term. With their basic needs provided for, and with career prospects reserved for party cadres, many Czechoslovaks retreated into a world of private hobbies and do-it-yourself activities, including electronics and computing—a phenomenon that Paulina Bren has called "private citizenship."[25]

Unlike the Brits, Czechoslovaks did not set out to build a profitable computing sector. Party technocrats saw computers as instruments of industrial automation, administrative control, and defense—not entertainment or personal consumption. Home computers were scarce due to a combination of import embargoes, lack of hard currency to purchase them from abroad, and disorganized domestic production. The authorities nevertheless granted support to programming education and hobby computing—not to create rock-star programmers, but rather "cadres ... for expeditious application of electronics and microelectronics in all branches of the national economy."[26] Around 1982, organizations such as the Socialistický svaz mládeže (Socialist Union of Youth) and Svazarm (Union for the Cooperation with the Army) opened their first cybernetics youth groups and paramilitary computer clubs. Ostensibly, they trained programmers for their work in factories, institutions, or the military; in fact, their activities comprised free-form tinkering, programming, and play. They were prime examples of what Alexei Yurchak has called *"vnye"* milieus—groups and collectives formally subsumed in the state apparatus but largely independent from state ideology and oversight.[27] The country's most influential and well-connected clubs at the time were Prague's Station of Young Technicians—primarily for kids of various ages—and the more adult-oriented club of the 602nd Basic Organization of Svazarm. Like most Svazarm clubs, the latter was known by its organization number and simply called "the 602." Other important clubs included the 482—a Prague-based competitor of the 602—and the 415, located in the city of Ostrava.

Simultaneously, electronics and computing enthusiasts individually imported computers from the West. Often, they had to mobilize their social network to find a friend or a relative with a travel permit. Many early computer users recruited from cosmopolitan professions: academics, artists, or tourism workers. Others were temporary workers in the "friendly" socialist countries of Africa and the Middle East, who could buy their machines during layovers in Western Europe. The prolific coder Tomáš Rylek, for example, got his computer—a Spectrum—from his dad, who worked as a geologist in Syria. The Spectrum was a typical choice among Czechoslovak fans. It was not only cheaper, but also physically smaller than other machines, and it was therefore easier to smuggle across the border—a practice prompted by prohibitively high customs fees. Even then, the computer would cost up to six months' worth of average Czechoslovak salary in the early to mid-1980s. The Rylek family eventually decided to split the cost with their neighbors, and Tomáš ended up sharing his machine with his friend Miroslav Fídler in an arrangement that was—as he remembers—"quite complicated, especially as we all wanted to sit at it for ten hours a day."[28] Together, however, the two youngsters, both of whom joined Prague's Station of Young Technicians, would write some of the earliest Czechoslovak *Manic Miner* clones.

Soon, they were joined by many more Spectrum owners who opted for this machine to benefit from the resources and know-how shared by the user community. While, like other Western computers, the Spectrum machines were considered status symbols (at least initially), they were also widely used in government-approved computer clubs. By 1986, an estimated 40,000 Spectrums were running in the country, the majority of them bought abroad or on the black market.[29] Although it was never advertised or continuously sold in the country, the Spectrum thus became the country's number-one home computer platform, opening doors to a strong and lasting British influence on Czechoslovak gaming communities.

It is difficult to pinpoint the exact moment when *Manic Miner* arrived in Czechoslovakia. A likely scenario is that a few weeks or months after its British release, a Czechoslovak fan picked it up at an electronics store somewhere in Western Europe, brought it home, and shared it with friends and colleagues in a computer club.[30] What we know for certain is that the game was already popular among local fans by summer 1984, the release date of its earliest preserved Czechoslovak conversion. Once the game arrived in the country, there were next to no barriers to its distribution. The domestic informal distribution network was described as "lightning fast," as it took as little as five days to two weeks for a program to reach the other side of the country.[31] There were three main reasons for this speed. First, computer games were under the radar of censors—they were too niche, too obscure, and not considered a medium capable of expressing political messages. Second, Czechoslovakia did not enforce copyright in the domain of computer software. Computer clubs generally believed that programs, including foreign commercial games, could be freely shared among club members. Third, even before the widespread adoption of computer networks, home computer technology made copying easy. Software for eight-bit computers circulated on regular audiocassette tapes, which were relatively available and affordable. Moreover, unlike analog video or audio recordings, software could be copied digitally (from tape to computer, then back to tape); therefore, the signal did not deteriorate when copied. In this way, each user could become a source of a potentially infinite number of copies of the same quality. Matters became more complicated when publishers started to employ copy-protection mechanisms, but even those were eventually broken.[32]

Copy protection techniques were introduced by British publishers to fight software piracy on their domestic market. But despite the existence of piracy, British users were well aware that *Manic Miner* could be bought in a shop as a mass-produced entertainment product in a plastic case that contained not only the original tape, but also an inlay with its paratextual elements—legal disclaimers, the manual, and the game's backstory.[33] In Czechoslovakia, conversely, nearly all copies of *Manic Miner* were unauthorized, having been stripped of the pieces of the original material culture and its paratextual supplements. Most users got a copy of the game in a club or from a friend, without ever seeing the original cover. Separated from the industrial infrastructures and media discourses of the UK entertainment industry, the game's meaning among Czechoslovak fans became very fluid.

## A Game to Program With

Due to the lack of computing or gaming periodicals in Czechoslovakia at the time, we have no firsthand accounts of *Manic Miner*'s reception in 1983 Czechoslovakia. It is safe to assume that Czechoslovak players appreciated its genre-defining design and enjoyed its core gameplay and wacky animations just as much as the Brits. In the recollections of my informants, the game is always described as "absolutely legendary" or "classic." In fact, it was canonized almost immediately. The earliest preserved computer club newsletter from 1985 calls *Manic Miner* a "classic game" only two years after its release.[34]

While the game was a classic in both countries, its reception differed in Czechoslovakia. For local users, it had the appeal of a cool Western product, but they soon made it fit their own language, interests, and ambitions. We know, for example, that some people pronounced the word *manic* in the same way as the Czech word *maník*, a colloquial expression referring to a low-ranking soldier, a worker, or just a "man" or "dude."[35] The game's cultural references were mostly lost on Czechoslovak players. Although Smith chose the main character's profession based on genre conventions rather than political sentiment, playing as a miner could be considered slightly subversive in

Britain at the time of Thatcher-era miner strikes. In Communist Czechoslovakia, on the other hand, mining was among the best-paid and favored professions, making the game seem like wholesome entertainment—especially in comparison to action games that featured American–Soviet conflict. But the main divergence in reception stemmed from the different values and practices of Czechoslovak user communities. Here, the use of home computers for entertainment was not nearly as normalized as in Britain. Around 1985, as more Western computer games were entering the country, club newsletters ran several articles about the computer game craze. Their authors, typically senior club members, observed the immense appeal of games, as well as their addictive nature (which was praised by the British press), noting "the infectious snobbery of the pseudo-users of microcomputers, many of whom sink deeper and deeper into the imaginary world of gaming high."[36] Their criticism was not aimed at the games' content. Rather, they feared that users would play ready-made games instead of engaging in active club work. At the same time, critics could not simply stop users from playing games. Instead, games were incorporated into the club discourses of tinkering and bricolage, and people were encouraged to use them as material for dissection and further creative endeavors—be they hacks, modifications, or conversions.

In the club environment, *Manic Miner*'s origin story became largely disconnected from the larger industry narrative and was retold to fit the local context. Very few users had access to British magazines, and those who did often lacked the English skills to grasp the nuances of journalistic discourse. The bits and pieces of information that circulated about miner Willy games were often truncated and distorted. As my informant Martin Malý pointed out: "We knew that *Manic Miner* was written by a fifteen-year-old. What we didn't know was that he made money on it, started to drink and do drugs, and ruined himself.... We—or at least I—didn't see the business behind it, because we didn't know about it."[37] Czechoslovak fans were familiar with labels like Bug-Byte or Software Projects, but they found it difficult to imagine the workings of a game industry, because nothing like it existed in Czechoslovakia.

Despite what many local users believed, Smith was not fifteen, but rather sixteen to seventeen years old when he made *Manic Miner*. His age was one of the very few behind-the-scenes facts that Czechoslovak computer club materials mentioned about *any* game, but they invariably portrayed Smith as younger than he actually was, reducing his age to fifteen or even thirteen.[38] His (presumed) young age must have made an impression on my informants, because they tend to remember these lower—and incorrect—figures.[39] The distortion probably arose as the story was relayed many times, with more and more exaggeration. But it also fit with the mission of Czechoslovak computer clubs, whose overt goal was to train young programmers. Unaware of his reputation as a "merchant of mayhem," young club members could look up to Smith as a role model—the boy who made games.[40]

At the time, most commercial games—*Manic Miner* included—were written in machine code or assembly language (which is, in essence, annotated machine code), because a higher programming language, such as BASIC or C, would run sluggishly on the era's slow mass-market micros. Program in machine code consists of instructions sent directly to the computer's CPU, and to the untrained eye, it looks like a jumble of hexadecimal numbers. Smith's story made it seem less intimidating. One club newsletter contributor explicitly recommended disassembling *Manic Miner* to learn machine code: "Only a few [programs] are polished into the state of perfection, attractiveness, and user-friendliness to the extent that computer games are. I do think that beginners should . . . delve into simple games, and take them apart. An extraordinarily suitable game is, for example, the good old *Manic Miner*, written by a fifteen-year-old."[41] In part, *Manic Miner*'s suitability as teaching material was due to Smith's ingenious development system. Aleš Martiník, the author of the earliest Czechoslovak conversion of *Manic Miner*, remarked that the code was "very well written" and "well structured" and rightly guessed that "his family must have had another computer, because he would not have been able to write it [with the Spectrum alone]."[42] All of this made the game's code easier to understand and therefore also easier to modify or convert to other types of computers.

### Remaking Miner Willy

Home computers, the Spectrum included, were open platforms that allowed users to dissect or alter any piece of software, *Manic Miner* and *Jet Set Willy* included. Unrestrained by copyright, many club members considered these games to be raw material for software bricolage. The following two sections will cover the results of their work, which ranged from *pokes* to *ports* and *conversions* and finally to *mash-ups* and *imitations*. Each of these categories captures a different relationship between the source game and the program derived from it, starting with minor modifications (*pokes*) and ending with almost entirely original games (*imitations*). Except for *pokes*, which was a vernacular term, all of these are terms that I have developed to distinguish between various shades of amateur programming practice.[43]

*Pokes*—named after the command that changes a single byte in the computer's memory—were small hacks that could be performed even by a novice programmer. In the case of *Manic Miner*, they could enable infinite lives, remove monsters, or make Willy invincible. While pokes were also popular in the West, Czechoslovak club newsletters enthusiastically encouraged poking as a pathway into machine code programming, leading to a proliferation of modified versions of various games.[44] *Conversions* were pieces of software that tried to recreate the original experience on another hardware platform but were usually programmed from scratch. *Ports*, on the other hand, followed the same goal but reused the original code with minor modifications. Porting of machine code was less demanding than converting but was only possible between machines with the same CPU. Thanks to its classic status, *Manic Miner* became the most frequently converted and ported game in the country, spreading onto platforms for which it was never officially released. In the friendly but competitive—and overwhelmingly male—environment of computer clubs, young amateurs often used games to prove their commitment to the community and showcase their coding skills. A conversion or a port offered an easier pathway into game making, as graphics and game mechanics were already in place and only programming was required.

The earliest preserved Czechoslovak conversion was created in 1984 for the ZX81, the Sinclair-produced predecessor to the ZX Spectrum.[45] At the time, its author, Martiník, was a student at the Brno University of Technology and a Svazarm club member. He had played *Manic Miner* on a friend's Spectrum in the dorms, and it was "love at first sight." Knowing that he would lose access to the game during summer break, he set out to rewrite it for his ZX81. However, the desire to play *Manic Miner* was just a part ("twenty percent") of his motivation. The remaining eighty percent "was the desire to prove to myself, but mainly others, that I am good enough to pull it off, at both of which I succeeded."[46] Remaking the game for the ZX81 did indeed seem like an impossible challenge. The ZX81 ran the same CPU but had less memory, and—unlike the Spectrum—it could not display individual pixels but only characters stored in the machine's read-only memory (ROM). Martiník's solution was to continuously hijack the character display routine and redirect it to a position in ROM that contained a graphic as close as possible to what needed to be drawn. The trick had its limitations, resulting in slightly jagged graphics (see fig. 7.2). Otherwise, the conversion was surprisingly faithful. To this day, the ZX81 version of *Manic Miner* is considered one of the most impressive programming achievements on this machine, even by the international retro gaming community.[47]

Another notable conversion was released for the PMD 85, a Czechoslovak machine introduced in 1985 by Tesla, the country's largest electronics manufacturer. The PMD 85 never became a home computer, as it was not sold in retail, but it was widely used in schools and computer clubs. Tesla did not provide any official software, so it was up to amateurs to equip it with

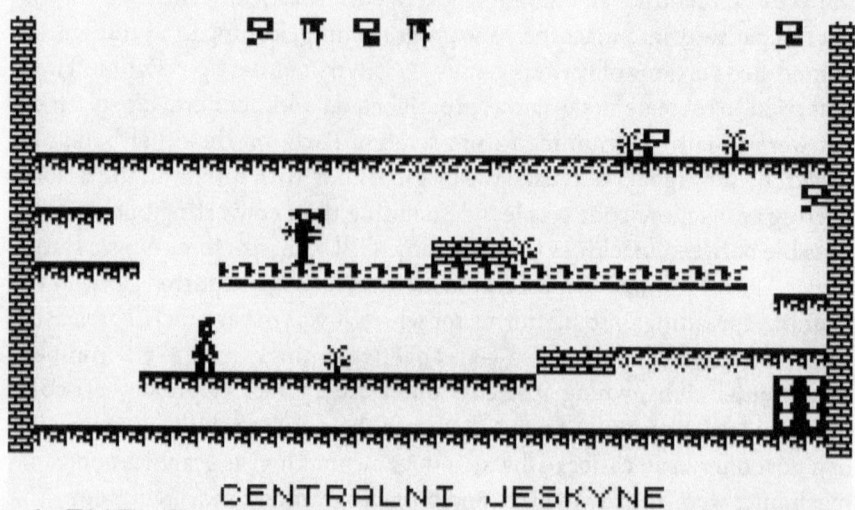

Figure 7.2. Aleš Martiník's ZX81 version of *Manic Miner* (with five lives) (frame grab).

games and utility programs. Its first version of *Manic Miner*, written by Vít Libovický and Daniel Jenne of Prague's 602 computer club, appeared shortly after the machine's 1985 launch.[48] Aiming for a 100 percent faithful conversion, the duo kept "one finger in [Smith's] original code." Libovický even unknowingly mimicked Smith's development process, as he assembled the code on a TRS-80-compatible machine and fed it into a PMD 85, both of which he borrowed from the club.[49] The resulting game played remarkably similarly, even on the PMD's inferior CPU (see fig. 7.3).

In 1987, another team ported *Manic Miner* to the Sharp MZ-800, a Japanese computer that was intermittently sold in Czechoslovak electronics stores but was obscure in the rest of Europe.[50] Additionally, we have reports of further versions that have not been preserved.[51] While all the ports and conversions tried to convey the experience of the original, their differences are illuminating. They tended to be more lo-fi, losing color, sound, and special effects—usually because they were converted to an inferior platform. In terms of gameplay, all surviving Czechoslovak versions lowered the game's difficulty by increasing the number of lives from three to five, six, or even eight in the case of PMD 85. The original's high difficulty level was likely inspired by the uncompromising coin-operated arcade games of the time, but the conversions were made in a context where poking the game to get more lives was so commonplace that extra lives were hardly considered a

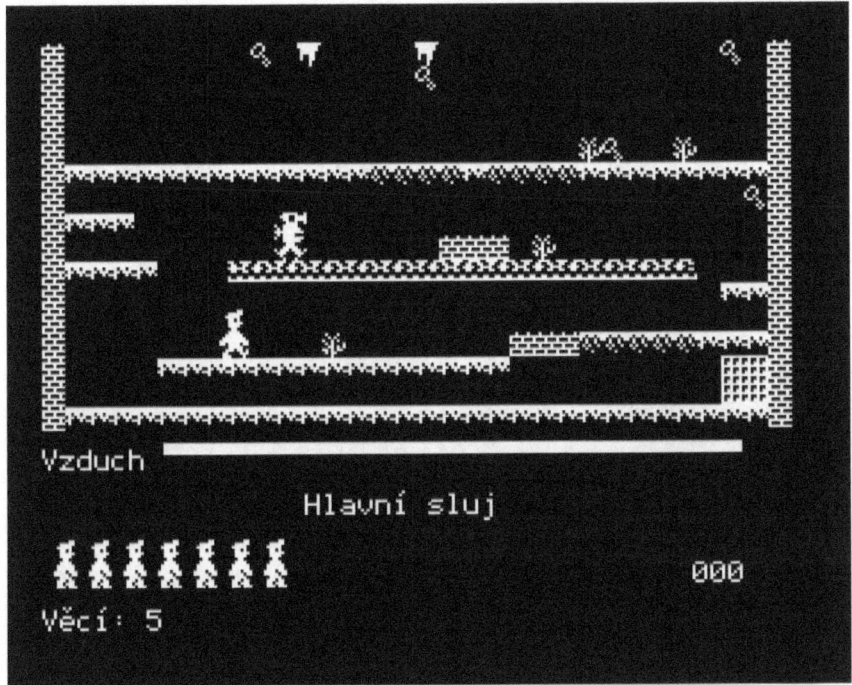

Figure 7.3. Vít Libovický and Daniel Jenne's PMD 85 version of *Manic Miner* (with seven additional lives, excluding the current one) (frame grab).

breach of the original design. Lastly, conversions invariably translated in-game text, including the names of individual caverns, into Czech or Slovak. Each version contained a few changes and misunderstandings. "The Warehouse" was once translated as "The War House," and "Menagerie" (featuring turkeys and spiders) became "Mine Management." Cultural references were lost in translation, with "Endorian Forest" becoming "Forbidden Forest"—this nod to *Star Wars* might not have been noticed in a country where the 1977 *Star Wars* film only officially premiered in 1991.[52] In some cases, local authors simply made up their own names; for example, a cavern originally called "The Vat" received the descriptive denomination "Cavern at the Three Kangaroos," which follows the conventional syntax of Czech toponyms.[53] Despite the converters' aim to mimic the original, they also contributed their interpretations of the game artifact.

### Miner Willy Visits a Restricted Military Area

In the British game industry, it was widely understood that any conversion or sequel to a miner Willy game had to be licensed by its copyright holder. Series such as *Dynamite Dan* and *Monty Mole* were clearly inspired by

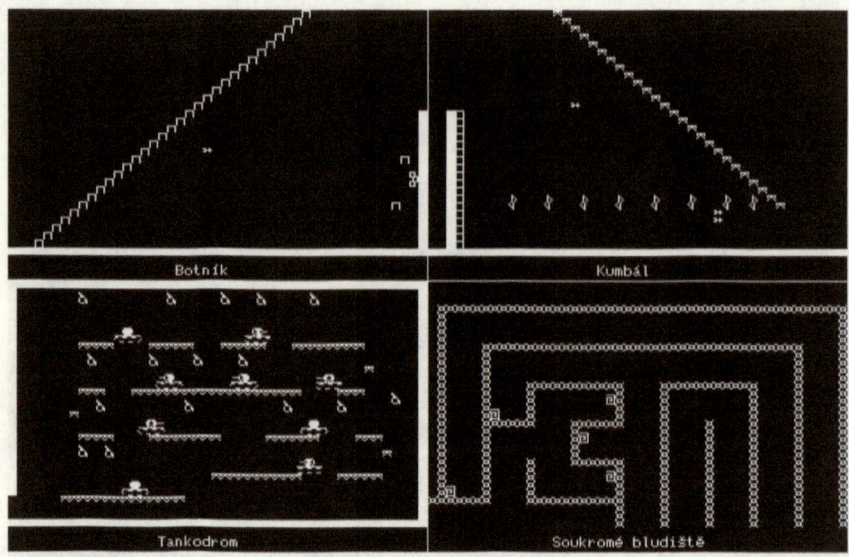

Figure 7.4. A small portion of the house layout in Karel Šuhajda's *Willy Walker*, cropped from a composite assembled by Vlastimil Veselý. The Tank Training Area (Tankodrom) is below the Shoe Rack (Botník) and Junk Room (Kumbál) and next to a Private Maze (Soukromé bludiště) (frame grab).

Smith's game but introduced different characters and expanded on the formula. In Czechoslovakia, no such rules applied. Some authors of ports and conversions did not even credit Smith—not for lack of respect, but because authorship was associated with writing the program rather than designing the game. The PMD 85 version of *Manic Miner* made this point explicit in its credit line, which read: "Authors: Vít Libovický and Daniel Jenne, screenplay and shapes: Matthew Smith."[54] In other cases, Czechoslovak programmers added a considerable amount of their own content, creating games that were *mash-ups* rather than simple conversions.

The 1985 game *Willy Walker* for the PMD 85 was written by Karel Šuhajda, who had played *Manic Miner* and *Jet Set Willy* on a friend's Spectrum and used them as an inspiration for his first major programming project.[55] At the time, he was attending the 482 club in Prague, unaware that his more experienced peers at the 602 were working on their conversion. Unlike them, he did not strive for a verbatim copy of the original, and he did not peek into its code. Accordingly, the credits said: "From foreign materials adapted and written by Karel Šuhajda." Like *Jet Set Willy*, the game took place in a large mansion, but one that was local rather than British. It followed the typical layout of a Czechoslovak house, and included a few surreal twists (see fig. 7.4). The game map featured a tank training area and a restricted

Figure 7.5. The intro screen of VBG Software's *Manic Miner* (frame grab).

military area, typical examples of restricted and possibly dangerous places in the Cold War–era Soviet Bloc. Despite the game's novel environments and massive size, Šuhajda was disheartened when he saw his peers' faithful conversion: "Their game was better in all respects—in terms of graphics, playability and entertainment. Mine had a larger map and was original, but that wasn't enough to outweigh its cons." But Šuhajda did not give up, and he went on to produce some of the most sophisticated games for the platform.

There was yet one more miner Willy game for the PMD 85, released in 1987 by VBG Software, a trio based at Ostrava's 415 club. The group specialized in conversions from other machines, ranging from faithful to loose. Entitled simply (and confusingly) *Manic Miner*, their take on the classic falls squarely into the latter category. The game offers entirely different levels than the original game and introduces new mechanics, such as the ability to climb poles and ladders. Its caverns are interconnected (perhaps an inspiration from *Jet Set Willy*) and feature completely new monsters, including crocodiles, elephants, and germ-like critters (see fig. 7.5). Although it features Willy, this version's different jumping physics, map layouts, and challenges create a distinct experience, much removed from Smith's classic.

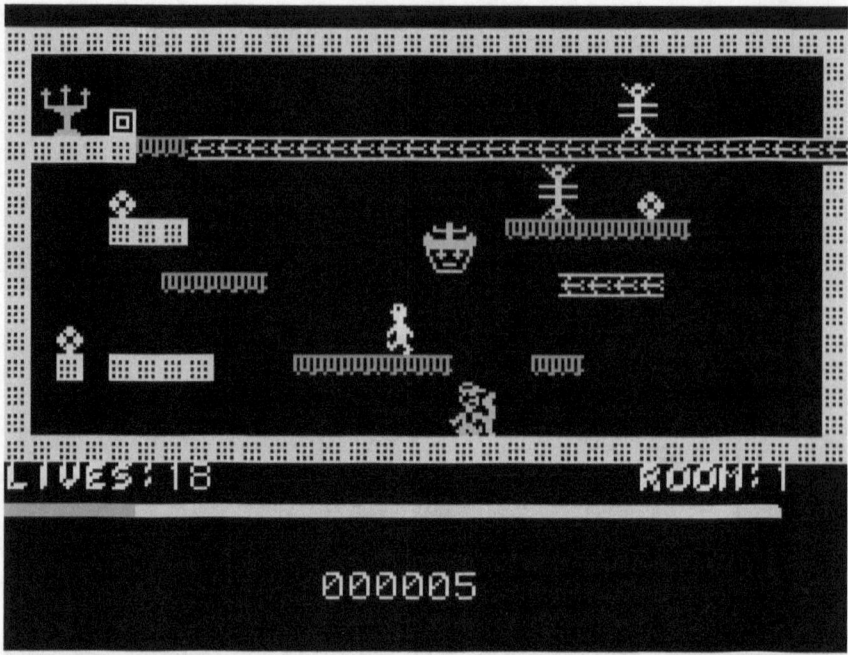

Figure 7.6. The opening level of *Maglaxians*, credited to Miroslav Fídler, bears similarities to *Manic Miner*'s Central Cavern (frame grab).

The final category of Willy-based games are *imitations*, or games that do not use elements of the original but heavily borrow from its structure and design; a slightly disparaging colloquial term would be *clones*. Although local computer owners had plenty of *Manic Miner* look-alikes to choose from, ambitious Czechoslovak programmers made their own even for the Sinclair machine. In 1985, Miroslav Fídler, with the help of Tomáš Rylek, released *Maglaxians* (see fig. 7.6) and *Itemiada*—imitations of *Manic Miner* and *Jet Set Willy*, respectively.[56] The games took place in abstract labyrinths that resembled neither houses nor caverns. Still, they contained references to the authors' lived experience. One of the game's enemies is a robot named Karel, a reference to KAREL, the popular Czechoslovak tool for teaching programming, in which the student gives instructions to the titular robot. Once again, after cutting their teeth on *Manic Miner* clones, both Fídler and Rylek became some of the top Czechoslovak coders, affirming the game's value as teaching material.

## Conclusion

Computer gaming communities of the 1980s were influenced by transnational flows of software, know-how, and inspiration. The parties involved in these exchanges were never on equal footing. Smith looked up to American designers, and Czechoslovak amateurs admired Smith. The flow of software from the West was one-sided, and before the widespread adoption of the internet, very few, if any, Soviet Bloc modifications made it to Britain. But even in the (relative) margins, people did not just consume culture from the (relative) centers; they also appropriated and localized it. At the peak of the local Willy mania, in 1985, at least one conversion, one mash-up, and two imitations of the game were made by Czechoslovak bricoleurs. This burst of activity cannot be explained by the popularity of the original game alone; instead, local modifications responded to the needs and ambitions of the local computing communities. Remaking *Manic Miner* for an obscure Czechoslovak computer, for example, brought immediate benefits to local players and earned respect and recognition for its authors. It made the machine "cooler" by allowing it to run a Western game, while also making miner Willy more at home at Czechoslovak computer clubs. Dissecting and rebuilding Smith's games was thus a way of actively participating in club life.

It is important to note that *Manic Miner* modifications were not an exclusively Czechoslovak or Soviet Bloc phenomenon. In the UK, several low-profile companies released editors for both *Manic Miner* and *Jet Set Willy*, which allowed users to create new graphics, rooms, and caverns for the game—which several fans did.[57] There is also a well-known 1985 unofficial sequel, *Manic Miner 2*, by a German-speaking author.[58] In Czechoslovakia, however, amateur modifications and conversions featured much more prominently among the bulk of preserved titles.

The trends and tastes among Czechoslovak gaming communities changed later in the decade. In the mid-1980s, Polish and Yugoslav pirates became essential middlemen in importing games into Eastern Europe, and Czechoslovak enthusiasts no longer had to rely on original copies purchased in Western European retail. *Manic Miner* soon became a thing of history, and new Spectrum games took over its role of inspiring domestic programmers. In the second half of the 1980s, many local programmers began writing text adventures—games that present interactive narratives through text descriptions of places and events.[59] Also initially inspired by Western titles, Czechoslovak amateurs used these games to tell their own stories and comment on current events. They even created satirical titles that made fun of Soviet war-hero narratives and military propaganda and several activist games that criticized the Communist regime and its suppression of peaceful protests.[60]

Throughout this chapter, I have pointed out the contextual factors that shaped *Manic Miner*'s reception in Czechoslovakia. In the UK, programming enthusiasts took advantage of commercial infrastructures of Tandy stores and gaming magazines and soon became part of an industry that framed games as entertainment products. In Communist-era Czechoslovakia, people congregated in government-sponsored computer clubs, where Western commercial games were recast as educational materials to train future specialists for state factories and institutions. While the commercial publishing model encouraged programmers to create new intellectual property, the Czechoslovak club-dominated environment allowed for the astounding range of modifications that gave Manic Miner a second life in Czechoslovakia. With the emergence of an online worldwide retro gaming community in the late 1990s, international fans could finally appreciate Czechoslovak versions of Manic Miner. One of them even reached Smith. In 2004, at the age of about thirty-eight, he gave several interviews after his long hiatus from gaming media. In one of them, he acknowledged that Martiník's ZX81 version was "very well done."[61]

The story of Manic Miner exemplifies broader trends in late Soviet-era culture and technology. Early Polish computer games also ran on imported technology and imitated Western titles. In fact, the first commercially released Polish game, Pandora's Box (Puszka Pandory) from 1986, positioned itself as a Polish-language substitute for English-language text adventure games.[62] As documented by Martin Thiele and Michael Geithner, East German bricoleurs produced scrappy handmade copies of non-digital tabletop games from West Germany and especially Monopoly, which embodied the allure of capitalism.[63] In the domain of music, Eastern European rock and electronic groups looked for inspiration in Western records and played instruments smuggled from the West. Such was the case of the Czechoslovak duo ORM, who made pioneering electronic music in their home studio and simultaneously wrote and produced disco hits for local pop singers.[64] Like the Manic Miner imitations, their music acknowledged the dominance of Western influences while recombining them into a distinctly local aesthetic. Far from being a niche practice, such bricolage was one of the defining modes of the period's cultural production.

## Notes

1. Smith, *Manic Miner*; and Smith, *Jet Set Willy*.
2. Fuka, *Počítačové Hry*, 6.
3. Smith arguably shared this status with the British studio Ultimate Play the Game.
4. See, for example, Bláhová, "The Good, the Bad, and the Un-American"; and Yurchak, *Everything Was Forever*.
5. Platinum Productions, *Raid Over Moscow*; and Pasanen, *Beyond the Pale*.
6. Švelch, *Gaming the Iron Curtain*.
7. Lobato, *Shadow Economies of Cinema*, 18.
8. Fassone, "Variantology of Italian Video Games."

9. Lévi-Strauss, *The Savage Mind*, 17.
10. In 1962, Tandy Corporation bought the US RadioShack retail network, but kept the original brand. However, Tandy's European electronics stores used the Tandy branding. The line of computers sold through the network was called TRS—Tandy RadioShack.
11. Wade, *Genealogy of 1980s British Videogames*.
12. Green and Drury, interview, August 10, 2010.
13. Ibid.
14. Smith, *Styx*.
15. Gazzard, "The Intertextual Arcade."
16. Nintendo, *Donkey Kong*; and Hogue, *Miner 2094er*.
17. "Penguins Make Life Perilous!"
18. Donovan, *Replay*.
19. Scriven, "Hitchcockian Nightmare," 16; and "Penguins Make Life Perilous!," 131.
20. The formation of discourse about games has been traced by Kirkpatrick. Kirkpatrick, *Gaming Culture*.
21. "Penguins Make Life Perilous!," 131.
22. Bourne, "Matthew Uncaged"; and A. Caulfield and N. Caulfield, *From Bedrooms to Billions*.
23. This and the previous quote from Bourne, "Matthew Uncaged," 92. The "merchant of mayhem" moniker was used in the teaser for this article on the front cover of the issue.
24. The episode is set in the 1980s British game industry, and Colin Ritman is an idol and mentor to the main character, the promising young programmer Stefan Butler. In one of the story branches, Colin and Stefan take LSD together. The Colin Ritman character seems to be an amalgamation of "British surrealist" game designers like Smith, Jeff Minter, Jon Ritman, and Chris and Tim Stamper. Slade, "Bandersnatch."
25. Bren, *The Greengrocer and His TV*.
26. Amatérské Radio, "Mikroelektronika."
27. Yurchak, *Everything Was Forever*.
28. Rylek, interview, January 15, 2015.
29. Myslík, "Mikro PF 86," 17–18.
30. Fuka, interview, August 28, 2008.
31. Libovický, interview, April 13, 2011; and Trojan, "Hráč," 2–3.
32. While *Manic Miner* was not copy protected, *Jet Set Willy* already was. The removal of copy protection is called *cracking*. See Wasiak, "Playing and Copying."
33. For a systematic treatment of paratextuality in relation to video games, see Švelch, "'Footage Not Representative.'"
34. "Programová nabídka mikrobáze," *Mikrobáze*, 66.
35. Lonský, interview, January 17, 2016.
36. Kš, "Program pro Vnoučata," 3.
37. Malý, interview, August 12, 2014.
38. "Počítačové hry jako společenský fenomén," *Sinclair 602*, 4–5; and KVT ZO Svazarmu Karolinka, *Poke č. 1*.
39. Malý, interview, August 12, 2014; and Martiník, interview, June 14, 2017.
40. See note 23 for reference.
41. "Počítačové hry jako společenský fenomén," *Sinclair 602*, 4.
42. Martiník, interview, June 14, 2017.
43. For a more detailed explanation of these categories, see Švelch, *Gaming the Iron Curtain*. In 1980s Czechoslovakia, ports, conversions, and mash-ups would all most likely be called remakes (*předělávky*).
44. MB, "Úpravy her pro ZX Spectrum," 44; and Bahenský, "Něco triků pro aktivní, spectristy," 28–30.
45. Martiník, *Manic Miner*.

46. All quotations from Martiník, interview, June 14, 2017.
47. Gasking, "Pushed To The Edge."
48. Jenne and Libovický, *Manic Miner*.
49. Libovický, personal communication with Švelch, September 2018.
50. *Manic Miner*, Unisoft.
51. The Sord M5 version has not been preserved, but its existence was confirmed by its author, Daniel Dočekal. Dočekal, interview, December 2, 2016. In addition, Libovický remembers remaking *Manic Miner* for two Czechoslovak computers—Tesla Ondra and the FK-1. Neither of these versions has been preserved.
52. Šrajer, "Tuzemská stopa."
53. The Czech or Slovak versions are, respectively, "Dům války" (on the PMD 85), "Správa baně" (Sharp MZ 800), "Zakázaný les" (PMD 85), and "Jeskyň U Tří klokanů" (ZX81).
54. Jenne and Libovický, *Manic Miner*.
55. Šuhajda, *Willy Walker*.
56. Fídler, *Maglaxians*; and Fídler, *Itemiada*.
57. Gromann, "List of Manic Miner and Jet Set Willy Games."
58. *Manic Miner 2*, Schultze.
59. See Montfort, *Twisty Little Passages*.
60. See Švelch, *Gaming the Iron Curtain*.
61. "The Wisdom of Matthew Smith," *Retro Gamer*, 27. Smith does not refer to Martiník by name, but there is little doubt that he refers to his work, as no other ZX81 version of *Manic Miner* has been preserved.
62. Budziszewski, "Poland."
63. Thiele and Geithner, *Nachgemacht*.
64. Soldan and Střelcová, "Meet the Duo."

## Bibliography

Amatérské Radio. "Mikroelektronika." *Amatérské Radio*, řada A 31, no. 1 (1982).
Bahenský, Zbyšek. "Něco triků pro aktivní, spectristy.'" *Elektronika* 3, no. 10 (1989).
Bláhová, Jindřiška. "The Good, the Bad, and the Un-American: The Czechoslovak Film Monopoly, Hollywood, and American Independent Distributors." *Post Script* 30, no. 2 (2011): 9–20.
Bourne, Chris. "Matthew Uncaged." *Sinclair User* 2, no. 33 (1984).
Bren, Paulina. *The Greengrocer and His TV: The Culture of Communism after the 1968 Prague Spring*. Ithaca, NY: Cornell University Press, 2010.
Budziszewski, P. Konrad. "Poland." In *Video Games around the World*, edited by Mark J. P. Wolf, 399–424. Cambridge, MA: MIT Press, 2015.
Caulfield, Anthony, and Nicola Caulfield. *From Bedrooms to Billions*. Gracious Films, 2014.
Dočekal, Daniel. Interview by Jaroslav Švelch. December 2, 2016.
Donovan, Tristan. *Replay: The History of Video Games*. East Sussex, England: Yellow Ant, 2010.
Drury, Paul, and Mark Green. "Matthew 'Manic Miner' Smith: Complete Transcript of 2005 Interview." *Pixelatron*, August 10, 2010. http://pixelatron.com/blog/matthew-manic-miner-smith-complete-transcript-of-2005-interview/.
Fassone, Riccardo. "Cammelli and Attack of the Mutant Camels: A Variantology of Italian Video Games of the 1980s." *Well Played Journal* 6, no. 2 (2017): 55–71.
Fídler, Miroslav. *Itemiada*. ZX Spectrum, Praha: Cybexlab, 1985.
———. *Maglaxians*. ZX Spectrum, Praha: Cybexlab, 1985.

Fuka, František. Interview by Jaroslav Švelch. August 28, 2008.

———. *Počítačové Hry: Historie a Současnost, 1 Díl*. Beroun: Zenitcentrum, 1988.

Gasking, Frank. "Pushed To The Edge." Oldschool Gaming, 2007. Accessed October 28, 2021. https://web.archive.org/web/20190615224253/http://www.oldschool-gaming.com/view_article.php?art=pushed_to_the_edge.

Gazzard, Alison. "The Intertextual Arcade: Tracing Histories of Arcade Clones in 1980s Britain." *Reconstruction* 14, no. 1 (2014). Accessed October 28, 2021. https://web.archive.org/web/20160319130044/http://reconstruction.eserver.org/Issues/141/Gazzard.shtml.

Gromann, Daniel. "List of Manic Miner and Jet Set Willy Games for the ZX Spectrum." JSW Central: Resource Centre for ZX Spectrum Games Using Manic Miner and Jet Set Willy Game Engines, 2018. Accessed September 8, 2021. http://www.jswcentral.org/index.html.

Hogue, Bill. *Miner 2094er*. Atari 8-bit: Big Five Software, 1982.

Jenne, Daniel, and Vít Libovický. *Manic Miner*. PMD 85, Praha: ViLiSoft & DaJeSoft, 1985.

Kirkpatrick, Graeme. *The Formation of Gaming Culture: UK Gaming Magazines, 1981–1995*. London: Palgrave Pivot, 2015.

Kš. "Program pro Vnoučata." *Mikrobáze* 2, no. 4 (1986).

KVT ZO Svazarmu Karolinka. *Poke č. 1*. Karolinka: Klub Výpočetní Techniky, ZO Svazarmu Karolinka, 1987.

Lévi-Strauss, Claude. *The Savage Mind*. London: Weidenfeld and Nicolson, 1966.

Libovický, Vít. Interview by Jaroslav Švelch. April 13, 2011.

———. Personal communication with Jaroslav Švelch. September 2018.

Lobato, Ramon. *Shadow Economies of Cinema: Mapping Informal Film Distribution*. London: Palgrave Macmillan, 2012.

Lonský, Jan. Interview by Jaroslav Švelch. January 17, 2016.

Malý, Martin. Interview by Jaroslav Švelch. August 12, 2014.

*Manic Miner*. Sharp MZ 800, Banská Bystrica: Unisoft, 1987.

*Manic Miner 2*. ZX Spectrum: Schultze, 1985.

Martiník, Aleš. Interview by Jaroslav Švelch. June 14, 2017.

———. *Manic Miner*. ZX81, 1984.

MB. "Úpravy Her Pro ZX Spectrum." *Mikrobáze* 2, no. 3 (1986).

Montfort, Nick. *Twisty Little Passages: An Approach to Interactive Fiction*. Cambridge, MA: MIT Press, 2005.

Myslík, Alek. "Mikro PF 86." *Amatérské Radio, Řada A* 35, no. 1 (1986).

Nintendo. *Donkey Kong*. Arcade: Nintendo, 1981.

Pasanen, Tero. *Beyond the Pale: Gaming Controversies and Moral Panics as Rites of Passage*. Jyväskylä: University of Jyväskylä, 2017.

"Penguins Make Life Perilous!" *Computer & Video Games* (September 1983).

Platinum Productions. *Raid Over Moscow*. ZX Spectrum: US Gold, 1985.

"Počítačové hry jako společenský fenomén." *Sinclair 602* 2, no. 4 (1988).

"Programová nabídka Mikrobáze (1/1985)." *Mikrobáze* 1, no. 1 (1985).

Rylek, Tomáš. Interview by Jaroslav Švelch. January 15, 2015.

Scriven, John. "Hitchcockian Nightmare." *Popular Computing Weekly*, September 22, 1983.

Slade, David. "Bandersnatch." *Black Mirror*. Netflix, December 28, 2018.

Smith, Matthew. *Jet Set Willy*. ZX Spectrum: Software Projects, 1984.

———. *Manic Miner*. ZX Spectrum: Software Projects, 1983.

———. *Styx*. ZX Spectrum: Bug-Byte Software, 1983.

Soldan, Olin, and Alexandra Střelcová. "Meet the Duo Who Smuggled Synths into Communist Czechoslovakia to Make Pioneering Electronic Music." *The Vinyl Factory*, January 3, 2017. http://thevinylfactory.com/features/orm-communist-czechoslovakia-pioneering-electronic-music/.

Šrajer, Martin. "Tuzemská stopa hvězdných válek." *Filmový přehled*, December 14, 2015. http://www.filmovyprehled.cz/cs/revue/detail/tuzemska-stopa-hvezdnych-valek.

Šuhajda, Karel. *Willy Walker*. PMD 85, Praha: 4004/482, ZO Svazarmu, 1985.

Švelch, Jan. "'Footage Not Representative': Redefining Paratextuality for the Analysis of Official Communication in the Video Game Industry." In *Contemporary Research on Intertextuality in Video Games*, edited by Christophe Duret and Christian-Marie Pons, 297–315. Hershey, PA: IGI Global, 2016.

Švelch, Jaroslav. *Gaming the Iron Curtain: How Teenagers and Amateurs in Communist Czechoslovakia Claimed the Medium of Computer Games*. Cambridge, MA: MIT Press, 2018.

Thiele, Martin, and Michael Geithner, eds. *Nachgemacht: Spielekopien aus der DDR*. Berlin: DDR Museum Verlag, 2013.

Trojan, Petr. "Hráč (rozhovor s Františkem Fukou)." *Informace pro Uživatele Mikropočítačů* 1, no. 2 (1989).

Wade, Alex. *Playback: A Genealogy of 1980s British Videogames*. New York: Bloomsbury, 2016.

Wasiak, Patryk. "Playing and Copying: Social Practices of Home Computer Users in Poland during the 1980s." In *Hacking Europe: From Computer Cultures to Demoscenes*, edited by Gerd Alberts and Ruth Oldenziel, 129–150. London: Springer, 2014.

"The Wisdom of Matthew Smith." *Retro Gamer* 1, no. 7 (2004).

Yurchak, Alexei. *Everything Was Forever, until It Was No More: The Last Soviet Generation*. Princeton, NJ: Princeton University Press, 2006.

**JAROSLAV ŠVELCH** is Assistant Professor of Media Studies at Charles University. He is author of *Gaming the Iron Curtain: How Teenagers and Amateurs in Communist Czechoslovakia Claimed the Medium of Computer Games*.

CHAPTER 8

BETWEEN SCRIPTS
## Radio Berlin International (RBI) and Its Swedish Audience in November 1989

Marie Cronqvist

This broadcast comes to you from Radio Berlin International—
the voice of the disappearing German Democratic Republic.
    Radio Berlin International, October 2, 1990

ON OCTOBER 2, 1990, THE ominous message above marked the end of a radio station with a global reach. For the very last time, Radio Berlin International's (RBI) tuning signal—the first eight notes of the GDR national anthem, "Auferstanden aus Ruinen"—sounded on the airwaves. This occurred in the context of the fundamental remapping of the European continent that took place between 1989 and 1991. The city of Berlin was at the heart of these changes, with the wall that separated Germans symbolically and physically torn down on November 9, 1989, making it possible for East and West Berliners to meet for the first time in decades. Although it was a moment of peaceful revolution, the autumn of 1989 was also a turbulent time for the GDR, not least for the country's governing Communist Party, the Socialist Unity Party (Sozialistische Einheitspartei Deutschlands, or SED). Other aspects of East German society, among them the media, also found themselves in between scripts. How were the new realities to be described, depicted, and made sense of in public life?

The aim of this chapter is not to once again tell the story of the political 1989 but to approach the peaceful revolution and Europe's remapping from the perspective of international radio and its audiences. It focuses on the East German broadcaster RBI and its Swedish-language broadcasts, relying on written manuscripts from the German Broadcasting Archive (Deutsche Rundfunkarchiv [DRA]) in Potsdam-Babelsberg. Through the manuscripts of the broadcasts from August through December 1989, we can approach the turbulence of this moment from a new angle, revealing some of the predicaments that RBI hosts encountered when trying to combine the old script of socialist state propaganda with a sensitivity to the unexpected and unprecedented events occurring both in the world and at home. In particular, the program *The Letterbox* (*Briefkasten/Brevlådan*), which consisted of letters to the Swedish studio in Berlin, testifies to how, even before the Berlin Wall crumbled, RBI hosts challenged the standard procedures of state-socialist broadcasting and sounded notes of disapproval of the SED government—soft at first, but with an increasingly critical tone. Within just a couple of weeks, a new RBI script was in the making—and from a distance, Swedes were listening and commenting on it.

### International Broadcasting during the Cold War

East German RBI was one of the most prominent international radio stations in the former Eastern Bloc. Officially founded on May 20, 1959 (although broadcasts in German, English, and French had already been introduced in 1956), it was situated within the GDR state radio station Rundfunk der DDR (1952–1991). From the fourth floor of the majestic Funkhaus Nalepastraße in East Berlin, the RBI shortwave signal went to powerful transmitters in Nauen, Königs Wusterhausen, and Leipzig, from which it was sent out to the world. In November 1989, RBI broadcast in eleven different languages: German, English, French, Swedish, Danish, Italian, Hindi, Arabic, Swahili, Portuguese, and Spanish. It is difficult to estimate the number of listeners, but according to one source, fifty-four million people around the world were tuning into RBI's broadcasts by the 1980s.[1] Most often, RBI staff seem to have been either foreign-born members of communist parties now living in Berlin or East German journalists, editors, teachers, or translators.[2]

RBI fell under the GDR's central authority for broadcasting activity, the State Radio Committee (Staatliches Komitee für Rundfunk). As one party official put it in the early 1960s, the committee's mandate was to use "radio and television [to] aid the construction and victory of socialism ... by means of ideological and educational broadcasts from the main centers of the republic."[3] This dissemination was to extend beyond the borders of the GDR: shortwave radio was seen as a powerful tool for reaching audiences in Africa, Asia, and on the other side of the Iron Curtain, and for informing these foreign audiences about East Germany. RBI's main content was thus news and information about the GDR; however, light entertainment such as East German (and later, even Western) pop music was a common feature of the broadcasts, showing global audiences the modernity and vitality of East German everyday life and popular culture.

Earlier research on the cultural Cold War has emphasized the role of radio—and especially shortwave radio, with its global reach—as a medium for propaganda that nurtured the antagonism between East and West.[4] Most of the existing scholarship tells the story of Western stations such as the BBC World Service, Voice of America, Radio Free Europe, and Radio Liberty, while much research remains to be done on Eastern broadcasting stations.[5] The few such studies that exist are mostly limited to the oldest and most influential Eastern station, Radio Moscow, which was founded in the late 1920s.[6] In the Cold War period, however, the English-language broadcasts of other significant stations had a broad reach, among them Radio Prague's, Radio Tirana's, and not least RBI's. Yet analyses or descriptions of RBI remain scarce, and surprisingly so, given the station's important position in the East German media landscape, as well as its rather significant role as an international media institution.[7] In James Wood's *History of International Broadcasting*, for instance, RBI is mentioned only in passing and in a chapter entitled "Broadcasting from the Federal Republic of Germany."[8]

Research on socialist media has historically emphasized strict centralization, censorship, and control. However, recent studies of socialist media systems in general and socialist television in particular have painted a much more nuanced picture, showing that, however controlled, these media industries were far from static and one-dimensional.[9] A telling example on the GDR is the impressive volume *Deutsches Fernsehen Ost (East German Television*, 2008), which synthesizes the findings of a large research program on GDR television. In the introduction, the authors state that their aim is not to simply see state-socialist television as a political instrument, but instead to look at television's instrumentalization in society—that is, to explore the role of television in a Durchherrschte Gesellschaft, a society drenched in authority. This, in turn, enables an investigation of how specific historical agents actively tested the limits to their freedom of action.[10] Similarly, as Alexander Badenoch, Andreas Fickers, and Christian Henrich-Franke argue in the volume *Airy Curtains in the European Ether*, the all-too-dominant "battle on the airways" approach to the history of Cold War broadcasting runs the risk of hiding other possible stories—those of European interaction or of the construction of cross-border media cultures.[11] Inspired by such recent research, I argue that since Cold War international radio broadcasters were at times able to connect and shape transborder media audiences, they were also key agents in creating meaning around the events of 1989 in European communication space.

## RBI's Swedish Broadcasts

The first broadcast of RBI's Swedish edition, *die Schwedische Redaktion*, included a report from the May Day demonstrations in Berlin on May 1, 1959.[12] For most of the period from the 1960s to 1990, RBI broadcast in Swedish for about an hour a day in the evening on middle and shortwave frequencies.[13] Swedish was the broadcaster's third foreign language (after the most obvious choices, French and English), and the decision to add a Swedish broadcast is unsurprising in light of the GDR's postwar political ambitions. In the first twenty-three years of the country's existence, its main goal was international diplomatic recognition, which it did not receive from any country but the Soviet Union until 1972. Relations with officially neutral countries were particularly important, and thus, early on, Sweden (along with countries such as Finland and Austria) was identified as a key target for political and cultural propaganda. Raising knowledge about and sympathy for the GDR in such key countries (Schwerpunktsländer) was considered essential both for recognition of GDR sovereignty and for the global advancement of the socialist worldview.[14]

Unlike the Soviet Union, the GDR underwent no process of political liberalization and *glasnost* in the mid-1980s. In this sense, it is noteworthy that the ideological differences between Sweden and the GDR did not hinder their deepening relationship in the fifteen years following Sweden's diplomatic recognition of the GDR in 1972. In the 1980s, bilateral contacts were strong and frequent on many levels and in many areas of society. This political friendship reached its peak with Swedish Prime Minister Olof Palme's 1984 visit with Erich Honecker in Stralsund, on Germany's Baltic coast. By this time, Swedish trade with East Germany had blossomed, and a large number of Swedish businesses had established themselves in Berlin, including IKEA, Volvo, ASEA, the Johnson group, and Electrolux. Yet contacts were not exclusively in politics and business. As Birgitta Almgren has shown in her research on cultural exchange between the two countries, a key target group was Swedish teachers of German.[15] Although most likely ideologically heterogeneous, this community of language teachers may have formed an important group of Swedes listening to the RBI broadcasts.

## The Letterbox

Twentieth-century international radio stations fostered close relationships with their listeners not only through audio broadcasts, but also through other media forms. In fact, radio relied heavily on written correspondence; by inviting listeners to write letters, radio stations encouraged participation and communication around a medium that might otherwise seem distant. In the 1980s, according to Heinz Odermann, RBI received as many as 180,000 letters yearly from listeners all over the world.[16] To meet these listeners' demands—or to increase their sympathy for the GDR—the station also produced and sent out a substantial amount of propaganda and publicity material.

*The Letterbox*, inaugurated in the 1980s and usually about fifteen minutes long, was a regular light program with a friendly and informal tone in which letters allegedly sent to RBI from Swedish (and sometimes Norwegian, Icelandic, or Finnish) listeners were read and commented on. The letters were most often highly enthusiastic, vividly praising the GDR's progressive politics, the efficiency of its health care system, the fundamental solidarity of the East German people, the country's work for world peace, and so on. Questions were also posed to the RBI staff, ranging from whether or not the stores in GDR offered fresh fruit to what the *dictatorship of the proletariat* really meant.

Sometimes the selection of letters answered in the Swedish program came from listeners in non-Nordic countries, in which case the program was renamed *The International Letterbox* (*Internationella brevlådan*). The inclusion of letters from listeners in countries such as India, Tunisia, Indonesia, and Colombia was not only designed to create an impression of the RBI signal's technical quality and international strength; it also constructed a very conscious image of global interest in and sympathy with the GDR and its struggle for socialism. A manuscript from October 1, 1989, cheerfully recites worldwide congratulations on the GDR's fortieth anniversary; in their letters, the listeners express their warmest appreciation for the country's leading work in the service of world peace and nuclear disarmament.[17]

Such programs were, of course, highly formulaic, and were in keeping with the government-sanctioned emphasis on the idea of an unfailingly triumphant GDR—even at a time when the country faced political, economic, and administrative problems of the most severe nature. For GDR citizens, the absence of democratic structures had also led to a fundamental distrust in the socialist system many had once held in high regard.[18] During the four decades of its existence, the country had developed into a repressive authoritarian state with a secret police that surveilled, registered, and imprisoned thousands of its own citizens. Toward the mid-1980s, it also became clear that the GDR's economic crisis was beyond repair. Nevertheless, the SED refused to acknowledge this and put on a sizable celebration of the country's fortieth anniversary shortly before the fall of the Berlin Wall. As a state propaganda instrument, RBI paid due attention to these festivities, vividly cheering them on. At the same time, dissent grew in East German society, which saw a series of demonstrations in the weeks leading up to November 9.

## The Listener

In his book *Listening on the Short Waves,* Jerome S. Berg writes that identifying the shortwave audience is at best "an inexact process."[19] The questions of how many listened to different stations and what stations they listened to are virtually impossible to answer. A reasonable guess is that a fair share of RBI listeners worldwide were simply shortwave enthusiasts belonging to the highly motivated community of so-called DXers, who were in it not for the program content, but for the thrill of tracing and collecting distant signals. Upon registering a signal from afar, the DXer would write a reception report as a form of detailed feedback to the radio station about time and frequency, the quality of the signal, and the content of the broadcast. To the DXers who sent in their reception reports to RBI, the station, like any other shortwave radio station, would return a written approval or verification of contact—a so-called QSL card or acknowledgement of receipt—which became a collector's item for the listener. RBI would also take the opportunity to send listeners GDR publicity, clothing, gifts, and souvenirs. This cultural practice is a key element in any study of shortwave radio and indicates that we need to understand shortwave radio as a system or an ensemble encompassing a range of different media: printed, material, visual, and auditory.

For the Swedish listener, the RBI signal did not need to travel very far, and it is unlikely that it was considered exotic in comparison with more distant signals from East Asia, Africa, or Australia. Quite possibly, a large portion of the Swedish listeners were actively seeking out the East German station, either for ideological reasons or simply in order to hear "another side of the story," which could be different from what they experienced domestically.[20] Some listeners' letters indeed indicate that this was the case; in the words of one, "I value the opportunity to be informed not only by our own media and their Western perspectives."[21] The act of tuning to the RBI (or any other shortwave radio station) could therefore have been intended to inform oneself by shifting one's ideological, cultural, and geographical horizon.

Both in responding to letters and in their other activities, the RBI hosts were obliged to follow a strict ideological protocol and were closely monitored by the State Committee for Radio. Their task was to give problems in GDR society a degree of visibility but to address these problems in a constructive tone, turning listeners' attention to the positive aspects of the

GDR's accomplishments (or to say that West Germany was really to blame for any hardships East Germans suffered, given the heavy war debts that the FRG still owed the GDR—a common theme in the reports as well as in the government's official historical narrative). A typical example of this occurred when engaged listener Erik, from Halmstad, Sweden, wrote that he doubted if the GDR, under the circumstances, would ever be able to fulfill its promised full-scale housing program.[22] The answer to Erik was sadly no, but "even if the GDR has been mismanaged in many ways that led the country into a deep crisis, many positive things have also happened. We *cannot* forget that."[23]

RBI established a particular relationship with its Swedish listeners, some of whom (like Erik) seem to have written frequently to the hosts, often addressing them directly by name—Jan, Jörgen, Volker, and so on. A listener from Åstorp asked if RBI could connect him with somebody in the GDR who wanted a pen pal in Sweden or if he could possibly stop by the radio station to visit the hosts. To both questions, the answer was no; however, if he ever found his way to Berlin, there would certainly be time for a coffee downtown.[24] And when a listener from Norway anxiously asked, in 1989, if her previous letters had arrived, she received a reassuring answer in the midst of the political turmoil: "No need to worry. To be sure, we have received the letters. But during these days there has simply been so much to do that we have neglected to confirm. I believe we have already thanked you for the beautiful postcard you sent on our 40th anniversary. Have we not?"[25]

An important ingredient of *The Letterbox*'s close connection with its Swedish listeners was the birthday greetings with which the program concluded. Another was the recurring GDR quiz, to which listeners could send in answers and whose winners were named and congratulated. Listeners could also request songs to be played in the program—"Neue Helden" by GDR pop group Puhdys or Western music like Kaoma's hit "Lambada." A recurring segment in the program was also the "Stevie Wonder Spot," where the singer's song "Happy Birthday" would be played.

Fostering listener engagement was, of course, not exclusive to RBI; it was a fundamental characteristic of both international and national radio throughout the twentieth century. Early on, radio was formed as a media companion with a distinct social relationship to its listeners. This has made some media scholars discuss radio as an intimate medium that touches at a distance. Radio lacks the visual intrusiveness of television; while television is one-to-many, radio is one-to-one, for the experience of radio is that of listening to a voice talking directly to the listener. Paddy Scannell has described this in terms of a "for-anyone-as-someone" structure; radio's address is personal, although not directed at a specific person.[26] In addition, Andrew Crisell and David Hendy have both pointed to radio's blindness, which lays a foundation for the production of images in the listener's mind. Thus, at least to a certain extent, Hendy argues, we can even talk about a "coproduction" of program content between station and listener.[27]

It is clear from reading *The Letterbox* manuscripts that the RBI hosts' familiar voices, sincere and friendly, were intended to nurture a continuing and courteous conversation with the listener in the informal mode of address made possible by radio, the ultimate everyday media companion. Again, we cannot be entirely sure that the letters were authentic, which means that the extent to which we can establish a relationship of coproduction or even communication is limited. However, to conceptualize RBI listeners as merely a silent audience passively subjected to propaganda would be to neglect the valuable insights that scholars of media audiences have given us over the last decades. And, as we shall see next, when the traditional RBI script was suddenly challenged, actual radio listeners did seem to have played an active part in the joint enterprise of making sense of the chaotic moment.

## The Emergence of an Alternative Script

In the autumn of 1989, Swedish listeners had a special reason to tune in to the RBI broadcasts and seek information about what was happening in Berlin, given the political turmoil leading up to the events in November. Thorbjörn from Lindesberg, for example, expressed excitement about being able to hear "open" and "interesting" reports from the center of events. The listeners also sent their warmest wishes on the basis of international solidarity and sometimes a sense of Northern European common history. Lennart from Jönköping wrote that he often thought about the GDR and its people against the background of Germany's twentieth-century history of war and destruction and was hoping for a peaceful transition.[28]

However, alongside such letters praising GDR society and confirmations from the hosts that everything was moving along nicely despite the political commotion, a new and more ambivalent script was introduced in the October and November broadcasts. It began with self-reflection on the part of the hosts. When a postcard from listener Bengt from Kungsbacka was read in the broadcast on November 26, saying "this is a development I have awaited for 20 years," RBI host Jan commented first by thanking Bengt for "not giving up on RBI." Jan then continued on a more personal note, telling the story of how he began working at RBI "about ten years ago" and how, over the years, he had felt that the dialogue with Bengt and other listeners had somehow diminished. "Many times," Jan said, "I thought about quitting my job, but then the [East German] October revolution came."²⁹ Jan described the peaceful revolution as a blessing, a long-awaited event that would keep him going. Although it is unclear why he thought his connection to listeners had declined, with this, Jan suddenly gave voice to a script that diverged considerably from the norm.

There were also instances when RBI's self-reflection transformed into self-criticism. Here it was often the listeners who were allowed to voice the sharpest critique, with which the hosts could then agree. On November 5, a letter by a French listener was cited in the broadcast: "So far I have had sympathy for your country. Mostly because of your antifascist agenda and your commitment to peace. I have also admired the accomplishments of your athletes. But recent events have been a cold shower for me. Why have you at RBI not even *tried* to explain what is happening, but just kept a stony—and no doubt baffled—silence??? I fear that other listeners have also condemned your silence. This has damaged your credibility."³⁰

The radio host answered the accusation in the French letter by turning directly to the (Swedish) listener: "However painful it may be, we have to admit that this criticism is justified. Only a few weeks ago, even we at the RBI preferred—like other media in our country—to tell a story of successes and achievements, instead of reporting about the real problems, contradictions, and sad circumstances here. We did it partly because we did not want anyone to have a bad impression of our country, and partly because we wanted to accommodate the official media policy."³¹

An interpretation of the last sentence could be that there was suddenly a window for the RBI hosts to say that they no longer wanted to follow "the official media policy." The traditional script was no longer valid; to say the least, everything was not OK in the GDR. The content of RBI's Swedish broadcasts could no longer be fully dictated by the SED—or rather, the SED no longer represented the people. And we can identify the use of *we* at least twice in the quote above: the "we have to admit" that embraced the listener as part of a transnational community and the "we at the RBI" that was responsible for the biased reporting. The mix of identification and shifts in address might reflect two simultaneous scripts—one existing and traditional, one emerging alternative—scripts that often also coexisted within each individual radio host.

Another listener, the above-mentioned Bengt from Kungsbacka, delivered extraordinarily harsh feedback about the content of the Swedish RBI broadcasts on October 29: "The stream of discontented GDR citizens is apparently interesting for the whole world . . . but does apparently not bother the GDR government, which continues to deny the existing problems. And no reforms are necessary. But why not ask all citizens in the GDR what they think is wrong with their country.... I hope that this arrogant and condescending attitude that has marked the comments in the Swedish-language broadcasts will be replaced by a more humble approach."[32]

Bengt's stern criticism, including his accusations of arrogance on the part of the RBI, was met with a reflexive comment—"What do you say when you get such a slap in the face?"—after which the host gravely addressed the whole radio audience: "Yes, we do agree with Bengt in most of his criticism. The GDR has suffered great human, political and economic losses. It is an open wound that will hurt for a long time. Everybody in this socialist society needs to ask how this could happen and what I personally, and all of us, have done wrong."[33]

This response mirrored another theme in the RBI's reporting on current events in autumn 1989: sorrow and guilt. On the evening of November 9, when people outside were dancing on the Berlin Wall, host Angelica introduced the broadcast with a sorrowful personal reflection, also adding to the impression that these broadcasts reflected multiple scripts. For while some hosts were openly pro-unification, others, such as Angelica, were more ambivalent:

> A warm welcome to Radio Berlin International and an autumnal Berlin! Learning how to respect and understand the paradoxes of life is hard and takes effort, but is very necessary. The GDR of today is contradictory... On the one hand, the people who have decided to stay here are active, energetic and even happy in a way. They really want to change and create something new, something of their own. On the other hand, the joy is ambiguous since so many of their countrymen no longer have the power and will to fight but instead choose to seek happiness in the promised land on the other side of the border. Naturally this feels extremely depressing.[34]

At other times a listener's letter was stereotypically cheerful, showing great trust in the GDR to overcome its titanic problems, but the radio hosts' comments were considerably more gloomy. On December 10, the hosts cited a letter from a Norwegian listener, who expressed his faith in coming reforms and the idea that the so-called refugee problem of thousands of East Germans escaping the country would soon be over. The radio host was, however, skeptical, and addressed this particular listener in a conversational one-to-one:

> Yes, the GDR is facing the beginning of a new era in which the people jointly want to save and rebuild the country, as you say. But I am not certain that our people are, at this point, prepared for absolute loyalty and diligence. To be sure, much has already changed here. The borders are open, a lot of restructuring

has taken place in different political authorities and on different levels, and free elections have been promised. But new scandals, cases of corruption, and other things are still rising to the surface. Old structures, old thinking, prohibit progress in so many areas.[35]

Toward the end of 1989, the RBI hosts sometimes even aired direct and explicit criticism of the country's leadership, unthinkable just a few months before. Their analysis was that the people of the GDR had been deceived by the SED and that the SED had failed to reform the country in its most difficult time. The massive criticism that had long been building up among dissidents and led to the fall of the Berlin Wall had, by December 1989, found its way into RBI, the main outlet for GDR state propaganda abroad. With this new or parallel script, RBI suddenly reflected not the official version of the future, but quite possibly East German people's wishes and hopes. It was a time of self-reflection and self-analysis. In *Broadcasting on the Short Waves*, Berg quotes an RBI announcer during a farewell program: "I think [we tried] to give as accurate a picture as possible under the circumstances . . . There was no choice but to stick to the rules and present the official views which quite often were a far cry from reality, particularly in the final stage of the old regime. And for that I feel that I have to apologize."[36]

## Off the Air

The years around 1990 were what historian John J. Ikenberry has called a "reordering moment" in history.[37] For GDR media, the reordering process was swift and relentless. Within a few months after the opening of the Berlin Wall, the formerly hegemonic State Radio Committee for Radio and its sister organization, the State Television Committee, were both completely dissolved, thus ending the socialist party's control over broadcasting.[38] And on October 3, 1990, the two Germanies merged into one.

"Davon geht die Welt nicht unter"—"The world will not end because of this"—Swedish singer Zarah Leander once sang confidently in the 1930s, but that October, it actually did. The German Democratic Republic no longer existed, RBI was shut down, and, as if a symbol of larger processes, the station's transmitters and frequencies were taken over by Deutsche Welle (DW), the former West German station. On the day before Germany's official unification (Tag der Deutschen Einheit), the final English-language broadcast contained melancholic comments from RBI hosts such as "that was it" and "the last day of the good old GDR," and the broadcast was accompanied by Swedish band Europe's "The Final Countdown" and Pink Floyd's "Goodbye Blue Sky."[39]

By zooming in on *The Letterbox*, this chapter has pointed to two different scripts that coexisted at RBI during this politically and socially turbulent moment—a traditional script determined by state-socialist propaganda and a new script that opened up a space for criticism and also an element of liveness and improvisation. On a general level, and in contrast to much other research on shortwave radio during the Cold War, this chapter has also argued for the need for perspectives on broadcasting that not only transcend the national framework (which is often taken for granted), but also take into account the international listener. On a specific level, it has supported recent research in arguing that not even state-sanctioned and strictly formalized GDR propaganda is simply propaganda. Indeed, broadcasting history, as Paddy Scannell and David Cardiff state in their much-cited book about the history of the BBC, cannot just take into account the sender and the content, but must, by necessity, be a social history. Broadcasting history, they argue, "embodies, always, a communicative intention which is the mark of a social relationship."[40] In the case of RBI, every radio program was shaped by considerations of its audience. The Swedish broadcasts were a point of exchange and circulation between RBI producers and the Swedish listener.

Such a social history of radio is a synthetic ambition that extends beyond radio itself and its institutional organization or output. We need to acknowledge that the audience, for example, is always a participant in or cocreator of even the most centralized broadcasting venture. And sometimes this audience is not at home, but far away. The traces of Swedes listening to RBI, writing letters to a station on the other side of the Iron Curtain, are but one such example. And although they present challenges as sources, the multivoiced manuscripts from *The Letterbox* program in the autumn of 1989 stand as documentation of a transborder dialogue about a reordering moment in history, an era of European remapping at the end of a Cold War.

NOTES

1. Odermann, *Wellen mit tausend Klängen*, 145.
2. Ibid., 38–39.
3. Paulu, *Radio and Television Broadcasting*, 229.
4. Hixon, *Parting the Curtain*; Nelson, *War of the Black Heavens*; Puddington, *Broadcasting Freedom*; Cummings, *Cold War Radio*; Schlosser, *Cold War on the Airwaves*; and Wasburn, *Broadcasting Propaganda*.
5. The BBC World Service was named the BBC Imperial Service (1932–1939) and the BBC External Service, including the BBC Overseas Service and the BBC European Service (1939–1962). See Ribeiro and Seul, "Revisiting Transnational Broadcasting."
6. von Geldern, "Radio Moscow"; Lommers, *Europe—On Air*; and Lovell, *Russia in the Microphone Age*.

7. Substantial research has been done on the GDR's media system, national radio, and television, but in these otherwise rich accounts, the East German international broadcasting station is nowhere to be found. For a general history of RBI, we have been left largely to rely on a few (rather GDR-apologetic) accounts by Fischer and Odermann, based on their own experiences working at RBI. See Odermann, *Wellen mit tausend Klängen*; and Fischer, "Radio Berlin International," 146–153. There are two MA theses on RBI: Röck, "Radio Berlin International"; and Fabian, "Die Selbstdarstellung der DDR im Auslandsrundfunk." For research on the GDR media system, see Holzweißig, *Die schärfste Waffe der Partei*; and Zahlmann, *Wie im Western, nur anders*. On GDR radio, see Arnold and Classen, *Zwischen Pop und Propaganda*; and Arnold, *Kalter Krieg im Äther*. On GDR television, see Steinmetz and Viehoff, *Deutsches Fernsehen Ost*; Behling, *Fernsehen aus Adlershof*; Gumbert, *Envisioning Socialism*; and Beutelschmidt, *Ost—West—Global*.

8. Wood, *History of International Broadcasting*, 153.

9. See Roth-Ey, *Moscow Prime Time*; Gumbert, *Envisioning Socialism*; Imre, *TV Socialism*; and Mihelj and Huxtable, *From Media Systems to Media Cultures*.

10. Steinmetz and Viehoff, *Deutsches Fernsehen Ost*, 22–23.

11. Badenoch, Fickers, and Henrich-Franke, *Airy Curtains in the European Ether*.

12. DRA Potsdam-Babelsberg, Digitalisierte Bestände, Sendepläne Hörfunk, Radio Berlin International, Schwedische Redaktion, R03030. Later the same year, on December 1, RBI started broadcasting in Danish. The prioritization of Danish could probably be explained by the fact that the country was the GDR's neighbor and therefore a strategically useful target for East German information, especially in the border region of Schleswig-Holstein. See Odermann, *Wellen mit tausend Klängen*, 251; Fabian, "Die Selbstdarstellung der DDR im Auslandsrundfunk"; and DRA Potsdam-Babelsberg, Digitalisierte Bestände, Sendepläne Hörfunk, Radio Berlin International.

13. Usually the broadcasts were on middle wave from 9:15 p.m. to 9:40 p.m. and on shortwave from 6:00 p.m. to 6:30 p.m. and 9:15 p.m. to 9:40 p.m. DRA Potsdam-Babelsberg, Schriftgut Hörfunk, RBI, Schwedische Redaktion, R01020.

14. Bohn et al., *Deutsch-skandinavische*; Linderoth, *Kampen för erkännande*; Friis and Linderoth, *DDR og Norden*; and Abraham, *Die politische Auslandsarbeit der DDR in Schweden*.

15. Almgren, *Inte bara Stasi*.

16. Odermann, *Wellen mit tausend Klängen*, 146.

17. DRA Potsdam-Babelsberg, Schriftgut Hörfunk, RBI, Hörerpost ab 1.1.1989 bis 31.12.1989, Schwedische Redaktion, 1989-11-01.

18. See Fulbrook, *The People's State*.

19. Berg, *Listening on the Short Waves*, 16.

20. An important question, of course, is whether or not we can trust RBI's manuscripts to give us the written words of actual listeners. We should be cautious in reading too much into the accounts without confirming them with other sources, especially given the fact that authentic letters stamped in Sweden are not saved in the archive.

21. DRA Potsdam-Babelsberg, Schriftgut Hörfunk, RBI, Hörerpost ab 1.1.1989 bis 31.12.1989, Schwedische Redaktion, 1989-11-05.

22. In Sweden, the relationship between the GDR and Swedish citizens is still a sensitive issue. For ethical reasons, I have therefore chosen to alter the names of the listeners in this text.

23. DRA Potsdam-Babelsberg, Schriftgut Hörfunk, RBI, Hörerpost ab 1.1.1989 bis 31.12.1989, Schwedische Redaktion, 1989-12-11.

24. DRA Potsdam-Babelsberg, Schriftgut Hörfunk, RBI, Hörerpost ab 1.1.1989 bis 31.12.1989, Schwedische Redaktion, 1989-08-03.

25. DRA Potsdam-Babelsberg, Schriftgut Hörfunk, RBI, Hörerpost ab 1.1.1989 bis 31.12.1989, Schwedische Redaktion, 1989-11-19.

26. Lacey, *Listening Publics*; and Scannell, "For-Anyone-as-Someone Structures." The understanding of sound "touching at a distance" is attributed to Schafer, *The Soundscape*.

27. Crisell, *Understanding Radio*; and Hendy, *Radio in the Global Age*, 115–122.
28. All quotations from DRA Potsdam-Babelsberg, Schriftgut Hörfunk, RBI, Hörerpost ab 1.1.1989 bis 31.12.1989, Schwedische Redaktion, 1989-12-10.
29. DRA Potsdam-Babelsberg, Schriftgut Hörfunk, RBI, Hörerpost ab 1.1.1989 bis 31.12.1989, Schwedische Redaktion, 1989-11-26.
30. DRA Potsdam-Babelsberg, Schriftgut Hörfunk, RBI, Hörerpost ab 1.1.1989 bis 31.12.1989, Schwedische Redaktion, 1989-11-05.
31. Ibid.
32. DRA Potsdam-Babelsberg, Schriftgut Hörfunk, RBI, Hörerpost ab 1.1.1989 bis 31.12.1989, Schwedische Redaktion, 1989-10-29.
33. Ibid.
34. DRA Potsdam-Babelsberg, Schriftgut Hörfunk, RBI, Hörerpost ab 1.1.1989 bis 31.12.1989, Schwedische Redaktion, 1989-11-09.
35. DRA Potsdam-Babelsberg, Schriftgut Hörfunk, RBI, Hörerpost ab 1.1.1989 bis 31.12.1989, Schwedische Redaktion, 1989-12-10.
36. Berg, *Broadcasting on the Short Waves*, 53.
37. Ikenberry, *After Victory*.
38. Stein, *Vom Fernsehen und Radio der DDR zur ARD*.
39. Internet Archive, "Radio Berlin International."
40. Scannell and Cardiff, *A Social History of British Broadcasting*, xi.

## BIBLIOGRAPHY

Abraham, Nils. *Die politische Auslandsarbeit der DDR in Schweden: Zur public diplomacy der DDR gegenüber Schweden nach der diplomatische Anerkennung 1972–1989*. Berlin: LIT, 2007.

Almgren, Birgitta. *Inte bara Stasi: Relationer Sverige-DDR 1949–1990*. Stockholm: Carlsson, 2009.

Arnold, Klaus. *Kalter Krieg im Äther: Der Deutschlandsender und die Westpropaganda der DDR*. Münster: LIT, 2002.

Arnold, Klaus, and Christoph Classen, eds. *Zwischen Pop und Propaganda: Radio in der DDR*. Berlin: Ch. Links, 2004.

Badenoch, Alexander, Andreas Fickers, and Christian Henrich-Franke, eds. *Airy Curtains in the European Ether: Broadcasting and the Cold War*. Baden-Baden: Nomos, 2013.

Behling, Klaus. *Fernsehen aus Adlershof: Das Fernsehen der DDR vom Start bis zum Sendeschluss*. Berlin: edition berolina, 2016.

Berg, Jerome S. *Broadcasting on the Short Waves: 1945 to Today*. Jefferson, NC: McFarland, 2008.

———. *Listening on the Short Waves: 1945 to Today*. Jefferson, NC: McFarland, 2008.

Beutelschmidt, Thomas. *Ost—West—Global: Das sozialistische Fernsehen im kalten Krieg*. Leipzig: VISTAS, 2017.

Bohn, Robert, Jürgen Elvert, and Karl-Christian Lammers, eds. *Deutsch-skandinavische Beziehungen nach 1945*. Stuttgart: Franz Steiner, 2000.

Crisell, Andrew. *Understanding Radio*. 2nd ed. London: Routledge, 1994.

Cummings, Richard. *Cold War Radio: The Dangerous History of American Broadcasting in Europe, 1950–1989*. Jefferson, NC: McFarland, 2009.

Fabian, Cornelia. "Die Selbstdarstellung der DDR im Auslandsrundfunk: Das Beispiel der dänischen Redaktion." MA Thesis, University of Göttingen, 2006.

Fischer, Klaus. "Radio Berlin International—die Stimme des Friedens und des Sozialismus aus Berlin." In *Erinnerungen von Pionieren und Aktivisten des Rundfunks der DDR. Band 2*, 146–153. Berlin: Lektorat Rundfunksgeschichte, 1990.

Friis, Thomas Wegener, and Andreas Linderoth, eds. *DDR og Norden: Østtysk-nordiske relationer 1949–1989*. Odense: Syddansk universitetsforlag, 2005.

Fulbrook, Mary. *The People's State: East German Society from Hitler to Honecker*. New Haven, CT: Yale University Press, 2005.

Gumbert, Heather. *Envisioning Socialism: Television and the Cold War in the German Democratic Republic*. Ann Arbor: University of Michigan Press, 2014.

Hendy, David. *Radio in the Global Age*. Cambridge: Polity, 2002.

Hixon, Walter L. *Parting the Curtain: Propaganda, Culture and the Cold War, 1945–1961*. New York: St. Martin's, 1996.

Holzweißig, Gunter. *Die schärfste Waffe der Partei: eine Mediengeschichte der DDR*. Köln: Böhlau, 2002.

Ikenberry, G. John. *After Victory: Institutions, Strategic Restraint, and the Rebuilding of Order after Major Wars*. Princeton, NJ: Princeton University Press, 2001.

Imre, Anikó. *TV Socialism*. Durham, NC: Duke University Press, 2016.

Internet Archive. "Radio Berlin International, October 2 1990." October 2, 1990. Accessed January 15, 2019. https://archive.org/details/RadioBerlinInternationalOctober21990.

Johnson, A. Ross. *Radio Free Europe and Radio Liberty: The CIA Years and Beyond*. Stanford: Stanford University Press, 2010.

Lacey, Kate. *Listening Publics: The Politics and Experience of Listening in the Media Age*. Cambridge: Polity, 2013.

Linderoth, Andreas. *Kampen för erkännande: DDR:s utrikespolitik gentemot Sverige, 1949–1972*. Lund: Historiska institutionen, 2002.

Lommers, Suzanne. *Europe—On Air: Interwar Projects for Radio Broadcasting*. Amsterdam: Amsterdam University Press, 2012.

Lovell, Stephen. *Russia in the Microphone Age: A History of Soviet Radio, 1919–1970*. Oxford: Oxford University Press, 2015.

Mihelj, Sabina, and Simon Huxtable. *From Media Systems to Media Cultures: Understanding Socialist Television*. Cambridge: Cambridge University Press, 2018.

Nelson, Michael. *War of the Black Heavens: The Battles of Western Broadcasting in the Cold War*. London: Brassey's, 1997.

Odermann, Heinz. *Wellen mit tausend Klängen: Geschichten rund um den Erdball in Sendungen des Auslandsrundfunks der DDR Radio Berlin International*. Berlin: Vistas, 2003.

Paulu, Burton. *Radio and Television Broadcasting in Eastern Europe*. Minneapolis: University of Minnesota Press, 1974.

Puddington, Arch. *Broadcasting Freedom: The Cold War Triumph of Radio Free Europe and Radio Liberty*. Lexington: University Press of Kentucky, 2000.

Ribeiro, Nelson, and Stephanie Seul. "Revisiting Transnational Broadcasting: The BBC's Foreign Language Services in the Second World War." *Media History* 21, no. 4 (2015): 365–377.

Röck, Claus-Dieter. "Radio Berlin International. Struktur und Entwicklung des Auslandsrundfunks der DDR." MA Thesis, Freie Universität Berlin, 1996.

Roth-Ey, Kristin. *Moscow Prime Time: How the Soviet Union Built the Media Empire That Lost the Cultural Cold War*. Ithaca, NY: Cornell University Press, 2011.

Scannell, Paddy. "For-Anyone-as-Someone Structures." *Media, Culture and Society* 22, no. 1 (2000): 5–24.

Scannell, Paddy, and David Cardiff. *A Social History of British Broadcasting, Volume One 1922–1939: Serving the Nation*. Oxford: Basil Blackwell, 1991.

Schafer, R. Murray. *The Soundscape: Our Sonic Environment and the Tuning of the World*. Rochester, VT: Destiny Books, 1994.

Schlosser, Nicholas J. *Cold War on the Airwaves: The Radio Propaganda War against East Germany*. Urbana: University of Illinois, 2015.

Stein, Reiner. *Vom Fernsehen und Radio der DDR zur ARD: Die Entwicklung und Neuordnung des Rundfunkwesens in den neuen Bundesländern*. Marburg: Tectum, 2000.

Steinmetz, Rüdiger, and Reinhold Viehoff. *Deutsches Fernsehen Ost: Eine Programmgeschichte des DDR-Fernsehens*. Berlin: Verlag für Berlin-Brandenburg, 2008.

von Geldern, James. "Radio Moscow: The Voice from the Center." In *Culture and Entertainment in Wartime Russia*, edited by Richard Stites, 44–61. Bloomington: Indiana University Press, 1995.

Wasburn, Philo. *Broadcasting Propaganda: International Radio Broadcasting and the Construction of Political Reality*. Westport, CT: Praeger, 1992.

Wood, James. *History of International Broadcasting, vol 2*. London: Peregrinus, 2000.

Zahlmann, Stefan, ed. *Wie im Western, nur anders: Medien in der DDR*. Berlin: Panama, 2010.

MARIE CRONQVIST is Associate Professor of Media History and Journalism at Lund University. She is editor (with Lina Sturfelt) of *War Remains: Mediations of Suffering and Death in the Era of the World Wars* (2018) and (with Rosanna Farbøl and Casper Sylvest) of *Cold War Civil Defence in Western Europe: Sociotechnical Imaginaries of Survival and Preparedness* (2022).

# PART III. TRANSLATION

CHAPTER 9

## ON SOVIET SPOKEN CINEMA

Elena Razlogova

ON A HOT JULY EVENING in 1965, M. U. Livshits took his wife to the movies. He later described his experience in a letter to the chairman of the State Committee for Cinematography of the Ukrainian Soviet Socialist Republic.[1] Livshits introduced himself as "not an art worker, but an ordinary Soviet person."[2] The couple bought tickets at more than double the regular price, not knowing the film titles—only that they were "prize-winning pictures from the latest Moscow film festival." They saw the double feature in a Palace of Sports, together with ten thousand Kiev residents. Livshits did not enjoy the screening. In the British comedy *A Stitch in Time* (dir. Robert Asher, 1963), the slapstick was clumsy, the plot unbelievable, and the translator from English, who was interpreting via loudspeaker over the original soundtrack, "kept mixing up the dialogue" (the picture was bought for distribution in 1964 but had not yet been dubbed). Livshits was equally shocked by the Italian melodrama *Time of Indifference* (*Gli indifferenti*, dir. Francesco Maselli, 1964). Its "dirty" love affairs could "elicit nothing but disgust from a Soviet person." The film was never purchased for distribution and thus was not dubbed either. Livshits pronounced both films lacking in "proper ideology" (*"bezydeinyi"*) and useful "content" (*"nesoderzhatel'nyi"*). He blamed film exhibitors' greed. "In our country, business profits matter least of all. But here the opposite was true," he argued. "The administration of the Palace of Sports took from me, and tens of thousands of workers like me, one ruble twenty kopeks for this: my wife and I sat for more than three hours high up near the dome roof, without any air circulation, and did not get any moral pleasure."

This delightful denunciation points to an alternative distribution circuit for foreign cinema in the Soviet Union. Foreign films considered for purchase were vetted by the Central Committee of the Communist Party of the USSR in the 1950s and a committee of political and cultural experts in the 1960s and 1970s. Sovexportfilm, the state film import and export organization, then bought approved films for distribution. Censors cut objectionable scenes, and actors dubbed each picture in a way that omitted suspect dialogue. A specific number of copies, depending on the film's political value and its potential audience, went into theaters.[3] Yet Livshits describes a public screening outside of Moscow or Leningrad, where several thousand ordinary spectators saw two foreign films uncut, with only a translator's voice coming through the loudspeaker over the original dialogue. This popular and profitable practice persisted in the Soviet Union until the late 1980s.

Throughout the Soviet Union, millions of people saw uncensored foreign films through this alternative film distribution network, which simultaneous film translation made possible. This network encompassed international film festivals, various public theaters, closed picture shows at cultural and scientific institutions and the dachas of the party elite, and provincial cineclubs and pirate screenings at makeshift venues. Each show incorporated a translator, who provided simultaneous Russian voice-over via a microphone from a special booth or from a jury-rigged station at the back of the room.[4] This exhibition format promoted a particular mode of spectatorship, where each film screening became a unique event because of the translator's live performance. Silent film historian Alain Boillat calls this practice "spoken cinema," to distinguish from "talking movies" with a recorded vocal track.[5] As Thai film scholar May Adadol Ingawanij and others have shown, spoken cinema survived beyond the silent era, in some regions into the 1980s, both in the socialist Second World and in the nonaligned Third World.[6]

Audiovisual translation theory focused on dubbing and subtitles cannot fully account for spoken cinema, a model associated with silent film commentators, from *benshi* in Japan to *bonimenteurs* in Québec. Theoretical critiques of translation in sound cinema—Ella Shohat and Robert Stam's Eurocentric "grafting" of translation, John Mowitt's "bilingual enunciation," and Abé Mark Nornes's "abusive subtitling," for example—focus on the film as a text and assume the finality of translation burned into the filmstrip as subtitles or an overdubbed soundtrack.[7] But spoken cinema was a live performance that precluded a stable text. The proper object for a history of cinema in live translation is not the film as a text but the encounter between the film and its audience during projection—or, as Tom Gunning puts it, "the place of the local in the history of a medium that aspires to the international, and indeed, the universal."[8] Live translation, in the Soviet Union and elsewhere, denaturalized the dominant modes of foreign sound-film exhibition.

This chapter addresses the crucial role of imperfect translation in the reception of foreign cinema in the USSR and of Soviet cinema at European festivals. It focuses on the Moscow International Film Festival (biannual after 1959) and the Tashkent Festival for Asian, African, and—eventually—Latin American Cinema (biannual after 1968, including Latin America after 1976), both of which aimed to one-up major European festivals by serving as the gateway to film cultures of socialist Eastern Europe and postcolonial Asia, Africa, and Latin America. Rossen Djagalov and Masha Salazkina propose that the Tashkent festival should be understood as a "contact zone," Mary Louise Pratt's term for colonial border zones where cultural and linguistic exchanges take place in the context of radical inequality.[9] Pratt borrows her term from linguistics, "where the term *contact language* refers to an improvised language that develops among speakers of different tongues who need to communicate with each other consistently, usually in the context of trade. Such languages begin as pidgins, and are called creoles when they come to have native speakers of their own. Like the societies of the contact zone, such languages are commonly regarded as chaotic, barbarous and lacking in structure."[10]

Much in this description applies to Soviet live film translation—it was also improvised, chaotic, and often criticized. Some foreign visitors cited loudspeaker translation as one of the major shortcomings of Soviet festivals, somewhere in between substandard competition lineups and abrasive toilet paper. Yet other spectators found it pleasurable and revealing. As a performance, simultaneous film translation foregrounded makeshift and fleeting ways of understanding another language. Arguing against "homolingual" linguistic transparency, theorist Naoki Sakai proposes a notion of "heterolingual address" that "does not abide by normalcy of reciprocal and transparent communication, but instead assumes that every utterance can fail to communicate because heterogeneity is inherent in any medium, linguistic or otherwise."[11] This chapter argues that improvised heterolingual Soviet film translation enabled transnational cinematic connections in the

Soviet Union and beyond, transgressing Soviet officials' original vision for live translation as an ideological weapon.

## Official Soviet Film Translation at European Festivals

The Soviet Union used live film translation to compete for primacy on the European film festival scene. This translation method had both plebeian and elite local precedents. In the 1920s, trained lectors combined political education and translation when they explained silent films from abroad and from various Soviet republics to multilingual worker and peasant audiences. In the Stalinist 1930s, the few foreign films in Soviet theaters were dubbed. But domestic and foreign films with Russian-language dialogue circulated in remote areas of Soviet republics without dubbing or subtitling in the local languages. In these regions, a 1938 note to party leadership complained, "unvetted, ignorant translators explain the dialogue during screenings, often distorting the meaning of the film."[12] On the elite end, Joseph Stalin and his circle watched foreign films regularly but banned professional interpreters from screenings. Instead, Minister of Cinema Ivan Bolshakov recited from memory the Russian lines for foreign dialogue, translated beforehand by professionals. Stalin preferred mysteries and Westerns and especially enjoyed onscreen brawls.[13]

These ad hoc domestic practices informed the Soviet policy for screening films in live translation at European film festivals. Benito Mussolini inaugurated the first international film festival in Venice in 1932. The Soviet Union countered in 1935 with a festival in Moscow, and France launched the Cannes film festival in 1939, though it was aborted by the Nazi invasion. After World War II, major European film festivals became Cold War battlegrounds, and in 1946, the USSR sent delegations to three such festivals: Cannes, Venice, and Karlovy Vary in Czechoslovakia. That year, the Resolution of the Council of Ministers of the USSR of July 22, 1946, cosigned by Stalin, proclaimed the most important goal of Soviet festival participation to be "the all-out popularization and promotion of Soviet films abroad, and before all, in the host festival countries."[14]

The Soviet leadership considered film translation indispensable for these promotional efforts. At the Venice festival, from August 31 to September 15, 1946, regulations required films to be shown entirely without translation, in their "original versions." That would not do for the Soviets. Sergei Budaev, head of the Soviet delegation at Venice, reported, "Italian spectators could understand an English, American, or French picture, because they more or less knew English and French. But most Italians do not speak Russian, and one cannot properly understand a film about life in the Soviet

Union without knowing Russian."[15] Overcoming the resistance of Venice festival organizers, the Soviet delegation brought professional announcers from Rome to translate all Soviet documentary and feature films. Thanks in part to this live commentary, Budaev claimed, Italian audiences loved the features *Chapayev* (dir. Sergei and Georgi Vasiliev, 1934), about a popular hero of the Russian Civil War, and *The Vow* (*Kliatva*, dir. Mikhail Chiaureli, 1946), a Stalin biopic, and responded well to documentary films on sports, parades, Central Asia, and other propagandist themes. Budaev reported that spectators applauded every time Stalin spoke, his words translated into Italian. "Our decision to show films with announcers' help completely justified itself," he concluded.[16]

At Cannes, from September 20 to October 5 of the same year, all films also played in their national, untranslated versions. Only the festival jury got special synopses explaining the plot. Again, the Soviets demurred. Soviet films, delegation head Mikhail Kalatozov argued, were different from others presented at the festival: "They possess ideological saturation and content and require detailed elucidation of the meaning and text of the picture."[17] Festival organizers and jury members from Great Britain, Egypt, Sweden, and the United States argued that showing a picture with translation using a microphone and a loudspeaker would give Soviets an unfair advantage over other countries, who did not prepare translations for their films. After six hours of wrangling, the Soviets were permitted to organize one experimental screening of the Soviet World War II documentary *Berlin* (dir. Yuli Raizman and Elizaveta Svilova, 1946). The Soviet delegation had invited, in advance, a qualified translator from Paris who had been recommended by the Central Committee of the French Communist Party. He had viewed the films and been trained especially for the job. "The demonstration of the picture 'Berlin' with translation completely justified itself," Kalatozov concluded after the screening. "The film was able to reach viewers not only via images, but the audience also understood the deep meaning of the text. For example, the words of comrade Stalin translated into French inspired ovations."[18]

During these 1946 screenings at Venice and Cannes, Russian voiceover also gave the Soviet Union an advantage over its main rival, the United States. The French newspaper *Laurent du Sud-Ouest* reported on September 20: "There is nothing more exhausting than spending several hours in a row in screenings where you don't understand a single word. The Russians perceived this from the first day, and they were the only ones who invited an announcer to translate their films. They couldn't have done anything better."[19] Because of such positive responses, midway through the festival the organizers allowed live commentary for all films. But other delegations could not conjure dialogue lists and find interpreters to read them on such short notice. The French *L'Avenir* and American *Variety* cited a US representative who complained, "Russian films are now accompanied with French commentary. On the other hand, we had been formally forbidden to add subtitles because the films had to be projected in their original version. We do not understand how, in such an important event as the Cannes Festival, the conditions of the competition can be thus modified in the midst of things."[20] In short, American and Soviet observers agreed that film translation had become a useful weapon in the cultural Cold War.

Eventually, major European festivals adopted a combination of subtitles for attendees and live translation via earphone for juries. Loudspeaker translation appeared only in an emergency—for example, at the 1968 Venice festival for John Cassavetes's *Faces* (1968), which was completed too soon before the festival to be subtitled.[21] Nevertheless, the Soviet Union used announcers for Soviet screenings at these same festivals into the 1970s. Kalatozov's report on Cannes in 1946 suggested that a subtitling studio be set up in Paris for all films competing at the festival. It was never built. And as late as 1973, film critic Rostislav Yurenev lauded the careful megaphone translation of Soviet films presented at the Italian Days of Cinema, a replacement for then-suspended Venice Mostra. The interpreter, a first-year Moscow State University philology student, received Russian dialogue lists in time to prepare and read her own literary translations into Italian during all screenings of *That Sweet Word: Liberty!* (*Eto sladkoe slovo—svoboda!*, dir. Vytautas Žalakevičius, 1973), a documentary about Chile before the 1973 coup, and *The Saplings* (*Nergebi*, dir. Rezo Chkheidze, 1972), a Georgian comedy. "This organizational trifle—a timely delivery of dialogue lists—contributed to the complete understanding and positive reception of Soviet films," Yurenev concluded.[22]

Throughout the 1960s and 1970s, festival guests often panned Soviet-style simultaneous translation. Indian critic Devendra Kumar, for instance, thought the Italian voice-over for Marlen Khutsiev's *I Am Twenty* (*Mne dvadtsat' let*, 1965) at the 1965 Venice festival "marred the charm of the film."[23] Yet Soviet officials valued live translation because it promised full control of the ideological message, total legibility, and maximum political effect—what Sakai would define as "homolingual address." Indeed, throughout the Cold War, these officials thought of international film festivals as an extension of Soviet diplomatic efforts, even if after 1953, diplomatic success was no longer gauged by spectators' applause at Stalin's translated words. The Moscow and Tashkent film festivals employed scores of simultaneous film translators working in dozens of languages, more than any other international cinema showcase. Each film was first translated into Russian, played through the theater's loudspeakers, and then translated into the languages of the various foreign guests, who listened through transistor headphones. This two-tier relay film interpretation system ensured that visitors from dozens of countries could see any film in their own language, and it improved on the simultaneous translation method developed during the Nuremberg Trials.[24] But this live translation system could not be controlled as easily as interpretation at an international summit—and informal practices at Soviet spoken cinema venues contradicted the government's political project.

### Cinema in Live Translation in the Soviet Union

Films in live translation were shown throughout the Soviet Union, beyond the official screenings during the Moscow and Tashkent festivals. The Filmmakers' Union (founded in 1957) and one of its arms, the Propaganda Bureau (founded in 1959), organized the films' distribution and collected the proceeds. Often, these public screenings took place following festivals, when foreign films, and often their filmmakers, traveled to at least four to six major cities around the country (including Leningrad, republican capitals like Kiev or Baku, major urban centers like Novosibirsk, and resort towns like Sochi). Half of the proceeds went to the host city, the other half to recoup the festival's expenses. In addition, every year from 1954, several national cinema weeks—for example, Indian, Polish, French, Syrian, and Senegalese—opened in Moscow and then traveled through the same network of major cities. Post-festival and film-week screenings usually took place in a House of Cinema (which were built for the local Filmmakers' Union chapters in every republican capital) or local movie theaters. Beginning in 1966, the Soviet State Film Repository, or Gosfil'mofond, also showed foreign movies from its vast collection in six to eight public screenings at each of its four theaters: Illuzion (opened in 1966) and its satellite, Red Textile Workers Club (1967) in Moscow, Kinematograf in Leningrad (1967), and Gazapkhuli in Tbilisi (1970).[25] Each theater employed a stable of interpreters, many of them famous among spectators as artists in their own right. To convey regional accents in Italian films, for example, celebrated Gazapkhuli interpreter Giovanni Vepkhvadze used a Mingrelian (a Kartvelian language spoken in Western Georgia) accent in contrast with standard Georgian. Once, he had a film character ask about local soccer results and gave the latest score in the response; the audience applauded.[26] Such heterolingual spoken cinema screenings blended multiple local and foreign languages and contexts.

In addition, from 1959, the Propaganda Bureau's traveling lecture program took excerpts from and entire foreign films to Houses of Cinema, cine-clubs, workers' clubhouses, and other venues around the country, including, in the 1980s, high-security prisons.[27] The film lecture program became a significant alternative supplement to official film distribution—one that, among other things, financed the activities of the Filmmakers' Union; in 1964, most of the union's budget, over six million rubles, came from the bureau's profits from print publications and public lectures accompanied by Soviet and foreign films.[28] At these, the lecturer or a local interpreter translated foreign films and excerpts into Russian. Before going out on a lecture tour about Ingmar Bergman, for instance, film historian Naum Kleiman—who did not know Swedish—studied the translation for the excerpts of Bergman's films, so as to be able to recite the dialogue from memory.[29]

Public screenings at these venues transgressed the general censorship standards for foreign film distribution; indeed, Soviet functionaries often berated Illuzion for showing forbidden or suspect movies during foreign film retrospectives. The Italian film week in December 1967 showed films by Giuseppe de Santis, Luchino Visconti, Michelangelo Antonioni, and Federico Fellini, including *8 1/2* (1963), which had won the top prize at Moscow in 1963 against the wishes of party officials and was never purchased for distribution. The program opened at Illuzion, the House of Cinema, and other Moscow venues and afterward traveled to Kiev. De Santis, who opened the retrospective, later published an article in the Italian Communist paper *Paese sera* praising Illuzion as an "oppositional" theater. As a result, the Moscow Communist Party Committee's film department, which was responsible for the political oversight of the city's film industry, summoned Illuzion programmers to inquire why an Italian director was praising the theater for showing the best Italian films despite Soviet censorship. In 1969, a Polish film retrospective at Illuzion showed over one hundred Polish films in a month and a half, many of them censored from general distribution.[30]

In addition to public events, closed film screenings served the creative, intellectual, and party elite, as well as their families, friends, and acquaintances. Filmmakers' Union chapters in Moscow, Leningrad, and republican capitals set up closed screenings for union members at Houses of Cinema. The All-Union State Film School (VGIK), the Higher Courses for Directors, and the Higher Courses for Screenwriters in Moscow, as well as film schools in Leningrad and other Soviet republics, showed foreign movies to their students, as Moscow, Leningrad, and republican film studios did for their employees. Film journal offices—from those of the premier cinema journal *Iskusstvo kino* (*Cinema Art*) to the popular magazine *Sovetskii ekran*

(*Soviet Screen*)—organized screenings for staff writers. Houses for other art workers—including writers, journalists, painters, and composers—borrowed 35mm reels from Gosfil'mofond or Sovexportfilm to show to their members, and scientific institutes did the same for their researchers. A special section of Gosfil'mofond served *sharashki* (closed research facilities) and the Communist Party leadership, who saw foreign films at their offices and their dachas. Most closed screenings were only nominally restricted to the elite: dentists, manicurists, hairdressers, and car mechanics could count on passes as thank-yous from authorized spectators.[31]

In addition to legitimate foreign film shows outside of general distribution, unsanctioned screenings took place. The first pirate shows used "trophy" musicals, comedies, and dramas seized in Germany at the end of the war and put into circulation between 1948 and 1953.[32] According to a 1957 investigation, a group of Moscow university students, all children of privileged parents, purchased retired trophy reels from projectionists and then circulated over two hundred different films in scientific and educational institutions in the city, preceded by live jazz performances.[33] In Moscow in the 1960s, at least until the 1968 Warsaw Pact invasion of Czechoslovakia, foreign films circulated through a similar network. The trophy films were dubbed or subtitled, but for all other films, an interpreter came in to provide a Russian voice-over. In 1967, a cine-club at Moscow State University was shut down the day after one such unauthorized spoken cinema screening: university administration clamped down on the "Maoist" propaganda of Jean-Luc Godard's *La Chinoise* (1967).[34]

Some evidence suggests that the provinces had their own illicit distribution systems. In 1966, for instance, A. V. Zagorsky, director of the Moldovan Propaganda Bureau, revived the pirate spoken cinema tradition. The Moscow Bureau had sent two Italian films to accompany local lectures: the raunchy omnibus picture *Boccaccio-70* (dir. Mario Monicelli, Federico Fellini, Luchino Visconti, and Vittorio De Sica, 1962) and the comedy *Yesterday, Today, and Tomorrow* (*Ieri, oggi, domani*, dir. Vittorio De Sica, 1963). After four authorized lectures at the House of the Moldovan Filmmakers' Union, Zagorsky took these films with him on his vacation to the Odessa district. He gave several lectures accompanied by the two films at four seaside resorts in exchange for free room and board. The pictures played to packed theaters, until an ill-wisher denounced the unauthorized screenings to the authorities. As one Moscow official later dryly remarked, "An event cannot remain secret when the lecture attracts a thousand people." The Moscow Filmmakers Union summoned Zagorsky and fired him after a brutal official reprimand. Committee members were particularly upset because Zagorsky's case laid bare an unofficial practice, common across Filmmakers' Union and Propaganda Bureau chapters in other Soviet republics. "We had already suffered because of this," admitted Aleksandr Karaganov, a Filmmakers' Union official.[35]

## LIVE FILM TRANSLATION AT SOVIET FESTIVALS

The frequency of unsanctioned screenings is difficult to gauge, but interviews and archival records suggest that they constituted a steady stream of events, rather than an occasional transgression. These semiofficial and illicit nationwide spoken cinema practices in turn formed the larger context for authorized international screenings at the Moscow and Tashkent festivals. Simultaneous translation at these festivals was a difficult job that began months before and continued weeks after a festival officially took place.

Festival translation involved multilingual publics and often more than two languages, a feature of its heterolingual address. At the Tashkent festival around 1976, a Hindi film could play with English subtitles, Russian loudspeaker voice-over, and earphone translation into French, English, Spanish, and Arabic. According to an internal report, fifty-eight simultaneous translators worked at the second Moscow festival in 1961. Out of 160 applications, twenty people were selected to translate into the official languages of the festival and thirty-eight to translate into Russian. Unique linguistic skills could overcome suspect politics: only thirty-one of the fifty-eight translators were Komsomol or Communist Party members. The translators' work began during the vetting period, when translators into Russian interpreted submitted films for the organizers and the commissions of the Ministry of Culture. That year, 263 films played at the festival, but written "dialogue lists" were provided for only twenty-seven of the thirty-three competition pictures. Of these, fifteen "particularly difficult ones" were translated into Russian.[36] But many films, in competition and out, arrived after the beginning of the festival. Most of the time, translators had to interpret extemporaneously by ear.

The translators who took this job came from all walks of life. Some had connections to the Communist Party elite, the KGB, or Sovexportfilm. Aleksei Mikhalev, who interpreted from Persian for Leonid Brezhnev, became known in Moscow art film circles in the 1970s as a translator from English and nationally in the 1980s as a translator's voice in pirated American blockbusters on video. But most translators had no connections to power. They could be college students studying linguistics, language, literature, or the history of a foreign country, or they could be students in an unrelated field whose parents had spent some time in a foreign country. Aleksandr Bondarev, who translated from Polish, was a graduate student in theoretical physics when he began working with films. Despite their proximity with foreign culture, film translators had a measure of political freedom. The interpreters who worked with delegations were specifically requested from foreign language institutes and VGIK and vetted by the KGB for political loyalty. Yet a dissident who knew a foreign language well could still get a job as a film translator.[37]

Since most festival films were shown with no Russian subtitles, film translators made the mass audiences at Soviet festivals possible. In 1959, the Moscow festival's more than half a million spectators brought in around five million rubles, and from then on, the festival was a profitable enterprise. "The organizing committee aimed not to imitate other festivals, but, using their experience, to conduct the Moscow festival as an open mass event," stated the final report for that year. "We succeeded. The participants and guests of the Moscow festival, and the press, noted the mass, popular character of the Moscow festival among the main differences from festivals in Cannes, Venice, and others."[38] In July 1961, at the Palace of Sports alone, 217,678 people attended forty-two screenings in twenty-one days, and 8,005 people showed up for the opening-night screening on July 9. Both attendance and earnings surpassed the plan.[39] In addition, throughout its history, the festival organized massive out-of-competition programs and sold tickets at double the regular price to increase profits. "Moscow Fans Finance Film Festival," *Variety* reported in 1975.[40] This ability to attract popular crowds distinguished Moscow from its major European counterparts—including the Karlovy Vary festival in socialist Czechoslovakia—all of which were closed to the general public.

Out-of-competition screenings, most of which were translated live, provided unique opportunities for both entertainment and art-film spectatorship at the Moscow festival. Many films were shown with the filmmakers present. The main draw for the general public was the screenings' range of entertainment films, shown for their popular appeal rather than their educational or ideological value. In 1965, these included the musicals *Mary Poppins* (dir. Robert Stevenson, 1964) and *My Fair Lady* (dir. George Cukor, 1964), the American comedy *It's a Mad, Mad, Mad, Mad World* (dir. Stanley Kramer, 1963), the French historical romance *Angélique, the Marquise of the Angels* (*Angélique, marquise des anges*, dir. Bernard Borderie, 1964), the swashbuckler *Black Tulip* (*La Tulipe noire*, dir. Christian-Jaque, 1964), and the British World War II epic *The Bridge on the River Kwai* (dir. David Lean, 1957).[41] Several of these films are considered classics today, but for many Moscow spectators, their genre attractions outweighed any artistic value. At the *My Fair Lady* screening at the Palace of Sports, when the translator tried to speak during musical numbers, ten thousand spectators stomped their feet and chanted "No translation!"[42] The tickets for the out-of-competition screenings sold out so quickly that the delegations that brought these films routinely complained that they received half or none of the complimentary tickets promised to them.[43]

The program also offered much for the art-film lover and the film critic, which meant thousands of cine-club movie buffs across geographic and class lines. During the 1965 Moscow festival, world-renowned art-film directors leaned on their producers to send their latest films. Michelangelo Antonioni came with *Red Desert* (*Il deserto rosso*, 1964). Jean-Luc Godard sent *Alphaville* (1965). Akira Kurosawa opened his *Red Beard* (*Akahige*, 1965) in Moscow before competing at Venice, where Toshiro Mifune subsequently won the award for the best performance.[44] Indeed, because very few foreign films were dubbed for general distribution, Soviet critical writing on foreign cinema largely drew on the films shown with live translation at festivals and foreign film weeks. A 1967 journal article on Antonioni focusing on *Red Desert* noted that it was shown at the 1965 festival and also analyzed his *Story of a Love Affair* (*Cronaca di un amore*, 1950), which had been shown during an Italian film week in Moscow in 1955.[45] While critics also analyzed films they saw at Gosfil'mofond, at foreign festivals, and during professional trips abroad, focusing on cinema from Soviet international festivals and film weeks allowed them to address a wider national community of art-film lovers and festivalgoers. And if out-of-town Soviet cinephiles timed their vacations to see Italian and French festival films unavailable in their local Soviet theaters, foreign guests came to see films they could not view in the West, both foreign and Soviet.

### LIVE TRANSLATION AND THE TRANSNATIONAL CIRCULATION OF CINEMA

Foreign guests suffered live translation together with millions of Soviet cinephiles. At all festival theaters in Moscow and Tashkent, an English-speaking guest would not hear the original soundtrack of an English-language picture, but rather an English translation of a Russian translation, which came half a minute after the original dialogue.[46] Occasionally, such free-form relay interpretation added humor to the film. One foreign journalist reported that he had heard, at a Soviet festival, "the English language expression, 'The spirit is willing but the flesh is weak' translated into a foreign language and then back into English as 'The drinks are pretty good, but the meat is lousy.'"[47] Yet this system also provided unique opportunities to see rare films, both Soviet and international. Writing in the 1970s, American filmmaker and critic

Gordon Hitchens, a representative of the Berlin and Leipzig festivals in the United States, recommended both Moscow and Tashkent as festivals where one could see films from Asia, Africa, and Latin America that were unavailable in the West.[48]

Because interpreters often had to work by ear, without preparation, they made errors that infuriated foreign participants. At the 1965 Moscow festival, Polish director Czesław Petelski complained that vocally challenged Soviet film translators "have jarring timbre, imprecise intonation, and don't always convey the meaning of the dialogue."[49] As a result, at a screening of Polish picture *Three Steps on Earth* (*Trzy kroki po ziemi*, dir. Jerzy Hoffman and Edward Skórzewski, 1965), the contrast between expository voice-over and the jocular vernacular dialogues—a central aesthetic device of the film—was completely lost. Petelski thought the botched delivery ruined his country's chances for a prize. Bad translation remained a typical foreign complaint at Soviet festivals into the 1980s.

At the same time, skilled translators from Russian into foreign languages could add their own slant to the dialogue. Hitchens witnessed such artistry at a screening of the Uzbek film *Riders of Revolution* (*Vsadniki revolutsii*, dir. Kamil Iarmatov, 1968) at the 1968 Tashkent festival. As Hitchens describes it, "The English language ear-phone translation of the Uzbek original was often very ironic." When a wounded Red Army scout escapes from the enemy lines and "collapses at the feet of the Bolshevik leaders, riddled with bullets and gasping out his last breath, the leader bends down to speak to him, and the voice on the earphones says, 'Well, now, what's the matter' in a rather petulant, irritated voice."[50] Such vocal interpretation exemplifies a unique heterolingual feature of multichannel live translation at festivals—only English-speaking guests got a shade of irony during this screening.

Simultaneous translation also helped dissident directors show their banned films to European festival programmers. In a notorious case from the 1975 Moscow festival, an ultimatum from Michelangelo Antonioni, who had threatened to leave the festival, forced officials to organize two last-minute special screenings of Andrei Tarkovsky's *The Mirror* (*Zerkalo*, 1975). The film was originally shelved as confusing and unpatriotic, so no subtitled copy existed.[51] The coveted screening, according to one participant, "was jammed with just about every delegation, whose various interpreters turned the theater into a horrifying Babel of translations."[52] Glowing reports of the two live-translated shows in the international press contributed to *The Mirror*'s prized place in film history, as cinematic art and as a political statement.[53]

Such informal screenings relied on the established channels of the Soviet alternative distribution system for films in live translation. Jay Leyda, an American film historian and an expert on Sergei Eisenstein, wrote to a friend in 1979 that Georgian director Otar Iosseliani, who was forbidden to show his films officially at the Moscow festival, each year "brings his own prints of his newest film, rents a small theater and a bus, [and] carts his foreign fans to a secret screening."[54] What Leyda perceived as a revolutionary activity was just an ordinary unofficial practice for Iosseliani and others, among them Naum Kleiman. Kleiman recalls how, during the 1975 Moscow festival, Iosseliani called him at home to invite him to an impromptu projection of his new film, *Pastorale* (*Pastorali*, 1975), at the offices of the magazine *Sovetskii ekran*. Leyda had just stopped by Kleiman's apartment, along with Ulrich Gregor, a cofounder of the Forum for Young Cinema at the Berlin International Film Festival. Kleiman took his visitors to see Iosseliani's film. Leyda understood Russian, but Gregor relied on Kleiman's extemporaneous whisper translation into German.[55] Impressed by the film, Gregor invited Iosseliani to the forum—although the director was only permitted to come in 1982, when *Pastorale* received a FIPRESCI (International Federation of Film Critics) prize. In these ways, underground screening practices and the unique live translation skills developed on the Soviet spoken cinema circuit enhanced and transformed foreign viewers' experience of Soviet festivals, contributing to the circulation of Soviet films at festivals in Europe and beyond.

## Conclusion

The Soviet translation project aimed to produce transparent communication within a stable geopolitical hierarchy, enshrining differences between languages, cultures, and the "three worlds"—capitalist, socialist, and nonaligned. The project succeeded only in part. Artisanal and inexact practices of live interpreting made assembly-line approaches impossible, and ambiguities in delivery and meaning invited spectators' critical attention.[56] Those who expected homolingual transparency left disappointed. Those who adopted a heterolingual approach to the rampant inefficiencies of the project made discoveries, aesthetic and political.

The Soviet case invites historians to reconsider the role of spoken cinema in the socialist world at large. Similar live translation practices took place across Eastern Europe, at festivals and elsewhere. Archival retrospectives and festival screenings in Yugoslavia, Romania, Czechoslovakia, Albania, and East Germany, for instance, were accompanied by live translation, while pirate video translation in the Soviet Union, Romania, and Bulgaria in the 1980s owed much to the translation styles developed in 35mm and 16mm spoken cinema in the preceding decades.[57] The transnational connections enabled by Soviet spoken cinema force us to reconsider these translation practices in a different light. We might ask, for example, why Roman Polanski was miffed about the simultaneous translation of his film *Tessa* (1979) at the Belgrade FEST. Was it simply a case of failure to "meet even basic screening standards," as one historian argued?[58] Or, perhaps, the film translator added another layer of meaning, humorous or critical, to the film screening as a unique spoken cinema event.

## Notes

I cite Russian archival documents according to their location as follows: fond/opis/ed.khr./page numbers. All translations are mine, unless otherwise indicated.

1. The letter only lists the last name of the addressee, Ivanov. This letter was forwarded to the national State Committee for Cinematography (Goskino).
2. All quotes in this paragraph come from Livshits's letter; Russian State Archive of Literature and Art, Moscow (RGALI), 2944/24/58/17–18.
3. Roth-Ey, *Moscow Prime Time*; and Zezina, "Kinoprokat i massovyi zritel' v gody ottepeli." On film dubbing, see Gilburd, *To See Paris and Die*.
4. For more on such screenings, see Razlogova, "Listening to the Inaudible Foreign"; Razlogova, "The Politics of Translation"; Razlogova, "The Liberation Politics of Live Translation"; and Hoffmann, "Soviet Estonian Cinema Clubs." Some examples in this essay also appear in my previous publications.
5. Boillat, "The Lecturer, the Image, the Machine and the Audio-Spectator."
6. Ingawanij, "Mother India in Six Voices" and "Itinerant Cinematic Practices." Other examples include Crowley, "Echo Translation" (Poland); Dwyer and Uricaru, "Slashings and Subtitles" (Romania); Li, "Cinematic Guerrillas in Mao's China"; and Srinivas, "Is There a Public in the Cinema Hall?" (India).
7. Shohat and Stam, "The Cinema After Babel" and *Unthinking Eurocentrism*; Mowitt, *Re-Takes*; and Nornes, *Cinema Babel*.
8. Gunning, "The Scene of Speaking," 68. For an excellent overview of film translation history, see Zanotti, "Historical Approaches to AVT Reception."
9. Djagalov and Salazkina, "Tashkent '68."
10. Pratt, *Imperial Eyes*, 8.
11. Sakai, *Translation and Subjectivity*, 8; and Sakai and Solomon, *Translation, Biopolitics, Colonial Difference*.
12. Russian State Archive of Socio-Political History (RGASPI) 17/114/956/209-212; reprinted in Maksimenkov et al., eds., *Kremlevskii kinoteatr, 1928–1953*, 504.
13. Mariamov, *Kremlevskii tzenzor*, 11.
14. de Valck, *Film Festivals*; Kötzing and Moine, *Cultural Transfer and Political Conflicts*; and RGALI 2456/4/103/3.
15. RGALI 2456/4/103/9.
16. RGALI 2456/4/103/9. On the Soviets at Venice in 1946, see Pisu, "The USSR and East-Central European Countries."
17. RGALI 2456/4/103/33.
18. RGALI 2456/4/103/33. On the 1946 Cannes festival, see Pozner, "Les 'Clefs de la propagande cinématographique en Europe.'"
19. *Laurent du Sud-Ouest* quoted in RGALI 2456/4/103/33-34.
20. Thierry, "Un Petard Sovietique," quoted in Pozner, "Les 'Clefs,'" 181; "Power Politics, Spearheaded by USSR, Marred Int'l Film Festival at Cannes," 12.

21. Moskowitz, "Boxoffice, Art, Politics."
22. Yurenev, "Festival' umer," 174.
23. Kumar, *World Cinema '65*.
24. Gofman, "K istorii sinkhronnogo perevoda"; and Gaiba, *The Origins of Simultaneous Interpretation*.
25. Fomin, *Istoriia kinootrasli v Rossii*; and Solov'ev, *Kinoteatr Gosfil'mofonda Rossii "Illuzion."*
26. Vepkhvadze, "Sinkhronist"; and Sherouse, "Russian Presence in Georgian Film Dubbing," 216.
27. A thank-you note with a poem from prisoners of OV156/3 to a translator, in author's possession.
28. Fomin, *Istoriia kinootrasli v Rossii*, 1073, 1138.
29. Kleiman, interview, September 10, 2018. On Estonian cine-club screenings with live translation, see Hoffman, "La traduction cinématographique," 222.
30. RGALI 2944/13/1078; Soloviev, *Kinoteatr Gosfil'mofonda Rossii "Illuzion,"* 44-45; and Golubev, *Professia—kinoman*, 41.
31. Fomin, *Istoriia kinootrasli v Rossii*; and Gilburd, *To See Paris and Die*.
32. Knight, "Enemy Films on Soviet Screens."
33. RGALI 2329/2/557; Zezina, "Kinoprokat i massovyi zritel v gody ottepeli."
34. Knight, "Enemy Films on Soviet Screens"; and Hoffman, "Soviet Estonian Cinema Clubs and Interpreting of Foreign Movies."
35. RGALI 2936/4/46/10.
36. RGALI 2936/1/1502/50–52.
37. YouTube, "Aleksei Mikhalev"; and Solov'ev, *Kinoteatr Gosfilmofonda Rossii "Illuzion."*
38. RGALI 2936/1/1324/9, 17.
39. RGALI 2936/1/1502/52d.
40. Zorkaya, "'Vchera' i 'segodnia' moskovskogo kinofestivalya"; and Werba, "Moscow Fans Finance Film Festival."
41. RGALI 2936/1/2059/6.
42. Golubev, *Professiia—kinoman*, 30–31.
43. RGALI 2936/1/1502/8.
44. RGALI 2936/1/2059/6.
45. Rubanova, "Posle 'Krasnoi pustyni.'"
46. This practice still survives at some festivals in Eastern Europe and former Soviet republics.
47. Unknown foreign journalist quoted in Hitchens, "Tashkent Festival" (typescript, 1968), box 1, folder 5, Papers of Gordon Hitchens, Wisconsin Historical Society Archives.
48. Hitchens, "Mind-Bending, Discomforts at USSR's Fest for Asia, Africa" and "Festival Report—Moscow."
49. RGALI 2936/1/2058/154.
50. Hitchens, "Tashkent Festival."
51. "Glavnaya tema—sovremennost."
52. Johnson, "Trends of Soviet Directors," 33.
53. Gillett, "Festivals 1975—Locarno, Berlin, Moscow"; Marshall, "Andrei Tarkovsky's 'The Mirror'"; and Tarkovsky, *Time Within Time*, 115.
54. Jay Leyda, draft of letter to an unknown recipient (1979), box 11, folder 5, Jay and Si-Lan Chen Leyda Papers, Tamiment Library and Robert Wagner Archives, New York University.
55. Kleiman, interview, September 10, 2018.
56. Soviet spoken cinema shared its politics of ambiguity and liveness with other socialist art practices. In this volume, Katie Trumpener argues that panoramic photography's "bends and distortions" produced a critique of socialist architecture in Czechoslovakia; see chapter 2. Likewise, Marie Cronqvist shows how international audiences shaped state-controlled East German broadcasting in 1989; see chapter 8.

57. On Romania, see Dwyer and Uricaru, "Slashings and Subtitles," 223. On the GDR, see Shtaier, "O mekhanizme sinkhronnogo perevoda."

58. Batančev, "The Belgrade FEST," 161.

## Bibliography

Batančev, Dragan. "The Belgrade FEST, or What Happened When Peckinpah Met Wajda." In *Cultural Transfer and Political Conflicts: Film Festivals in the Cold War*, edited by Andreas Kötzing and Caroline Moine, 153–165. Gottingen: Vandenhoeck & Ruprecht, 2016.

Boillat, Alain. "The Lecturer, the Image, the Machine and the Audio-Spectator." In *Cinema Beyond Film: Media Epistemology in the Modern Era*, edited by François Albera and Maria Tortajada, 215–231. Amsterdam: Amsterdam University Press, 2010.

Crowley, David. "Echo Translation." Faktografia.com. November 16, 2014. Accessed June 25, 2015. http://faktografia.com/2014/11/16/echo-translation/.

De Santis, Giuseppe. "Illuzion—Oppositional Theater." *Paese sera*, 1968.

de Valck, Marijke. *Film Festivals: From European Geopolitics to Global Cinephilia*. Amsterdam: Amsterdam University Press, 2008.

Djagalov, Rossen, and Masha Salazkina. "Tashkent '68: A Cinematic Contact Zone." *Slavic Review* 75, no. 2 (2016): 279–298.

Dwyer, Tessa, and Ioana Uricaru. "Slashings and Subtitles: Romanian Media Piracy, Censorship and Translation." In *A Reader on International Media Piracy: Pirate Essays*, edited by Tilman Baumgärtel, 207–230. Amsterdam: Amsterdam University Press, 2015.

Fomin, Valery. *Istoriia kinootrasli v Rossii: Upravlenie, kinoproizvodstvo, prokat*. Moscow: VNIIK VGIK, 2012.

Gaiba, Francesca. *The Origins of Simultaneous Interpretation: The Nuremberg Trial*. Ottawa: University of Ottawa Press, 1998.

Gilburd, Eleonory. *To See Paris and Die: The Soviet Lives of Western Culture*. Cambridge, MA: Belknap, 2018.

Gillett, John. "Festivals 1975—Locarno, Berlin, Moscow." *Sight and Sound* (autumn 1975): 214.

"Glavnaya tema—sovremennost." *Iskusstvo kino* 3 (1975): 1–18.

Gofman, E. "K istorii sinkhronnogo perevoda." *Tetradi perevodchika* 1 (1963): 20–26.

Golubev, Vladimir. *Professiia—kinoman*. Moscow: Globus-press, 2015.

Gunning, Tom. "The Scene of Speaking: Two Decades of Discovering the Film Lecturer." *Iris* 27 (1999): 67–80.

Hitchens, Gordon. "Festival Report—Moscow." *American Film*, November 1, 1975.

———. "Mind-Bending, Discomforts at USSR's Fest for Asia, Africa." *Variety*, June 12, 1974.

Hoffmann, Tiina. "La traduction cinématographique en Estonie soviétique: contextes, pratiques et acteurs." PhD diss., University of Tartu, 2021.

Ingawanij, May Adadol. "Itinerant Cinematic Practices In and Around Thailand during the Cold War." *Southeast of Now: Directions in Contemporary and Modern Art in Asia* 2, no. 2 (2018): 9–41.

———. "Mother India in Six Voices: Melodrama, Voice Performance, and Indian Films in Siam." *BioScope: South Asian Screen Studies* 3, no. 2 (2012): 99–121.

Johnson, Albert. "Trends of Soviet Directors." *Variety*, July 30, 1975.

Kleiman, Naum. Skype interview by author. September 10, 2018.

Knight, Claire. "Enemy Films on Soviet Screens: Trophy Films during the Early Cold War, 1947–52." *Kritika* 18, no. 1 (2017): 125–149.

Kötzing, Andreas, and Caroline Moine, eds. *Cultural Transfer and Political Conflicts: Film Festivals in the Cold War*. Gottingen: Vandenhoeck & Ruprecht, 2016.

Kumar, Devendra. *World Cinema '65*. Delhi: Time & Tide, 1966.

Li, Jie. "Cinematic Guerrillas in Mao's China." *Screen* 61, no. 2 (2020): 207–229.

Maksimenkov, Leonid, Kirill Anderson, Liudmila Kosheleva, and Larisa Rogovaia, eds. *Kremlevskii kinoteatr, 1928–1953: Dokumenty*. Moscow: ROSSPEN, 2005.

Mariamov, G. *Kremlevskii tzenzor: Stalin smotrit kino*. Moscow: Kinotsentr, 1992.

Marshall, Herbert. "Andrei Tarkovsky's 'The Mirror.'" *Sight and Sound* (spring 1976): 94.

Moskowitz, Gene. "Boxoffice, Art, Politics Not All That Complicates Fest O'seas; Also Lingo." *Variety*, September 25, 1968.

Mowitt, John. *Re-Takes: Postcoloniality and Foreign Film Languages*. Minneapolis: University of Minnesota Press, 2005.

Nornes, Abé Mark. *Cinema Babel: Translating Global Cinema*. Minneapolis: University of Minnesota Press, 2007.

Pisu, Stefano. "The USSR and East-Central European Countries at the Venice International Film Festival (1946–1953)." *Iluminace* 25, no. 3 (2013): 51–63.

"Power Politics, Spearheaded by USSR, Marred Int'l Film Festival at Cannes." *Variety*, November 13, 1946.

Pozner, Valérie. "Le bonimenteur 'rouge': Retour sur la question de l'oralité à propos du cas soviétique." *Cinémas* 14, no. 2–3 (2004): 143–178.

———. "Les 'Clefs de la propagande cinématographique en Europe': Les Soviétiques au premier Festival de Cannes 1946." *1895*, no. 83 (2017): 137–199.

Pratt, Mary Louise. *Imperial Eyes: Travel Writing and Transculturation*. London: Routledge, 1992.

Razlogova, Elena. "The Liberation Politics of Live Translation: Global South Cinemas at Soviet Tashkent." *Journal of Cinema and Media Studies* 59, no. 4 (2020): 183–188.

———. "Listening to the Inaudible Foreign: Simultaneous Translators and Soviet Experience of Foreign Cinema." In *Sound, Speech, Music in Soviet and Post-Soviet Cinema*, edited by Lilya Kaganovsky and Masha Salazkina, 162–178. Bloomington: Indiana University Press, 2014.

———. "The Politics of Translation at Soviet Film Festivals during the Cold War." *SubStance* 44, no. 2 (2015): 66–87.

Roth-Ey, Kristin. *Moscow Prime Time: How the Soviet Union Built the Media Empire That Lost the Cultural Cold War*. Ithaca, NY: Cornell University Press, 2011.

Rubanova, Irina. "Posle 'Krasnoi pustyni.'" *Voprosy kinoiskusstva* 10 (1967): 318–343.

Sakai, Naoki. *Translation and Subjectivity: On Japan and Cultural Nationalism*. Minneapolis: University of Minnesota Press, 1997.

Sakai, Naoki, and Jon Solomon, eds. *Translation, Biopolitics, Colonial Difference*. Hong Kong: Hong Kong University Press, 2006.

Sherouse, Perry. "Russian Presence in Georgian Film Dubbing: Scales of Inferiority." *Journal of Linguistic Anthropology* 25, no. 2 (August 1, 2015): 215–229.

Shohat, Ella, and Robert Stam. "The Cinema After Babel: Language, Difference, Power." *Screen* 26, no. 3–4 (1985): 35–58.

———. *Unthinking Eurocentrism: Multiculturalism and the Media*. New York: Routledge, 1994.

Shtaier, B. "O mekhanizme sinkhronnogo perevoda." *Tetradi perevodchika* 12 (1975): 101–111.

Solov'ev, Vladimir, ed. *Kinoteatr Gosfilmofonda Rossii Illuzion: Vchera, segodnia, zavtra*. Moskva: RID Interreklama, 2008.

Srinivas, S. V. "Is There a Public in the Cinema Hall?" *Framework* 42 (2000). Accessed September 9, 2021. https://8ba99043-46ef-443e-8e66-bc36aco1fd7b.filesusr.com/ugd/32 cb69_95584ff57df547febaf04c3e0bafa3fc.pdf.
Tarkovsky, Andrei. *Time Within Time: The Diaries, 1970–1986.* London: Faber and Faber, 1994.
Thierry, Gaston. "Un Petard Sovietique." *L'Avenir*, October 5, 1946.
Vepkhvadze, Dzhovanni. "Sinkhronist." In *Dzhovanni rasskazyvaet.* Tblilisi: Kalmosani, 2013. Accessed September 9, 2021. http://alves415.narod.ru/G.Vephvadze-6.html.
Werba, Hank. "Moscow Fans Finance Film Festival." *Variety*, July 30, 1975.
YouTube. "Aleksei Mikhalev—Interv'iu s korolem sinkhronnogo perevoda." Accessed May 9, 2019. http://www.youtube.com/watch?v=1FT15Hnb-Sc.
Yurenev, Rostislav. "Festival' umer. Da zdravstvuet festival'!" *Iskusstvo kino* (March 1974): 168–183.
Zanotti, Serenella. "Historical Approaches to AVT Reception: Methods, Issues and Perspectives." In *Reception Studies and Audiovisual Translation*, edited by Elena Di Giovanni and Yves Gambier, 133–158. Amsterdam: John Benjamins, 2018.
Zezina, Maria. "Kinoprokat i massovyi zritel' v gody ottepeli." In *Istoriia strany, istoriia kino*, edited by S. S. Sekirsky, 389–412. Moscow: Znak, 2004.
Zorkaya, Neya. "'Vchera' i 'segodnia' moskovskogo kinofestivalia." *Iskusstvo kino*, December 1995.

ELENA RAZLOGOVA is Associate Professor of History at Concordia University. She is author of *The Listener's Voice: Early Radio and the American Public.*

CHAPTER 10

A GDR WRITER IN AMERICA
## Christa Wolf's Visit to Oberlin and the Circulation of Her Writing as World Literature

Brangwen Stone

GERMAN AUTHOR CHRISTA WOLF, WHO died in 2011, is often named as the most internationally successful writer to have emerged from the former German Democratic Republic (GDR).[1] Wolf's work is available in over thirty languages, and she enjoyed "almost cultish popularity" in English translation in the 1980s.[2] In fact, few German-language authors from West Germany or Switzerland rivaled her level of international recognition in the postwar era.[3] However, during the nearly two months that she spent as a writer-in-residence at Oberlin College in 1974 (March 28–May 20), she was only just gaining recognition outside the GDR and West Germany.[4] Wolf's entry into the English-speaking world followed the English translation of her 1968 novel, *Nachdenken über Christa T*, published as *The Quest for Christa T* (*Christa T*) in 1970 by Farrar, Straus & Giroux (FSG). Yet when she visited Oberlin, most GDR citizens had only been able to visit the United States for two years, and Wolf was just the second East German writer to spend time at a US university.[5] She thus saw her visit to the US as an opportunity to create connections and help improve the image and prestige of GDR literature.[6] And indeed, 1974 is generally acknowledged as the year when, in the US, the field of German studies first really took notice of the literature of East Germany.[7]

Through an exploration of Wolf's visit to Oberlin, how it was reflected in her writing, and the publication of her work in the US, this chapter considers two core dimensions of literary traffic between the East and the West during the Cold War: literary exchanges and translation.[8] Wolf's time in the United States, the chapter argues, not only underscores the degree to which authors and their literature moved across the Iron Curtain in this period; it also demonstrates East German literature's ability to function as world literature in David Damrosch's sense—the circulation of literary texts beyond their country and language of origin.[9]

## Literary Exchange Visits between East and West during the Cold War

The East/West binary of the Cold War has traditionally been assumed to extend to the realm of culture, but in recent years, scholars have begun to show that there were cultural connections and mutual influences across the Iron Curtain.[10] This assumption extended to literature, and the global or transnational turn in literary studies of the last two decades is often represented as directly resulting from the globalization that followed the collapse of the Iron Curtain. However, as Christine Moore and Christina Spittel write, this model ignores the lasting cultural impact of socialist and left aesthetics in literatures across the globe, "for example, in the independence movements of Indonesia or South Africa, in critiques of nationalist imperialism in Japan and Korea, or in the leftist cultural nationalism informing settler literatures mid-century in the USA and Australia."[11] Rossen Djagalov, for instance, details how the Soviet Union deliberately attempted to build literary relationships with the Third World and argues that as a consequence of the resulting literary (and cinematic) network, Anglo-American postcolonial theory owes more to Soviet thought and experience than has previously been acknowledged.[12] Michael Denning reminds us, too, of an earlier globalization of literature in the form of the socialist interwar literary "international," whose influence continued after World War II. He argues that this movement "enfranchised a generation of writers, often of plebeian backgrounds, and ... was the first self-conscious attempt to create a world literature," listing writers including Maxim Gorky, Gabriel García Márquez, Lu Xun, and Isabel Allende as examples of the "novelists' international."[13] Indeed, this is a tradition that the GDR's first minister of culture, writer Johannes R. Becher, drew on in 1956, when he declared "an age of new classicism ... under the banner of the international of socialist realism."[14]

Literary exchange visits between European socialist nations and Western nations began in the late 1950s and early 1960s, following the signing of bilateral cultural exchange agreements.[15] These included an agreement between France and the Soviet Union (USSR) in 1957; between the US and the USSR in 1958; French-Romanian, Hungarian-Finnish, and British-Soviet agreements in 1959; and an agreement between Poland and Denmark in 1960.[16] While the most high-profile visits to result from these agreements were often those of musicians and dancers, exchanges of academics and writers also took place.[17] Literary exchange visits between the US and USSR began soon after their first cultural exchange agreement was signed. In 1963, for instance, Edward Albee and John Steinbeck each spent a month in the Soviet Union.[18] Other well-known US writers, such as Arthur Miller and E. L. Doctorow, followed later; however, until the 1970s, Soviet writers usually only visited the US as part of delegations.[19] With the beginning of détente in the 1970s, some Soviet writers were also able to accept invitations by American universities and to travel individually.[20] The University of Kansas had a writer-in-residence program specifically for Soviet (mostly Russian) writers in the 1970s and '80s, and the Iowa Writer's Workshop also hosted writers from a number of East European socialist countries; the Soviet Union nevertheless declined Iowa's invitations until 1986, when Boris Zakhoder attended.[21]

While much of the scholarship on literary exchange visits between East and West during the Cold War has focused on writers from socialist nations visiting the US, there were also literary exchange visits between other East European and Western nations from the early postwar years onward. The Foundation for European Intellectual Cooperation fellowships, for instance, allowed writers, artists, and academics from East European socialist countries (including the GDR) to spend one to two months in West European nations.[22] There were also literary exchange visits between countries with no official agreements. Well-known Swiss writers/playwrights Friedrich Dürrenmatt and Max Frisch made a number of trips to the Communist East, and Dürrenmatt's play *The Physicists* (*Die Physiker*) had already been performed two hundred times in Poland by 1964, even though Switzerland did not have any cultural exchange agreements with the socialist nations of East Europe.[23]

The GDR's situation was complicated by the fact that most other nations did not officially recognize the country until the early 1970s, supporting the Federal Republic of Germany's (FRG) claim that it was the only German nation. The FRG's Hallstein Doctrine (1955–1969), which stated that the FRG would regard it as an unfriendly act if third countries were to recognize the GDR or maintain diplomatic relations with it (with the exception of the USSR), led to the GDR being largely isolated internationally, and the two German states did not officially recognize each other's sovereignty until

December 1972, when the Grundlagenvertrag (Basic Treaty) was signed.[24] The former Allies implicitly recognized the existence of the GDR with the Four Power Agreement on Berlin in 1971, and formal recognition followed a couple of years later (for instance, by France and the United Kingdom in 1973 and the US in 1974); other Western nations soon followed suit. As a consequence, the GDR did not initiate cultural exchange with the US and other nations until the early 1970s.[25]

Gerrit-Jan Berendse details how most East German writers were able to travel abroad once cultural exchange agreements between the GDR and other Western countries were signed; academics in the UK, France, Italy, and the Netherlands also began to regularly invite GDR writers to visit.[26] Wolf had been preceded in the US by Gisela May, a well-known singer of Brecht-Weill songs, and by writer Günter Kunert; she would be followed by a number of well-known GDR authors, including Ulrich Plenzdorf, Heiner Müller, Jureck Becker, Stefan Heym, Monika Maron, and Helga Schütz, who usually visited universities.[27]

For the GDR, artists' visits to the West—whether writers' visits, tours by symphony orchestras and singers, or art exhibitions—were intended to create a positive image of the socialist state's cultural politics.[28] In addition to showcasing the GDR and socialism generally, they were also, Ian Wallace argues, intended to distinguish the GDR from the capitalist FRG.[29] The GDR's desired outcomes of cultural exchange with the West thus mirrored those of the Soviet Union, as summarized by Mari Elisabet Herrala: "To strengthen the cultural and ideological influence of the Soviet Union, advertise its successes, and promote a picture of Soviet superiority in the eyes of its cultural exchange counterpart[s]."[30] Indeed, this was the central aim of cultural diplomacy on both sides of the Iron Curtain, as encapsulated in the commonplace claim that the Cold War was won by "jazz and blue jeans."[31] Yet this increased mobility also had complex internal ramifications: Alison Lewis, for instance, suggests that the initiation of cultural exchange in the 1970s was one of the main contributing factors to the high level of Stasi surveillance of the GDR literary scene, as it meant the regime needed a new and subtler approach to the growing issue of internal dissent to make sure it was able to identify writers critical of the regime and ensure they were not able to travel.[32]

## Christa Wolf's Visit to Oberlin

Arriving with her husband, Gerhard Wolf, in early April 1974, Wolf was the seventh writer-in-residence at Oberlin College (fig. 10.1). Oberlin's German department was the first in the United States to introduce a writer-in-residence

Figure 10.1. Writer Hermann Kant (right) congratulates Gerhard Wolf (left) on the award of the Heinrich Mann Prize, as Christa Wolf (center) looks on, on March 26, 1974, just a day or two before the Wolfs flew to New York, where they would spend a few days before traveling to Oberlin. © Bundesarchiv, Bild 183-N0326-034. Photo by Vera Stark-Katschorowski.

program for German-language writers, beginning in the academic year 1967–1968.[33] This was made possible by the Max Kade Foundation (New York), established by the German-born philanthropist of the same name.[34] Wolf was the first GDR writer at Oberlin, though she followed Helga Novak (1973), who had begun her career in the GDR and then moved to West Germany.[35] Shortly before traveling to the US, Wolf wrote to West German writer and playwright Peter Weiss and said she was traveling to the US "with mixed feelings."[36] After returning to Germany, she would emphasize how important the journey had been to her in other letters to friends, writing to Christa Dixon, for instance, that "the trip was a very important experience for me, and continues to have a strong and lasting effect."[37]

Although Wolf wrote fondly of the people she encountered at Oberlin both in these letters and in a later text remembering her stay at the college, she was fairly critical of the actions of the US government and of tendencies she saw in US society during her stay.[38] In an interview with East German literary journal *Sinn und Form*, she discusses "what occupied me a lot [at the time of writing her novel *Kindheitsmuster*] and continues to occupy me: a visit to the US and what I felt as though I saw there."[39] Though she does not specify in the interview what exactly she saw, both her letters and *Kindheitsmuster*, which she was writing during her time in Oberlin, give some indication. To Carlfried Claus, for instance, she writes that she found the certainty of Middle Americans that they are "living in the richest and freest country in the world" hard to bear in the long term and further describes Americans as "a mass of happy infantile consumers."[40]

Wolf's visit also confirmed the commonly held GDR perception of the US as racially divided. The GDR had officially signaled its anti-racist stance through a state-sponsored solidarity program to "Free Angela" during Black Panther Angela Davis's imprisonment from October 1970 to June 1972.[41] As a German-speaking member of the US Communist Party, Davis, who had visited East Berlin several times during her time as Theodor Adorno's graduate student in Frankfurt (1965–1967), was a particularly potent symbol of US racism for the GDR.[42] After her release from prison, Davis received an honorary doctorate from Karl-Marx University in Leipzig in 1972 and led the US delegation to the World Youth Festival in East Berlin in 1973 (see fig. 10.2).[43] In a letter during her stay at Oberlin to her friend, GDR writer Stephan Hermlin, Wolf wrote that "the Black ghettos in the cities are unbelievable." Writing to Christa Dixon soon after her stay, she expressed her agreement with James Baldwin's observations about the US; she also commented that Black and white children sit separately in school buses and classrooms in Oberlin.[44] In *Kindheitsmuster*, the narrator wonders whether the Black residents of American cities will ever revolt and declares her solidarity with Angela Davis.[45]

In other respects, too, Wolf indicated her support for the oppositional politics of what Davis termed "the other America" ("das andere Amerika") in her acceptance speech for the GDR Star of People's Friendship in 1972, awarded by head of state Walter Ulbricht.[46] At regular intervals in *Kindheitsmuster*, Wolf's narrator draws parallels, explicit and implicit, between contemporary atrocities in which the US was implicated—in Vietnam, Chile, and Laos, for instance—and the crimes of the Nazi era. While the narrator never goes as far as labeling the US fascist, in the interview with *Sinn und Form*, Wolf explicitly states that she saw "fascist and fascistoid developments" in the US during the period in which she was writing the novel.[47]

This sparked conflict with her editor at FSG when *Kindheitsmuster* was being translated in 1980. On February 10, Wolf wrote to Nancy Meiselas, her

Figure 10.2. Erich Honecker meets Angela Davis on September 11, 1972, and hands her an invitation to the World Youth Festival the following year. © Bundesarchiv, Bild 183-L0911-029. Photo by Peter Koard.

editor at FSG, declaring that she could not agree to Meiselas's suggested cuts of passages concerning the US and arguing that the novel's structure relies on associative comments on the political events that took place during the period of writing; one chapter, she wrote, was drafted entirely in Oberlin.[48] She would later realize that some abridgments, including the omission of several overtly critical references to US actions in Vietnam, had been undertaken without her permission when her French translator notified her after consulting the English translation.[49] The cuts included a line in which the narrator worries that current events like the US bombing of Vietnam could sink into oblivion, as she fears the events of the Nazi era already have.[50]

Despite her mixed feelings toward the US, Wolf saw her visit as an opportunity to network and boost the reputation of GDR literature, and she strongly supported the quest of Richard Zipser, an associate professor at Oberlin, to create a handbook on GDR literature. In a February 1975 letter, she assured the secretary of the GDR Writers' Union, Gerhard Henninger, that Zipser had no interest in "distorted depictions of our conditions or literature" and emphasized that this represented an opportunity to wrest control of GDR literature's international representation from the West German federally funded Goethe Institute.[51] Zipser's Stasi file further indicates that

Wolf characterized him as a "progressive US citizen" to the Writers' Union.[52] She was very frustrated when Zipser was initially refused permission to come to the GDR and interview authors, writing to Hermlin, "What is the point of traveling overseas, when everything one has painstakingly built up, is destroyed with the stroke of a pen when one gets back!"[53] In this instance, a project intended to showcase the GDR and its literature abroad—and thus seemingly in direct alignment with the GDR's goals for cultural exchange—appears to have been hampered by an inherent suspicion of the US and its citizens.[54]

### The Reception of Christa Wolf and GDR Literature in the United States

In the mid-1970s, when Zipser wanted to travel to East Germany to start work on his handbook, little GDR literature was read in the US. Although the English-language GDR publishing house Seven Seas had circulated a limited number of GDR literary works in translation since 1960, these books were often more widely distributed outside the US (and the UK), in leftwing bookshops in former English colonies, principally India but also South Africa and Australia.[55] Peter D. McDonald explains that this was "in part because of the protective copyright agreements but also because American customs officials were hostile to books emanating from communist countries."[56]

Indeed, GDR literature was hardly read anywhere outside the GDR until the 1970s. Even in the neighboring FRG, little GDR literature was published in the 1950s and 1960s, but by the 1970s, most West German literary publishers had East German authors in their program.[57] As Wolfgang Emmerich notes, West German and other foreign literary criticism only took notice of GDR literature around 1970.[58] This was partly due to the fact that there was a tendency in the immediate postwar years not to distinguish between FRG and GDR literature outside Germany, as many of the well-known authors of the time (such as Bertolt Brecht and Thomas Mann) were still associated with the culture of Germany before World War II.[59]

As Marc Silberman argues, 1974 (the year of Wolf's visit to Oberlin) was pivotal for GDR studies in the US.[60] Yet he notes that what seems like a sudden spike in scholarly interest actually represented the convergence of a number of factors. The most important of these was the improvement of political relations between the GDR and the US, but Silberman also outlines a variety of other elements, including the rise of the New Left and a shift from the earlier perception that all GDR literature was political propaganda.[61] After 1974, there was a great interest in GDR studies among US German

Studies scholars, resulting in conferences, journals, Modern Language Association (MLA) panels, associations, and a variety of student and academic exchange programs.[62] As of 1975, it was also possible for US academics to obtain International Research and Exchange Board (IREX) stipends to visit the GDR.[63]

Yet this level of scholarly interest in GDR literature was not reflected in the amount of GDR literature published in the US, which remained small and mainly encompassed short stories and poems in journals and literary magazines.[64] Indeed, David Bathrick argues that if one looks at indicators such as US bestseller lists, book reviews, and influence on American writers, "there is practically no reception of GDR literature in the US."[65] However, as Mark Rectanus points out, West German novels were not commonly published or widely reviewed in the US during the years of the GDR's existence, either.[66] Moreover, he suggests that the general American reading public continued not to make any distinction between East and West German literature, as was the case immediately after the war.[67] Wolf was an exception, having been both published and widely reviewed in the US.[68]

Wolf's texts began to circulate as world literature, in Damrosch's sense of the term, as soon as they were first translated, though the dissemination of *Divided Heaven*, her first work in English translation, was limited.[69] Damrosch argues that "a literary work *manifests* differently abroad than it does at home." He writes: "Works of literature take on a new life as they move into the world at large, and to understand this new life we need to look closely at the ways the work becomes reframed in its translation and in its new cultural contexts."[70] Wolf showed an awareness of this reframing in a letter to her first editor at FSG, Roger W. Straus, on the receipt of the proofs for the dust jacket of *Christa T* in 1971. Starting by noting that she does not like the dust jacket, she continues, "The lady on the cover teeters between demonic and classy, and neither fits the person whom I thought I had written about.... she has probably been translated into American, and has thus become completely foreign to me. This is probably one of the unavoidable aspects, or transformations, which literature must undergo when it is translated not only into foreign languages, but also into foreign worlds of experience."[71] Wolf understands that her work is not only being translated into a new language, but that it is also moving into a new cultural context—or world of experience, as she phrases it, a point she also emphasizes by referring to the new language as "American," rather than "English." Yet while Damrosch views this process as potentially positive, writing that "far from inevitably suffering a loss of authenticity or essence, a work can gain in many ways," Wolf seems to find the experience discomfiting and imagines her central character becoming completely foreign to her, suggesting that at some level she believes the GDR and US are culturally fundamentally different.[72]

While Wolf did not let this initial apprehension about how her work would mutate as it moved into a new cultural context stop her from publishing further translations with FSG, her work *was* received differently in the US than it was in either the FRG or GDR, as scholarly interpretation most often emphasized its feminist tendencies. Indeed, a phrase from Wolf's novel *Christa T*—"the difficulty of saying I"—was taken up as a catchphrase by American feminists.[73] The feminist reception of Wolf's work in the US, which extended to feminist scholars outside of German studies, is briefly noted by Pascale Casanova, who describes Wolf as "an East German writer who has become well known in feminist circles in the US as well."[74] Yet a variety of German studies scholars have criticized American feminists' tendency to sideline the cultural and political context of Wolf's work in order to emphasize her feminist stance. Angelika Bammer, for instance, argues that it is problematic that as Wolf "is incorporated into the feminist canon, she tends to be read less as a German (much less than a GDR-German) writer, than as a woman—indeed a Great Woman—writer."[75] Bathrick contends that some feminist readings of Wolf attempt to "locate Wolf completely within a feminist position and to see her ideological orientation and her GDR history as of considerably less importance."[76]

Bathrick suggests that US feminist readings of Wolf's work not only decontextualize but also *recontextualize* her work, thus implying, like Damrosch, that a literary work is not inevitably diminished in translation, but can also gain in a new cultural context.[77] Yet in an essay first published in 1978, Wolf indicates that while she admires the solidarity, spontaneity, and creativity of Western feminist movements, she does not believe that "sect-like" movements focused solely on women—resulting from the absence of a strong workers' movement, in her opinion—can address the issues facing society as a whole.[78] For Wolf, the enduring problems with women's position in GDR society, despite the progress made under socialism, illustrate the damage that patriarchal class society has inflicted on its objects and the long time period that it will take for them—whether male or female—to become subjects.[79]

While Wolf's approach to the dust jacket may indicate hesitancy about the *recontextualization* (Bathrick) or *reframing* (Damrosch) of her work in the US, elsewhere she emphasized that her work (and GDR literature more generally) had universal appeal and even suggested that literary works that do not function in other cultural contexts are parochial, responding to University of Massachusetts German studies scholar Sigrid Bauschinger's question of "whether GDR literature is incomprehensible outside the GDR" with the answer "now that would be pretty sad, because it would mean that GDR writers depict people and formulate problems that do not occur in the rest of the world or can at least not be understood ... of course—a certain part of the literature of a people or a country—the weaker part—will always remain provincial and therefore only have local meaning."[80] Wolf went on to emphasize that after her "experiences in Oberlin especially, [she] can say decidedly that the audience could access our poems and stories despite the very different social structures from which our and American literature, for instance, originate."[81]

Damrosch argues that a "work can enter world literature by embodying what are taken to be universal themes and values, so that local cultural detail can be considered secondary or even irrelevant."[82] Following this pattern, the 1973 *Kassandra*, which would become Wolf's most successful novel in the English-speaking world, did not directly allude to the contemporary GDR, although the ancient context can be read as an allegory for conditions in East Germany. Yet US readings of *Cassandra*, the English translation published in 1984, focused largely on the text's critique of patriarchy and war, supported in this by the novel's paratexts, especially its cover, which featured a stylized image of Cassandra dwarfing both title and author and a blurb describing *Cassandra*'s narrative as a "pressing monologue whose inner focal points are war and patriarchal society."[83] As Caroline Summers notes, the emphasis on universal themes in Wolf's work by English-language translators, editors, and reviewers sidelines the East German, socialist, humanist, and self-critical identity Wolf wished to embody.[84] Nevertheless, there is an inherent and seemingly unresolved tension between the realization that universal themes will appeal to a wider audience (as Wolf herself noted) and the desire for a culturally specific context to be retained and understood.

## Conclusion

When Wolf visited Oberlin in the spring of 1974, the GDR's international isolation, which had hindered GDR authors from traveling and their work from circulating as world literature, had recently ended. In Wolf's writings of this moment, she critiques the tendencies she sees during her time in the US—particularly relating to race—and voices her support for, and agreement with, oppositional figures such as Angela Davis and James Baldwin. In later years, Wolf would continue to emphasize the importance of maintaining contact with friends and acquaintances in the US. At the beginning of the Reagan era, for instance, she wrote to Helen Fehervary (a German literature professor at the Ohio State University) that, particularly at times when Europeans were concerned about US politics, it was important to remain "in contact and in conversation."[85]

Yet, as this chapter has argued, in this process of contact and conversation, Wolf's work was *reframed* (Damrosch) or *recontextualized* (Bathrick) in the US cultural context. The most prominent way in which this occurred was in the predominant focus on it as feminist, which emphasized the oppression of women as a universal ill while ignoring both the cultural and political context of the GDR and Wolf's resistance to political movements that focused solely on women's position in society. Other instances of reframing Wolf's work in a US context, intended to make her novels more palatable to a broader readership, included cover designs and even the omission of passages overtly critical of the US government. In the attempt to bring Wolf's literature to the American reading public—at a time when the supposed cultural differences between East and West figured prominently in the Cold War imagination—context was lost.

## Notes

1. Summers, "Patterns of Authorship," 378.
2. Kuhn, *From Marxism to Feminism*, 191.
3. Rectanus, "GDR Literature," 14; and Romero, "Rezeption in den USA," 363. Wolf's legacy has, however, been muddied by post-reunification controversies following both the 1990 publication of the autobiographical novella *Was bleibt* (*What Remains*), which focused on Stasi surveillance and was interpreted as an attempt by Wolf, who had been a privileged intellectual in the GDR, to be seen as a victim of the state, and the 1993 revelation that she had operated as an unofficial informant for the Stasi from 1959 to 1962.
4. She had already been successful in the GDR for more than a decade and was also well known in West Germany since the publication of *Nachdenken über Christa T* in 1968.
5. The first was Günter Kunert, who was a poet-in-residence at the University of Texas at Austin in 1972/1973.
6. Before 1972, GDR citizens had not been permitted to visit the US unless they also had a Western passport.
7. While there had been few US publications, conferences, or even conference panels on GDR literature previously, in 1974, there was: a special issue of *New German Critique* on GDR literature, a first major conference on the GDR at Washington University in St. Louis with 150 participants, and conference panels at both the American Association of Teachers of German and MLA conferences. Silberman, "Readings and Misreadings?," 611.
8. As Djagalov details, these processes were also at the core of attempts to create literary traffic between the Second and Third World during the Cold War. Djagalov, *From Internationalism to Postcolonialism*, 75.
9. Damrosch argues that there are a number of features of literary texts that can enable them to become world literature, but in Wolf's case, the most prominent seems to have been that the themes and values in her works were seen to be universal. Damrosch, *What Is World Literature?*, 213.
10. See, for instance, Mikkonen and Suutari, *Music, Art and Diplomacy*.

11. Moore and Spittel, "South by East," 4.
12. Djagalov, *From Internationalism to Postcolonialism*, 31.
13. Denning, *Culture in the Age of Three Worlds*, 53. See also Clark, who explores how the Soviet Union promoted "world literature" in the 1930s, both for domestic consumption and as an emblem of the antifascist movement: Clark, *Moscow*, 169–209.
14. Becher, "Von der Größe unserer Literatur," 408.
15. Djagalov tracks a similar timeline for literary exchange visits between USSR and Afro-Asian states but notes that while literary exchanges between the Soviet Bloc and the West usually involved Western leftists, Afro-Asian cultural producers were often representing their state rather than its opponents. Djagalov, *From Internationalism to Postcolonialism*, 73–74.
16. It should be noted that these agreements were generally for a fixed term, and thus the bilateral agreements mentioned here were often just the first in a series of agreements. The first two-year cultural exchange agreement between the FRG and USSR, signed in 1959, was an exception, as it was never really implemented or renewed due to the unresolved question of Berlin. See Großman, "Dealing with 'Friends'," 206.
17. Indeed, Herrala notes that "music and dance were often mentioned first in the bilateral cultural exchange agreements signed from the end of the 1950s." See Herrala, "Pianist Sviatoslav Richter," 100. See also Tomoff, *Virtuosi Abroad*.
18. Richmond, *Cultural Exchange and the Cold War*, 153.
19. Ibid., 154.
20. Ibid.
21. Ibid., 155, 157.
22. Popa, "'Discrete' Intermediaries," 164–165.
23. Gillabert, "Cultural Diplomacy of Switzerland," 91.
24. The FRG severed diplomatic relations with Yugoslavia in 1957 and Cuba in 1963, following each country's establishment of diplomatic relations with the GDR. Lightbody, *The Cold War*, 71.
25. GDR writers had visited other Western nations even before these developments, but none seem to have visited the US earlier; for example, Günter Kunert and Manfred Bieler had attended the Cheltenham Festival for Literature in the UK in 1965 (Wallace, "The GDR's Cultural Activities in Britain," 396) and Stefan Heym appeared at the Adelaide Writers Festival in Australia in 1970 (Moore and Spittel, "South by East," 17).
26. Berendse, "The Politics of Dialogue," 149, 156.
27. Wessel, *Bild und Gegenbild*, 50. On May, see Klemm, *Eine Amerikanerin in Ostberlin*, 44.
28. Klemm, *Eine Amerikanerin in Ostberlin*, 44.
29. Wallace, "The GDR's Cultural Activities in Britain," 394–95.
30. Herrala, "Pianist Sviatoslav Richter," 87.
31. Von Eschen, *Satchmo Blows Up the World*, 253. As Von Eschen further notes, the US jazz ambassadors' program was intended to amend the perception that the US was racist, although "America was still a Jim Crow nation." Ibid., 4.
32. By the late 1970s, most members of the Writers' Union were under some form of surveillance. Lewis, "Tinker, Tailor, Writer, Spy," 184. Richard Zipser writes that though the Writers' Union did not initially attempt to determine which writers were invited to Oberlin, they indicated in 1985 that they wished to decide who was invited in the future. See Zipser, "Reading My Stasi File," 166–167.
33. The program is open to all German-language writers, and writers-in-residence have included Germans, Swiss, and Austrians, in addition to German-language authors of other nationalities. Kaufmann, *Willkommen und Abschied*, x.
34. Ibid.
35. Ibid., xi.
36. Wolf, *Man steht sehr bequem zwischen allen Fronten*, 236.
37. Ibid., 243.

38. The text written later remembering her stay was for a volume about the German writers who had visited Oberlin: Kaufmann, *Willkommen und Abschied*, 55–58. In this text, there is no criticism of the American government or ideology; instead, the only negative reported impressions are related to the experience of a tornado and the unfamiliar American food: white sliced bread and flavored oatmeal. I use the German title of the novel (*Kindheitsmuster*) for clarity, as it was first entitled *A Model Childhood* and then later *Patterns of Childhood* in English.
39. "Diskussion mit Christa Wolf," 888.
40. Wolf, *Man steht sehr bequem zwischen allen Fronten*, 242.
41. Hagen, "Ambivalence and Desire," 157.
42. Kaplan, *Dreaming in French*, 183; and Davis, *An Autobiography*, 140.
43. Kaplan, *Dreaming in French*, 215.
44. Wolf, *Man steht sehr bequem zwischen allen Fronten*, 240, 244.
45. Wolf, *Kindheitsmuster*, 600.
46. Kirchmann, "Mit vollen Löffeln genießen."
47. "Diskussion mit Christa Wolf," 888.
48. Wolf, *Man steht sehr bequem zwischen allen Fronten*, 396.
49. Ibid., 397.
50. Wolf, *Kindheitsmuster*, 20.
51. Wolf, *Man steht sehr bequem zwischen allen Fronten*, 253.
52. Zipser, "Reading My Stasi File," 372.
53. Wolf, *Man steht sehr bequem zwischen allen Fronten*, 254.
54. The three-volume handbook was finally published in 1985 as *DDR-Literatur im Tauwetter: Wandel – Wunsch – Wirklichkeit*.
55. Moore and Spittel, "South by East," 16. Seven Seas also published texts by non-GDR writers, and Djagalov notes that a number of works by politically engaged African authors owed their first publication worldwide to Seven Seas. Djagalov, *From Internationalism to Postcolonialism*, 9.
56. McDonald, *The Literature Police*, 109.
57. Rectanus, "GDR Literature," 11–12.
58. Emmerich, "The GDR and Its Literature," 12.
59. Rectanus, "GDR Literature," 13.
60. Silberman, "Readings and Misreadings?," 611.
61. Ibid., 611–613.
62. Ibid., 614–616.
63. Klemm, *Eine Amerikanerin in Ostberlin*, 91. They had been available for other East European countries from 1968. Zipser traveled to the GDR with IREX funding in 1977 and 1978.
64. Gerber and Pouget, *Literature of the German Democratic Republic*, 4.
65. Bathrick, "Productive Mis-Reading," 1–2.
66. Rectanus, "GDR Literature," 13.
67. Bathrick, "Productive Mis-Reading," 2.
68. Rectanus, "GDR Literature," 14.
69. *Der geteilte Himmel* was published as *Divided Heaven* by the English-language GDR imprint Seven Seas. However, this flawed translation, which "eliminated the very features of the text that had destabilized ideological readings in the East," altering it to reflect the "masculine aesthetics of Socialist Realism," attracted little attention in the English-speaking world (von Ankum, "The Difficulty of Saying 'I'," 229).
70. Damrosch, *What Is World Literature?*, 6, 24.
71. Wolf, *Man steht sehr bequem zwischen allen Fronten*, 186.
72. Damrosch, *What Is World Literature?*, 6.
73. See, for instance, Rich, "Notes Towards a Politics of Location," 75.
74. Casanova, *The World Republic of Letters*, 167.
75. Bammer, "The American Feminist Reception of GDR Literature," 20.

76. Bathrick, "Productive Mis-Reading," 4.
77. Ibid. It is beyond the scope of this chapter to enter into the nuances of the debate about world literature, but it should briefly be noted that these criticisms of American feminist readings of Wolf's work raise some of the problems with world literature's blindness to linguistic and cultural specificity, as taken up by Apter in *Against World Literature*.
78. Wolf, *Werke*, 122–125.
79. Ibid., 122.
80. Wolf, *Man steht sehr bequem zwischen allen Fronten*, 245.
81. Ibid.
82. Damrosch, *What Is World Literature?*, 213. As Damrosch discusses in detail elsewhere in his monograph, earlier universalist approaches to Kafka ceded to approaches that focused on the particular from the 1980s onward (Damrosch, *What Is World Literature?*, 187–208).
83. Summers, "Hostage to Feminism?," 232–233.
84. Summers, "World Authorship as a Struggle for Consecration," 149.
85. Wolf, Man steht sehr bequem zwischen allen Fronten, 417.

## Bibliography

Apter, Emily. *Against World Literature: On the Politics of Untranslatability*. London: Verso, 2013.

Bammer, Angelika. "The American Feminist Reception of GDR Literature (With a Glance at West Germany)." *GDR Bulletin* 16, no. 2 (1990): 18–24.

Bathrick, David. "Productive Mis-Reading: GDR Literature in the USA." *GDR Bulletin* 16, no. 2 (1990): 1–6.

Becher, Johannes R. "Von der Größe unserer Literatur. Rede zur Eröffnung des IV. Deutschen Schriftstellerkongresses am 9. Januar 1956." In *Dokumente zur Kunst-, Literatur-und Kulturpolitik der SED. Band 1: 1949–1970*, edited by Elimar Schubbe, 408. Stuttgart: Seewald, 1972.

Berendse, Gerrit-Jan. "The Politics of Dialogue: Poetry in the GDR." In *Rereading East Germany: The Literature and Film of the GDR*, edited by Karen Leeder, 143–159. Cambridge: Cambridge University Press, 2015.

Casanova, Pascale. *The World Republic of Letters*. Translated by M. B. DeBevoise. Cambridge, MA: Harvard University Press, 2004.

Clark, Katerina. *Moscow, the Fourth Rome: Stalinism, Cosmopolitanism and the Evolution of Soviet Culture, 1931–1941*. Cambridge, MA: Harvard University Press, 2011.

Damrosch, David. *What Is World Literature?* Princeton, NJ: Princeton University Press, 2003.

Davis, Angela. *An Autobiography*. New York: Random House, 1974.

Denning, Michael. *Culture in the Age of Three Worlds*. London: Verso, 2004.

"Diskussion mit Christa Wolf." *Sinn und Form*, no. 4 (1976): 861–888.

Djagalov, Rossen. *From Internationalism to Postcolonialism: Literature and Cinema between the Second and the Third Worlds*. Montréal: McGill-Queen's University Press, 2020.

Emmerich, Wolfgang. "The GDR and Its Literature: An Overview." In *Rereading East Germany: the Literature and Film of the GDR*, edited by Karen Leeder, 8–34. Cambridge: Cambridge University Press, 2015.

Gerber, Margy, and Judith Pouget. *Literature of the German Democratic Republic in English Translation: A Bibliography*. Lanham, MD: University Press of America, 1984.

Gillabert, Matthieu. "Cultural Diplomacy of Switzerland and the Challenge of Peaceful Coexistence, 1956–75." In *Beyond the Divide*, edited by Simo Mikkonen and Pia Koivunen, 82–100. New York: Berghahn, 2015.

Großman, Sonja. "Dealing with 'Friends': Soviet Friendship Societies in Western Europe as a Challenge for Western Diplomacy." In *Beyond the Divide*, edited by Mikkonen and Koivunen, 196–217. New York: Berghahn, 2015.
Hagen, Katrina. "Ambivalence and Desire in the East German 'Free Angela Davis' Campaign." In *Comrades of Color: East German in the Cold War World*, edited by Quinn Slobodian, 157–187. New York: Berghahn, 2015.
Herrala, Meri Elisabet. "Pianist Sviatoslav Richter: The Soviet Union Launches a 'Cultural Sputnik' to the US in 1960." In *Music, Art and Diplomacy*, edited by Mikkonen and Suutari, 87–106. New York: Routledge, 2016.
Kaplan, Alice. *Dreaming in French: The Paris Years of Jacqueline Bouvier Kennedy, Susan Sontag, and Angela Davis*. Chicago: University of Chicago Press, 2012.
Kaufmann, Dorothea, ed. *Willkommen und Abschied: Thirty-Five Years of German Writers-in-Residence at Oberlin College*. Rochester, NY: Camden House, 2005.
Kirchmann, Hans. "Mit vollen Löffeln genießen." *Die Zeit*, September 22, 1972.
Klemm, Sibylle. *Eine Amerikanerin in Ostberlin: Edith Anderson und der andere deutsch-amerikanische Kulturaustausch. Histoire*. Bielefeld: Transcript Verlag, 2015.
Kuhn, Anna. *From Marxism to Feminism: Christa Wolf's Utopian Vision*. Cambridge: Cambridge University Press, 1988.
Lewis, Alison. "Tinker, Tailor, Writer, Spy: GDR Literature and the Stasi." In *Rereading East Germany: The Literature and Film of the GDR*, edited by Karen Leeder, 180–196. Cambridge: Cambridge University Press, 2015.
Lightbody, Bradley. *The Cold War*. London: Routledge, 1999.
McDonald, Peter D. *The Literature Police: Apartheid Censorship and Its Cultural Consequences*. Oxford: Oxford University Press, 2010.
Mikkonen, Simo, and Pia Koivunen, eds. *Beyond the Divide: Entangled Histories of Cold War Europe*. New York: Berghahn, 2015.
Mikkonen, Simo, and Pekka Suutari, eds. *Music, Art and Diplomacy: East-West Cultural Interactions and the Cold War*. New York: Routledge, 2016.
Moore, Christine, and Christina Spittel. "South by East: World Literature's Cold War Compass." In *Australian Literature in the German Democratic Republic: Reading Through the Iron Curtain*, edited by Christine Moore and Christina Spittel, 1–32. London: Anthem, 2016.
Popa, Ioana. "'Discrete' Intermediaries: Transnational Activities of the Fondation pour une entraide intellectuelle européenne, 1966–91." In *Beyond the Divide*, edited by Mikkonen and Koivunen, 151–176. New York: Berghahn, 2015.
Rectanus, Mark. "GDR Literature in the International Book Market: From Confrontation to Assimilation." *GDR Bulletin* 16, no. 2 (1990): 11–18.
Rich, Adrienne. "Notes Towards a Politics of Location." In *Arts of the Possible: Essays and Conversations*, 62–82. New York: W. W. Norton, 2001.
Richmond, Yale. *Cultural Exchange and the Cold War: Raising the Iron Curtain*. University Park: Penn State University Press, 2003.
Romero, Christiane Zehl. "Rezeption in den USA." In *Christa Wolf Handbuch: Leben - Wirken - Werk*, edited by Carolina Hilmes and Ilse Nagelschmidt, 363–369. Stuttgart: J. B. Metzler, 2016.
Silberman, Marc. "Readings and Misreadings?: The GDR and the GSA." *German Studies Review* 39, no. 3 (2016): 611–620.
Summers, Caroline. "Hostage to Feminism? The Success of Christa Wolf's *Kassandra* in its 1984 English Translation." *Gender & History* 30, no. 1 (2018): 226–239.

———. "Patterns of Authorship: The Translation of Christa Wolf's *Kindheitsmuster*." *German Life and Letters* 67, no. 3 (2014): 378–398.

———. "World Authorship as a Struggle for Consecration: Christa Wolf and *Der geteilte Himmel* in the English-Speaking World." *Seminar: A Journal of Germanic Studies* 51, no. 2 (2015): 148–172.

Tomoff, Kiril. *Virtuosi Abroad: Soviet Music and Imperial Competition during the Early Cold War, 1945–1958*. Ithaca, NY: Cornell University Press, 2015.

von Ankum, Katharina. "The Difficulty of Saying 'I': Translation and Censorship of Christa Wolf's *Der geteilte Himmel*." *Studies in Twentieth Century Literature* 17, no. 2 (1993): 223–241.

Von Eschen, Penny M. *Satchmo Blows Up the World: Jazz Ambassadors Play the Cold War*. Cambridge, MA: Harvard University Press, 2006.

Wallace, Ian. "The GDR's Cultural Activities in Britain." *German Life and Letters* 53, no. 3 (2000): 394–408.

Wessel, Daisy. *Bild und Gegenbild: die USA in der Belletristik der SBZ und der DDR (bis 1987)*. Opladen: Leske & Budrich, 1989.

Wolf, Christa. *Kindheitsmuster*. München: Deutscher Taschenbuch, 1995.

———. *Man steht sehr bequem zwischen allen Fronten: Briefe 1952–2011*. Berlin: Suhrkamp, 2016.

———. *Werke*, vol 8. Edited by Sonja Hilzinger. München: Luchterhand, 2000.

Zipser, Richard. "Reading My Stasi File." *Colloquia Germanica* 39, no. 3/4 (2006): 367–382.

> BRANGWEN STONE is Chair of the Department of Germanic Studies at the University of Sydney. She is author of *Heimkehr? Narratives of Return to Germany's Former Eastern Territories 1965–2001*.

CHAPTER 11

TRANSLATING COLD WAR INTERNATIONALISM
*Allegoresis in Ryszard Kapuściński's Literary Reportage*

Marla Zubel

RENOWNED IN HIS HOME COUNTRY of Poland and abroad, Ryszard Kapuściński would become one of the most celebrated literary journalists of the twentieth century. Between the 1950s and 1970s, he built a reputation as a chronicler of Third World national liberation movements in works of literary reportage that were informed by the Socialist Bloc's Cold War politics of solidarity with the decolonizing world. His writing appeared in major Polish newspapers and magazines of the era (*Sztandar Młodych, Trybuna Ludu, Kultura,* and *Polityka*) and was reprinted in popular book-length volumes, among them *Black Stars* (*Czarne gwiazdy*, 1963), *If All of Africa* (*Gdyby cała Afryka*, 1969), *Christ with a Rifle on His Shoulder* (*Chrystus z karabinem na ramieniu*, 1975), and *The Soccer War* (*Wojna futbolowa*, 1978). This body of work forms an essential category of contemporary world literature as it was conceived under actually existing socialism.

But in the 1980s, as the Cold War came to a close, Kapuściński was refashioned (and arguably refashioned himself) as a dissident writer, rather than a fellow traveler.[1] The complex personal political trajectory that led to this transformation is chronicled by Artur Domosławski, whose important (and controversial) biography, *Ryszard Kapuściński: A Life* (2013), goes to great lengths to examine Kapuściński's shifting, and at times contradictory, political commitments.[2] This chapter, in contrast, is concerned with the way the English translation and "transediting" of select works by Kapuściński

193

eclipsed these works' socialist and anti-colonial valences at a time when anglophone publishers sought to adapt the literary cosmopolitanism of a waning socialist internationalism to the emergent political-economic paradigm of neoliberal globalization.[3]

This process of adaptation and reframing reflected broader trends in the anglophone publishing world in the last decade of the Cold War, as publishers energetically translated and marketed works by writers on the other side of the Iron Curtain. Harcourt Brace Jovanovich, *Granta* magazine/Granta Books, and Penguin Books all commissioned translations and built book series and lists that sought to bring modern and postmodern Eastern European literature to a wider readership and into the canon of twentieth-century world literature. In many respects, these initiatives are exemplary of what Pascale Casanova has called *littérisation*—or the process by which publishers, critics, and academics in the West come to regard a text from beyond Western Europe and the United States as being of literary value and worthy of attention. Scholars of contemporary world literature have tended to mobilize Casanova's conceptual framework to understand the political, economic, and racial hierarchies that inform the publication and circulation of literature of the Global South in the Global North.[4] The publishing dynamics of works of world literature that managed to cross the Iron Curtain have gone comparatively underexamined.[5]

Yet the anglophone translation of Cold War–era Eastern European literature provides a particularly rich area of study for understanding the geopolitical dynamics that shaped conceptions of world literature in the latter half of the twentieth century.[6] As David Damrosch has argued, it is the social and aesthetic values of the culture into which a work is being translated—what he calls the "host culture"—that largely determine whether and how a foreign text finds its way into translation and circulation in that culture.[7] These values are far from politically neutral. During the Cold War, publishing initiatives often participated (intentionally or otherwise) in the assimilation of Eastern European literature into aesthetic and political categories that held anticommunist dissidence to be the only authentic form of cultural expression in the region, resulting in an oversimplification or misrecognition of the complex political commitments that shaped the original works.

The publication history of Kapuściński's most popular and widely translated work, *Cesarz / The Emperor: Downfall of an Autocrat* (1978; 1983 in English), serves as a compelling case study for this process of assimilation. As a magical realist account of the excesses and abuses of Haile Selassie I's dictatorship in Ethiopia, *The Emperor* was widely interpreted by Polish readers to be an allegory for the political dysfunction of the Polish socialist state. The work was the first of Kapuściński's books to be translated into English, and its allegorical quality also enabled its reception in the anglophone world, where *The Emperor* was enthusiastically received as a parable for the political and economic failures of both the Second and Third Worlds. In its English translation, I argue, the work participated in the ideological containment of the global socialist and anti-imperialist movements that had in the 1960s posed serious threats to US interests. Moreover, in Poland, the publication of *The Emperor* marked the end of a political culture of solidarity with Third World peoples, even as the work reflected and inspired the political sentiments that would soon give rise to Poland's Solidarność (Solidarity) movement.

## Socialist Internationalist Reportage as World Literature

Before looking more closely at *The Emperor*, it is necessary to situate the form and content of Kapuściński's reportage in the broader contexts of socialist internationalism and aesthetics. Nurtured by the interwar East Central European and Soviet avant-gardes, literary reportage became a formal paradigm of Socialist Bloc journalism during the Cold War, when, amid the global upheaval of Third World decolonization, the genre was mobilized in the service of socialist internationalism. This hybrid literary-journalistic form, which had proved useful for chronicling life on collective farms and construction sites from the 1920s through the 1950s, was now tasked with fostering a culture of solidarity and friendship between Second and Third World peoples that reflected the Socialist Bloc's renewed commitment to an anti-imperialist foreign policy agenda.[8]

This was Kapuściński's beat. And while his success abroad set him apart from many of his contemporaries, he was certainly not the only Polish journalist to turn to literary reportage to cover Third World struggles. In the 1960s, while writing for the weekly newsmagazine *Polityka*, Kapuściński was part of a group of journalists known as "Rakowski's gang" ("banda Rakowskiego") after the magazine's editor, Mieczysław Rakowski.[9] The gang included, among others, Daniel Passent, who reported on the Vietnam War and published his collected reportage on that conflict in a volume titled *Every Day, War* (*Co dzień wojna*, 1968), and Marian Turski, who, like Kapuściński, wrote about the decolonization of Africa in the early 1960s. Turski also covered the Civil Rights movement in the United States, where he participated in and reported on the march from Selma to Montgomery.

In addition to appearing in newsmagazines, Polish internationalist reportage was published by Iskry State Publishing House in the book series "The World Is Changing" ("Świat się zmienia"). Between 1960 and 1972, the series published over two dozen titles, including Witold Zalewski's *View of the Yellow River* (*Widok Żółtej Rzeki*, 1960), Klemens Kęplicz's *Old India in a New World* (*Stare Indie w nowym świecie*, 1964), Wojciech Giełżyński's *Indonesia, Archipelago of Unrest* (*Indonezja, archipelag niepokojów*, 1966), and Ryszard Bańkowicz and Aleksander Ziemny's *Eyes on Mexico* (*Oczy na Meksyk*, 1968). As works of nonfiction, these texts documented Second World encounters with the Third World at the height of the Cold War. Their shifting geographical focus—from Africa to Asia and then to Latin America—reflected critical developments in the politics and practices of global socialism as it positioned itself against colonialism and neocolonialism, in alliance with the politics of Non-Alignment and Tricontinentalism.[10]

I do not wish to suggest that the writers of this vast body of work ascribed to one political ideology, which they uniformly propagandized through their reportage and travelogues. Rather, these texts may be understood to be works of socialist internationalism insofar as the geopolitical formations and networks in which they worked (including where they went and with whom they interacted) were broadly determined by the Soviet Union's Cold War alliances.[11] Socialist internationalist reportage did not simply cover Third World national liberation struggles; it participated in the worlding of these struggles through sympathetic characters, compelling narratives, and engaged first-person narration that fostered support for anti-imperialist policies and practices. This literary quality is critical for understanding Kapuściński's oeuvre. But more than serving as a reflection of the official program of Socialist Bloc solidarity with the Third World, Kapuściński's writing frequently attempted to push the Socialist Bloc's embrace of anti-imperialism to its logical conclusion in the Second World. Through the use of allusion and allegory, Kapuściński's work often gestured beyond its journalistic content to express criticism of Poland's historical position as an intra-European colony of Imperial Russia and its contemporaneous position as a Soviet satellite state. His reportage drew parallels between the histories of foreign control and local government corruption in both Poland *and* the decolonizing world. In this way, it adhered to the Socialist Bloc's stated commitment to anti-imperialism while also drawing attention to the inconsistent application of this commitment within the bloc itself, as many Eastern European republics were prevented (under the threat of Soviet invasion) from developing national paths to socialism that diverged from the Soviet model. Kapuściński's reportage, therefore, functioned simultaneously as news and allegory as it sought to bring the politics of anti-imperialism to bear on the Polish national context.[12]

By the late 1970s, however, the allegorical qualities of Kapuściński's reportage came to eclipse its role as journalism. The publication of *The Emperor* in 1978 marked a move away from the journalistic foundations of the genre and toward a more literary and interpretive style of writing in which the Third World merely served as a pretense for commenting on conditions at home. Whereas earlier works like *Black Stars* (1963) and *Christ with a Rifle on His Shoulder* (1975) were works of journalism that contained subtle moments of self-referentiality, *The Emperor* was primarily a literary work. The overthrow of Selassie was not so much reported on (indeed, the hard facts of the event are somewhat opaque in the text) as transfigured into an allegory for a larger—and supposedly universal—truth: state socialism and Third-worldism had both emphatically failed.

### THE EMPEROR ALLEGORY IN POLAND

In 1974, while on assignment for the Polish Press Agency (PAP), Kapuściński traveled to Addis Ababa to report on the military coup that overthrew Haile Selassie I—the once-beloved anti-colonial leader who had ruled Ethiopia with an iron fist for nearly forty-five years. Several years later, in 1978, Kapuściński published a series of articles about the events surrounding the coup d'état in the Polish weekly *Kultura* under the collective title "Trochę Etiopii" / "A Bit of Ethiopia." These articles served as the basis for *The Emperor*, which was published later that year.

The book was an immediate success in Poland, selling over a hundred thousand copies in the first four years.[13] Its popularity had much to do with the fact that it offered not only an account of Selassie's deposing, but also a sumptuously written fable about the seemingly inevitable demise of a political regime propped up on fear and favors that basked in luxuries enjoyed at the expense of the people. This was a way of governing that, to many Polish readers, appeared to have a great deal in common with that of their own country, as the regime of Edward Gierek attempted to quell the popular unrest that had resulted from a series of economic and political crises in the mid-1970s. This unrest would coalesce around the formation of the Solidarność trade union and would lead not only to Gierek's removal in 1980, but also to the end of Communist Party rule by the end of the decade.

*The Emperor* presents life under the Selassie regime as a series of testimonies told to the Polish reporter by former dignitaries and servants of the Ethiopian government who, wishing to remain anonymous for fear of violent reprisal, are identified only by their initials. Because they are told from an insider's (rather than detractor's) point of view, lamenting the downfall of the regime, these accounts speak of the excesses of Selassie's rule with an absurd matter-of-factness and nostalgic tone. Kapuściński's commentary, interspersed throughout the text and set off from the testimonies with italics, grounded the otherwise fantastical tales of everyday life in the palace. The reported narratives unfold in a magical realist style that seems to reflect the absurd surreality of a regime that has moved beyond logic and reason. This is a world in which the emperor's small dog is allowed to urinate on the shoes of dignitaries—"august gentlemen who were not allowed to flinch or make the slightest gesture when they felt their feet getting wet."[14] A palace servant is charged solely with the task of wiping the urine from their shoes with a satin cloth. While the country is stricken with widespread poverty and famine, an extra palace is constructed in the Ogaden Desert, fully stocked and maintained by a staff of servants on the off chance that Selassie might one day need to stop there for the night.

In addition to documenting the eccentricities of the regime, *The Emperor* is concerned with the broader cultural impact of Selassie's rule. According to one of Kapuściński's informants, the emperor's favor and the granting of assignments would provoke physical transformations in otherwise normal citizens: "The facial features become solemn, almost stiffened . . . set to create no possibility of psychological contact . . . Nor is the Emperor's favorite eager to talk, since a change in speech is another post-assignment symptom. Multiple monosyllables, grunts, clearings of the throat, meaningful pauses, changes of intonation, misty words, and a general air of having known everything better and for a longer time replace simple, full sentences."[15]

But when such a man is inevitably demoted and removed from the palace, "the effects of the promotion disappear. The physical changes reverse themselves, and the one who has hit the street returns to normal . . . as if it had been some illness not worth mentioning."[16] Of the proliferation of secret police and spies in the final years of Selassie's reign, Kapuściński writes: "Ears appeared everywhere, sticking out of the ground, glued to the walls, flying through the air, hanging on doorknobs, hiding in offices, lurking in crowds, standing in doorways, jostling in the marketplace."[17] As a result, people learned to speak "another language, mastered it, and became so fluent in it that we simple and uneducated folk suddenly became a bilingual nation . . . one tongue served for external speech, the other for internal."[18] Here, in one of the work's many self-referential moments, Kapuściński employs magical realism (the descriptions of ears and a secret language) as a form of doublespeak in order to cue readers into the book's internal allegory.

*The Emperor*'s allegorical qualities were so apparent at the time of its publication that Minister of Culture Józef Tejchma noted in a diary entry dated March 16, 1978, "It's about Ethiopia, but it's just as much about today's Poland."[19] Nevertheless, the Central Committee Press Department chose not to censor the book or prevent the publication of subsequent editions. Censoring a work for being allegorical would mean legitimating its interpretation as such, potentially conferring on it even greater power. As Kapuściński later recalled in an interview, "We decided that if anybody in censorship tried to make trouble for us we would report them to the Party Control Bureau, saying there is somebody who dares to compare this corrupt fascist dictatorship of Haile Selassie with the excellent leadership of Comrade Gierek. Who could say such a thing? Who could dare to see the text in this way?"[20]

Authorial intent is difficult to prove, and the text always exceeds it. This is true even of allegorical works, for allegoresis is as much a mode of reading as it is a mode of writing. Thus, the threat *The Emperor* presented to the regime had less to do with the book's content than with the impossibility of controlling its popular interpretation. As Kapuściński later explained in an essay titled "From Warsaw, 1982" ("Z Warszawy, 1982"): "In Poland every text is read as allusive, every written situation—even the most distant in space and time—is immediately, without hesitation, applied to the situation in Poland. In this way, every text is a double text, and between the printed lines we search for sympathetic messages."[21]

In *The Emperor*, these messages are transmitted through particularly effective use of what Marcel Cornis-Pope has called "Aesopian language," or language that conveys an innocuous message to censors but contains a second, more subversive meaning to readers in the know.[22] Many scholars of Kapuściński's work emphasize the degree to which he (and other writers of socialist-era Polish reportage) developed strategies for "subverting the documentary techniques of communist propaganda and using them for other ends."[23] But what is often lost in the discussion of double texts, Aesopian language, and subversion is the fact that these "other ends" were not always ideologically anticommunist. In Kapuściński's writing about Ghana and Congo in the 1960s, for example, critiques of the political situation in Poland were conveyed through expressions of solidarity with experiments in Third World postcolonial governance that seemed (at least for a time) to offer new forms of state socialism, alternatives to the Soviet model. But by the late 1970s, as the era of decolonization came to a close, the commitment to Third World solidarity that had once been at the core of Kapuściński's reportage underwent a dramatic shift. The allegorical qualities of his work ceased to function as a literary strategy for cultivating alliances with the decolonizing and postcolonial world and instead served to undermine these alliances.

As allegory, *The Emperor* flies off the page, as both the writer and reader are set free from reportorial fidelity to the Ethiopian context. To a certain degree, this abandonment of reality is fundamental to allegory, which works by stripping that which is represented of its immediate context and elevating it to a universal truth. As Walter Benjamin theorized in *The Origin of German Tragic Drama*, in allegory, "all of the things that are used to signify derive, from the very fact of their pointing to something else, a power which makes them appear no longer commensurable with profane things, which raises them onto a higher plane, and which can, indeed, sanctify them."[24] As a result, "the profane world is both elevated and devalued" in what Benjamin called the "antinomies of allegoresis."[25]

In the context of a work of reportage about a Third World nation, this simultaneous devaluing and sanctifying of the original object of the allegorical work becomes deeply problematic. Through allegoresis, the profane world represented in *The Emperor* (the fall of Selassie) loses its meaning in the Ethiopian context and takes on another meaning that not only refers to Poland, but comes to occupy a higher plane of truth: the inevitable fall of all dictators and decadent regimes. With the Third World demoted from concrete geopolitical ally to allegorical space, Polish readers were no longer invited to understand themselves to be in a common struggle with real Third World peoples, as their cultural and political equals (as they had been encouraged to do in internationalist reportage of the 1960s and early 1970s). Instead, the Third World became an imaginary space onto which the Polish national context could be superimposed—in effect evacuating that space of political meaning on its own terms and reducing its people to stereotypes.

For example, throughout *The Emperor*, Kapuściński's informants use increasingly over-the-top honorifics to refer to Selassie, such as "His Most Virtuous Highness" (*przezacny pan*), "His Benevolent Majesty" (*dobrotliwy pan*), "His Merciful Highness" (*miłościwy pan*), and "His Most Puissant Majesty" (*osobliwego*).[26] In his critical review of the book, Ethiopia scholar Harold G. Marcus points out that the use of such honorifics is pure fiction: "Those of us who take Amharic and its usage seriously are insulted by the artistic license taken by Kapuscinski when he ostensibly replicates conversations with informants . . . a simple 'Jahnhoy' or 'Majesty' would have sufficed."[27] Thus, although *The Emperor* uses the Ethiopian context as a pretense for criticizing the Polish government (in which case, the real target of criticism is Poland, not Ethiopia), such moments of artistic license invite allegoresis by reproducing the colonial and neocolonial discourse that framed African nations as unfit for self-rule. Polish self-recognition (even if it is a self-deprecating recognition) is made possible by appealing to the readers' deeply embedded assumptions of European cultural superiority over Africa. *The Emperor* is effective as political allegory because it relies on negative identification. When Polish readers are made to see reflections of themselves in Ethiopians, they become aware of just how bad things have become. The Third World is no longer a source of political inspiration, and the story of Selassie's regime is a wake-up call; Poles must not allow themselves to become like Africans.

Without a doubt, imperialist tropes were detectable in Kapuściński's earlier reportage, but when compared with *The Emperor* and especially with works published after the collapse of socialism, these aspects of his writing are comparatively restrained. It is telling that they found their fullest expression toward the end of and after the Cold War, when Thirdworldism, as both an international movement and a political standpoint, began to wane. Whereas the internationalist political culture of the Socialist Bloc in the 1960s had required representations of non-Western peoples as self-determining subjects, the opposite was demanded by the culture on the other side of the Iron Curtain. And the triumph of the capitalist countries gave rise to a new form of literary internationalism under the banner of neoliberal globalization.

## THE EMPEROR ALLEGORY ABROAD

The publication of *The Emperor* in English (now with the added subtitle *Downfall of an Autocrat*) coincided with a major political crisis in Poland, on which the West's eyes were fixed. From December 1981 until July 1983, General Wojciech Jaruzelski, the newly appointed First Secretary of the Polish Communist Party, instituted martial law—a state of emergency that resulted in mass arrests and governmental repression throughout the country. Jaruzelski's crackdown was largely in response to strikes that had paralyzed the Gdańsk shipyards in 1980 and led to the formation of Solidarność, the first independent worker's organization in the Socialist Bloc.[28]

In 1983, with Poland cut off from the rest of the world by martial law and the United States imposing economic sanctions against the country, Kapuściński entered the world literary market when the New York–based publisher Harcourt Brace Jovanovich published an English-language edition of *The Emperor* translated by William R. Brand and Katarzyna Mroczkowska-Brand. With Central European émigré Helen Wolff at its helm (her late husband, Kurt Wolff, had been Kafka's publisher in Germany before World War II), the publishing house had made a name for itself publishing English translations of works by Günter Grass, Boris Pasternak, Max Frisch, and Italo Calvino. Kapuściński's work of magical realism about Selassie's downfall seemed to fit nicely on their list of modernist and postmodernist continental writers. Moreover, as Domosławski has argued, the political crisis in Poland meant that Kapuściński's dissident voice was eagerly and urgently received by American readers who were already captivated by newspaper headlines about Polish resistance to the Communist regime.[29]

By all measures, *The Emperor* was an immediate success in the anglophone world. "[*The Emperor's*] reception among literati in the West," John Ryle noted in his review of Kapuściński's *The Shadow of the Sun* (2001), "was conditioned by an awareness of its doubly exotic origin—a book about a far-off country by an author who was himself a *rara avis*, a master of the new journalism, sprung miraculously from within the Soviet bloc."[30] John Updike reviewed *The Emperor* favorably in *The New Yorker*, as did Tariq Ali in *The New Statesman*. Ali called *The Emperor* the "most powerful piece of non-fiction I have read in years; it is a stunning mosaic of history, journalism, and literature."[31] Salman Rushdie named it the book of the year in a review for the *Sunday Times*. "Always concrete and observant," Rushdie wrote, "[Kapuściński's writing] conjures marvels of meaning out of minutiae. And his book transcends reportage, becoming a nightmare of power depicted as a refusal of history that reads as if Italo Calvino had rewritten Machiavelli."[32]

None of these reviewers concerned themselves with the text's inaccuracies, exaggerations, and generalizations about Ethiopia. As Harold G. Marcus aptly observed at the time: "Instead of seeking out knowledgeable reviewers, [the media] chose political activists, novelists, librarians, and others remote from Ethiopian studies [to review *The Emperor*]. They inactively conspired to hoodwink the public into believing that a bad book on one subject was really a good book on another.... those that preside over reviews are uninterested in Africa and therefore do not take the continent or its problems seriously."[33]

Since the work was clearly allegorical, reviewers were all too willing to grant Kapuściński permission to shirk responsibility for providing an accurate and culturally sensitive representation of the political situation in Ethiopia. After all, its readers, both at home and abroad, were primarily concerned with current events in Poland, not Ethiopia.

Although the allegorical aspects of *The Emperor* were not lost on Western readers, it is important to note that this process of allegoresis was different from that which took place in Poland. As Frederic Jameson has observed, contrary to traditional understanding, allegory is not fixed, but shifts according to the context of reception: "Our traditional conception of allegory... is that of an elaborate set of figures and personifications to be read against some one-to-one table of equivalences.... [But] such equivalences are themselves in constant change and transformation at each perpetual present of the text."[34]

In English translation, the allegory of *The Emperor* offered an occasion for anglophone readers to laugh at the absurd "backwardness" of *both* Africa and Eastern Europe. When, for example, Kapuściński writes that young people who had gone abroad to be educated in the universities of the West would return to Ethiopia, "put their heads in their hands, and cry, 'Good God, how can anything like this exist,'" the meaning for American readers was more insidious than it would have been for the original audience.[35] Where Polish readers would have been encouraged to recognize similarities between their own experiences and those of the Ethiopian people, American readers would find confirmation of Western cultural superiority over both of these parts of the world. Being in on the work's thinly veiled critique of the Polish government at a time when the United States was lending support to the country's emergent anticommunist movement allowed American readers to experience the work from a position of moral authority. *The Emperor* seemed to provide confirmation that they were on the right side of history.

A *Newsweek* review of the book by Peter Prescott gave voice to this self-assuredness: "An allegory of totalitarian governments today? Almost certainly. Haile Selassie is a stand-in for Stalin, for Big Brother, the ruler who brings his country to a condition of near perfect stasis. It's a fascinating performance, seductively written and translated as if there were no language barrier."[36] Prescott's insistence on the unique communicative capacity of the work not only obscures the highly mediated nature of literary translation; it also denies the existence of cultural barriers that might potentially limit the work's intelligibility in a different cultural context. In fact, when read from within the political context in which *The Emperor* was conceived, the allegorical meaning of the text is not quite as straightforward as Prescott's review would suggest. After all, in *The Emperor*'s "downfall of an autocrat" narrative, Selassie was overthrown by Marxists, and the Provisional Military Administrative Council (the "Dergue") that replaced Selassie was backed by the Soviet Union. This council was, in Kapuściński's words, composed of "bright, intelligent men, ambitious and embittered patriots conscious of the terrible state of affairs in their homeland, of the stupidity and helplessness of the elite, of the corruption and depravity, the humiliating dependence of the country on stronger states."[37]

Moreover, while Kapuściński's account of the coup d'état lends support to the Dergue's actions, it also gives Selassie credit for the modernization of Ethiopia. Among the regime's many accomplishments, Kapuściński notes the abolition of the slave trade, reforms to the legal system and capital punishment, the publication of the country's first newspaper, the electrification of the nation, and the creation of the postal service. Sitting with the contradictions embodied by the emperor, Kapuściński reflects:

> There existed two images of Haile Selassie. One, known to international opinion, presented the Emperor as a rather exotic, gallant monarch distinguished by indefatigable energy, a sharp mind, and a profound sensitivity, a man who made a stand against Mussolini, recovered his empire and his throne, and had ambitions of developing his country and playing an important role in the world. The other image, formed gradually by a critical and initially small segment of Ethiopian opinion, showed the monarch as a ruler committed to defending his power at any cost, a man who was above all a great demagogue and a theatrical paternalist who used words and gestures to mask the corruption and servility of a ruling elite that he had created and coddled. And, as often happens, both these images were correct.... He ruled a country that knew only the cruelest methods of fighting for power (or of keeping it).... He was out of touch with the new world.[38]

In contrast, the opposition "had workers and students behind them ... the members of the Dergue were people of great courage. And also, to some extent, desperados."[39] *The Emperor* is thus not simply the story of a corrupt regime; it is more precisely a story of the ongoing struggle for national liberation, embodied first by Selassie and then by a generation of young Marxists informed by the spirit of 1968. When read in this light, *The Emperor*'s allegory is no longer principally an anticommunist one. It has to do, instead, with young militants attempting to take the next steps toward the actualization of the postcolonial Communist project in an effort to correct its grotesque deformation.

Notably, this project was shared by certain segments of the Polish workers' movement in the 1970s and early 1980s. For many, the formation of Solidarność—which grew out of an organization called the Workers' Defense Committee (Komitet Obrony Robotników, or KOR)—initially seemed to signify the beginning of a new phase of class struggle in the Socialist Bloc.[40] In a 1983 article titled "Solidarity and Egalitarianism," Henryk Flakierski noted that Solidarność's program was "one of the most egalitarian ever formulated in a socialist country. No Communist Party in the last 50 years, not even in Maoist China, has gone so far."[41] Tellingly, in 1985, conservative thinker Piotr Wierzbicki criticized "the vision of a future independent Polish society" put forward by the opposition at the time, which was "not against socialism, only its distortions, and aimed to improve it by establishing a harmonious existence between the state-run economy, trade unions, and local governments, hitherto unknown anywhere in the world."[42] And in 1992, with the perspective of hindsight and speaking from the left, Raymond Taras emphasized Solidarność's fundamentally socialist tenets. "While there are various interpretations of the Solidarity movement," he noted, "the most convincing ... is as a revolutionary movement of the industrial (especially highly-skilled) working class on whose bandwagon other social groups subsequently jumped."[43] After the collapse of the Soviet Union, the global narrative of the movement as a thoroughly anticommunist one solidified in accordance with the broader narrative of capitalist triumphalism. But as with other periods of upheaval in Eastern Europe, the early Solidarność movement's antigovernment agenda was not necessarily ideologically anticommunist. Keeping this in mind allows one to interpret the allegory of *The Emperor*—both its production and its reception—with greater political nuance and to re-situate the text in relation to the socialist and anti-imperialist commitments expressed in so much of Kapuściński's earlier writing.

As Kapuściński was an Eastern European journalist whose work had been informed by the socialist internationalism of the 1960s and 1970s, his reportage was a somewhat unlikely fit for the neoliberal cosmopolitanism of the West in the 1980s. His work, therefore, had to be framed to fit the sensibilities of what Timothy Brennan has called the "actually existing Western aesthetics" of the period.[44] Like the literature of Kapuściński's non-Western contemporaries—the novels of the Latin American Boom of the 1970s or works by postcolonial writers like Salman Rushdie, Derek Walcott, and Wole Soyinka—his reportage offered readers an experience of hybridity and difference. At the same time that modern literature of the Global South was being discovered by the West, US and UK publishers began to offer their readers Eastern European literary experiences of a very particular kind (i.e., not socialist). Kapuściński's first English-language publisher, Harcourt Brace Jovanovich, was among those who helped to facilitate the Western perception of an Eastern European literary renaissance, but the most influential of these publishing projects was arguably Penguin Books' "Writers from the Other Europe" series. Under the general editorship of Philip Roth, the series (which ran from 1974 to 1989) published major literary works by Eastern European writers, including Milan Kundera and Danilo Kiš, who were largely unknown to American readers at the time. Both Roth's series and the "old world" list of Harcourt Brace Jovanovich partook in a Cold War–inflected process of *littérisation* whereby select works of literature from Europe's periphery were annexed to the literary centers of the West so that anglophone readers could discover foreign writers who fit the Free World's literary and political categories.

In the case of Kapuściński's *The Emperor*, these categories were multiple and overlapping—and at times contradictory. When lifted from its original political and cultural context, the work could now be made to fit the ideological demands of the anglophone audience's imperialist gaze (often expressed in the 1980s as a cosmopolitan fascination with postcolonial cultures) *and* its anticommunism. As a hybrid subject of the culturally and geographically liminal space of Eastern Europe, Kapuściński offered readers glimpses of exotic Third World landscapes that he—by virtue of his in-between status as both European and of the Cold War East—seemed uniquely positioned to both understand and interpret, all the while leaving Western cultural superiority safely intact.

This could not be said of Kapuściński's earlier works of reportage, which were patently critical of the Western powers and the economic and cultural legacy of their imperialist endeavors. It is notable that, with the exception of the edited and condensed versions of essays that were republished in the volume *The Soccer War* (1978; 1991 in English), most of these early works have not been translated into English. *The Emperor*, by contrast, fit easily into American cultural assumptions about both the Second and Third Worlds. Insofar as the book's representation of Ethiopia played to stereotypes of both the excesses of the Third World despot and the totalitarianism of the Socialist Bloc, the English edition of *The Emperor* reinforced US cultural and political hegemony in the twilight of the Cold War.

It should come as no surprise, then, that Kapuściński's subsequent works of reportage, including *Imperium* (1993; 1994 in English) and *Heban* (1998; *The Shadow of the Sun*, 2001, in English)—works written during and after the dissolution of the Socialist Bloc, and with English translation in mind—helped establish a greater cultural and political alliance with the West, against both the former Soviet Union and the Third World. *The Shadow of the Sun*, a memoir about Kapuściński's experiences as a journalist in Africa in the 1960s and 1970s, is rife with troubling—and indeed racist—generalizations about the so-called African psyche, which the author frequently juxtaposes to the supposedly more rational European mentality. The material and cultural parallels between Eastern Europe and the Third World that had structured Kapuściński's Cold War–era reportage are emphatically disavowed in *The Shadow of the Sun* in favor of a clash-of-civilizations discourse that pits the West against the rest and attempts to establish postsocialist Poland as a member of the West.

## Conclusion

The publication of *The Emperor* in Poland appears to have marked the beginning of the end of a Cold War geopolitical context that had once made representations of a dignified and agential Third World *Other* politically necessary in the Socialist Bloc. Kapuściński's socialist-era reportage had been grounded in the understanding that Polish and Third World liberation were fundamentally bound up with one another. The end of the Cold War dissolved this understanding and established new alliances. These alliances were prefigured in *The Emperor*'s anglophone reception, where the work's generalized antitotalitarian allegory seemed to point to the inevitability of capitalism's victory over the supposed irrationality of both the Socialist Bloc and the Third World.

Today, as the former New World Order that emerged from the wreckage of the Soviet and Third World socialist experiment begins to undergo a reconfiguration characterized by the breakdown of trade agreements, the resurgence of nationalism, and the rise of new global superpowers, the study of twenty-first-century world literature would benefit from a deeper examination of the ways Eastern European texts moved across the Iron Curtain in the last decade of the Cold War. Not only would this serve to complicate the North/South coordinates that the study of contemporary world literature often seems to take for granted, but it would also remind us that the gains or losses of translation depend on whether a host culture shares the political commitments and struggles of a work's culture of origin. It is under such shared conditions that, during the Cold War, an alternative concept of world literature as the literature of international solidarity briefly found form in Second World literary reportage—even as that form strained under the challenges and responsibilities of representing Third World peoples.

## Notes

1. Domosławski makes the case that, after the publication of *The Emperor*, Kapuściński opportunistically shifted the political framework of his writing and molded his self-image to appeal to the tastes and sensibilities of the West, knowing this was a prerequisite for international acclaim and celebrity. For more on this, see Domosławski, *Ryszard Kapuściński*.

2. For another authoritative Kapuściński biography, see Nowacka and Ziątek, *Ryszard Kapuściński: Biografia pisarza*.

3. I borrow the term "transediting" from Wirtén to refer to the combined work of translation and editing that makes a foreign book legible to a target readership. See Wirtén, *Global Infatuation*.

4. See, for example, Brouillette, *Postcolonial Writers*.

5. Although, as Brennan argues in "The Cuts of Language," the Cold War haunts the North/South divide. Brennan observes the presence of the "ghost of belief" of anticommunism that haunts the problem of translation, even as postcolonial theorists prefer to avoid framing it in these terms.

6. Casanova, *The World Republic of Letters*, 136.

7. For more on the role of the "host culture" in shaping a translated work's translation and publication processes, see Damrosch, *What Is World Literature?*.

8. Anti-imperialism had been a major tenet of the interwar Third International but was largely abandoned during the United Front era. In 1956, the Soviet Union resumed a policy of supporting Third World anti-imperialist struggles. For more on this, see Prashad, *The Darker Nations*.

9. Domosławski, *Ryszard Kapuściński*, 104. In the 1980s, Mieczysław Rakowski would go on to become the First Secretary of the Polish Communist Party, the last prime minister of Communist Poland.

10. The Non-Aligned Movement (NAM) was an international organization established in Belgrade in 1961 to assert ideological independence from the two Cold War superpowers. NAM membership countries (which included much of the Global South and the former Yugoslavia) were aligned with neither the Soviet Union nor the United States and sought ways to meet the needs of their countries that broke from the capitalist and socialist models prescribed by the two blocs. In 1966, the Tricontinental Conference in Havana, Cuba, brought together 500 delegates from eighty-two countries to discuss anti-imperialist politics and strategy at a time when the Soviet Union seemed to be more committed to an agenda of peaceful coexistence with the West than with confronting colonialism and neocolonialism. The conference founded the Organization of Solidarity of the Peoples of Africa, Asia, and Latin America (OSPAAAL). For more on NAM, see Prashad, *The Darker Nations*. For more on the Tricontinental, see Mahler, *From the Tricontinental*.

11. For more on the way internationalism influenced the production and circulation of literature and film in the Soviet Union and its allies, see Djagalov, *From Internationalism to Postcolonialism*.

12. For more on how Kapuściński's coverage both reported on and stoked anti-imperialist politics, see Zubel, "Black Stars, Red Stars" and "Translating Che in the Socialist Bloc."

13. Kapuscinski.info, "Cesarz. Spis wydań."
14. Kapuściński, *The Emperor*, 5.
15. Ibid., 35.
16. Ibid., 36.
17. Ibid., 94.
18. Ibid.
19. Qtd. in Domosławski, *Ryszard Kapuściński*, 242.
20. Qtd. in Tighe, "Interview with Ryszard Kapuściński," 934.
21. Kapuscinski, "Z Warszawy 1982" (1990). Trans. and qtd. in Tighe, "Interview with Ryszard Kapuściński," 933–934.
22. For a discussion of Aesopian language in Polish literature, see Cornis-Pope, "An Anxious Triangulation."
23. Greenberg, "Kapuściński and Beyond," 130.
24. Benjamin, *The Origin of German Tragic Drama*, 175.
25. Ibid.
26. Kapuściński, *The Emperor*, 35, 39, 128. It is worth noting that in the original Polish, these titles are somewhat less extravagant than they are in English translation. Nevertheless, the use of a range of honorifics seems intended to invoke the absurdity of the informants' devotion to Selassie.
27. Marcus, "Prejudice and Ignorance," 374.
28. For more on this, see Falk, *The Dilemmas of Dissidence*.
29. See Domosławski, *Ryszard Kapuściński*.
30. Ryle, "Tales of Mythical Africa."
31. Ali, "Review of Ryszard Kapuściński *The Emperor*," 26.
32. Domosławski, *Ryszard Kapuściński*, 284.
33. Marcus, "Prejudice and Ignorance," 377.
34. Jameson, "Third-World Literature," 73.
35. Kapuściński, *The Emperor*, 52.
36. Domosławski, *Ryszard Kapuściński*, 284.
37. Kapuściński, *The Emperor*, 140.
38. Ibid., 101.
39. Ibid., 141.
40. For more on the relationship between KOR and Solidarność, see Falk, *The Dilemmas of Dissidence*.
41. Flakierski, "Solidarity and Egalitarianism," 380–381.
42. Wierzbicki, "Myśli staroświeckiego Polaka," 72.

43. Taras, "Marxist Critiques of Political Crises in Poland," 87.
44. Brennan, *At Home in the World*, 1.

## Bibliography

Ali, Tariq. "Review of Ryszard Kapuściński's *The Emperor*." *The New Statesman*, October 21, 1983.
Benjamin, Walter. *The Origin of German Tragic Drama*. Translated by John Osborne. London: Verso, 2003.
Brennan, Timothy. *At Home in the World: Cosmopolitanism Now*. Cambridge, MA: Harvard University Press, 1997.
———. "The Cuts of Language: The East/West of North/South," *Public Culture* 13, no. 1 (2001): 39–63.
Brouillette, Sarah. *Postcolonial Writers in the Global Literary Marketplace*. New York: Palgrave MacMillan, 2007.
Casanova, Pascale. *The World Republic of Letters*. Translated by M. B. Debevoise. Cambridge, MA: Harvard University Press, 2004.
Cornis-Pope, Marcel. "An Anxious Triangulation: Cold War, Nationalism and Regional Resistance in East-Central European Literatures." In *Cold War Literature: Writing the Global Conflict*, edited by Andrew Hammond, 160–175. London: Routledge, 2007.
Damrosch, David. *What Is World Literature?* Princeton, NJ: Princeton University Press, 2003.
Djagalov, Rossen. *From Internationalism to Postcolonialism: Literature and Cinema Between the Second and the Third Worlds*. Montreal: McGill-Queen's University Press, 2020.
Domosławski, Artur. *Ryszard Kapuściński: A Life*. Translated by Antonia Lloyd-Jones. London: Verso, 2013.
Falk, Barbara. *The Dilemmas of Dissidence in East-Central Europe*. Budapest: Central European University Press, 2003.
Flakierski, Henryk. "Solidarity and Egalitarianism." *Canadian Slavonic Papers* 25, no. 3 (1983): 380–391.
Greenberg, Susan. "Kapuściński and Beyond: The Polish School of Reportage." In *Global Literary Journalism: Exploring the Journalistic Imagination*, edited by Richard Lance Keeble and John Tulloch, 123–140. New York: Lang, 2012.
Jameson, Fredric. "Third-World Literature in the Era of Multinational Capitalism." *Social Text* 15 (1986): 65–88.
Kapuściński, Ryszard. *The Emperor: Downfall of an Autocrat*. Translated by William R. Brand and Katarzyna Mroczkowska-Brand. New York: Vintage, 1989.
———. "Z Warszawy 1982." *Lapidarium*. Warsaw: Czytelnik, 1990.
Kapuscinski.info. "Cesarz. Spis wydań." November 5, 2010. http://kapuscinski.info/cesarz-spis-wydan.html.
Mahler, Anne Garland. *From the Tricontinental to the Global South: Race, Radicalism and Transnational Solidarity*. Durham, NC: Duke University Press, 2018.
Marcus, Harold G. "Prejudice and Ignorance in Reviewing Books about Africa: The Strange Case of Ryszard Kapuściński's *The Emperor* (1983)." *History in Africa* 17 (1990): 373–378.
Nowacka, Beata, and Zygmunt Ziątek. *Ryszard Kapuściński: Biografia pisarza*. Warsaw: Znak, 2008.
Prashad, Vijay. *The Darker Nations: A People's History of the Third World*. New York: The New Press, 2008.
Ryle, John. "Tales of Mythical Africa." *Times Literary Supplement*, July 27, 2001.

Taras, Raymond. "Marxist Critiques of Political Crises in Poland." In *The Road to Disillusion: From Critical Marxism to Postcommunism in Eastern Europe*, edited by Raymond Taras, 81–113. Armonk, NY: M. E. Sharpe, 1992.

Tighe, Carl, trans. "Interview with Ryszard Kapuściński." In *The Works*, edited by N. Jenkins, 933–934. Swansea: Welsh Union of Writers, 1991.

Wierzbicki, Piotr. *Myśli staroświeckiego Polaka*. London: Puls Publications, 1985.

Wirtén, Eva Hemmungs. *Global Infatuation: Explorations in Transnational Publishing and Texts: The Case of Harlequin Enterprises and Sweden*. Uppsala: Uppsala University Press, 1998.

Zubel, Marla. "Black Stars, Red Stars: Anti-Colonial Constellations in Ryszard Kapuściński's Cold War Reportage." *Postcolonial Studies* 19, no. 2 (2016): 131–149.

———. "Translating Che in the Socialist Bloc: Ryszard Kapuściński's Guerilla Reportage." *The Global South* 13, no.1 (2019): 125–144.

MARLA ZUBEL is Assistant Professor of World Literature and Film at Western Kentucky University. Her work is published in *Genre: Forms of Discourse and Culture, Postcolonial Studies, Studies in Eastern European Cinema*, and *Cultural Critique*.

CHAPTER 12

TRAVELING WITH THE PRESIDENT
*Finnish-Soviet State Visits and
1970s Television Diplomacy*

Laura Saarenmaa

THE IMAGE IS FAMILIAR. THE visitor appears from the airplane door, waving energetically, and then steps down the wobbly stairs to meet hands eagerly outstretched for warm greetings and welcome. However cold the Cold War world political climate may have been, these oft-repeated state-visit gestures indicate friendship and respect between the visiting and welcoming parties and were iconically captured in televised welcoming ceremonies at the airport. This chapter discusses the symbolic significance of the televisualization of state visits within Cold War iconography, focusing on current affairs reports produced by the Finnish Broadcasting Company (Yleisradio, YLE), the country's license-fee-funded public service television station.[1]

As a militarily neutral state balanced politically between the Cold War power blocs, Finland had a strong interest in establishing and maintaining good relations with the neighboring Soviet Union and the socialist states allied to it. The Finnish-Soviet Agreement of Friendship, Cooperation, and Mutual Assistance (1948–1992) set the tone for this so-called friendship policy, and YLE played a fundamental role in maintaining and deepening the notion of friendship as the cornerstone of Finnish-Soviet diplomatic relations. While earlier literature on YLE during the Cold War has focused on the state's political control of the company's management, my interest here is in the significance of the *television medium* itself and how it helped frame East-West diplomatic interactions.[2] Through television news and current affairs programming, Finnish citizens were informed about Finnish state-level communication with the Soviet Union and the socialist states and guided in how to understand it.

I analyze the role of the journalism professionals involved in televising state visits as well as the televisual images and sounds themselves, which earlier research has neglected, deeming them purely ceremonial and hence lacking historic value.[3] This focus on the image and sound shifts the discussion from journalists' ethical integrity to the affordances of the medium and, more broadly, to the seldom-discussed role of European public service television as an instrument of Cold War state diplomacy.[4] I focus on two 1977 documentary programs produced by the YLE news and current affairs department. *What UKK Saw in the Soviet Union* (*Mitä UKK näki Neuvostoliitossa?*) is a twenty-nine-minute documentary program about the fourth official state visit to the Soviet Union by Finnish President Urho Kekkonen in May 1977, which took the president to faraway Kyrgyzstan and the industrial city of Minsk in Belarus.[5] The documentary *Visit from a Friend* (*Tasavallassa tapahtuu: Ystävä kylässä*) follows Soviet Prime Minister Aleksei Kosygin on his unofficial friendship visit to Finland in March 1977.[6] To shed light on the editorial choices behind the programs, I have conducted background interviews with two YLE journalists who had central roles in the programs' production: the former head of YLE news, Yrjö Länsipuro, and YLE's former foreign correspondent in Moscow, Reijo Nikkilä.[7] These programs emphasized not only Kekkonen's decisive role in Finnish foreign policy, but also YLE's role as a trusted fellow traveler, mediator, and interpreter of events. The YLE television crew was allowed to enter the chambers of power and even take a peek backstage as a response to the 1970s hunger for the unmediated, intimate, and personal behind ceremonial scenes.

State visits are the highest expression of friendly bilateral relations between two sovereign states and are characterized by an emphasis on official public ceremonies. During the Cold War, state visits were loaded with expectations. One such occasion was Nikita Khrushchev's visit to the United States in 1964. The visit, publicized under the banner of peace and friendship, is regarded as a historic venture that had the potential to mitigate the Cold War climate of fear. According to Viorela Dana Papuc, Khrushchev's visit paved the way for the end of the Cold War and temporarily replaced the threat of war with hopes of peace and agreement between the world's two superpowers.[8] President Richard Nixon's visit to China has been seen as a comparable Cold War turning point.[9]

The Cold War was also an era of intensive state visits within Europe. Consequently, Finnish television news constantly aired reports on presidents, ministers, and other political leaders traveling to numerous official and unofficial visits around the continent.[10] State visits were of particular national significance, as they showed how, in the international game of public diplomacy, tiny Finland was a sovereign player that enjoyed good relations with Western leaders as well as with the East. The ideal of friendly relations in all directions was at the heart of Cold War–era Finnish foreign policy and the Finnish national self-image. Thus, state visits to and from Finland were considered important news events and strongly prioritized.[11] When Kekkonen, the main architect of the Finnish-Soviet friendship policy, departed for his numerous visits, television news crews were at the airport to send him off; when he returned, they were waiting for him, also ready to welcome the political personalities visiting Finland.[12]

The archetypal documentation of state visits consisted of the welcome and farewell ceremonies at the airport. The main reason for this was technical. In the 1960s and early 1970s, television news was still shot on film, making location shooting demanding. Airport ceremonies—so often repeated—allowed crews to follow an established protocol and were therefore simple to film. In addition, the YLE newsroom had good contacts with the presidential office and a shared understanding about the political significance of documenting and reporting the visits.[13] More pragmatically, state visits were seen as opportunities to encounter the political elite in person. As the former head of the YLE news recounts, in the 1960s and 1970s, it was often difficult to get information beyond the official foreign-political phraseology. State visit ceremonies, however, offered the chance to approach politicians with questions.[14]

### Sharing the Presidential View

Contemporary state visits have become shorter, but in the 1960s and 1970s, they could take a week or more and involved a wide range of unofficial activities, leisure-time programs, and opportunities to socialize with the hosts. The televised reports and programs about the visits gave viewers opportunities for imaginary travel and to see the wonders of the world through presidential eyes.[15] Seeing is, indeed, the theme of the documentary on Kekkonen's state visit to the Soviet Union, appearing even in its title—*What UKK Saw in the Soviet Union*. In the opening sequence, a sound bite from an interview with the president runs as a voice-over alongside footage of the welcome ceremony at the Moscow airport: "During the visits, I see things that I could not have seen and learned in any other way."

Throughout the documentary, Kekkonen is shown in a viewer's position. In a section filmed in the Kirghiz Soviet Socialist Republic, we see him watching folk dances and a riding show and listening to a presentation about Vladimir Lenin and the revolutionary headquarters Smolny in Saint Petersburg. We also see masses of Kirghiz people watching in return; standing by the street, they wave and greet "the first foreign state leader ever" to visit the republic. According to a Kirghiz senior citizen interviewed later in the documentary, Finland's president had arrived from a "neighboring country." Yet Kirghizia was located at the Chinese border, circa 3,700 kilometers southeast from Finland's eastern frontier, and it is fair to assume that knowledge of Finland among the Kirghiz people (and vice versa) in the mid-1970s was relatively modest. It is thus also quite likely that people seen standing by the street and waving at the black cars were recruited there by the hosts expressly for the television cameras.

In this section, there is a strong sense of setting the stage for the cameras, particularly in scenes depicting a riding show at a Kirghiz hippodrome. We see Kekkonen sitting in a private booth, accompanied by his hosts. From here, we cut to tightly framed shots of the local audience enjoying the show, all of them men dressed in tailored suit jackets, white-collared shirts, dark ties, and fedoras—clearly enlisted in service of the Soviet Union's self-presentation as a well-organized, modern state that shared Western styles and standards of living, even in its rural communities. The only crack in the otherwise stylized mise-en-scène is a close-up of a laughing face, revealing the poor condition of a man's teeth.

Indeed, according to Finnish journalists with experience on Soviet assignments, independent journalism was impossible on trips to the country, with so-called "everyday life" filming opportunities strictly controlled by Soviet propaganda authorities.[16] Every program required extensive, time-consuming bureaucracy, and information about the filming circumstances was hard to come by in advance.[17] At the Kirghiz state visit, the Finnish television crew's equipment was simply transported to the location, and the group had to start filming without any planning, scripts, or storyboards.[18]

Yet there were exceptions to this omnipresent control. The sequence at the riding show, for instance, includes glimpses of other cameras documenting the show. At one point, a car drives alongside a horse and its rider, and we see a cameraman filming from the car window. This was a Moscow film group making a film about the event to be archived in Moscow and used for diplomatic occasions.[19] For Finnish television viewers, these glimpses of photographers and camera operators in the frame likely created a sense of presence and a reality effect characteristic of the documentary and news feature genre—something otherwise missing in the filming circumstances.[20] On the other hand, the explicit reference to the cameras implies that the riding show was structured for a Soviet (and Finnish) television public as much as for the diplomatic guests, accentuating the central role of television in 1970s Cold War public diplomacy.

In the sequence following the riding show, the television cameras relocated to a grand yurt, where a festive banquet for the Finnish president and his entourage was served. According to the evidently impressed voice-over, the menu included "several appetizers, two different kinds of soups, trout in *smetana* [sour cream]—and so on." Attention to local delicacies is a common feature in the "television diplomacy" Cold War state visits performed, making use of broadcast television's medium-specific ability to provide views about foreign countries and interpret state-level diplomatic relations.[21] In the scene shot inside the yurt, the television cameras and reporters were there to witness the host state's high standards of living and the hospitality the president of Finland enjoyed abroad.

The final sequence of the documentary captures a more somber side of Cold War television diplomacy—namely Soviet engagements with the Second World War. At the Victory Monument in Minsk, a Soviet World War II memorial, we see Kekkonen laying a wreath with blue and white ribbons (the colors of the flag of the Republic of Finland). "The German occupiers burned down 136 Belarussian Soviet villages, including their inhabitants," the reporter's voice-over recollects. "Throughout the visit, the eternal flames reminded the president of Finland of Soviet soldiers' burdensome but critical role in in defeating Nazi Germany. In Moscow at the Tomb of the Unknown Soldier, in Leningrad at the Monument to the Heroic Defenders of Leningrad, and at the Piskaryovskoye Memorial Cemetery, memorializing the half-million dead inhabitants of the city of Leningrad."

This memorial sequence follows the common practice in 1970s Finland of adhering to the Soviet narrative about the war, emphasizing the country's role in defeating Nazi Germany while overlooking the history of Soviet-Finnish conflict, notably the 1939 Soviet attack on Finland. The commemoration of Soviet war victims could be seen as a discursive strategy for overcoming the past by focusing on shared sacrifice and loss, while the focus on Soviet civilian casualties was perhaps intended to inspire empathy among the Finnish people within the Cold War geopolitical situation, which involved considerable political pressure on Finland from the Soviet Union. This, in turn, emphasizes a Finnish Cold War cultural and foreign-political strategy of focusing on managing the present rather than wallowing in the past. As media historian Raimo Salokangas notes, Finnish television journalists knew that they were serving the interests of the Soviet Union, but more importantly, they felt they were serving Finland's official foreign policy.[22]

However, the journalists interviewed for this study remarked that the YLE editorial staff was politically far more diverse than existing scholarship on the company's management and editors indicates, and sometimes political tensions among the staff were even seen in programming.[23] Thus, if we turn our focus to the television image rather than the voice-over, we may read the close-up of Kekkonen carefully organizing the wreath's blue and white ribbons in patriotic terms. The shot emphasizes the power of televisual repetition. The image of the president with the wreath resembles scenes seen numerous times before at Finnish war memorials—the same, solitary president; the same wreath; the same ribbons with the same patriotic phrases; the same expressions of gratitude for people's sacrifices for the sake of the homeland. Many historians have criticized YLE for viewing the Soviet Union through rose-colored glasses in the 1970s.[24] But images such as these could equally be seen as an enunciation of sovereignty—both for Kekkonen and for the nation he embodied.

### The Promise of the Backstage

Kekkonen visited the Soviet Union thirty-five times during his three decades in office (1956–1981); he was first hosted by Nikita Khrushchev and then Leonid Brezhnev from 1964 onward.[25] Soviet leaders' visits to Finland, however, were rarer. During his time in office, Khrushchev visited Finland only once, in 1957. Brezhnev visited twice, in 1961 and again for the Conference on Security and Cooperation in Europe, held in Helsinki in 1975. A more familiar figure in Finland was Kosygin, who was on good terms with Kekkonen. In March 1977, Kosygin visited Finland to prepare for Kekkonen's state visit to the Soviet Union in May 1977. The documentary about this visit reflects not only the warm relations between the Soviet and Finnish political leadership, but also YLE foreign news reporters' exceptional access to politicians' off-scene interactions. The documentary was introduced by the program's producer, Hannu Vilpponen, who acted as a studio host:

> Last week we Finns had a friend visiting. The chair of the Soviet minister council, Aleksei Kosygin, made an official visit of friendship to Finland. We tried to follow this visit as closely as possible. The official side of the visit has already been covered thoroughly in the news. However, this kind of visit consists of many other things besides official negotiations. This time we got a chance to take a peek behind the scenes. We got permission to shoot some discussion in a sauna, and we joined the presidential morning coffee on a train to the city of Raahe. You are invited to spend the next 45 minutes in the company of the prime minister of the Soviet Union.

This, remarkably, underlines the promise of backstage venues such as the sauna and the train car, perhaps speaking to audiences' growing hunger for the people and events behind the scenes, as Leo Lowenthal describes in his 1980s study of the rising popularity of biographies.[26]

The program's first sequence starts by showing a backstage view of the Finnish protocol personnel discussing the red carpet on the platform at Helsinki Central Station. We see two cadets rolling out the carpet and hear a female voice talking to someone almost outside the microphone's reach: "Too close to the train... if you can pull it afterwards... just roll it open, yeah, it is easier to pull when it is spread... just grab the sides and pull." We see close-ups of the carpet being brushed with brooms and rows of cadets standing at attention, followed by the president and his adjutants taking their positions at the platform. We see the train moving slowly toward the platform and a close-up of the president, who is smiling, as if eagerly awaiting a reunion with an old friend. The train stops, and Kosygin almost leaps down the stairs with his arm stretched forward, seemingly ready to greet his beloved host. We see (although do not hear) the exchange of greetings that follows. Something funny is said, as Kosygin and Kekkonen both lean their heads back in relaxed laughter.

The leaders then step into black diplomatic cars and drive away as the voice-over summarizes the underlying motive for diplomatic exchange: direct contact and communication between the parties. "And to gain this, one does not have to discuss serious issues all the time. The discussion can just as well be about quitting smoking." The remark forms a bridge to the following sequence, where we see Kekkonen, Kosygin, and the accompanying party sitting in the ornate Yellow Hall at the presidential palace at small coffee tables scattered around the room. The camera gets closer to the president's table, where people are discussing the tobacco industry. Kosygin explains the industry's growing sales figures, remarking that he does not smoke himself: "I quit smoking the day the war was officially over. We were gathered at home with some friends, spending the day drinking cognac, thinking about how we could make the day special, and we decided to all quit smoking."

The direct references to the Second World War show Kekkonen and Kosygin's uncomplicated relationship insofar as they fought as enemies during the conflict. The atmosphere stays cheerful as Kekkonen, in his charmingly humorous manner, blurts out, "But you did not consider giving up drinking."

"No, that I could not have managed," Kosygin responds.

The sequence ends with an image of Kekkonen and Kosygin sitting side by side, raising their cognac glasses for a sip, and sharing a laugh. These kinds of intimate moments were apt to invoke empathy, acceptance, and trust among Finnish television viewers. Alcohol was central to this: in the Finnish cultural mindset of the 1960s and 1970s, alcohol served a particular role in the modernization of society and in the destruction of hierarchies between different social backgrounds, ages, and genders. It also had a significant role in the growing bilateral trade with the Soviet Union.[27] The intimate images of Kekkonen and Kosygin sharing informal moments of closeness with drinks in hand thus corresponded to the idea that alcohol encouraged closeness, contact, and communication between parties.

In another such moment, we see Kekkonen and Kosygin sitting side by side at the opening ceremony of the Loviisa nuclear power station. The ceremony took place outdoors in the apparently cold early spring weather. Because of the temperature, the men have gray woolen blankets on their laps. Kekkonen seems to be enjoying the comfort of the blanket, while Kosygin has pushed his casually aside. We can only speculate on the underlying reasons behind Kosygin's choice. Were there perhaps concerns about the blanket's implication of physical weakness or about the intimacy implied by the image of two people sitting next to each other under blankets? Nevertheless, the sequence's depiction of the political leaders' physical closeness corresponds well with the voice-over narration about the countries' long-term interdependence in energy policy.

As a televisual mode of expression, such intimacy drew on the widespread interest, in the 1970s, in seeing politicians as personalities.[28] Kekkonen shared this interest and frequently highlighted the personal and informal side of state-level diplomacy. Throughout his long career, he was open to fresh ideas, new modes of expression, and the input of the younger generation. At the time, television was a young medium and was the domain of young male professionals interested in its particular technical possibilities. According to Länsipuro, *Visit from a Friend* was a technically innovative project, as it required two camera crews who communicated with each other through walkie-talkies. The sense of the everyday and the intimate was made possible by techniques borrowed from cinema vérité; the quiet Arriflex film cameras allowed cameramen to get close to the subjects without disturbing the soundscape, while the sound was recorded with portable Nagra audio recorders attached to microphones.[29]

The advantages of this technology are evident in the sequence shot in the president's train car as it travels across the Finnish countryside toward the industrial city of Raahe. We see a group of men in gray suits sitting at a table full of coffee mugs, yogurt cups, plates of cold cuts and rolls, and glasses of orange juice. We hear the familiar sounds of breakfast: chewing mouths and spoons tinkling on porcelain. The sequence has a strong sense of everyday informality and closeness, enabled by the quiet camera and audio recording. The overheard discussion of the average size of a Finnish farm reflects the visitors' genuine interest in and curiosity about the subject and their relaxed nonchalance about the presence of the camera crew.

The intimate mode reaches its peak in the sauna sequence, where we see the prime minister of the Soviet Union and the president of Finland relaxing after bathing. The sequence starts with a glimpse of a naked man running across the frame, accompanied by male laughter. We see Kekkonen sitting barefoot on a bench wearing a linen bathrobe. The president's face glows red while he rubs his famously bald head with a linen towel. His gestures convey genuine enjoyment and relaxation, while Kosygin—whom we see standing at the other side of the room, as if seeking escape from the camera—buttons his shirt hastily, expressing apparent unease about the camera intruding in the intimate space. It appears that there was a shared understanding of the concessions that needed to be made for the media. However, there were evidently differences in the participants' comfort with the television camera intruding on their private sphere.

Nevertheless, the editor's voice-over frames the sauna as an occasion for deep engagement in issues: "Finnish sauna diplomacy has a firm reputation. Whether the discussions in the sauna were about nuclear waste issues or the extension of the CSCE was not revealed." And indeed, sauna bathing is a typical form of hospitality in Finland, intended to convey a sense of togetherness and reciprocal trust. The expression *sauna diplomacy*, however, carries a mildly sarcastic undertone and was used in reference to Kekkonen's habit of pursuing his political goals through sauna meetings.[30] Perhaps more than anything else, the sauna sequence was addressed to the Finnish people by a president who was preparing for yet another election in 1978 and was thus interested in showcasing his close relations with Soviet political authorities.[31]

The sequence—and the documentary as a whole—was also a personal achievement for Länsipuro, who is shown conversing privately, in Russian, with Kosygin.[32] At the time, it was highly unusual for journalists to approach Soviet leaders directly and for the leaders to converse casually and reply to questions outside of prepared talks and official statements. In this casual conversation with the Finnish foreign reporter, Kosygin confirms long-term plans in the field of nuclear technology and for joint construction projects, such as the mining city of Kostamus in Soviet Karelia, which was expected to be extremely profitable for Finland.[33] Economic concerns dominate the documentary. Kosygin is not at any point challenged about social or environmental issues in relation to the planned construction in Soviet Karelia; such concerns arose only later in the news media and public awareness.

What was novel in the second half of the 1970s was access to intimate moments behind the ceremonial scenes, images that perhaps paved the way for more realistic reporting about the Soviet Union.

### Easygoing Cold War Companions

Starting in the 1990s, uncritical 1970s Finnish reporting about the Soviet Union was reevaluated harshly. The Finnish mainstream media, including YLE, was accused of "sidestepping the reality of conditions in the Soviet Union and Eastern Europe" and of a "depressingly dishonest atmosphere maintained by the whole system of power."[34] According to one of the fiercest public critics, journalist Max Rand, "The most shameful aspect with regard to the journalistic profession in Finland was the fact that, with only a few exceptions, we [journalists] were part of this atmosphere."[35]

Adopting the point of view of the political power elite in journalism, however, is hardly a Finnish phenomenon. Criticism of the proximity between journalists and politicians grew in the United States in the 1960s and 1970s and eventually led to the American news media's transformation from a relatively passive institution into one with an oppositional relationship to political authority.[36] In Finland, the debate about journalists' relations to official sources, closeness to the political elite, and support for political authority developed substantially later, with Kekkonen's resignation in 1981 representing an important turning point.[37] However, the development of journalistic integrity and critical distance toward the elite did not extend to the coverage of foreign policy before the fall of the Berlin Wall in 1989.[38] And thus, to avoid retrospective readings and anachronism, television documentaries about state visits must be understood in their broader professional, cultural, and political context, in particular the context of the television medium. The documentary programs discussed in this chapter show that, in Finland, 1970s television newsroom ambitions lay not in confrontation, but in the display of intermediation, reconciliation, and intimacy, framing Finnish public service television as a "warm" rather than a "cool" medium.[39]

This warmth was accentuated in both YLE documentaries discussed here. The informal, intimate style of expression can be seen in the films' visual and verbal content as well as in their narrative structure. *What UKK Saw in the Soviet Union* opens with a thirty-three-second folk-dancing scene whose bold orchestral music continues over shots of Kekkonen stepping down from the airplane, creating a comic parallel between the state diplomatic ceremonies and carefully executed choreography. *Visit from a Friend* highlighted its informal approach by showing the preparations for the welcoming ceremony at the train station. The programs are of course different in terms of their subject matter. The documentary filmed in the Soviet Union includes showy events and the exoticism of the geopolitical *other*, while its counterpart in Finland focuses on intimate indoor locations, resembling the Finnish self-image as nonhierarchical, laid-back, and easygoing companions.

Remarkably, Soviet television was not involved in these productions, and the programs produced by YLE were not exported to the Soviet Union or elsewhere. The YLE documentaries were made by Finnish television journalists for Finnish television viewers to bolster the Finnish self-image and support Finnish foreign policy. Indeed, Finland was not as important for Soviet public diplomacy as the Soviet Union was for Finland. However, the participation of the Soviet leadership indicates that television's significance was recognized at the highest level of Soviet politics. In other words, television's value lay not only in creating visibility and a favorable public image for the two states, but also in emphasizing the diplomatic bonds and close personal relations between state representatives.

Cold War diplomatic interaction should thus be analyzed not only in the framework of Cold War foreign policy, but also in the framework of television, particularly that of the developing news and current issues genre. While YLE is an example of how public service television played a crucial role as a mediator and interpreter of diplomatic interaction, reflecting public service broadcasting's assimilation with the perspectives of state authority—something that has been strongly criticized by post–Cold War Finnish historians—focusing on actual televisual images and sounds and the views of program makers opens a nuanced understanding of state visits as televised media events. This reminds us that the judgmental tone in contemporary criticism is part of an ongoing debate—rather than the final truth—about these events and their meanings.

## Notes

1. The Finnish Broadcasting Company was regulated (from 1948) by an Administrative Council that consisted of members of Parliament, including opposition parties in proportion to their parliamentary strength. In turn, the Administrative Council nominated a Program Council to examine and approve the programming plans and review the broadcast programs in retrospect. Until 1985, there were two national television channels, which broadcast commercial Mainos-TV's (MTV) programs side by side with the YLE's public service programs. See Salokangas, "In the Shadow of the Bear," 68–69; and Ruoho, *Utility Drama*, 24.

2. See Salokangas, "In the Shadow of the Bear"; Lounasmeri, "Through Rose or Blue and White Glasses?"; and Salminen, *The Silenced Media*.

3. Derix, "Facing an Emotional Crunch," 118.

4. See Lounasmeri, "Through Rose or Blue and White Glasses?"; Salminen, *The Silenced Media*; and Uskali, *"Älä kirjoita itseäsi ulos."*

5. *Mitä UKK näki Neuvostoliitossa?*, aired June 13, 1977.

6. *Tasavallassa tapahtuu: Ystävä kylässä (Kosyginin vierailu)*, aired March 31, 1977.

7. The interviews reveal background details that do not manifest in the programs themselves. One of these is that in addition to YLE, the state visit to the Soviet Union and the trips to Kyrgyzstan and Belarus were accompanied by a group of sixteen Finnish journalists from television and radio, as well as the biggest daily newspapers and party newspapers. The state visit was reported from various angles, ranging from the economy to political analysis. *What UKK Saw in the Soviet Union* is hence only one of the numerous stories and reports about the journey. This, again, illustrates the exceptionality of the visit.

8. Papuc, "A Thawing in the Cold War?"
9. Tudda, *A Cold War Turning Point*.
10. This remark is based on search results in YLE's digital database Metro on foreign news and current issues reporting between 1970 and 1989.
11. Länsipuro, interview, August 20, 2017.
12. Pernaa, *Uutisista hyvää iltaa*, 60.
13. Länsipuro, interview, August 20, 2017.
14. Ibid.
15. Pernaa, *Uutisista hyvää iltaa*, 60.
16. Lounasmeri, "Through Rose or Blue and White Glasses?," 95.
17. Salokangas, "In the Shadow of the Bear," 76.
18. Nikkilä, interview, March 2, 2018.
19. Ibid.
20. Scannel, "Television and History."
21. Saarenmaa and Cronqvist, "Cold War Television Diplomacy."
22. Salokangas, "The Shadow of the Bear," 77; see also Lounasmeri, "Through Rose or Blue and White Glasses?"
23. Nikkilä, interview, March 2, 2018.
24. Vihavainen, *Kansakunta rähmällään*; Salminen, *The Silenced Media*; and Seppinen, *Suomettumisen syövereissä*.
25. In comparison, Kekkonen made twenty-three visits to Sweden, four to Yugoslavia (1963, 1967, 1975, 1980), three to the United States (1961, 1970, 1979), two to the UK (1961, 1969) and Hungary (1963, 1976), and one to West Germany (1979), Poland (1967), Romania (1969), and Czechoslovakia (1969).
26. Lowenthal, *Literature and Mass Culture*.
27. The background lies in the history of the strict Finnish alcohol policy, prohibition (1919–1932), and the tradition of home-brewed liquor feeding the culture of heavy drinking. The legalization of beer sales in grocery stores in 1969 has been seen as a pivotal point in the country's mental modernization. Kuusi, *Viinistä vapautta*.
28. Stayner, *Intimate Politics*; and van Zoonen, *Entertaining the Citizen*.
29. Länsipuro, interview, February 28, 2018. This style was still quite unusual in television news and current affairs programming.
30. Nowadays, sauna diplomacy also carries negative connotations because of the exclusion of women, as the Finnish public sauna is strictly gender segregated. See Saarenmaa, "Playboys and Politicians."
31. Aunesluoma and Rainio-Niemi, "Neutrality as Identity?," 56–57. In the 1970s political climate, Kekkonen's personal relations with the Soviet leadership were seen as an assurance of peace and security, and this strongly influenced domestic politics in Finland.
32. According to Länsipuro's recollection, the sequence was recorded spontaneously, and it was Kosygin himself who approached him. Länsipuro tried to take advantage of the unexpected opportunity with his basic Russian. Länsipuro, interview, February 28, 2018.
33. Kostamus was a major project executed by Finnish companies in Soviet Karelia between 1977 and 1985. It was the largest construction project ever executed by Finnish companies abroad, including the building of the city of Kostamus and an iron ore mine. The project employed 1,500

people per year, led to the economic growth of the Finnish construction industry, and resulted in substantial profits for shareholders.

34. Salminen, *The Silenced Media*, 33.
35. Ibid.
36. However, as Daniel Hallin argues in his critical study of the coverage of the Vietnam War in the US news media, the "transformation" was not as uniform as is often narrated, and the movement toward stronger professional integrity and clearer norms of objectivity took much longer than has often been argued. See Hallin, "The Media, The War in Vietnam, and Political Support."
37. Aula, "Perässä tullaan, Amerikka?"
38. Ibid., 19.
39. The original claim that television was a "cool" medium was made by Marshall McLuhan in the 1960s. See Doherty, *Cold War, Cool Medium*.

## Bibliography

Aula, Maria Kaisa. "Perässä tullaan, Amerikka? Ajatuskoe suomalaisen poliittisen julkisuuden murroksesta." *Tiedotustutkimus*, no. 2 (1992): 10–21.

Aunesluoma, Juhana, and Johanna Rainio-Niemi. "Neutrality as Identity? Finland's Quest for Security in the Cold War." *Journal of Cold War Studies* 18, no. 4 (2016): 51–78.

Derix, Simone. "Facing an 'Emotional Crunch': State Visits as Political Performances during the Cold War." *German Politics & Society* 25, no. 2 (2007): 117–139.

Doherty, Thomas. *Cold War, Cool Medium: Television, McCarthyism, and American Culture*. New York: Columbia University Press, 2003.

Hallin, Daniel. "The Media, The War in Vietnam, and Political Support: A Critique of the Thesis of an Oppositional Media." *The Journal of Politics* 46, no. 1 (1984): 1–24.

Kuusi, Hanna. *Viinistä vapautta: Alkoholi, hallinta ja identiteetti 1960-luvun Suomessa*. Helsinki: Suomalaisen Kirjallisuuden Seura, 2004.

Länsipuro, Yrjö. Phone interview by Laura Saarenmaa. August 20, 2017.

———. Phone interview by Laura Saarenmaa. February 28, 2018.

Lounasmeri, Lotta. "Through Rose or Blue and White Glasses? Decades of News about the Soviet Union in the Finnish Press." *Nordicom Review* 34, no. 1 (2013): 105–123.

Lowenthal, Leo. *Literature and Mass Culture: Communication in Society, Volume 1*. London: Transaction Books, 1984.

Nikkilä, Reijo. Phone interview by Laura Saarenmaa. March 2, 2018.

Papuc, Viorela Dana. "A Thawing in the Cold War? Examining Nikita Khrushchev's Visit to the USA, 15–27 September 1959." *Flinders Journal of History and Politics* 25 (2008): 55–78.

Pernaa, Ville. *Uutisista hyvää iltaa*. Helsinki: Karttakeskus, 2009.

Ruoho, Iiris. *Utility Drama: Making of and Talking about the Serial Drama in Finland*. Tampere: Tampere University Press, 2001.

Saarenmaa, Laura. "Playboys and Politicians: Men's Magazines as Political Counterpublics." In *A Man's World? Political Masculinities in Literature and Culture*, edited by Kathleen Starck and Birgit Sauer, 181–193. Newcastle: Cambridge Scholars Publishing, 2014.

Saarenmaa, Laura, and Marie Cronqvist. "Cold War Television Diplomacy: The German Democratic Republic on the Finnish Television." *Nordicom* 41, no 1 (2020): 19–31.

Salminen, Esko. *The Silenced Media: The Propaganda War between Russia and the West in Northern Europe*. London: Palgrave McMillan, 1999.

Salokangas, Raimo. "In the Shadow of the Bear." In *The Nordic Media and the Cold War*, edited by Henrik Bastiansen and Rolf Werenskjold, 67–100. Göteborg: Nordicom, 2015.

Scannel, Paddy. "Television and History: Questioning the Archive." In *Media History and the Archive*, edited by Craig Robertson, 40–54. London: Routledge, 2011.

Seppinen, Jukka. *Suomettumisen syövereissä*. Helsinki: WSOY, 2011.
Stayner, James. *Intimate Politics: Publicity, Privacy and the Personal Lives of Politicians*. Cambridge: Polity, 2013.
Tudda, Chris. *A Cold War Turning Point: Nixon and China, 1969–1972*. Baton Rouge: Louisiana State University Press, 2012.
Uskali, Turo. "Älä kirjoita itseäsi ulos." *Suomalaisen Moskovan-kirjeenvaihtajuuden alkutaival 1957–1975*. Jyväskylä: Jyväskylän yliopisto, 2003.
van Zoonen, Liesbet. *Entertaining the Citizen: When Politics and Popular Culture Converge*. Lanham: Rowman & Littlefield, 2005.
Vihavainen, Timo. *Kansakunta rähmällään: Suomettumisen lyhyt historia*. Helsinki: Otava, 1991.

## Filmography

*Mitä UKK näki Neuvostoliitossa?* Aired June 13, 1977. Edited by Reijo Nikkilä and Liisa Laine, produced by Yrjö Länsipuro. 29:23 minutes.

*Tasavallassa tapahtuu: Ystävä kylässä* (*Kosyginin vierailu*). Aired March 31, 1977. Edited by Yrjö Länsipuro, produced by Hannu Vilpponen. 48:14 minutes.

LAURA SAARENMAA is Senior Lecturer of Media Studies at the University of Turku. Her work is published in *Nordicom Review, WiderScreen*, and *Media History*.

# PART IV. INFRASTRUCTURE AND PRODUCTION

CHAPTER 13

# HOLLYWOOD GOING EAST
## State-Socialist Studios' Opportunistic Business with American Producers

Petr Szczepanik

THE YEAR 1968 WAS SPECIAL, not just in the political and social history of both Western and Eastern Europe, but also in international film-business relations between the East and the West. Around that year, most of the major Hollywood studios were involved in one way or another in planning, producing, or at least cofinancing films (mostly historical dramas) in collaboration with the state-run industries across Eastern Europe.[1] United Artists was not an exception, backing *The Bridge at Remagen* (dir. John Guillermin, 1969), a World War II epic shot partly on locations near Prague, in the Barrandov Studios, and in the Czech city of Most.

This chapter uses a case study of *The Bridge at Remagen* and Barrandov to propose a revisionist, industry-studies account of the early history of the US "runaway production" behind the Iron Curtain and of Eastern Europe's pragmatic dealings with Hollywood.[2] *The Bridge at Remagen*'s location shooting collided with the Warsaw Pact invasion of Czechoslovakia in August 1968, and its complicated production history shows how Cold War reality seemed to work against the emerging business ties between the state-socialist studios and Hollywood. Indeed, the surreal encounter between the old US military equipment used by *The Bridge at Remagen*'s crew and Soviet soldiers outside Prague gave rise to conspiracy theories about the film's supposed role in the Soviets' case for the invasion and speculations about the catastrophic consequences for the international reputation of Czechoslovak

227

State Film (Československý státní film, the state-run film corporation). Yet the aim of this chapter is to show that the presence of American filmmakers in Prague in 1968 was not surprising and would become part of a longer industry history both before and after 1989.

In the existing literature on the history of Hollywood's globalizing production, the Iron Curtain plays a negligible role; Hollywood's collaboration with state-socialist regimes and Eastern Europe's position in the industry imagination at the time of Hollywood's transformation into a global production network have been mostly overlooked.[3] On the other hand, research on Eastern European cinemas' international relations has so far tended to focus on cinema's role in the cultural Cold War, its links to cultural-diplomatic objectives, and the ideological perils of coproductions between Eastern and Western countries, disregarding a longer tradition of opportunistic production services that eventually became the economically dominant industry mode across the region after 1989.[4] This revisionist case study thus could also be seen as a prehistory of East-Central European studios' current business model, which is based predominantly on servicing foreign producers, a type of economically driven collaboration that falls under what Mette Hjort calls "opportunistic transnationalism."[5]

The economic and cultural logic of runaway production has been diagnosed as an integral part of post-Fordist global capitalism. After the so-called Paramount decree in 1948, Hollywood majors gradually started disintegrating and disaggregating. Instead of films produced in a serial manner, with fixed assets and in-house talent and crews, the flexible "package-unit" or project-based system has dominated the US film economy since the mid-1950s. For each project, a specific business strategy is developed, studio space is rented, and freelance creative as well as below-the-line workers are hired on a temporary basis.[6] The process of vertical disintegration was complemented by the geographic dispersal of the studios' production process; various stages and tasks of a single film's production could now be accomplished by specialized firms around the world connected by constantly changing collaborative arrangements. In today's global production networks, peripheral studio facilities like Barrandov function as vehicles for reaggregating elements of physical production in one place, while Hollywood and other "media capitals" remain the centers of command and control, where the increasingly complex strategic functions of developing, deal-making, coordinating, and financing occur.[7]

With the arrival of West European and Hollywood runaways to Eastern Bloc countries in the 1950s and especially the 1960s, two distinct production systems and cultures collided: a centralized, state-controlled, command-economy model—what I elsewhere call the "state-socialist mode of production"[8]—versus the US/Western European flexible, project-based organization, or the egalitarian, self-censoring culture of state-socialist studios' permanent employees versus the highly hierarchical work world and competitive informal networks of freelance above-the-line talent and below-the-line labor. The success of the Western runaway strategy and the Eastern endeavor to reach new sources of hard currency depended not so much on finding themes of joint interest (as in coproductions), but rather on the ability of both sides to understand and mediate between these two production systems and cultures.

### Eastern Europe as Location and Soundstage

In the second half of the 1960s, the Hollywood trade press reported not only about the slow decline of traditional runaway production in Western Europe, but also about opportunities for (and the challenges of) shooting behind the Iron Curtain.[9] As veteran distributor and producer Alan Shapiro wrote, "In recent years production overseas meant London, Paris, Rome or Madrid. Now the cameras are turning further east, and Yugoslavia is at the crossroads of this new frontier for top motion picture production."[10] Josip Broz Tito's Yugoslavia, the most Hollywood-friendly service provider of all socialist countries since the mid-1950s—sometimes called the "California of Europe"[11]—became a testing ground for moving further behind the Iron Curtain. Czechoslovakia, Hungary, Romania, and even the USSR were now targeted as promising new production locales.[12]

West European producers such as Carlo Ponti and Dino De Laurentiis from Italy, Constantin Film from Germany, and Franco London Films from France had already started coproductions and their own versions of runaway shooting in Eastern Europe, and they became industry mediators between Eastern and Western production systems.[13] They acted as informers, partners, and competitive drivers of Hollywood's activities in the East. One of them, the Italian Moris Ergas, played a minor mediating role in initial negotiations between the Czechoslovaks and *The Bridge at Remagen*'s American producer, David Wolper.[14]

Industry observers noticed that political and economic liberalization in Czechoslovakia, as in Yugoslavia a decade before, had stimulated an increase in film trade with the West. The import of American movies had been rising for some time, though it was hampered by Czechoslovakia's censorship and lack of hard currency.[15] Hollywood's attention thus turned to new opportunities via foreign location shooting, overtures that Prague met with keen interest.[16] The sense was that "of all the socialist states, Czechoslovakia has been most receptive to Western filmmakers."[17] And in reports about the making of *The Bridge at Remagen*, the first big-budget Hollywood movie shot in the country, US trade journalists and filmmakers voiced their outright fascination with the Socialist Bloc: "No one questions that several Iron Curtain countries could, like Yugoslavia now, become regular production centers for Western films. . . . And all throughout Europe this summer, industryites who had visited the set or had some firsthand knowledge of the production found themselves constantly besieged by questioners. Every producer, every director, property master, special effects specialist—*everyone* seemed to know just who in their field had been the one to take on the pioneering assignment of making a film in Prague. And all anxiously asked, 'How are they getting on?'"[18]

The press in the Eastern Bloc was not as vocal about promoting new collaborations with the West; even the presence of Hollywood stars in Prague didn't create much buzz. Nonetheless, studio managers behind the Iron Curtain were taking resolute steps to make the production-service business with the West easier and to compete against one another.

### Barrandov as the East European Hub of Western Production

The foreign-service approach was nothing new for Barrandov. The studios, built with state support in 1932 by Czech film entrepreneur Miloš Havel, were from the beginning designed to attract foreign clients (the best-known incoming production in the 1930s was Julien Duvivier's *Golem*). During World War II, Barrandov became a key part of the Third Reich film industry and hosted around eighty German productions, some of them shot in color, with Germans investing heavily in the modernization of the facilities. After the war, Soviets capitalized on the well-preserved and newly nationalized infrastructure, skilled local crews, and color film know-how by moving some of their projects to Prague. Although the resulting seven epic effects-heavy movies shot in Barrandov between 1945 and 1949 were meant to be a part of the USSR's never-materialized project of an international production network, in retrospect, they look more like a prefiguration of Western "runaway productions."[19]

After the Communist takeover in 1948, Barrandov took part in dozens of international coproductions and provided services to numerous socialist as well as Western producers. Following a period of relative isolation in the early 1950s, the state-run industry slowly opened to the outside world, both in distribution and in production. First, in the second half of the 1950s, eight coproductions with socialist countries were shot in Czechoslovakia.

Coproductions with Western Europe followed from 1957, but they really took off in the second half of the 1960s, driven by the international fame of the Czechoslovak New Wave. The first Czechoslovak-UK feature, *Ninety Degrees in the Shade* (directed in 1965 by Jiří Weiss, who had been a wartime refugee in Britain), was shot in Czech and English versions. In 1966, a deal was negotiated between Czechoslovak Film and Ponti (assisted by Ergas, his business partner) for seven Czech-Italian coproductions to be directed by prominent Czechoslovak filmmakers, some in English and intended for American distribution.[20] After several years of talks, Czechoslovakia signed bilateral coproduction agreements with France and Italy in the spring of 1968. Although Ponti's involvement with Czechoslovak Film ended in mutual disillusionment, all of his coproduction plans failed, and the bilateral agreements brought negligible results, these activities attracted Hollywood's attention.[21] *Variety* labeled Ponti a "catalyst of the growing momentum in joint east-west film trade" and his Czechoslovak deal "a point of reference in future pact-making."[22]

Czechoslovak-US talks and meetings took place in 1966, indicating that "some sort of 'mutual agreement' possibly leading to a 'coparticipation entente'" between the state-run Czechoslovak Film and the Motion Picture Association of America (MPAA) was being considered.[23] Czechoslovak Film hired a US agent to negotiate distribution, coproduction, and service deals with Hollywood: Gerald J. Rappoport (International Film Exchange), who distributed several New Wave films in the US and claimed in 1966 that there were already three coproduction deals and six service productions with US indie interest in negotiation.[24] Although no real start in US-Czechoslovak coproduction followed (apart from the 1969 independent film *Adrift*, directed by the Oscar-winning duo Ján Kadár and Elmar Klos), the reestablished contacts were soon used in negotiating production service deals.

Production services developed in parallel to coproductions. First, a group of agreements were signed between Czechoslovakia and other socialist countries between 1958 and 1962 to exchange so-called reciprocal production services without transfers of foreign currencies, based on an idea of international division of labor and specialization within the Eastern Bloc. But the real business was elsewhere, and as in other parts of the world, manual labor-intensive animation became the pioneering field of film production offshoring (i.e., relocating a production process to a foreign country).[25] In 1959, Czechoslovak Film's animated film division started working on commissions for US producer William L. Snyder (Rembrandt Films), including MGM's revived *Tom and Jerry* series (1961–1962). Snyder sent American (soon-to-be Oscar winner) animation director Gene Dietch to Prague to supervise Czech animators; Dietch stayed on and was labeled "the most prominent non-Communist American living permanently in Eastern Europe" by the *LA Times* in 1974.[26] Driven by the worldwide rise of television, other profitable animation commissions followed, and Czechoslovak Film created a special production unit for them.[27]

Disillusioned by coproductions with other socialist countries and conscious of its increasing technological underdevelopment, Barrandov, inspired by Yugoslavia, started providing services to Western feature productions in 1963, soon reaching an average of three features per year.[28] The key difference from coproductions was that the services provider acquired no right to influence the creative content and no share of international distribution rights; instead, direct payments in hard currency were exchanged for services. In 1957, a state-owned company was established under the name Czechoslovak Filmexport (Československý filmexport, modeled on the USSR's Sovexportfilm) to manage the import and export of films. In 1963, Filmexport started coordinating production services as well, operating as the exclusive legal representative of the Czechoslovak film industry vis-à-vis foreign producers. In the same year, Barrandov established a foreign production services department to manage all foreign commissions.

With this organizational consolidation, a more standardized system of international production emerged (and lasted until 1990), divided into three sectors: coproductions with either Eastern Bloc or Western countries, subject to ideological control of screenplays, without direct financial payments in foreign currency (each partner was expected to cover a part of the production costs in their local currency in exchange for a corresponding share of distribution rights), following the strategic objective of international exposure and cultural diplomacy; "reciprocal services" exchanged between Soviet Bloc countries, mostly East Germany and the USSR, with the aim of mutually complementing individual national studios' specializations; and production services to Western countries, mostly West Germany but also the UK, US, and others, based on one-time contracts, with direct payments in hard currency as the main objective.

The first group of production-services commissions came from the West German company Independent Film (the 1963 TV film *The House in Karp Lane / Das Haus in der Karpfengasse*, directed by Kurt Hoffmann and set in the Jewish district in Prague's Old Town in 1939) and Constantin Film (a group of West German/French/Italian genre films, including the Western *Massacre at Marble City / Die Goldsucher von Arkansas*, directed by Paul Martin in 1964), which attracted local attention by featuring prominent Czech actors. The first (atypical and unsuccessful) US-interest commission soon followed: in early 1966, the sport comedy *Ski Fever*, directed by Kurt Siodmak, was shot in the Slovak High Tatras (standing for the Alps) with several Czech production department heads and including Czech actors in minor roles.[29] In the mid-1960s, the volume of foreign production services quickly increased, reaching a total of a hundred million CZK in 1970, or the equivalent of approximately thirty Czech feature films a year—thus equaling the total annual number of domestic features. But at the same time, Barrandov executives realized that competition with other Eastern Bloc countries (mainly Hungary, Yugoslavia, and Romania) for Western commissions was intensifying and a more active business approach was needed. Hungary was luring the same West German or Austrian producers to Budapest instead of Prague, offering better prices (due to a favorable hard currency exchange rate provided to the local studios by the state)—a situation reminiscent of the post-2004 "subsidy race" between the two production centers, which Hungary has been winning with the help of its tax incentives, effectively becoming the EU leader in foreign production services.[30]

Services to Western producers were judged in economic, not ideological or aesthetic, terms (despite authorities' occasional claims to the contrary), because they were clearly profitable, unlike cooperations with socialist countries, which were increasingly perceived as bothersome and loss-making obligations.[31] As negotiation protocols reveal, the reasons to reject a project were typically based on the lack of studio capacity, appropriate locations, technology, or expertise on the Czechoslovak side or on the lack of financial credibility on the client's side, which would make cooperation too risky. Western productions brought desperately needed hard currency, which enabled Barrandov to buy high-quality Eastmancolor film stock and modern technology such as cameras and sound recording and lighting equipment that would be otherwise inaccessible.

While coproductions allowed Czechoslovak executives and filmmakers, at least potentially, to have an equal say and share and were meant to be compatible with the state-socialist mode of production, servicing Hollywood was very different. All creative decisions, above-the-line talent, and key crew members were the Western producers', while local input was strictly limited to technical, supportive tasks. The unpredictable regime of production services, the dependence on foreign commissioners' requirements, budgets, and timelines, and the crucial importance of overtime—and more generally, post-classical, project-based organization—required Barrandov staff to adapt their work methods and mindsets. In the first place, it took them some time to understand how Western media industries had changed since 1948, especially in Hollywood. A report from a business trip by Barrandov representatives to New York and Los Angeles in early 1969 is surprising in the effort it devotes to describing the basics of Hollywood industry organization, financing, and independent producing and its stress on the need for a permanent Czechoslovak Film office in Hollywood.[32] Step by step, Barrandov executives learned new networking and negotiation skills, cultivated informal networks of contacts, realized how to judge the credibility and financial strength of foreign partners, learned how to meet Western standards of quality, and eventually devised a way to mediate all of this to the supervising political authorities.

### THE MAKING OF *THE BRIDGE AT REMAGEN*: POLITICAL HISTORY MEETS FILM HISTORY

*The Bridge at Remagen* was primarily Wolper's project. The young—yet already renowned—documentary film producer wanted to continue his recent expansion into feature film while using his nonfiction skills to produce an authentic World War II spectacle. He managed to get United Artists' backing and assembled an estimated budget of $4.5 million. During preproduction, he undertook a worldwide search for a site that resembled the Ludendorff Bridge at Remagen, whose capture allowed the US Army to cross the Rhine for the first time, despite German forces' repeated attempts to destroy it. In March 1967, Wolper's representative contacted the Czechoslovak Ministry of Transport, which proposed several possibilities. Wolper first visited Prague in July of the same year and, with production designer Alfred Sweeney, decided on a bridge in Davle, outside Prague. According to Wolper, the bridge was absolutely crucial to the war movie's realistic effect. When questioned about the reasons for moving production to Czechoslovakia, Wolper insisted that his project was not a pragmatic kind of runaway: "We didn't go there because of cheap labor costs, but because we couldn't duplicate that bridge anywhere."[33] In reality, though, there was more to it than that.

In October 1967, Wolper's business affairs vice president, Harvey Bernhard, signed a contract with Filmexport. The contract was "on strictly a rental basis; no coproduction involved."[34] For $750,000, Wolper was promised carte blanche cooperation, including locations, studio sets (for interiors), and film processing at Barrandov, 5,000 Czechoslovak extras (300 of them Czechoslovak Army soldiers), several professional Czechoslovak actors for minor roles, some 188 technicians and other support staff (three assistant directors, grips, electricians, property and soundmen, drivers, numerous interpreters, etc.), accommodations for cast and crew, a demolition team, and old German weapons and uniforms. The most prominent Czech crew members had previous experience with coproductions and production services: art director Bohuslav Kulič (who previously worked on *Ninety Degrees in the Shade*) and makeup artist Miloslav Jandera (on production services for West German TV). Wolper's incoming thirty-five-member team consisted of the main cast (including the star trio Ben Gazzara, Robert Vaughn, and George Segal), director John Guillermin, experienced department heads (cinematographer Stanley Cortez and production designer Alfred Sweeney among them), and British and American crews. Wolper's closest collaborators were associate producer Julian Ludwig and production manager Milton Feldman, who had worked on many foreign-location movies before. A fifteen-week shoot was planned entirely in Czechoslovakia.[35]

In February 1968, construction of the complex set started, "transforming Davle bridge into multi-towered Remagen facsimile ... [an] 80-foot railroad tunnel is blasted into mountainside and the bridge raised 14 feet."[36] American military equipment, including M-24 tanks, was rented from Austria and supplemented by German weapons supplied by the Czechoslovak side. The film started shooting on June 6, 1968, in the north Bohemian city of Most, where Wolper was allowed to blow up three blocks to imitate the Remagen battle (the blocks were already scheduled for demolition due to their location on top of coal mines). From Most, the crew moved to Prague and Davle to continue shooting.

Yet the presence of the American military equipment in Czechoslovakia attracted unwanted attention. In early May 1968, before shooting began, the East German newspapers *Berliner Zeitung* and *Neues Deutschland* reported that the film was a cover-up for smuggling weapons and US soldiers into the country. The Czech police and army reacted by inspecting the explosives and putting the weapons under guard. Wolper wrote a letter to Czechoslovak Film's director general Alois Poledňák asking for help and threatened to move the production out of the country. Poledňák responded by publicly denouncing the East German reports as propaganda. The Czechoslovak press followed, accusing East Germany of using the occasion to attack Alexander Dubček's liberalization process, by that point in full swing.[37]

After the Warsaw Pact invasion on August 21, Soviet troops surrounded the International Hotel, where the foreign filmmakers were accommodated, and shooting was interrupted. Wolper's publicist Bob Silverstein noted that "never before had a Hollywood film unit encountered a location snag quite like this. On what would have been director John Guillermin's 61st day of filming, the production report carried but one line. It read: 'No shooting today because of shooting.'"[38] All American and British cast and crew were quickly evacuated to Austria. While Wolper managed to find a replacement for Barrandov and the Davle bridge in Studio Hamburg and the Castel Gandolfo region in Italy, the second unit director, William Kronick, went back in October 1968 to shoot critical missing scenes in Davle, with Czechoslovak soldiers dressed as American GIs, under the constant supervision of Soviet troops.[39] As Wolper recalls in his memoir: "The actors get on the bridge in Czechoslovakia, remove explosives from under the bridge in Germany, and get off the bridge in Italy."[40] On November 19, 1968, Guillermin completed principal photography. In the meantime, Barrandov executives had to deal with Wolper's demands related to the interrupted shooting, which involved negotiation with his lawyers in Vienna and with the Soviets in Prague; the final sum Barrandov received from Wolper was lower than originally expected: $600,000.[41]

### The Show Must Go On

It could be expected that such a spectacular failure and the ensuing political change would thwart any further collaboration across the Iron Curtain. In November 1968, Wolper told *Variety* that "the events last August overnight wiped out Prague's tremendous progress toward becoming one of the world's major motion picture centers—comparable to London and Rome. Before the invasion, production representatives of almost all the big American companies could be found in Prague hotel lobbies drawing up plans for US production." He added, "It will now be a long time before an American company invests dollars for picture making in Czechoslovakia."[42]

But what was happening on the ground? In the interim, the politically ambivalent period of 1969, the Czechoslovaks were trying to persuade their Western partners that the Soviet occupation changed nothing; Czechoslovak Film's representatives were sent to London, New York, and Hollywood to negotiate further commissions, and *Variety* reported that "Prague authorities are anxious to obtain hard currency (dollars, pounds, francs, etc.) and thus are in a continuing mood to deal with western traders."[43] It indeed seemed for a while that the purges that inaugurated the post-1969 period of Normalization would put an end to the opportunistic business model: in early 1970, Filmexport's management was replaced, and Czechoslovak Film's new director general, Jiří Purš, conducted a thorough inspection of the post-1963 Western commissions, accompanied by a politically motivated press campaign pointing at supposed fraudsters among pre-1969 Filmexport and Barrandov management.[44] In reality, however, the inflow of Hollywood production to Prague was interrupted only for a little more than a year, quietly continuing when Universal brought another World War II movie to Czechoslovakia: *Slaughterhouse-Five* (dir. George Roy Hill, 1972). Universal executives and Hill arrived in Prague for talks in May 1970, after which production services department head Jan Klement wrote enthusiastically to newly appointed Barrandov head Miloslav Fábera: "In this case, we are dealing directly with one of the biggest film corporations in the world, unlike the previous case of Mr. Wolper, who is an independent producer working for these major studios, and we are convinced that we could not only earn important hard currency and secure a share to buy Eastmancolor stock or technical equipment for our own production, but also achieve significant profitability."[45]

Universal used the same location in Most as *The Bridge at Remagen*, rented local military equipment, hired four hundred soldiers as extras, and—quite untypically—employed Czech cinematographer Miroslav Ondříček, known for his collaborations with Miloš Forman; the commission's worth was only slightly lower than *The Bridge at Remagen*: $620,000.[46]

Despite the political repression of Normalization, the total volume of Western commissions increased dramatically during the 1970s: while it totaled 11 million DM in the first half of the decade, it increased by 86 percent in the second half to reach 20.5 million DM, the vast majority coming from West Germany.[47] Americans kept coming, too: in 1974, Warner Bros. backed *Operation: Daybreak* (dir. Lewis Gilbert, 1975), about Czech paratroopers assassinating SS General Reinhard Heydrich in Prague; *All Quiet on the Western Front* (dir. Delbert Mann, 1979), using Most once again; United Artists' *Yentl* (dir. Barbra Streisand, 1983), where a Czech location stood in for a Polish shtetl in the early 1900s; and *Amadeus* (dir. Miloš Forman, US, 1984), which made great use of historical Prague architecture and contributed to the city's long-lasting popularity among US producers.[48] Such collaborations became even more pragmatic in ideological terms, extending to West German genre films and TV series and the B-horror movie *Howling II: Stirba—Werewolf Bitch* (dir. Philippe Mora, US, 1985).

The growing opportunism influenced coproductions, too. While joint projects with other socialist countries prevailed in the 1950s and 1960s, and while 1960s coproductions with the West concentrated on the strong authorial voices of the Czechoslovak New Wave, West Germany became the most frequent coproducer with Czechoslovakia in the 1970s, focusing mostly on commercially successful children's and family films and TV series. Czechoslovak Film didn't stop actively searching for US commissions; it appointed an additional US representative to join Gerald Rappoport in 1981, Jitka Markvartová, who claimed that her area of concentration would be "'the area where the most money can be made,' mainly in luring foreign producers to locations and soundstages."[49] The infrastructure, crews, and mediators involved in production services to Western producers became key agents of continuity in Barrandov after 1990, one of the reasons why the studios survived in the free market, unlike the Koliba studios in Bratislava.

## Conclusion: East European Runaways' Opportunistic Business Model

From the perspective of state-socialist studios, commissions such as *The Bridge at Remagen* were a great opportunity to earn hard currency that would allow them to modernize film equipment and buy quality film stock. The motivations of Western producers were more complex. In the early days, some were intrigued by East European films' festival successes and awards, such as the Oscars for *The Shop on the Main Street* (*Obchod na korze*, dir. Kadár and Klos, 1965) and *Closely Watched Trains* (*Ostře sledované vlaky*, dir. Jiří Menzel, 1966). They were interested in the kind of production facilities these filmmakers had at their disposal and the production methods they used. But in the actual decision-making processes, purely business speculation was most important. This went beyond cheap labor, locations, and studio rentals; even more crucial, although less publicized, were the advantages of working with the centrally managed state-run industries. Central government control allowed for a different kind of deal than business collaboration in the West—carte blanche or package deals, which provided all services in one inexpensive bundle, making it unnecessary to negotiate with a number of private parties. As *Variety* commented on the day of the invasion: "If Czechoslovakia appeals to Western filmmakers as a production locale it is precisely as a result of its being a Communist country."[50]

Perhaps even more importantly, a Hollywood producer could ask for things that would be impossible or very difficult in a democratic country: suspending traffic on a bridge or a river for three months, blowing up several blocks of an abandoned town district, hiring hundreds of army personnel as extras, and so on. State control didn't necessarily mean more transparency and predictability, though. As Wolper recalls in his memoir: "One of the freedoms in which the Czechs were already expert was the art of bribe. I could get anything I wanted done—as long as I paid for it. The head of the Czech film industry told me I could hire soldiers from the Czech army as my extras for about a dollar a soldier—if I deposited $5,000 in American dollars in his Swiss bank account. We also made deposits in Swiss banks for some of the army officers."[51]

These comments, however exaggerated they might be, need to be considered as balance to Wolper's "creative runaway" claims (i.e., the supposedly perfect double of the Ludendorff Bridge as the only reason for moving the shoot to Czechoslovakia). The relatively low service and labor costs together with unique locations (easily used as selling points in promotional campaigns) made East European production services similar to their West European predecessors. Yet the package deals, the massively exploitative and laissez-faire use of locations, the pitfalls of the rigid studio administration, and—paradoxically—the potential of the informal economy specific to state-socialist societies differentiated them from their Western counterparts.

Although the opportunistic business model offered many potential benefits, it was also risky for both parties. Not used to making deals with capitalist businessmen, Czechoslovak executives struggled to specify their own terms vis-à-vis the Western business partners and even to agree what their own chain of command should be. This applied particularly to repeated jurisdictional struggles and turf wars between Barrandov and Filmexport that led to mismanagement, poor judgement, and bad decisions. Inexperienced executives repeatedly signed contracts with dubious Western companies that proved to be insolvent or even went bankrupt before paying their debts.[52]

Moreover, unlike US-based runaways in Western Europe, labeled by Daniel Steinhart "a more flexible mode of production," Hollywood producers coming to Eastern Europe couldn't rely on a network of foreign studio offices and trusted insiders.[53] While shooting on East European locations, American crews remained rather isolated from their local colleagues and everyday reality. As the memoirs quoted above illustrate, they perceived Czechoslovakia as a fascinating but rather alien, incomprehensible, or even dangerous country. This only strengthened the barriers already created by fundamental differences in language, financial and administrative realities, production modes, and work habits, adding to a sense of unpredictability. As a result, Hollywood and East European production systems, communities, and practices didn't mutually influence and hybridize each other to the extent that Hollywood had done with the UK, Italy, or France.[54]

The production history of *The Bridge at Remagen* is a spectacular example of a filming process drastically interrupted by force majeure—a World War II fiction invaded by Cold War reality. The turbulent events of August 1968 earned their place in memoirs by Wolper and the lead actors, who mostly expanded on the World War II analogy and the *political history meets film history* theme first offered in Wolper's publicity.[55] Indeed, both Wolper and Guillermin were originally documentarists praised for their hard, realistic styles. By overcoming all the obstacles, they claimed to have achieved the authentic eyewitness feel of history in the making. According to Wolper, the release campaign "will remind one and all that *Remagen* was the picture mass communications media world-wide had identified as the American film project caught up in the Warsaw Pact invasion of Czechoslovakia."[56] However, this chapter has also shown that *The Bridge at Remagen*'s production history is a reminder of another history: the early history of the globalization of film production that is so visible in today's Prague, Budapest, and elsewhere in Central and Eastern Europe. The current business of foreign production services—based on a global search for attractive locations, cheap and nonunionized labor, and above all, financial incentives—doesn't differ much from the runaways of the 1960s. On the occasion of the fiftieth anniversary of the Warsaw Pact invasion, Czech media repeated speculations about *The Bridge at Remagen*'s role in it. Film historians, on the other hand, should also pay attention to how the film's legacy is still visible in today's local industry structure and in Czech cinema's constrained, peripheral place in global production networks.

## Notes

*Acknowledgment*: This work was supported by the European Regional Development Fund project "Creativity and Adaptability as Conditions of the Success of Europe in an Interrelated World" (reg. no.: CZ.02.1.01/0.0/0.0/16_019/0000734).

Sources used in reconstructing the production history include USC's David L. Wolper Collection and files related to Barrandov in the National Film Archive in Prague (NFA) and the Czech National Archive (NA).

1. Columbia was perhaps the most active, backing *Man on Horseback* (*Michael Kohlhaas—Der Rebell*, dir. Volker Schlöndorff, 1969), which was partly shot in Bratislava and in Moravia, *The Night of the Generals* (dir. Anatol Litvak, 1967) in Poland, and a number of films shot in Yugoslavia, such as *Castle Keep* (dir. Sidney Pollack, 1969). Universal was involved in *Isadora* (dir. Karel Reisz, 1968), shot on numerous locations in Yugoslavia. MGM produced *The Fixer* (dir. John Frankenheimer, 1968) in Hungary and *Kelly's Heroes* (dir. Brian G. Hutton, 1970) in Yugoslavia. Paramount Pictures backed Laurentiis's productions *Waterloo* (dir. Sergei Bondarchuk, 1970), shot on locations in the USSR with Russian troops, although the Waterloo battle scenes were initially planned for Czechoslovakia, and *Fräulein Doktor* (dir. Alberto Lattuada, 1969), shot on locations in Budapest and Yugoslavia. Twentieth Century-Fox shot *A Walk with Love and Death* (dir. John Huston, 1969) in Austria; Huston also originally intended to use a Carthusian monastery in the Czech city of Brno, but his crew was stopped at the border by invading Warsaw Pact troops. See "Czech Thrust May Cost USSR Par-Italo Deal"; and Brooks, "Wolper's 'Bridge' Unit Caught in Czech Invasion."

2. Barrandov was the biggest Czechoslovak production facility, built in 1932 and nationalized in 1945. The term *runaway production* refers to Hollywood films shot entirely or partially overseas, primarily for financial reasons; it was coined in the late 1940s by Hollywood labor unions critical of jobs leaving the Los Angeles area. Alternative, more neutral terms include *overseas production, foreign production*, or *mobile production*, but *runaway production* has attracted most industry and academic attention.

3. See Miller et al., *Global Hollywood 2*; Siegel, "The Lives of Kong"; Yale, "Runaway Film Production"; Steinhart, "All the World's a Studio"; and Donoghue, *Localising Hollywood*.

4. See Silberman, "Learning from the Enemy"; Michaels, "Mikhail Kalatozov's *The Red Tent*"; Siefert, "Co-producing Cold War Culture"; Skopal, "Barrandov's Co-productions"; and Shaw, "Nightmare on Nevsky Prospekt." Marsha Siefert describes the intricate connections between cultural-political and economic motives in 1960s East-West film collaboration in "Meeting at a Far Meridian."

5. On opportunistic transnationalism, see Hjort, "On the Plurality of Cinematic Transnationalism," 19–20. For the overview of East-Central European studios' production-services business model, see Szczepanik, *Screen Industries in East-Central Europe*, 109–138.
6. See Bordwell et al., *The Classical Hollywood Cinema*, 571–576.
7. Curtin, "Thinking Globally."
8. Szczepanik, "The State-Socialist Mode of Production."
9. See, for example, "West 'Finds' East Locales." Runaway production's decline in the 1960s was a result of Hollywood below-the-line labor's long-term anti-runaway campaign, the strengthening of Western European film industries and the related increase in production costs in Western Europe, and a revision of Hollywood's runaway strategy itself, due to unpredictable financial losses while shooting overseas. See Yale, "Runaway Film Production," 84–132; and Steinhart, "All the World's a Studio," 10–13.
10. Shapiro, "Avala Studio Speaks English." See also Tusher, "Europe Lensing Losing Lure," 1, 3.
11. Tusher, "Europe Lensing Losing Lure."
12. "Hungary Hungry for U.S. Film Locationing," 1, 11; Weaver, "Hungary Welcomes MGM 'Fixer' Crew with Open Arms," 9, 14; "Romania Joins Race to Woo U.S. Pix Prod'n"; Luft, "Rumanian Film Industry Alive and Thriving," 1, 22–23, 40; and Pozner, "Sovinfilm, New USSR Body, to Oil Machinery for Co-prod. with West."
13. On Italian-Soviet coproductions, see Stefano Pisu, "Envisioning the Revolutionary South," in this volume (chap. 14).
14. For his role, Ergas unsuccessfully demanded 10 percent of the final fee from Barrandov. NA, f. P ÚV KSČ (1261/0/5), sv. 130, a. j. 206.
15. From zero to five US features annually in the 1950s and early 1960s to about ten per year in the mid-1960s and twenty-five toward the end of the decade.
16. See "Czechs Shopping for More U.S. Pix to Show or Co-produce There."
17. Werba, "Czechoslovak Invasion."
18. Byron, "Czechs Want Western Production."
19. See the dossier of Soviet archival documents edited by Fomin, *Kinovedcheskye zapiski*.
20. This slate never materialized. See NFA, f. ÚŘČSF, k. R8/B1/4P/7K.
21. "Czechs Pushing Co-production with the U.S.," 1–2; and "Czechoslovak Coproduction." On the failure of Ponti's plans, see Di Chiara and Skopal, "Příliš kruté pro Američany."
22. Werba, "Ponti's Czech Deals Could Blaze Trail There for U.S. Films," 1, 18.
23. "Czechs Talk MPAA Understanding."
24. "Czech Films Seek Co-production Deal."
25. See Yoon and Malecki, "Cartoon Planet," 239–271.
26. Longworth, "The Dietch Odyssey." Dietch married a Czech production manager, lived in Prague until his death in 2020, and published a biography. Dietch, *For the Love of Prague*.
27. See report on Western animation commissions from May 13, 1960, in NFA, f. ÚŘČSF, k. R9/B2/5P/4K.
28. On inspiration by Yugoslavia, see an interview with the then-head of Filmexport, Ladislav Kachtík, by Skopal and Skupa in *Hoří, má panenko*, 162.
29. During the shooting, the original producer, Gaumont International, proved to be insolvent; the contract was canceled, but the film was finished. Czechoslovak Film sold the rights to US distributor Allied Artists for an expected share in revenues and for four Allied Artists films (see NFA, f. ÚŘČSF, k. R5/B1/5P/3K). The film is usually credited as a US/Austrian/West German/Czechoslovak coproduction.
30. NFA, f. ÚŘČSF, k. R5/A1/1P/7K, R5/A1/1P/3K, k. R5/B1/5P/3K.
31. In 1975, Czechoslovak Film's director general circulated a memo claiming that not only coproduction but also production services should follow ideological objectives as an instrument of "active foreign policy," "infecting" foreign films with "preferred cultural-political tendencies." NFA, f. ÚŘČSF, k. R12/A2/4P/6K.

32. NFA, f. ÚŘČSF, k. R11/B2/4P/4K.
33. "Wolper Dickers to Shoot More Czech 'Bridge' Scenes."
34. Beigel, "Borrow Span, Blow up Town."
35. Bob Silverstein, "The Bridge at Remagen, Background Highlights and Production Notes," USC Warner Bros Archive, David L. Wolper Collection, The Bridge at Remagen; and Loynd, "'Remagen' Location Costs."
36. Lightman, "Photographing 'The Bridge at Remagen,'" 839.
37. See USC Warner Bros Archive, David L. Wolper Collection, The Bridge at Remagen; see also Kraus, "Americké tanky v ČSSR"; and Petr, "Kachny, nebo politika."
38. Silverstein, "Revised Production Notes," USC Warner Bros Archive, David L. Wolper Collection, The Bridge at Remagen.
39. "Wolper Dickers to Shoot More Czech 'Bridge' Scenes"; and "2D Unit Winds Czech 'Remagen' Scenes."
40. Wolper, *Producer*, 173.
41. See NFA, f. ÚŘ ČSF, k. R12/B1/1P/9K, NA, f. P ÚV KSČ (1261/0/5), sv. 130, a. j. 206.
42. Werba, "Czechoslovak Invasion."
43. "Czech Pic Biz Still Woos West Deals."
44. NFA, f. ÚŘČSF, k. R5/B1/5P/3K; NA, f. P ÚV KSČ (1261/0/5), sv. 130, a. j. 206; and "Potěmkinovy vesnice Filmexportu," 1–2.
45. Jan Klement to Miloslav Fábera, October 6, 1970, NFA, f. ÚŘČSF, k. R5/B1/5P/3K.
46. NFA, f. ÚŘČSF, k. R5/B1/5P/3K.
47. Zach, "Vztah Československého filmexportu a zahraniční zakázkové skupiny FSB," 16.
48. See Holloway, "Many Filmmakers from West Take Czech Coproduction Route."
49. "Markvartova with Rappoport to Hypo Czech Films & Locations," 6.
50. Byron, "Czechs Want Western Production."
51. Wolper, *Producer*, 167.
52. NFA, f. ÚŘČSF, k. R5/B1/5P/3K.
53. Steinhart, "All the World's a Studio," 65.
54. Ibid.
55. Vaughn, *A Fortunate Life*, 243–244; and Gazzara, *In the Moment*, 139–140.
56. Werba, "Czechoslovak Invasion."

## BIBLIOGRAPHY

Beigel, Jerry. "Borrow Span, Blow up Town. Czechs Big Aid to U.S. Feature." *Variety Weekly*, November 8, 1967.

Bordwell, David, Janet Staiger, and Kristin Thompson. *The Classical Hollywood Cinema: Film Style and Mode of Production to 1960*. New York: Columbia University Press, 1985.

Brooks, Dick. "Wolper's 'Bridge' Unit Caught in Czech Invasion; Fox Unit Nearby." *Motion Picture Daily*, August 23, 1968.

Byron, Stuart. "Czechs Want Western Production; Package Deals, But Problems Too." *Variety*, August 21, 1968.

Curtin, Michael. "Thinking Globally: From Media Imperialism to Media Capital." In *Media Industries: History, Theory, and Method*, edited by Jennifer Holt and Alisa Perren, 108–119. Malden, MA: Wiley Blackwell, 2009.

"Czech Films Seek Co-production Deal." *Hollywood Reporter*, January 12, 1966.

"Czechoslovak Coproduction. Strong Prague Woo of Deals." *Variety Weekly*, April 13, 1966.

"Czech Pic Biz Still Woos West Deals & Soviet Apparently Gives Greenlight." *Variety Weekly*, July 23, 1969.

"Czechs Pushing Co-production with the U.S." *Hollywood Reporter*, April 5, 1966, 1–2.

"Czechs Shopping for More U.S. Pix to Show or Co-produce There." *Variety Daily*, April 21, 1966.
"Czechs Talk MPAA Understanding." *Variety Weekly*, December 7, 1966.
"Czech Thrust May Cost USSR Par-Italo Deal." *Daily Variety*, August 29, 1968, 3.
Di Chiara, Francesco, and Pavel Skopal. "Příliš kruté pro Američany. Carlo Ponti, česká nová vlna a barrandovské koprodukce se západní Evropou." In *Hoří, má panenko*, edited by Anna Batistová, 56–79. Praha: NFA, 2012.
Dietch, Gene. *For the Love of Prague*, 6th ed. Praha: Baset Books, 2008.
Donoghue, Courtney Brannon. *Localising Hollywood*. London: British Film Institute, 2017.
Fomin, Valerij, ed. *Kinovedcheskye zapiski*, no. 71 (2005).
Gazzara, Ben. *In the Moment: My Life as an Actor*. New York: Carroll & Graf, 2004.
Hjort, Mette. "On the Plurality of Cinematic Transnationalism." In *World Cinemas, Transnational Perspectives*, edited by Nataša Ďurovičová and Kathleen Newman, 12–33. New York: Routledge, 2010.
Holloway, Ron. "Many Filmmakers from West Take Czech Coproduction Route." *Variety Weekly*, October 24, 1984.
"Hungary Hungry for U.S. Film Locationing." *Variety Daily*, November 9, 1967, 1, 11.
Kraus, J. "Americké tanky v ČSSR." *Rudé právo*, May 11, 1968, 3.
Lightman, Herb A. "Photographing 'The Bridge at Remagen.'" *American Cinematographer*, September 1968, 839.
Longworth, L. C. "The Dietch Odyssey: Cartoonist in a New Frame." *LA Times*, August 3, 1974.
Loynd, Ray. "'Remagen' Location Costs." *Hollywood Reporter*, August 19, 1968.
Luft, Herbert G. "Rumanian Film Industry Alive and Thriving." *LA Times*, December 28, 1969, 1, 22–23, 40.
"Markvartova with Rappoport to Hypo Czech Films & Locations." *Variety Weekly*, October 7, 1981, 6.
Michaels, Paula A. "Mikhail Kalatozov's *The Red Tent*: A Case Study in International Coproduction Across the Iron Curtain." *Historical Journal of Film, Radio and Television* 26, no. 3 (2006): 311–325.
Miller, Toby, Nitin Govil, John McMurria, Richard Maxwell, and Ting Wang. *Global Hollywood 2*. London: British Film Institute, 2008.
Petr, Milan. "Kachny, nebo politika." *Kulturní tvorba*, May 16, 1968, 15.
"Potěmkinovy vesnice Filmexportu." *Zemědělské noviny*, July 7, 1970, 1–2.
Pozner, Vladimir. "Sovinfilm, New USSR Body, to Oil Machinery for Co-prod. with West." *Variety Weekly*, February 11, 1970.
"Romania Joins Race to Woo U.S. Pix Prod'n." *Variety Daily*, February 20, 1968.
Shapiro, Irvin. "Avala Studio Speaks English." *Variety Weekly*, January 3, 1968.
Shaw, Tony. "Nightmare on Nevsky Prospekt. *The Blue Bird* as a Curious Instance of U.S.-Soviet Film Collaboration during the Cold War." *Journal of Cold War Studies* 14, no. 1 (2012): 3–33.
Siefert, Marsha. "Co-producing Cold War Culture: East-West Filmmaking and Cultural Diplomacy." In *Divided Dreamworlds? The Cultural Cold War East and West*, edited by Peter Romijn, Giles Scott-Smith, and Joes Segal, 73–94. Amsterdam: Amsterdam University Press, 2012.
———. "Meeting at a Far Meridian: US-Soviet Cultural Diplomacy on Film in the Early Cold War." In *Cold War Crossings: International Travel and Exchange Across the Soviet Bloc, 1940s–1960s*, edited by Patryk Babiracki and Kenyon Zimmer, 166–209. Arlington: Texas A&M University Press, 2014.

Siegel, Andrea. "The Lives of Kong: Labor and Moviemaking in Three Acts." PhD diss., City University of New York, 2009.
Silberman, Marc. "Learning from the Enemy: DEFA-French Co-productions of the 1950s." *Film History* 18, no. 1 (2006): 21–45.
Skopal, Pavel. "Barrandov's Co-productions: The Clumsy Way to Ideological Control, International Competitiveness and Technological Improvement." In *Cinema in Service of the State: Perspectives on Film Culture in the GDR and Czechoslovakia 1945–1960*, edited by Pavel Skopal and Lars Karl, 89–106. New York: Berghahn, 2015.
Skopal, Pavel, and Lukáš Skupa. Interview with Ladislav Kachtík. In *Hoří, má panenko*, edited by Anna Batistová, 162. Praha: NFA, 2012.
Steinhart, Daniel. "All the World's a Studio: The Internationalization of Hollywood Production and Location Shooting in the Postwar Era." PhD diss., University of California, Los Angeles, 2013.
Szczepanik, Petr. *Screen Industries in East-Central Europe*. London: Bloomsbury, 2021.
———. "The State-Socialist Mode of Production and the Political History of Production Culture." In *Behind the Screen: Inside European Production Cultures*, edited by Petr Szczepanik and Patrick Vonderau, 113–134. New York: Palgrave Macmillan, 2013.
Tusher, William. "Europe Lensing Losing Lure." *The Film Daily*, September 13, 1967, 1, 3.
"2D Unit Winds Czech 'Remagen' Scenes; USSR Troops Stand By." *Variety Daily*, October 23, 1968.
Vaughn, Robert. *A Fortunate Life*. New York: Thomas Dunne and St. Martin's, 2008.
Weaver, Gordon. "Hungary Welcomes MGM 'Fixer' Crew with Open Arms." *Motion Picture Herald*, February 14, 1968, 9, 14.
Werba, Hank. "Czechoslovak Invasion, Winds His 'Remagen.'" *Variety*, November 27, 1968.
———. "Ponti's Czech Deals Could Blaze Trail There for U.S. Films." *Variety Daily*, January 31, 1967, 1, 18.
"West 'Finds' East Locales." *Variety Weekly*, January 24, 1968, 17.
Wolper, David L. *Producer: A Memoir*. New York: A Lisa Drew Book and Scribner, 2003.
"Wolper Dickers to Shoot More Czech 'Bridge' Scenes; $1 Mil Loss." *Variety Daily*, October 4, 1968.
Yale, Camille K. "Runaway Film Production: A Critical History of Hollywood's Outsourcing Discourse." PhD diss., University of Illinois at Urbana-Champaign, 2010.
Yoon, Hyejin, and Edward J. Malecki. "Cartoon Planet: Worlds of Production and Global Production Networks in the Animation Industry." *Industrial and Corporate Change* 19, no. 1 (2010): 239–271.
Zach, Juraj. "Vztah Československého filmexportu a zahraniční zakázkové skupiny FSB." Diploma thesis, FAMU, 1982.

PETR SZCZEPANIK is Associate Professor of Film Studies at Charles University. He is author of *Screen Industries in East-Central Europe*. He is editor (with Pavel Zahrádka, Jakub Macek, and Paul Stepan) of *Digital Peripheries: The Online Circulation of Audiovisual Content from the Small Market Perspective* and (with Patrick Vonderau) of *Behind the Screen: Inside European Production Cultures*.

CHAPTER 14

ENVISIONING THE REVOLUTIONARY SOUTH
## *The Soviet-Italian Coproduction* Life Is Beautiful *(1979)*

Stefano Pisu

Antonio Murillo refuses to machine-gun women and children during an antiguerilla operation in Angola in the mid-1960s. He is subsequently discharged from the army and becomes a taxi driver in his homeland. Despite his decision to distance himself from the revolutionary turmoil that has captured his country's spirit, he plays a part in the arrest of Alvarado, a key leader of the underground opposition movement. He aims to protect his young girlfriend Maria and her uncle João, who are involved in the underground movement and are friends of Alvarado. However, in doing so, Antonio falls into a trap laid for him by a young and ambitious investigating judge, thus involuntarily causing the arrest of several members of the underground movement. Viewed widely as a traitor, Antonio organizes an escape plan [for himself and the prisoners]. Maria, however, retains her full confidence in him, and helps him convince Alvarado and his friends to use this final opportunity to escape before their trial begins. By distracting the guards, Antonio is able to escape with Alvarado and the others. Together with Maria, pursued by the police until the very last moment, he successfully achieves his bid for freedom.[1]

The film is set in a Mediterranean country with a totalitarian regime. At the center of the plot is the love story of two young people, Antonio and Maria. Their personal relationship is closely intertwined with the social problems in their country. The fundamental idea behind the film is that man cannot and must not remain impassive in face of the events unfolding in the society in which he lives. Sooner or later, he is forced to make a choice, even if he must pay a high price for it.[2]

The first quotation above is a synopsis of the Italian-Soviet film *Life Is Beautiful* (*La vita è bella/Zhizn' prekrasna*, 1979) by Grigory Chukhrai; it was presented by the Italian production company Quattro Cavalli Cinematografica as part of its request for permission to distribute the film in Italian cinemas. The second quotation is a Soviet synopsis of the same film, preserved in the archive of Goskino, the state committee that managed the Soviet film industry. This was a unique project; it was an Italian-Soviet coproduction, which made its development and creation significantly more complex than would have been the case had the partners been film industries on the same side of the Iron Curtain. In addition, it had an unusual subject: the underground opposition to an authoritarian regime in a Southern European state, easily identifiable as Portugal before the 1974 Carnation Revolution.[3] This was politically sensitive terrain. It involved a dictatorship, underground opposition, and political revolution in a Southern context (a "totalitarian" and "Mediterranean" context, according to the Soviet synopsis) only a few years after the fall of several authoritarian regimes in Southern Europe—Portugal's and Greece's in 1974, Francoist Spain in 1975—and it dealt with political violence at a moment when armed struggles and terrorism were widespread, including in Italy. This raises the question of how the film's Italian and Soviet partners negotiated the practicalities of its production—and, more broadly, of how an East-West film collaboration could represent revolutionary Southern Europe at the end of the 1970s.

This chapter considers *Life Is Beautiful* against the background of the history of Italian-Soviet cinematic coproductions during the Cold War, examining the film's initial conception and the economic, financial, and political issues that impeded its creation via documents from the Russian State Archive for Literature and Art (RGALI) in Moscow and the State Central Archive (ACS) in Rome. In addition, it considers the development of the screenplay and how its most sensitive elements—particularly the theme of terrorism—were refined. I argue that the material possibilities each party brought to the coproduction relationship—the Soviet film industry's consistent availability of financial and human resources, as a state-sponsored body, and Italian producers' ability to distribute films internationally, especially in the West—made them natural allies in the historical context of the late 1970s. This case study also reveals in broad terms the extent to which East-West film cooperation was possible in and of itself.

### A Brief History of Italian-Soviet Coproductions

Coproductions between the Cold War East and West were often encouraged by official cultural agreements between individual countries, many of them made during the post-Stalin thaw of the late 1950s and early 1960s.[4] They were subsequently institutionalized by intergovernmental protocols for joint film production and, at the end of 1968, by the creation of Sovinfilm, a Soviet body charged with organizing coproductions and providing services to foreign companies willing to shoot films in the USSR.[5] Between 1953 and 1983, the USSR coproduced more than one hundred films, many of them in collaboration with countries beyond the Iron Curtain, such as France, Italy, Norway, and Japan.[6]

In the context of East-West cinematic relations, coproductions offered the valuable—and often rare—opportunity for filmmakers to share professional experience across the Iron Curtain. Yet Italian-Soviet coproduction posed numerous challenges. First, it required collaboration between the USSR's entirely nationalized film industry and its Italian counterpart, which was privately owned (yet also partially supported by public funds), involving the amalgamation of the two different production models embedded within these industries. Second, like nearly all coproductions, it involved negotiation between different cultural, artistic, and symbolic frameworks. In sum, as Marsha Siefert argues, this mode of coproduction represented a "multilayered dynamic process in the negotiation and export of cultural influence during the Cold War."[7]

Despite attempts by a number of Italian producers to initiate negotiations with Soviet film organizations in the 1930s and once again in the mid-1950s, the first Italian-Soviet coproduction was not made until the 1960s. The project, Giuseppe De Santis's 1964 *Attack and Retreat* (*Italiani brava gente/ Oni shli na vostok*, coproduced by Mosfilm and Italian producer Nello Santi's company Galatea Spa), was facilitated on the Italian side by the country's Communist Party.[8] On the Soviet side, it was enabled by a series of legislative provisions and *ad hoc* bodies established in the late 1960s to support coproductions with Western film companies. In 1967, aiming to facilitate joint projects from a financial and technical standpoint, the USSR signed intergovernmental coproduction agreements with France and Italy, countries with strong domestic Communist Parties and whose governments were interested in strengthening commercial and industrial partnerships behind the Iron Curtain.[9]

Why did both sides find such projects so appealing in the 1960s and 1970s? Although the Italian Communist Party was the initial instigating force, Italian production houses themselves developed relationships with the USSR. Their motives for doing so differed from the Communist Party's and lay in the hope of gaining support from the Soviet film industry in the form of services (e.g., extras and locations for crowd scenes). As Eitel

Monaco, president of the Union of Italian Film Producers (ANICA), noted, "Soviet cinema exceeds Italian cinema decisively in terms of the scale of its investment in production over the last few years. Yet the number of new films going into production does not exceed 120 per year. In addition, exports of Soviet films to Western markets, and thus the profits that accrue from them, are significantly lower than... Italian film exports."[10]

Indeed, while the Soviet film industry had enormous spending power, especially in terms of material resources, the country's films circulated primarily in Eastern Europe and nonaligned countries and performed relatively poorly in the lucrative Western market. By contrast, Italian cinema—faced with increasing competition from television and the general crisis in the Italian economy—had limited financial means yet performed well abroad and had a vast network of distributors. On paper, then, collaboration between the two countries could compensate for their cinemas' respective weaknesses. Italian film producers' interest was also indicative of broader industrial trends: numerous Italian entrepreneurs attempted to forge relations with the USSR in the 1960s and 1970s, both for commercial reasons and in pursuit of more practical forms of cooperation. This attention to business with the USSR was favored by *neoatlantism,* a post-1957 turn in Italian foreign policy that sought a more autonomous place for the country in the international arena, albeit always within NATO.[11]

There were several reasons for the Soviets to work with Italy in the cinematic field. Some of these were cultural-diplomatic: coproductions brought prestige and could improve the superpower's image overseas, especially in the West. Others were economic, underscoring that—as recent historiography has shown—the film industry was a money-making venture for the USSR.[12] Not only did coproductions provide a means to penetrate Western markets and thus to obtain the foreign currency the USSR needed (often in exchange for services), the films themselves could also be screened in Soviet cinemas, alongside the foreign films that the country had imported in ever-greater numbers since the 1960s.[13] While such imports increased during the détente of the 1970s, coproductions offered a "softer" way for the USSR to enlarge its film supply and reduce the number of films it imported from the West.[14] In sum, as Birgit Beumers has argued, the goal of commercial success helped support the Soviet film industry's internationalization during a moment when, faced with the rise of television, cinema audiences decreased.[15]

Collaboration between the USSR's lead production house, Mosfilm, and Italian film producers reached a peak between the late 1960s and the mid-1970s, with films such as *The Red Tent* (*La tenda rossa/Krasnaia palatka,* 1968, dir. Mikhail Kalatozov, prod. Vides di Franco Cristaldi), *Waterloo* (1970, dir.

Sergei Bondarchuk, prod. Dino De Laurentiis), *Sunflower* (*I girasoli/Podsolnukhi*, 1970, dir. Vittorio De Sica, prod. Carlo Ponti), and *Unbelievable Adventures of Italians in Russia* (*Una matta, matta, matta corsa in Russia/ Neveroiatnye prikliucheniia ital'iantsev v Rossii*, 1974, dir. Eldar Riazanov, prod. De Laurentiis).[16] Belatedly, in 1975, a mixed Italian-Soviet committee met for the first time to discuss cinematic collaboration.[17] The committee was subsequently reformed at four-year intervals, in 1979 and again in 1983, and coproductions were always at the top of the agenda, although discussions never went beyond a general call to strengthen collaboration.[18] The year 1979 also saw the release of *Life Is Beautiful*, which was novel in the history of Italian-Soviet films. Whereas most earlier coproductions interpreted relationships between Italians and Soviets through generic lenses (such as war, comedy, and drama), *Life Is Beautiful* offered an original narrative in an unfamiliar location. Collaboration between the East and the West, here, was transposed to Portugal under military dictatorship. In turn, this location became a metaphor for Southern European authoritarian regimes and opposition movements.

## The Project's Conception: Political and Artistic Difficulties

According to producer Santi, the idea for the film originated with screenwriter Gian Gaspare Napolitano in the mid-1960s, but negotiations with the deputy director of Goskino, Vladimir Baskakov, were interrupted "because we had underestimated the film's political and artistic significance, and were looking at it from a purely commercial point of view."[19] The project resumed over a decade later, between May and June 1977. On the Italian side, it initially involved the renowned Titanus production house, managed by Goffredo Lombardo and his associate, Santi.[20] Representing the USSR were the general director of Mosfilm, Nikolai Sizov, and the president of Sovinfilm, the Georgian Otar Teneishvili. The film's working title was *Attack on State Security/Attentato alla sicurezza dello Stato*—later changed to *Lone Man In Revolt/Uomo solo in rivolta*—and it was agreed that the Italians would not only retain the author's rights to the script, but also oversee the final screenplay and a search for "an internationally renowned director."[21] However, the situation grew complicated at the beginning of the new year, when Santi wrote to Teneishvili to report a conversation with Lombardo, who had just returned from Los Angeles:

> [Lombardo] maintains that it is essential to make an agreement with an American co-producer who could provide a director, screenwriters, and actors. The

situation in Italy is becoming ever more difficult, and we do not feel that we alone should oversee such a demanding production, at such a delicate moment for our national cinema. Our English co-producer, Lew Grade, has not confirmed his availability, as the Incorporated Television Company board considers the film to be too politically engaged. The same was expressed by Paramount. We now await the answer of Joe Levine, who, in addition to being a personal friend of mine, has already achieved commercial success in the distribution of political films, such as our own *Attack and Retreat*.[22]

Here, Lombardo was relying on established partnerships to secure financial support for the project. American distributor Joseph Levine had arranged American actors and overseas distribution for the very first Soviet-Italian coproduction, *Attack and Retreat*, and an American role was maintained in subsequent productions: Sean Connery acted in *The Red Tent*, Paramount served as international distributor for *Waterloo*, and Levine, once again, for *Sunflower*. If this underscored how Soviet commercial objectives overrode the USSR's prejudices against cooperation with capitalist countries (including the American antagonist), *Attack on State Security* once again proved exceptional in its politically delicate subject matter. Even Levine declined to collaborate, and Antonio Caputo's filmmaking company Quattro Cavalli Cinematografica eventually managed the production, with Santi as associate producer.

The film's direction also grew complicated. Renowned Soviet director Chukhrai was selected and spent two months in Italy drafting the screenplay's final version with young Italian screenwriter Gianfranco Clerici. In a report to Sovinfilm, Chukhrai described how creative negotiations entered into crisis, as Clerici's proposals regarding the opening scenes revealed opposing approaches to the project: "In a bid to provide entertainment, my coauthor has filled the opening scenes of the screenplay with a great many standardized elements typical of Western commercial cinema, from a bedroom scene to some lines of a rather vulgar nature."[23] Chukhrai was explicit about the divergent ideological approaches to cinema underlying this conflict: "Although we are in complete agreement on the general issues and principles, our system of values is entirely different to theirs. I was never under any illusions regarding 'the freedom of creation in the West,' but this conflict has made clear to me the extent to which their artists are in fact not free, but rather slaves to the conditions dictated by the capitalist market."[24]

Only Santi's mediation would allow the collaboration between Chukhrai and Clerici to proceed, and ultimately, the Soviet filmmaker confirmed that the film could indeed achieve "both commercial success and prestige."[25]

## Asymmetry between Coproducers and the Geopolitics of Film Markets

In June 1978, a preliminary agreement was signed for the film, which held the double title *Lone Man in Revolt / Attack on State Security* (*Uomo solo in rivolta / Attentato alla sicurezza dello Stato*). Reaching this agreement was by no means simple and exposed a lack of equity in terms of the film's potential returns. The USSR had proposed retaining the right to distribute the film in socialist or pro-Soviet countries and giving the Italians distribution rights in capitalist or anticommunist countries. However, Santi noted that this arrangement, which largely followed the logic of geopolitical equilibrium, did not reward the financial risk assumed by the more financially exposed Italian coproducer, particularly in light of the crisis in the Italian and global cinematic markets as well as American and British producers' refusals to participate in the project. He proposed that the USSR be given the rights to distribute the film in socialist countries, Cuba, and Africa (with the exception of South Africa, Morocco, Algeria, and Tunisia) and that Italy receive the rights to sales in Western Europe, English-speaking countries, Latin America, the Near and Far East, Japan, and Korea.[26]

In a letter to Sizov and Teneishvili sent two days before the signing, Santi criticized Goskino for the purely commercial focus of the USSR's distribution proposal:

> Since Goskino represents an ideological organization, I cannot believe that the minister who leads it wishes to include, as a necessary condition, elements of a purely commercial nature, such as dividing the markets in the proposed manner. Only the conditions I presented will allow me to carry out this project . . . I, your old and devoted friend, went about my work, despite the difficulties it posed. And I believed it necessary to do everything possible to produce this film, giving first priority to its political significance, and only then considering it from a commercial point of view . . . It seems strange and contradictory that all the work carried out hereto may be rendered useless, merely due to the trivial matter of dividing the markets.[27]

This, again, overturns the traditional categories through which we have interpreted cinemas in the Iron Curtain's East and West: Santi accused the Soviets of being interested primarily in the project's money-making potential, whereas the Italians focused on its political value. Santi's error, however, was in considering Goskino's commercial interest to be contradictory and incorrectly defining the organization as an ideological entity; as this essay has discussed, economic considerations had long been central to the Soviet film industry.

Ultimately, the preliminary agreement (signed June 9, 1978) was decidedly more favorable to the Soviets, who were awarded distribution rights for the Scandinavian countries and Greece, as well as for North Africa and Asia (excluding South Korea, Hong Kong, Singapore, Israel, and Indonesia). The rights for Japan and the Philippines were to be divided equally.[28] Santi had tried desperately to modify the division of distribution zones in Italy's favor, in February requesting distribution rights for the Philippines (and therefore the connected Hong Kong market) and in early spring asking Sovinfilm for the rights to Scandinavian distribution.[29] This outcome highlights the imbalance of power between the Soviet film industry and the Italian production company, as well as the USSR's intransigence and pragmatic attitude in negotiating with Western partners—even long-standing friends like Santi, who had pioneered Italian-Soviet film ventures.

In November 1978, a final agreement was signed between the Soviets and Quattro Cavalli Cinematografica stipulating the equal division of expenses and the production of the film's soundtrack directly in English for international distribution. It was also agreed that the film would be shot not only in the USSR and in Italy, but also in Portugal and/or Spain.[30] In January 1979, Chukhrai wrote to Mosfilm to propose, for the first time, the title that would become definitive: *Life Is Beautiful* (*La vita è bella*)—a choice inspired by the ironies that defined the protagonist's experience.

### A Revolutionary—but Nonviolent—South: Censoring Terrorism

Beyond the geopolitical conflicts underpinning the film's production and distribution, difficulties and risks lay in coproducing a film that portrayed a generic revolutionary Southern Europe during the 1970s, a time during which armed organizations committed to terrorism had established themselves on an international scale (Antonio and Maria, after all, are members of an underground group).[31] According to Santi, the decisively political nature of the screenplay would render it "almost impossible, in the current geopolitical situation, to sell for distribution in countries such as Spain, Portugal, and Latin America"—countries, he implied, where viewers could identify its setting.[32] *Life Is Beautiful*'s southern milieu, as well as the characters' Latin names, could indeed have provoked unpredictable reactions, especially in Portugal, where, despite its post-1974 transition to democracy, the coproducers harbored fears of being denied filming permits.[33] Moreover, the many military dictatorships in Latin America meant that the film risked being refused for distribution there, as it could foment revolutionary actions.[34]

In post-Francoist Spain, the danger likely lay in links to ETA (*Euskadi Ta Askatasuna*, Basque Homeland and Liberty) terrorism.[35]

To this end, shortly after the November 1978 agreement, Mosfilm and Quattro Cavalli Cinematografica signed an additional document formalizing a number of changes to the screenplay—among them a Soviet request to define the resistance leaders (including Antonio) as nonviolent "partisans of a mass democratic movement."[36] This request had particular resonance in Italy, where in the spring of 1978, while the screenplay was being developed, the extreme left-wing terrorist group Brigate Rosse kidnapped and murdered Aldo Moro, president of the Italian Republic's majority party, the Christian Democrats.[37] Moro's murder was the culmination of the Years of Lead, a period of terror attacks carried out by neofascist groups or the so-called extra-parliamentary left; the aim—dubbed the *strategia della tensione* (tension strategy)—was to destabilize the institutional and political balance of Italian democracy.[38] In this context, the USSR's prudence (as well as the Italian coproducer's) is easily understood. The Soviets could not be seen to support projects that could be accused of legitimizing acts of terrorism, even if they were directed against regimes the Soviets viewed as dictatorial and reactionary. In spring 1979, Chukhrai reported to Sovinfilm that these changes had been requested personally by the president of Goskino, Filipp Ermash:

> Ermash has expressed his wish that a scene contained in the screenplay be removed: the airport scene (provoked by the fascist police, the film's protagonist Antonio gives a bag containing explosives to a passenger).... Ermash advised me that issues surrounding the complex and intricate matter of terrorism should be avoided entirely. Obviously, satisfying such a request was not a simple task. The film, by its very nature, is dedicated to one of the problems of terrorism ... the problem of political provocations carried out by a reactionary group. However, I understand the nature of the president's recommendations and request, and I have done everything within my power to respect them.[39]

Even after filming had concluded, there was a further appeal, this time by editors at Mosfilm, to "clarify the aims and methods employed by the progressive groups in their fight against social injustice. These people must not look and act like terrorists."[40] In other words, the Soviets wanted the film not only to avoid justifying armed struggle and terrorism, but also to make no reference to it at a time when Italy was still shaken by Moro's execution—and when the Soviet capital itself had recently been the target of terrorist attacks. These, in January 1977, resulted in the deaths of seven people; the Armenian nationalists charged with the attacks were sentenced to death in January 1979, just a few months before Ermash issued his request.

Although the Italian producers were also wary of the topic of terrorism, members of the creative team were not. Italian screenwriter Clerici refused to "clean up" the script (albeit presumably not for political reasons)—for which Santi fired him, hiring Augusto Caminito as the third Italian screenwriter involved in the project.[41] A letter from Chukhrai to Aleksandr Surikov summarizes the final version of the screenplay: "It remains the story of a young man who, over the course of the film, rises from an apolitical and semi-bourgeois condition to an active anti-fascist position, in a desperate situation, and who organizes an escape from prison for the leaders of the anti-fascist movement. In this new version, the theme of terrorism has been completely eliminated."[42]

The gradual process through which references to terrorism were eliminated is clearly visible both in the above quotation and in a comparison between the initial script by Giovanni Fago, Massimo Felisatti, and Fabio Pittorru and the final version of the film. The initial script draws an exact comparison with events in Portugal in 1968, before António de Oliveira Salazar's death and during the war with Portugal's Angolan colony, which only came to an end after the Carnation Revolution. It begins with the sabotage of the International Telephone Exchange in Lisbon during a plenary meeting between NATO members, indicating that "everything goes according to predefined plan, and precisely at midday, a tremendous explosion shakes the Telephone Exchange building. Lisbon remains isolated from the outside world for a good nineteen hours. It is the latest in a series of sensational attacks carried out by the Portuguese resistance against the dictatorial government that ruled Portugal for over forty years."[43]

However, in the final version of the film, violence has been eradicated from the opening scene. Antonio is the pilot of a warplane given a mission to hit a group of Africans (Angolans, although this is not specified) near the coast. Unwilling to carry out the mission, he is forced to leave the army and work as a taxi driver. The film's opening scene, set on what the screenplay refers to as the "African coast," was one of the last to be filmed and was shot in Cuba. This comprised a curious relocation of the southern line from Angola to the Caribbean island—shortly after the Cuban armed intervention in Angola's civil war.[44]

The first version of the screenplay also contains several references to acts of police torture committed by the dictatorial regime. The Italian insistence on such violent episodes was mainly due to the screenwriters' experience in Italian action-crime (*poliziottesco*) films, known for their strong violence.[45] Yet, once again, the final version of the film contains no allusions to the use of terrorist methods by the underground opposition. This change is also perceptible in the evolution of the film's title. The more semantically subversive initial version—*Attack on State Security*—was altered to retain the revolutionary idea yet focus solely on the protagonist (*Lone Man in Revolt*). There followed a period when the screenplay was entitled *Antonio Machado, Master of Tricks and Poet* (*Antonio Machado, maestro di trucchi e poeta*), strengthening the link to the protagonist while eliminating any reference to subversion or even to the underground resistance.[46] The final title confirmed this shift from violent revolution to indisputable optimism, as Chukhrai himself explained: "From his [Antonio's] lips, the expression sounds like both an appeal and an ironic comment, but above all expresses his insatiable optimism. The Italian figures, who were solely interested in a commercial title, proposed to change the initial title from *Uomo solo in rivolta* to *La vita è bella!* (*Life Is Beautiful*). They are convinced that this will bring in more viewers. In my role as an author, I support their request, as it best expresses the position of the author [Antonio]. Life is beautiful, as is man's eternal aspiration for freedom and social justice."[47]

## Conclusion

As Chukhrai made clear, this shift in the film's title, like Santi and Ermash's common determination to eliminate terrorism from the narrative, united the figures involved in the project.[48] Indeed, although Italy and the USSR had already coproduced films for approximately fifteen years, *Life Is Beautiful* was a singular undertaking, both in its fraught political subject and its lack of direct references to either Italy or the USSR. This brought with it a series of conflicts, both practical—differences in creative approaches between screenwriters, for example—and ideological. Although Chukhrai balked at the Italian insistence on including scenes of pure entertainment, this underscored a divide between the artists that resulted from their position vis-à-vis the Iron Curtain. At the same time, however, Santi's surprise and irritation at Soviet intransigence regarding the film's distribution calls into question Cold War dichotomies between capitalist commercial cinema and socialist artistic and political cinema.

The film's politics brought with it a further element of difficulty, initially frightening off potential American and British coproducers and eventually unnerving even the Soviets, whose requests to mitigate the film's violent tone were supported by Santi, probably as a result of the Moro case. This, in turn, conditioned the film's representation of revolutionary Southern Europe. It is no coincidence that, while the original draft of the screenplay ended with the 1974 Carnation Revolution, the final version of the film ended simply with

Antonio and Maria's escape from prison, implying continued resistance but also serving as a classic happy ending to an individualistic love/adventure story. This shift to bourgeois narrative structures in which melodrama prevailed over politics was encapsulated perfectly in the film's final title: no longer an *Attack on State Security*, but *Life Is Beautiful*.

## Notes

1. Ministry of Tourism and Show Business, Directorate of Show Business, *Revision Application n. 74514*, December 5, 1979, in Italian Central State Archives (hereafter ACS), Ministry of Tourism and Show Business (MTS), Coproductions, CO1583, *La vita è bella*.

2. "*Life Is Beautiful*: Annotation," in Russian State Archives for Literature and Art (hereafter RGALI), fond 2944, opis. 4, delo 4993, list 38.

3. See Chilcote, *The Portuguese Revolution*.

4. An Italian-Soviet cultural agreement was first signed in early 1960. On East-West coproductions with a focus on collaborations between the US and USSR, see Siefert, "Co-producing Cold War Culture," 73–94; see also Siefert, "Meeting at a Far Meridian," 166–209.

5. On Sovinfilm, see Mityurova, "Tra apertura e diffidenza."

6. Siefert, "Co-producing Cold War Culture," 73.

7. Ibid. On East-West film coproductions not involving the USSR, see, for example, Petr Szczepanik's essay in this volume (chap. 13). On coproductions within the Socialist Bloc, see, among others, Karl and Skopal, *Cinema in Service of the State*. On coproductions in a cross-bloc European perspective, see Palma and Pozner, *Mariages à l'européenne*.

8. On the form of this mediation, see Pisu, "Coesistenza pacifica e Cooperazione."

9. See Rey, "Le cinéma dans les relations franco-soviétiques." On USSR-Italy intergovernmental and economic relations after Stalin's death, see Salacone, *La diplomazia del dialogo*.

10. Eitel Monaco, "L'industria cinematografica negli anni 1966–1967: Relazione all'assemblea generale dell'Anica," cited in Corsi, "Italian Film Producers," 86.

11. See Martelli, *L'altro atlantismo*, 2008.

12. On the contradiction between the Soviet film industry's self-identification as an anticommercial art and its supposed capacity to draw huge audiences and guarantee revenues for the state, see Roth-Ey, *Moscow Prime Time*, especially chapter 1.

13. See Kozovoï, "Défier Hollywood," 67–68.

14. See Zhuk, *Rock and Roll in the Rocket City*, 125, 126, 166, and *Soviet Americana*, especially chapter 5. See also Shaw and Youngblood, *Cinematic Cold War*, 53.

15. See Beumers, *A History of Russian Cinema*, 146–150.

16. In fact, *Sunflower* is a French-Italian coproduction made with the external collaboration of Mosfilm (which provided locations, actors, and extras). On the history of Italian-Soviet film coproductions from the 1950s through the 1970s, see Pisu, *La cortina di celluloide*.

17. This body had been described in the 1967 Italian-Soviet agreement on coproductions and should have met every year. It did not, however, probably due to bureaucratic challenges.

18. See Pisu, "Les coproductions italo-soviétiques," 56–57.

19. Nello Santi to Nikolai Sizov and Otar Teneishvili, "Some considerations for the Soviet coproducer," Moscow, June 7, 1978, RGALI, 3160/2/2908/84.

20. See Di Chiara, *Generi e industria cinematografica in Italia*.

21. Sizov, Teneishvili, Alberto Soffientini, Santi, "Memorandum on the Italian-Soviet film coproduction 'Attack on State Security'," Moscow, June 3, 1977, RGALI, 3160/2/2908/47; and Titanus to Teneishvili, "Attack on State Security," Rome, November 23, 1977, RGALI, 3160/2/2908/16. The

script was written by Giovanni Fago, Massimo Felisatti, and Fabio Pittorru, and the final screenplay was to be drafted by Giorgio Arlorio and an as-yet-unidentified American screenwriter.

22. Santi to Teneishvili, Rome, February 21, 1978, RGALI, 3160/2/2908/24.

23. Grigorii Chukhrai, "Report on screenplay 'Antonio Machado, master of tricks and poet,'" Moscow, October 27, 1979, RGALI, 3160/2/2909/58.

24. Ibid.

25. Ibid., list 61.

26. "Santi-Caputo delegation's proposals on the issues of the coproduction 'Uomo solo in rivolta,'" RGALI, 3160/2/2908/88.

27. Santi to Sizov and Teneishvili, "Some Considerations for the Soviet Co-producer," Moscow, June 7, 1978, cit., list 84.

28. "Preliminary Agreement on the Italian-Soviet film coproduction 'Uomo solo in rivolta' (Attentato alla sicurezza dello Stato)," Moscow, June 9, 1978, RGALI, 3160/2/2908/62.

29. "Tape of phone conversation with the producer Nello Santi," Moscow, February 9, 1979, RGALI, 3160/2/2910/10.

30. "General Agreement on the Italian-Soviet film coproduction provisionally entitled 'Uomo solo, in rivolta,'" ACS, MTS, Coproductions CO 1583. A copy of the same document is also preserved in RGALI, 3160/2/1247/15–25.

31. These organizations had different goals and structures (for example, the ETA in Spain, the IRA in Northern Ireland, or the Palestinian Black September Organization). For a chronological database, see the University of Maryland's project on global terrorism, "National Consortium for the Study of Terrorism and Responses to Terrorism," accessed March 27, 2019. http://www.start.umd.edu/gtd/.

32. Santi to Sovinfilm, without date but likely March or April 1979. RGALI, 3160/2/1247/32.

33. Chukhrai to Sizov, Moscow, January 10, 1979. RGALI, 3160/2/1247/3.

34. Military dictatorships were in power in many Latin American countries. See Dávila, *Dictatorship in South America*.

35. In 1974, a terror attack in Madrid by the Basque nationalist and separatist organization ETA caused the deaths of twelve people. In 1976 at San Sebastian, a councillor of the Kingdom was assassinated by the same group.

36. "Additional Agreement on the Italian-Soviet film coproduction provisionally entitled 'Uomo solo, in rivolta,'" RGALI, 3160/2/2910/2908/64.

37. On the Moro case, see Giovagnoli, *Il caso Moro*. On the Brigate Rosse and extreme-left terrorism, see Della Porta, *Il terrorismo di sinistra*.

38. See Lazar and Matard-Bonucci, *Il libro degli anni di piombo*.

39. Chukhrai to Aleksandr Surikov, Moscow, April 9, 1979, RGALI, 3160/2/2910/36.

40. Beliaev, "Resolution on G. Chukhrai film 'Life Is Beautiful,'" after November 1, 1979, RGALI f. 2944/4/4763/46.

41. Clerici's refusal might be explained by his expertise in horror, *giallo*, and crime-action screenplays.

42. Chukhrai to Surikov, Moscow, April 9, 1979, cit., list 36–37.

43. "'Lone Man in Revolt' (Attack in State Security)," plot by Giovanni Fago, abridged script by Giovanni Fago, Massimo Felisatti, Fabio Pittorru, p. 1, ACS, MTS, Coproductions CO 1583, *La vita è bella*.

44. See Pons, *La rivoluzione globale*, 351–353.

45. See Curti, *Italia odia*, 2006.

46. Teneishvili to Boris Pavlenko, Moscow, October 19, 1978, RGALI, 3160/2/2909/37.

47. Chukhrai to Surikov, Moscow, April 9, 1979, cit., list 37.

48. Such violence was also exploited by a prolific strand of 1970s Italian cinema, which also proved popular in the USSR. See Zhuk, "'Ideological Threat of Italian Movies.'"

# Bibliography

Beumers, Birgit. *A History of Russian Cinema*. New York: Bloomsbury, 2008.
Chilcote, Ronald H. *The Portuguese Revolution: State and Class in the Transition to Democracy*. Plymouth: Rowman and Littlefield, 2010.
Corsi, Barbara. "Alle origini del crisi. Industria e mercato." In *Storia del cinema italiano, Vol. XIII 1977–1985*, edited by Vito Zagarrio, 329–346. Venezia-Roma: Marsilio-Edizioni di Bianco & Nero, 2005.
———. "Italian Film Producers and the Challenge of Soviet Coproductions: Franco Cristaldi and The Case of *The RED TENT*." *Historical Journal of Film, Radio and Television* 40, no. 1 (2020): 84–107.
Curti, Roberto. *Italia odia. Il cinema poliziesco italiano*. Torino: Lindau, 2006.
Dávila, Jerry. *Dictatorship in South America*. Chichester: Wiley-Blackwell, 2013.
Della Porta, Donatella. *Il terrorismo di sinistra*. Bologna: Il Mulino, 1990.
Di Chiara, Francesco. *Generi e industria cinematografica in Italia: il caso Titanus (1949–1964)*. Torino: Lindau, 2013.
Giovagnoli, Agostino. *Il caso Moro. Una tragedia repubblicana*. Bologna: Il Mulino, 2005.
Halliday, Fred. *The Making of the Second Cold War*. London: Verso, 1983.
Karl, Lars, and Pavel Skopal, eds. *Cinema in Service of the State: Perspectives on Film Culture in the GDR and Czechoslovakia, 1945–1960*. New York: Berghahn, 2017.
Kozovoï, Andrei. "Défier Hollywood: la diplomatie culturelle et le cinéma à l'ère Brejnev." *Relations Internationales*, no. 147 (2011): 67–68.
Lazar, Marc, and M. A. Matard-Bonucci, eds. *Il libro degli anni di piombo. Storia e memoria del terrorismo italiano*. Milano: Rizzoli, 2013.
Martelli, Evelina. *L'altro atlantismo. Fanfani e la politica estera italiana (1958–1963)*. Milano: Guerini e Associati, 2008.
Mityurova, Ekaterina. "Tra apertura e diffidenza: il Sovinfilm e le coproduzioni cinematografiche franco-sovietiche negli anni della distensione." In *La storia internazionale e il cinema. Reti, scambi e transfer nel '900*, special issue of *Cinema e Storia. Rivista di studi interdisciplinari*, no. 1 (2017), edited by Stefano Pisu and Pierre Sorlin, 175–191.
"National Consortium for the Study of Terrorism and Responses to Terrorism." Global Terrorism Database. University of Maryland, July 2018. Accessed March 27, 2019. http://www.start.umd.edu/gtd/.
Pisu, Stefano. "Coesistenza pacifica e Cooperazione culturale nella guerra fredda: il film Italiani brava gente e l'avvio delle coproduzioni italo-sovietiche." *Mondo Contemporaneo*, no. 1 (2016): 35–62.
———. "Les coproductions italo-soviétiques (1950–1970): coopération réelle entre Est et Ouest ou occasion manquée?" In *Mariages à l'européenne. Les coproductions cinématographiques intra-européennes depuis 1945*, edited by Paola Palma and Valérie Pozner, 51–71. Paris: AFRHC, 2019.
———. *La cortina di celluloide. Il cinema italo-sovietico nella Guerra fredda*. Milano: Mimesis, 2019.
Pons, Silvio. *La rivoluzione globale: Storia del comunismo internazionale 1917–1991*. Torino: Einaudi, 2012.
Rey, Marie-Pierre. "Le cinéma dans les relations franco-soviétiques: Enjeux et problèmes à l'heure de la détente (1964–1974)." In *Culture et guerre froide*, edited by Georges-Henri Soutou and Jean-François Sirinelli, 159–172. Paris: PUPS, 2008.

Roth-Ey, Kristin. *Moscow Prime Time: How the Soviet Union Built the Media Empire That Lost the Cultural Cold War*. Ithaca, NY: Cornell University Press, 2011.
Salacone, Alessandro. *La diplomazia del dialogo: Italia e Urss tra distensione e coesistenza pacifica (1958–1968)*. Roma: Viella, 2017.
Shaw, Tony, and Denise J. Youngblood. *Cinematic Cold War: The American and Soviet Struggle for Hearts and Minds*. Lawrence: University Press of Kansas, 2010.
Siefert, Marsha. "Co-producing Cold War Culture: East-West Film-Making and Cultural Diplomacy." In *Divided Dreamworlds? The Cultural Cold War in East and West*, edited by Peter Romijn, Giles Scott-Smith, and Joes Segal, 73–94. Amsterdam: Amsterdam University Press, 2012.
———. "Meeting at a Far Meridian: US-Soviet Cultural Diplomacy on Film in the Early Cold War." In *Cold War Crossings: International Travel and Exchange across the Soviet Bloc, 1940s–1960s*, edited by Patryk Babiracki and Kenyon Zimmer, 166–209. College Station: Texas A&M University Press, 2014.
Zhuk, Sergei I. "'Ideological Threat of Italian Movies': The KGB, Mafia, Punk-Rock and Rise of Neo-Fascism among Soviet Youth, 1979–1985." Working paper presented at "Culture and International East-West Relations (1945–1990): Film, Music, TV," University of Perugia, November 14–15, 2019.
———. *Rock and Roll in the Rocket City: The West, Identity, and Ideology in Soviet Dniepropetrovsk, 1960–1985*. Baltimore: Johns Hopkins University Press & Washington, DC: Woodrow Wilson Center Press, 2010.
———. *Soviet Americana: The Cultural History of Russian and Ukrainian Americanists*, London: I. B. Tauris, 2018.

STEFANO PISU is Assistant Professor of Contemporary History at the University of Cagliari. He is author of four monographs in Italian, most recently *La cortina di celluloide. Il cinema italo-sovietico nella Guerra fredda* (2019).

CHAPTER 15

DIVIDING THE COSMOS?
*INTELSAT, Intersputnik, and the Development of Transnational Satellite Communications Infrastructures during the Cold War*

Christine Evans and Lars Lundgren

IN 1976, NORTH AMERICAN SCHOLARS began to debate the outcome of nearly a decade of international negotiations in the field of satellite communications, which had culminated in the creation of two ostensibly rival international commercial satellite networks: INTELSAT, a US-led network created in 1964 and refounded on the basis of a new treaty in 1971, and Soviet-led Intersputnik, announced in August 1968 and formalized in 1971. For some commentators, the United States' failure to create a single global network for satellite television and telephone transmission was a betrayal of communication satellites' *technologic imperative,* a form of technological determinism that saw new technologies as having inherent, unalterable qualities that obliged human policy makers to take action to reshape the world to meet the demands of the new technology's inherently global form.[1] Other commentators, often former participants in the negotiations themselves, found the failure to create a single global satellite network unsurprising given the very divergent perspectives within INTELSAT's membership, not to mention between the US and the USSR.[2] Both groups of commentators generally agreed, however, that, as one former participant in the negotiations put it, the failure to negotiate a cooperative agreement across the Iron Curtain would "remain one of the real pities of the development, to date, of satellite communications."[3] In the coming years, many more regional satellite communications consortiums would be formed, laying the foundation for today's multicentered communications satellite (comsat) industry and making the idea of a single global satellite network seem like a distant and implausible dream.

Given the dramatic changes in the satellite communications industry since the 1970s and the collapse of the Soviet Union in 1991, the story of the creation of INTELSAT and Intersputnik have been largely forgotten. To the extent that this era in the development of satellite communications has been remembered, however, it has been subsumed into a larger story about unambiguous US victory over the USSR in satellite communications, downplaying the significance of Soviet activities in this sphere and ignoring the feeling of failure among US officials and observers after the INTELSAT negotiations of 1969–1971.[4]

Recent work in media studies addressing satellite communication from cultural, technical, and geopolitical perspectives, part of an emerging field sometimes called critical studies of media infrastructures, has largely followed this pattern.[5] James Schwoch, for example, in his rich and insightful history of the role of satellites in transforming television into a global medium, concludes by arguing that the development of communications satellites marked a larger victory for American science, one that paved the way for US domination of the processes of economic and technological globalization.[6] Lisa Parks' foundational work on satellite cultures and infrastructures similarly emphasizes US global power and sees Soviet satellites as marginal.[7] Together, Parks and Schwoch have helped found the emerging field of the critical study of satellite media infrastructures—a field that is, nonetheless, implicitly predicated on the assumption that US state and corporate power require our critical attention precisely because they were victorious in the Cold War technology race.

We argue that a competitive space-race model does not fully describe the development of satellite communications networks and institutions as media infrastructures, because it conceals the extensive interaction, mimesis, and shared goals that characterized Soviet and US efforts to establish a satellite communication infrastructure. In this essay, we draw on Soviet and US archival records in order to reexamine the origins of Intersputnik and the negotiation of its relationship to INTELSAT in the late 1960s. Emphasizing the role of transnational interaction and mutual influence, rather than discrete, competitive national satellite communications projects, we argue that the outcome of these negotiations was neither a missed opportunity for global integration, as officials at the time saw it, nor an unequivocal US triumph. Rather, we present it as a revealing early episode in the globalization of communications and of space, one that offers a new perspective not only on satellite communications history, but also on Cold War media and economic and technical relations across the Iron Curtain more generally. The creation and negotiation of the INTELSAT and Intersputnik agreements, we argue, demonstrate the surprising similarities between plans for satellite networks on both sides of the Iron Curtain, the shared desire for an integrated global satellite network, and the socialist world's active role in shaping the direction and institutions of economic and media globalization.[8]

Instead of a story of division and failure, therefore, we offer an account of how INTELSAT and Intersputnik were interconnected from the beginning, reflecting their origins in pre–satellite era broadcast exchanges and partnerships across the Iron Curtain. This drive to integrate the networks, despite political rhetoric on both sides, reflected the fact that by the second half of the 1960s, all participants in the creation of these networks, including the US, the Soviet Union, their Western and Eastern European partners, and their developing-world clients, sought to benefit from either selling access to or manufacturing components for this emerging high-tech sector.[9] The story of INTELSAT and Intersputnik reveals a great deal of political and economic common ground among negotiating partners on both sides of the Iron Curtain when it came to infrastructure construction.[10] The relationships established during these negotiations laid the groundwork for future collaboration across the Iron Curtain in space exploration, research, and commerce.[11]

## Global Communication by Satellite: Origins of a Vision

In the mid-1960s, communications administrators' and diplomats' calls for a global satellite system were shaped by a long tradition of envisioning international communications.[12] Satellites themselves had long been anticipated as a telecommunications tool, most famously in Arthur C. Clarke's foundational 1945 paper, "The Space Station: Its Radio Application."[13] As Asif Siddiqi has documented, starting in the early 1950s, Soviet popular science enthusiasts and rocket scientists transformed their shared dream of space exploration into a successful campaign to convince the (otherwise uninterested) Soviet leadership to launch the first experimental satellite in 1957.[14] While communication satellites were still only in the ideation phase, the first postwar decade produced a wide array of ideas and technologies that aimed to make possible the global transmission of television broadcasts, including via satellite.[15] Some of the proposals for a global network were modeled on existing technologies, such as David Sarnoff's 1948 RCA Ultrafax proposal and a global microwave TV network called UNITEL, an airborne relay system proposed in the early 1950s that would reflect signal transmissions much like later satellites and carry television as well as telegraph and telephone services. Both UNITEL and Ultrafax were planned as global media systems but were never fully realized.[16]

While UNITEL, Ultrafax, and other efforts to achieve what Schwoch calls "the holy grail of the transatlantic crossing" for television failed, Europe in the 1950s saw the emergence both of communication networks capable of carrying television images across greater distances and continuing cooperation between national broadcasters, even over the East–West divide.[17] This started in the early 1950s with bilateral broadcasts such as the coronation of Queen Elizabeth II in 1953, which was shown live in England and France, and continued with a series of exchanges in Europe before culminating with the European-wide broadcast of Yuri Gagarin's return to Earth, and Moscow, in April 1961.[18] In addition to these media spectaculars—based on efforts to temporarily link television networks by cable and microwave relay—there was increasingly extensive ongoing cooperation in program exchange and in the creation of separate but interrelated television networks, Intervision in Eastern Europe and Eurovision in Western Europe.[19] These collaborative precedents also shaped demands and expectations for the new kinds of cooperation and integration communications satellites would make possible.

During the 1960s, these transnational initiatives moved into the sphere of satellite communications. Already in 1962, the first transatlantic satellite transmission was carried by Telstar, and three years later, the first geosynchronous and commercial satellite, Intelsat I (nicknamed Early Bird), was launched. Early Bird was the first satellite to be launched by the INTELSAT organization, which had been founded one year earlier, in 1964.

### Visions of Integration: INTELSAT's Overtures to the Soviet Bloc

Given all of this, when Lyndon B. Johnson used his August 14, 1967, "Special Message to the Congress on Communication Policy" to invite the Soviet Bloc countries to join INTELSAT in a single global communications network, he was continuing a long tradition of similar calls. "I urge the Soviet Union and the nations of Eastern Europe to join with the United States and our 57 partners as members of INTELSAT," Johnson said. "INTELSAT is not a political organization," Johnson stressed. "It holds no ideological goal," he asserted, "except that it is good for nations to communicate efficiently with one another."[20] This claim, of course, glossed over significant concerns—especially as the US was drawn more deeply into the Vietnam War—about the country's ability to profit from its enormous investment in communication satellite technology. Indeed, during the mid-1960s, the INTELSAT organization was riven by conflicts between the US Comsat organization (the

US representative within INTELSAT) and INTELSAT's Western European partners. The former sought to maximize profits by buying the lowest-cost technology, generally produced by US manufacturers, while the latter wanted a guaranteed share of INTELSAT's contracts to develop their own high-tech manufacturing sectors in return for their substantial investment in the organization.[21] These conflicts led INTELSAT's Western European members to insist that the organization's initial structure, created in 1964 and heavily weighted toward US interests, be based on interim agreements only, with a renegotiation set for 1969.

It was in this context of financial urgency and conflict that INTELSAT sought to expand its membership as rapidly as possible, including through renewed outreach to the Soviet Bloc. In his August 1967 statement, Johnson acknowledged the difficulties in negotiating the terms for a global system in which the US and the Comsat corporation would play such an important and dominating role. Johnson's invitation also came only two months after the Soviet Union and several other Eastern European countries withdrew from the global *Our World* broadcast and less than two years before the final agreement on INTELSAT had to be signed.[22] With the withdrawal in fresh memory, it may have seemed more difficult than ever to create a truly global satellite system joining the US and Soviet Union. Indeed, from the US perspective, the Soviet Union had been unresponsive to previous invitations, and there was no immediate official Soviet response to the August 1967 invitation, either.

Nonetheless, as with the rhetoric surrounding the *Our World* broadcast, the failure to include the Soviet Bloc was a significant obstacle to INTELSAT's claim that it was a truly global network. Moreover, as the 1969 INTELSAT negotiations approached, many Western European members felt strongly that INTELSAT should seek Eastern European membership as energetically as possible. This was an economic and political, rather than technical, challenge. As Johnson's "Special Message" pointed out, there was "no insurmountable technical obstacle to an eventual linking of the Soviet domestic satellite broadcasting system, Molniia, with the INTELSAT system," and there were many reasons to do so.[23] Johnson's statement reiterated long-standing US arguments in favor of a single global network, which he claimed would reduce international conflict by facilitating global communication and exchange.[24] It was also politically important for the US to avoid the impression of excluding socialist countries and possibly alienating potential members within the developing world. Internally, however, the US and its Western European partners indicated that the most important reason to include the Soviet Union in INTELSAT was to prevent "unnecessary competition" for INTELSAT.[25] That is, their objective was to prevent a Soviet-led network from undercutting INTELSAT's prices and to retain US and Western European control over the lucrative work of manufacturing high-tech components and constructing "earth stations"—new infrastructural facilities featuring the large parabolic antennae ("satellite dishes") needed to send and receive radio signals from satellites in space—around the globe.

In this sense, the satellite communications negotiations of 1967–1969 constituted a failure for INTELSAT. Their outcome was precisely the creation of a rival global network led by the USSR that did indeed threaten to create "unnecessary competition," although the Soviet network's significance as a competitor for market share was limited until it became operational in the second half of the 1970s. However, the networks were truly never as separate as they seemed, and cooperation, exchange, and integration across the Cold War political divide were central goals from the beginning, particularly on the Soviet side. While Soviet reluctance to join INTELSAT was sometimes attributed to exclusively political motives, such as an ideological objection to INTELSAT's commercial goals and organizational structure, this was far from the case.[26]

## The Intersputnik Proposal

Efforts to create a Soviet-led international satellite network that would provide an alternative to INTELSAT had begun by April 1967 at a meeting in Moscow of Interkosmos, an organization for international scientific cooperation in space led by the Soviet Academy of Sciences and founded in November 1965.[27] In August 1967, the Ministry of Communications presented a draft plan to an Interkosmos working group. Finally, just after the Molniia network began regular domestic television broadcasting service in the USSR in December 1967, technical specialists from the future founding members of what would become the Intersputnik network (Bulgaria, Hungary, the GDR, Cuba, Mongolia, Poland, Romania, and Czechoslovakia) were invited to Moscow to work out technical plans for such an organization.[28] The working group's correspondence in spring 1968 was characterized by some urgency, since the head of Interkosmos, academician B. N. Petrov, hoped to officially announce the creation of the organization at the UN meeting on Peaceful Uses of Outer Space in Vienna in August 1968.[29] At a June 1968 meeting in Budapest, the participants approved the proposed articles as working drafts and selected the name Intersputnik.[30]

Intersputnik draft articles of agreement emphasized that this network was to be founded on very different principles than INTELSAT had been. "This project," the articles claimed, "is built on principles of international cooperation, equality, and mutual benefit of all participants."[31] The main basis for this claim was the proposed decision-making body, a council (not unlike the UN General Assembly) in which each member country would receive one vote, regardless of its level of investment in or use of the network's infrastructure or services.[32] INTELSAT, by contrast, was governed by a body that used weighted voting, giving countries that invested in and used the network a greater share of decision-making power and leaving the US with more than 50 percent of the votes. Like INTELSAT, however, Intersputnik was intended to be global in its ambition and membership; the articles' authors proposed sounding out "other countries, like France, the Arab countries, India, Pakistan, Burma, and others, to clarify the possibility of their participation in the proposed system."[33] The proposed socialist-led international comsat network was thus presented as both a rebuke and a rival to INTELSAT.

Yet how strong a rebuke was it? The Soviet Bloc was proposing a network that was explicitly designed to attract nonsocialist members and in fact strongly resembled what Western European members of INTELSAT were seeking in that organization's permanent arrangement negotiations, including a new organizational structure that would balance the United States' overwhelming dominance.[34] Indeed, the Soviet announcement in August 1968 had been supported behind the scenes by France and Switzerland, who hoped, at a minimum, to weaken US influence in INTELSAT's upcoming negotiations and bring about a proliferation of regional comsat organizations, of which one would be Western European. In the months after the announcement in Vienna, they continued these efforts. On September 25, 1968, for example, a diplomat in the Soviet Embassy in Washington, V. A. Racheev, met for lunch with his Swiss counterpart in charge of space affairs, Reinhold Steiner. Steiner urged the USSR to release information about Intersputnik's capacity and the date when it would come into service in order to "strike another blow" to the US position within INTELSAT.[35] In response, Racheev pointed out that the timing of Intersputnik's realization was unclear because they did not yet know whether the Europeans, who could help fund it, would in fact join. At the same time, he noted, "We are getting the impression that some members of 'Intelsat' would like to speed up the creation of our system only in order to strengthen their position in negotiations with the US, and do not seriously intend to participate in Intersputnik."[36] The best outcome, Steiner insisted, was multiple regional commercial satellite systems, including US-, Soviet-, and European-led networks.[37] On several occasions, the French made similar overtures to the Soviets on behalf of a European satellite program.[38]

As the regionalist vision articulated by Western European countries in negotiations with the Soviets suggests, however, the idea that Intersputnik was genuinely different *in principle* from INTELSAT was not very well founded. Instead, as both sides acknowledged internally, Intersputnik's organizational structure was closely modeled on that of INTELSAT. Intersputnik was conceived from the beginning as an independent commercial entity that would eventually own its own space segment (satellites). As with INTELSAT, earth stations would belong to the countries in which they were located.[39] Soviet claims about the superior egalitarianism of Intersputnik's one-country, one-vote governance structure concealed the fact that the rest of its articles resembled INTELSAT's 1964 structure, with only minor adjustments that reflected changes Western Europeans sought within INTELSAT.[40] Thus, despite arguments that the Soviet Union objected to INTELSAT's private commercial structure, the Intersputnik proposal that was made public in August 1968 reflected not a uniquely socialist alternative to INTELSAT, but rather a consensus position forged in interactions across the Cold War divide.

Moreover, via talks with the US embassy and other channels between August and December 1968, Soviet diplomats conveyed their willingness to concede or limit the only real distinguishing feature of the Intersputnik proposal, the one-country, one-vote structure. In a telegram dated August 17, 1968, just days after the Intersputnik proposal was announced in Vienna, the US Deputy Chief of Mission in Moscow, Emory Swank, reported that Soviet diplomats had raised the subject of terms for Soviet entry into INTELSAT. Soviet diplomats told their US interlocutors that they were flexible about requiring a one-country, one-vote decision-making body within INTELSAT as a precondition to joining, since they knew it was unacceptable to the US. Instead, they stressed that "some assurances re: purchase and use [of] Soviet communications equipment in third countries" might serve as an adequate incentive for Soviet membership.[41]

At the same time that it wooed Western European members with offers that closely resembled those countries' demands toward INTELSAT, Interkosmos also sought to engage future Eastern European Intersputnik members with access to manufacturing contracts. Like their Western European counterparts, Soviet Bloc countries sought to participate in the manufacturing of high-tech components for satellite communications. During the summer of 1968, in the months before a June meeting in Budapest where the Intersputnik proposal was to be finalized, the Soviet Ministry of Communications signed agreements to conduct joint research and component production with the GDR, Bulgaria, and Czechoslovakia.[42] Interkosmos's Soviet leadership also explicitly promised its Eastern European participants that Intersputnik's prices would be lower than those of INTELSAT for the same services.⁴³ In the summer of 1969, moreover, a Soviet diplomat told a US counterpart in Geneva that in the network's first phase, members would be granted use of Soviet satellites without charge.⁴⁴ Thus, while US diplomats tended to characterize socialist countries' decisions to join Intersputnik as entirely political, economic incentives were also an important part of the negotiations within the Socialist Bloc in advance of the Vienna announcement.⁴⁵

The early phases of Intersputnik's creation were thus characterized by significant mimesis of INTELSAT's structure and were directly shaped by the contemporaneous renegotiation of its governing structure. Soviet communications officials were even mindful that INTELSAT had taken years to negotiate and build; their network, they cautioned, would likely require a similar amount of time to develop.⁴⁶ But this was not simply a case of political or economic imitation or of competition between two separate, opposing networks. Instead, the boundaries between the two networks were initially not firmly set at all, and indeed the possibility of Soviet Bloc entry into INTELSAT remained open at least through February 1969. Negotiations in the late 1960s revealed that integration, rather than maintaining two separate, opposing networks, was fundamental to how both sides envisioned the relationship between Intersputnik and INTELSAT.

## Deciding How to Integrate

Internal discussions in both the US and USSR reveal that some form of integration of the Soviet domestic satellite network, Molniia, with INTELSAT was always the expected outcome. The question was not whether, but on what terms, this integration should occur. Even before the Intersputnik proposal, no one on either side seems to have considered the possibility that the Soviet domestic satellite network would not eventually be linked to a global system (i.e., INTELSAT). As a March 25, 1968, report by the US State Department Bureau of Intelligence and Research pointed out, the integration of the Molniia system into INTELSAT's network without Soviet membership was likely the most desired outcome on the Soviet side. Such an arrangement would allow the Soviets both political and economic benefits: it could "stay out of what it may feel is a US-operated club, yet at the same time plug Molniia into a world hookup and accordingly enhance its international standing and earnings."⁴⁷ The State Department was open to this possible arrangement; on November 25, 1968, it informed its embassies that it saw no objections to allowing non-INTELSAT members "direct access" to the system, provided financial terms were set so that nonmembers did not have an advantage over members.⁴⁸

Soviet negotiations with likely Intersputnik member states also made clear that integration and exchange with INTELSAT would be a central function of the new network. In the summer of 1967, Interkosmos sent out surveys asking whether and when each potential member country would require access to the INTELSAT system.[49] Several of the respondents clearly saw Intersputnik as a route to greater global integration and exchange, particularly of television programming. In the fall of 1967, Polish representatives proposed new text for the agreement, including that "the technical parameters of the International System of Communication Satellites must take into account the possibility of cooperation with other systems [in 1967, this could only mean INTELSAT], creating the conditions for the future organization of a single global system, accessible to all countries"—a striking echo of Johnson's invitation to the socialist world to join INTELSAT.[50] When the Intersputnik proposal was finalized in June 1968, it included a chapter on cooperation with "capitalist-country satellite systems," which concluded that it would be useful to include "one or two rebroadcast stations [*retransliatsionnye stantsii*] that will be able to work simultaneously with multiple satellite communications systems."[51]

Indeed, for Soviet diplomats, integration was a higher priority than creating a separate international network in the first place. This became evident when the hoped-for interest from countries outside the Soviet Bloc failed to materialize. As of December 15, 1968, an internal memorandum reported that thirty-two countries (beyond the founding members) had received the Soviet Intersputnik proposal, and not one had yet replied. This could be explained, the report continued, by the fact that many of these countries were heavily invested in INTELSAT; their future relationship with Intersputnik depended on what happened at the forthcoming INTELSAT negotiations.[52] The memorandum outlined several possible next steps, depending on how many and which countries ultimately decided to join Intersputnik. If a large number of countries agreed to do so, the network could move forward. The same was possible if only "a small number of countries wish to join" but they were "countries with significant scientific and manufacturing resources." It could also proceed if a larger number of developing countries, which lacked resources to invest but would "agree to rent channels on the satellite," decided to join.[53] In other words, as long as there were wealthy coinvestors from outside the Socialist Bloc *or* there was a clear market for Intersputnik's services in the developing world, plans for the Intersputnik network could go forward after March 1969, reflecting a planning process that was chiefly about economic viability.

However, even if Intersputnik was not created, the memo confirmed that "steps would be taken to develop possible forms of cooperation between the international system 'INTELSAT' and [the Soviet] regional communication system with geostationary satellites."[54] This cooperation could take place via "mutual use of communication channels, or the acceptance of traffic from countries belonging to INTELSAT by [Socialist Bloc] earth stations and the further transmission of this traffic via land lines to countries that are not members of INTELSAT. Other forms of cooperation could be possible as well," the memo concluded.[55] In effect, the Soviet Ministry of Foreign Affairs' position in advance of the INTELSAT negotiations of February 1969 was almost entirely flexible and contingent; the only consistent part of their plan was the goal of integrating the Soviet domestic satellite system with INTELSAT.

Soviet flexibility on the specific form of satellite network integration naturally reflected the Soviet Union's weak negotiating position in light of the fact that INTELSAT was already well established and rapidly gaining new members. Despite the failure of the Intersputnik proposal to attract a significant number of capitalist- or developing-world members, however, it did have an impact within the US government and, ultimately, on the governing structures of INTELSAT itself. In a memo to Secretary of State Dean Rusk about the Intersputnik announcement in Vienna, Assistant Secretary of State for Economic Affairs Anthony Solomon acknowledged that the Intersputnik proposal was "structurally similar to the existing INTELSAT arrangements, except that it provides for decision-making in a Council with voting by one-country/one-vote."[56] In response, he proposed that the State Department consider reviving a 1967 proposal to create an annual assembly within INTELSAT that would have "quite limited powers" but a one-country, one-vote structure. "It is my belief," Solomon continued, "that so long as the assembly is not transformed into a body making basic commercial or systems decisions, we can and should be prepared to make the voting in the assembly simply one-nation/one-vote."[57] The memo that Rusk sent to Johnson a few days later likewise concluded that, looking ahead to the INTELSAT negotiations in February 1969, "we should be prepared to make such changes in the structure as are necessary and acceptable to continue the very broad support this organization has built."[58]

## Conclusion

As the negotiations in the crucial years 1967–1969 suggest, even the signing of 1971's two, seemingly separate, network agreements did not prevent interaction, exchange, and—with time—integration within the context of a competitive system of multiple regional satellite networks with their own space segments, including Arabsat, created in 1976 to serve Arab League member countries, and Eutelsat, created by seventeen European countries in 1977. One outcome of the Nixon–Brezhnev Moscow summit of 1972 was the construction of two INTELSAT ground stations on Soviet territory, one near Moscow and another outside Lviv.[59] Already in Richard Nixon's first months in office, moreover, US officials were proposing a reorientation and dramatic expansion of US–Soviet space cooperation driven in part by lessons learned in the recent INTELSAT negotiations.[60]

The rapid arrival of multiple regional satellite networks, and the beginnings of direct satellite broadcasts to the home by the second half of the 1970s saw swift and dramatic transformations in satellite communications from the late 1970s onward. Nonetheless, we should not ignore this key early phase in the creation of global satellite infrastructure. Instead, the INTELSAT and Intersputnik negotiations of the late 1960s suggest how Cold War ideological claims have obscured the significant overlap and common objectives between socialist and capitalist systems in this new technological realm. Moreover, it was precisely the intersection of Soviet Bloc and Western European commercial interests that shaped the institutional structures that still underlie communication satellite organizations in the present. Despite the Soviet Union's genuine economic weakness relative to the US in the postwar decades, the USSR and its Eastern European allies actively sought integration while working successfully with Western European governments to reshape communication infrastructures and institutions, reducing US dominance and driving economic and media globalization forward in pursuit of shared goals. The Soviet Union's active, if asymmetrical, role in reshaping what began as US-dominated media infrastructures offers a revised picture of the origins of global satellite media networks as the product of a shared, mutually negotiated Cold War understanding of what global media in the space age should be.

## Notes

List of Acronyms:
ARAN- Arkhiv Rossiiskoi Akademii Nauk (Archive of the Russian Academy of Sciences)
NACP- National Archives at College Park

1. See, for example, Smith, *Communication via Satellite*.
2. McWhinney, "Review: Communication via Satellite," 834–835.
3. Ibid., 835. See also Kildow, *Intelsat*; Downing, "The Intersputnik System and Soviet Television"; Hultén, "The Intelsat System"; and McDanie and Day, "INTELSAT and Communist Nations' Policy."
4. See, for example, Butrica, *Beyond the Ionosphere*, xv; and Slotten, "Satellite Communications."
5. Key works in the critical study of media infrastructures include Schwoch, *Global TV*; Parks, *Cultures in Orbit*; Parks and Schwoch, *Down to Earth*; and Volkmer, "Satellite Cultures in Europe." On media infrastructures more generally, see Appel et al., *The Promise of Infrastructure*; Graham

and Marvin, *Splintering Urbanism*; Larkin, *Signal and Noise*; Näser-Lather and Neubert, *Traffic*; Parks and Starosielski, *Signal Traffic*; and Starosielski, *The Undersea Network*.

6. Schwoch, *Global TV*, 153.
7. See, for example, Parks, *Cultures in Orbit*; Parks and Schwoch, *Down to Earth*.
8. For a recent reevaluation of the Soviet relationship to globalization along these lines, see Sanchez-Sibony, *Red Globalization*, and Mark, Kalinovsky, and Marung, *Alternative Globalizations*.
9. On Western European and US economic motives, see Kildow, *Intelsat*, 52–57.
10. Communication satellites infrastructure followed, on a global scale, the pattern European historians of technology have described as "hidden integration," in which technical networks, such as gas pipelines, to mention only Per Högselius's landmark study, connected European countries in ways that often directly undermined prevailing geopolitical logics. See Misa and Schot, "Inventing Europe," as well as the other articles in this special issue. On gas pipelines as an example of hidden integration, see Högselius, *Red Gas*, 2–3. The broader historical literature has also begun to interrogate Cold War binaries. See, for example, Mikkonen and Koivunen, *Beyond the Divide*; Autio-Sarasmo, "Stagnation or Not"; and Romijn et al., *Divided Dreamworlds*.
11. On Soviet-US cooperation in space, see Jenks, *Collaboration in Space*.
12. See Lemberg, *Barriers Down*; Hay, "The Invention of Air Space." For the vision of television as a global medium, see Burns, *Television*; Mosco, *The Digital Sublime*, 132–40; and Marvin, *When Old Technologies Were New*, 157.
13. Clarke, "The Space Station."
14. Siddiqi, *The Red Rockets' Glare*.
15. For the fullest account of the US vision of global television, see Schwoch, *Global TV*, 139–149. See also Winston, *Media, Technology and Society*.
16. Schwoch, *Global TV*, 84.
17. Schwoch, *Global TV*, 11.
18. Lundgren, "Live From Moscow," 45–55.
19. Eugster, *Television Programming*; Beutelschmidt, *Ost—West—Global*; and Lundgren, "Transnational Television in Europe."
20. Johnson, "Special Message." See also Schwoch, *Global TV*, 150–153.
21. Kildow, *Intelsat*, 52–57.
22. On "Our World," see Parks, *Cultures in Orbit*; and Evans and Lundgren, "Geographies of Liveness."
23. Johnson, "Special Message."
24. Ibid.
25. "US mission to the United Nations to Department of State," New York, Telegram 6920, October 8, 1968, Folder 10-1-68, File Economic: TEL 6 7/1/68-11/1/68, 1967–69, SNF, Record Group 59 (RG59): Department of State Central Files, NACP, College Park, MD.
26. For one example of this view, see Buck, *The Global Commons*, 160. Schwoch, by contrast, notes Soviet openness to cooperation. Schwoch, *Global TV*, 150–153.
27. "Academic B. N. Petrov, Chairman of Interkosmos, to Academic L. Kristanov, Chairman of the Bulgarian Academy of Science's Committee for Study of the Cosmos," September 4, 1967, ARAN, Moscow, Russia, F. 1678 "Sovet po mezhdunarodnomu sotrudnichestvu v oblasti issledovaniia i ispol'zovaniia kosmicheskogo prostranstva 'Interkosmos'," op.1 d. 9, l. 63. Burgess and Vis, *Interkosmos*, 2–3; and Beutelschmidt, *Ost—West—Global*, 277.
28. "Plan mezhdunarodnykh sviazei Sovetskogo Soiuza s sotsialisticheskimi stranami v oblasti issledovaniia i ispol'zovaniia kosmicheskogo prostranstva v mirnykh tseliakh na IV kvartal 1967 g," ARAN F. 1678, op. 1, d. 1, l. 152.
29. See Petrov's May 7, 1968, letter to the Chair of the Hungarian Committee for Space Research, urging him to organize a meeting to approve the draft agreement before the August UN meeting in Vienna. ARAN F. 1678 op. 1 d. 34, l. 13.

30. "Zakliuchitel'nyi protokol, g. Budapesht 24–29 iiunia 1968 g," ARAN F. 1678 Sovet "Interkosmos," op. 1, d. 34, l. 91.

31. "Ob"iasnitel'naia zapiska," draft agreement for Mezhdunarodnaia sistema sputnikovoi sviazi, March 1968, ARAN, F. 1678 op. 1 d. 34, l. 24.

32. The connections between the Soviet Intersputnik proposal, as well as, to a lesser extent, the INTELSAT interim agreements of 1964, and the basic organizational structure of the United Nations is not surprising, given that these satellite networks were conceived as *both* intergovernmental and commercial agreements. At the same time, the US and likely the USSR both sought to avoid subordinating satellite communication agreements to the United Nations Committee on the Peaceful Use of Outer Space (formed in 1959), something that some smaller countries, such as Sweden, had proposed.

33. Understandably, both INTELSAT and Intersputnik were interested in recruiting India and Pakistan, given their size and economic power. Both India and Pakistan were among thirteen countries prioritized by the US, meaning the Department of State would support the development of Earth Stations in the selected countries. See "Memorandum: Communication Satellite Earth Stations Construction in Less Developed Countries," December 31, 1966, Tel 6 1/1/67 to Tel 6 7/1/67, Economic, Central Foreign Policy Files 1967–1969, RG 59: Department of State Files, NACP; and ARAN F. 1678 op. 1 d. 34, l. 23–24.

34. Slotten, "Satellite Communications," 348–349.

35. V. A. Racheev, Counselor of the Soviet Embassy to the United States, "Notes from conversation with Counselor Steiner [Switzerland], 30 Sept. 1968. From the counselor's diary from 25 Sept. 1968," ARAN F. 1678 op. 1 d. 34, l. 142.

36. Ibid. l. 142–145.

37. Notably, other Swiss officials had taken a different line with US Deputy Assistant Secretary for Transportation and Communications Frank Loy earlier in the summer, saying they felt regional networks should not undermine "logic or economics" of a worldwide system. Loy, "Notes on Talks with Swiss Officials, June 18, 1968," 2, Folder 7/1/68, File Economic: TEL 6 7/1/68-11/1/68, 1967–69, SNF, RG 59, NACP.

38. See, for example, "Otchet Sovetskoi delegatsii o komandirovke vo Frantsiiu /Parizh s 16 po 29 maia 1967 g. na soveshchanie rabochei gruppy No. 2/ kosmicheskaia sviaz'/ sozdannoi v sootvetstvii s protokolom ot 12 oktiabria 1966 goda/ g. Moskva/ o nauchno-tekhnicheskom sotrudnichestve mezhdu SSSR i Frantsiei v oblasti kosmicheskoi sviazi." ARAN f. 1678 op. 1 d. 8 l. 109; and "Otchet o rabote rabochei gruppy No. 2 (kosmicheskaia sviaz') Parizh, 1–11 Oktiabria 1968 g," ARAN F. 1678 Soviet "Interkosmos," op. 1, d. 36, l. 56.

39. "Proekt soglasheniia ob uchrezhdenii mezhdunarodnoi organizatsii po ispol'zovaniiu iskusstvennykh sputnikov zemli dlia tselei sviazi," ARAN F. 1678 "Interskosmos," op. 1, d. 9, l. 43–44.

40. This included Intersputnik's status as an independent, commercial entity with "legal personality," allowing it to own its space segment and/or lease space capacity from other countries on behalf of its members. See Ibid., ll. 43–44. On European requests for a "legal personality" for INTELSAT, see "European Conference on Satellite Communications. Swiss Contribution. Working Party on the definitive Arrangement for INTELSAT. Legal Personality of the Organization to Succeed INTELSAT," May 7, 1968, Folder 7/1/68, File Economic: TEL 6 7/1/68-11/1/68, 1967–69, SNF, RG 59, NACP.

41. "US Embassy Moscow to Department of State, re: Intersputnik and Intelsat," Telegram number 5125, August 17, 1968, Folder 8-1-68, File Economic: TEL 6 7/1/68-11/1/68, 1967–69, SNF, RG 59: Department of State Central Files, NACP.

42. See, for example, ARAN F. 1678 Sovet "Interkosmos," op. 1, d. 34, ll. 29–82. Intellectual property that resulted from the networks' work was also to belong to all member countries, regardless of who invented it. See "Proekt soglasheniia ob uchrezhdenii mezhdunarodnoi organizatsii po ispol'zovaniiu iskusstvennykh sputnikov zemli dlia tselei sviazi," ARAN f. 1678 op. 1, d. 9, l. 54.

43. "Zakliuchitel'nyi protokol g. Ulan-Bator 10–17 marta 1970 g," ARAN F. 1678 Sovet "Interkosmos," op. 1, d. 68a, l. 10.

44. "US Mission Geneva to Secretary of State, Subject: Satellite Direct Broadcast Working Group," August 8, 1969, Folder 7-20-69, File Economic: Tel 6 7/1/69 to Tel 6 11/1/69, Central Foreign Policy Files 1967–1969, RG 59, NACP.

45. See, for example, "Department of State to the President, Subject: Soviet INTERSPUTNIK proposal," September 3, 1968, 1, Folder 9-1-68, File Economic: TEL 6 7/1/68-11/1/68, 1967–69, SNF, RG 59, NACP.

46. "Letter from Academic B. N. Petrov, chair of Interkosmos, to N. V. Talyzin, Vice Minister of Communications of the USSR," August 12, 1967, ARAN f. 1678 op. 1, d. 9, l. 61–62.

47. Holly, *Foreign Relations of the United States*.

48. "US Department of State to all US diplomatic posts, Subject: re: 'Intelsat Conference,'" 8, Airgram CA-12775, Folder 12-17-68, File Economic: TEL 6 11/11/68-1/1/69, 1967–69, SNF, RG 59, NACP.

49. See, for example, Mongolia's response to the survey, "From Academic B. Shirendyb to Academic Petrov," July 20, 1967, ARAN f. 1678 "Interkosmos," op. 1, d. 9, l. 3.

50. "Mnenie pol'skoi storony otnositel'no voprosnika po dannym dlia podgotovki predvaritel'nogo proekta MSSS," n.d. (1967), ARAN f. 1678 "Interkosmos," op. 1, d. 9, l. 126.

51. "Zakliuchitel'nyi protokol, g. Budapesht 24–29 iiunia 1968 g." ARAN f. 1678, Sovet "Interkosmos," op. 1, d. 34 l. 98.

52. "Tezisy doklada "O mezhdunarodnoi sisteme kosmicheskoi sviazi "Intersputnik" i predstoiaschei konferentsii chlenov "Intelsat" na zasedanii Soveta "Interkosmos" 20 dek. 1968," ARAN f. 1678, Sovet "Interkosmos," op. 1, d. 34, ll. 186–187.

53. Ibid.

54. Ibid., l.187. While the existing Soviet Molniia system used a highly elliptical orbit, the Interkosmos discussion referred to a future Intersputnik system, which would employ Soviet geostationary satellites.

55. Ibid., l. 188.

56. Anthony Solomon to Secretary of State, "Subject: The Intersputnik proposal of the Soviet Union—Action Memorandum," August 30, 1968, 1, Folder 9-1-68, File Economic: TEL 6 7/1/68-11/1/68, 1967–69, SNF, RG 59, NACP.

57. Anthony Solomon to Secretary of State, "Subject: The Intersputnik proposal of the Soviet Union—Action Memorandum," August 30, 1968, 2, Folder 9-1-68, File Economic: TEL 6 7/1/68-11/1/68, 1967–69, SNF, RG 59, NACP.

58. "Secretary of State to the President, Subject: Soviet Intersputnik Proposal," September 3, 1968, Folder 9-1-68, File Economic: TEL 6 7/1/68-11/1/68, 1967–69, SNF, RG 59, NACP.

59. Smith, *Communication via Satellite*, 288, n. 101.

60. These new efforts focused on "coordination of separate efforts rather than corporate efforts," with extra attention to the interests of Western European partners. Holly, *Foreign Relations of the United States*, 3.

## Bibliography

Appel, Hannah, Nikhil Anand, and Akhil Gupta, eds. *The Promise of Infrastructure*. Durham, NC: Duke University Press, 2018.

Autio-Sarasmo, Sari. "Stagnation or Not? The Brezhnev Leadership and the East-West Interaction." In *Reconsidering Stagnation in the Brezhnev Era: Ideology and Exchange*, edited by Dina Fainberg and Artemy Kalinovsky, 87–104. Lanham, MD: Lexington Books, 2016.

Beutelschmidt, Thomas. *Ost—West—Global: Das Sozialistische Fernsehen Im Kalten Krieg*. Leipzig: Vistas, 2017.

Buck, Susan. *The Global Commons: An Introduction*. Washington, DC: Island, 2012.
Burgess, Colin and Bert Vis. *Interkosmos: The Eastern Bloc's Early Space Program*. London: Springer, 2015.
Burns, Russel W. *Television: An International History of the Formative Years*. London: Institution of Engineering and Technology, 1998.
Butrica, Andrew J., ed. *Beyond the Ionosphere: Fifty Years of Satellite Communication*. Washington, DC: NASA, 1997.
Clarke, Arthur C. "The Space Station: Its Radio Application." In *Exploring the Unknown: Selected Documents in the History of the US Civilian Space Program*, vol. 3, edited by John M. Logsdon, Roger D. Launius, David H. Onkst, and Stephen J. Garber. Washington, DC: NASA, 1998.
Downing, John. "The Intersputnik System and Soviet Television." *Soviet Studies* 37, no. 4 (1985): 465–483.
Eugster, Ernest. *Television Programming Across National Boundaries. The EBU and OIRT Experience*. Dedham, MA: Artech House, 1983.
Evans, Christine, and Lars Lundgren. "Geographies of Liveness: Time, Space, and Satellite Networks as Infrastructures of Live Television in the Our World Broadcast." *International Journal of Communication* 10 (2016): 5362–5380.
Graham, Stephen, and Simon Marvin. *Splintering Urbanism: Networked Infrastructures, Technological Mobilities and the Urban Condition*. London: Routledge, 2001.
Hay, James. "The Invention of Air Space, Outer Space, and Cyberspace." In *Down to Earth: Satellite Technologies, Industries and Cultures*, edited by Lisa Parks and James Schwoch, 19–41. New Brunswick, NJ: Rutgers University Press, 2012.
Högselius, Per. *Red Gas: Russia and the Origins of European Energy Dependence*. New York: Palgrave MacMillan, 2013.
Holly, Susan K., ed. *Foreign Relations of the United States, 1964–1968*, vol. XXXIV, Energy Diplomacy and Global Issues. Washington: Government Printing Office, 1991. Document 100. Accessed February 21, 2020. https://history.state.gov/historicaldocuments/frus1964-68v34/d100.
Hultén, Olof. "The Intelsat System: Some Notes on Television Utilization of Satellite Technology." *International Communication Gazette* 19, no. 1 (1973): 29–37.
Jenks, Andrew. *Collaboration in Space and the Search for Peace on Earth*. Anthem Series on Russian, Eastern European, and Eurasian Studies. London: Anthem Press, 2021.
Johnson, Lyndon B. "Special Message to the Congress on Communication Policy." August 14, 1967. In The American Presidency Project, edited by Gerhard Peters and John T. Wooley. Accessed November 5, 2021. https://www.presidency.ucsb.edu/documents/special-message-the-congress-communications-policy
Kildow, Judith. *Intelsat: Policy Maker's Dilemma*. Lexington, MA: Lexington Books, 1973.
Larkin, Brian. *Signal and Noise: Media, Infrastructure, and Urban Culture in Nigeria*. Durham, NC: Duke University Press, 2008.
Lemberg, Diana. *Barriers Down: How American Power and Free-Flow Policies Shaped Global Media*. New York: Columbia University Press, 2019.
Lundgren, Lars. "Live From Moscow: The Celebration of Yuri Gagarin and Transnational Television in Europe." *VIEW: Journal of European Television History and Culture* 1, no. 2 (2012): 237–256.
———. "Transnational Television in Europe: Cold War Competition and Cooperation." In *Beyond the Divide: Entangled Histories of Cold War Europe*, edited by Simo Mikkonen and Pia Koivunen, 237–256. New York: Berghahn, 2015.

Mark, James, Artemy M. Kalinovsky, and Steffi Marung, eds. *Alternative Globalizations: Eastern Europe and the Postcolonial World*. Bloomington: Indiana University Press, 2020.
Marvin, Carolyn. *When Old Technologies Were New*. Oxford: Oxford University Press, 1990.
McDanie, Drew, and Lewis A. Day. "INTELSAT and Communist Nations' Policy on Communications Satellites." *Journal of Broadcasting* 18, no. 3 (1974): 311–322.
McWhinney, Edward. "Review: Communication via Satellite: A Vision in Retrospect, by Delbert D. Smith." *The American Journal of International Law* 71, no. 4 (1977): 834–835.
Mikkonen, Simo, and Pia Koivunen, eds. *Beyond the Divide: Entangled Histories of Cold War Europe*. New York: Berghahn, 2015.
Misa, Thomas J., and Johan Schot. "Inventing Europe: Technology and the Hidden Integration of Europe." *History and Technology* 21, no. 1 (2005): 1–19.
Mosco, Vincent. *The Digital Sublime: Myth, Power, and Cyberspace*. Cambridge, MA: MIT Press, 2004.
Näser-Lather, Marion, and Christoph Neubert, eds. *Traffic: Media as Infrastructures and Cultural Practices*. Leiden: Brill, 2015.
Parks, Lisa. *Cultures in Orbit: Satellites and the Televisual*. Durham, NC: Duke University Press, 2005.
Parks, Lisa, and James Schwoch, eds. *Down to Earth: Satellite Technologies, Industries and Cultures*. New Brunswick, NJ: Rutgers University Press, 2012.
Parks, Lisa, and Nicole Starosielski, eds. *Signal Traffic: Critical Studies of Media Infrastructures*. Chicago: University of Illinois Press, 2015.
Romijn, Peter, Giles Scott-Smith, and Joes Segal, eds. *Divided Dreamworlds? The Cultural Cold War in East and West*. Amsterdam: Amsterdam University Press, 2012.
Sanchez-Sibony, Oscar. *Red Globalization: The Political Economy of the Soviet Cold War from Stalin to Khrushchev*. Cambridge: Cambridge University Press, 2014.
Schwoch, James. *Global TV: New Media and the Cold War, 1946–69*. Chicago: University of Illinois Press, 2009.
Siddiqi, Asif. *The Red Rockets' Glare: Spaceflight and the Russian Imagination 1857–1957*. Cambridge: Cambridge University Press, 2010.
Slotten, Hugh R. "Satellite Communications, Globalization and the Cold War." *Technology and Culture* 43, no. 2 (2002): 315–350.
Smith, Delbert D. *Communication via Satellite*. Leiden: A. W. Sijthoff, 1976.
Starosielski, Nicole. *The Undersea Network*. Durham: Duke University Press, 2015.
Volkmer, Ingrid. "Satellite Cultures in Europe: Between National Spheres and a Globalized Space." *Global Media and Communication* 4, no. 3 (2008): 231–244.
Winston, Brian. *Media, Technology and Society. A History: From the Telegraph to the Internet*. London: Routledge, 1998.

CHRISTINE EVANS is Associate Professor of History at the University of Wisconsin-Milwaukee. She is author of *Between Truth and Time: A History of Soviet Central Television*.

LARS LUNDGREN is Associate Professor of Media and Communication Studies at Södertörn University. His work is published in *Media History*, *European Journal of Cultural Studies*, and *International Journal of Communication*.

CHAPTER 16

SPY FROM THE CLOUD
*From Big Brother to Big Data*

Anikó Imre

Spies were the quintessential agents of Cold War popular media, both by profession as fictional representatives of powerful intelligence agencies and in their allegorical role as superhero-like liaisons in the international diplomacy between the two superpowers. Descended from Mata Hari and other master spies of World War I, James Bond and his many heroic, crafty, campy, or melancholic brothers and sisters who populated Cold War cinematic and literary spy fiction skillfully traversed the Iron Curtain, reassuring their viewing publics of the triumph of the good side or at least of the moral superiority of their own nations. It is no surprise that the spy genre enjoyed its heyday in the 1950s and '60s, at the height of Cold War hostilities, and declined in its classic form with the thawing and eventual demise of the conflict.[1]

TV and movie spies have made a remarkable international comeback since the early 2010s. Many of these recent series and feature films draw on the Cold War for historical parallels, antecedents, or representational elements. They include blockbusters such as *Atomic Blonde* (dir. David Leitch, 2017), *Red Sparrow* (dir. Francis Lawrence, 2018), *The Spy Who Dumped Me* (dir. Susanna Fogel, 2018), and *Tinker Tailor Soldier Spy* (dir. Tomas Alfredson, 2011), as well as popular television dramas such as *The Americans* (FX, 2013–2018), *Counterpart* (Starz Network, 2017–), *Comrade Detective* (Amazon, 2017), *Homeland* (Showtime, 2011–), *The Handmaid's Tale* (Hulu,

2017–), *A Very Secret Service* (Arte, 2015), *Deutschland 83, 86,* and *89* (AMC Networks and RTL, 2015–), *1983* (Netflix, 2018–), *Secret City* (Netflix, 2016–), *The Spy* (Netflix, 2019–), and others.

What is obvious at first glimpse is that most of these recent products deploy familiar nostalgic Cold War aesthetic and narrative elements to convey a decidedly contemporary sense of ambiguity, allegory, and dystopia that is associated with the global crisis of neoliberal markets, the erosion of trust in democratic institutions (and, indeed, in the value of truth), and the emergence of autocratic regimes worldwide. In this chapter, I probe this association further and ask why and how the memory of the Cold War is resurrected through its favored genre to lend a representative platform to current, globally shared structures of feeling. On the one hand, I argue that the implied historical parallels yield a contemporary reevaluation of the Cold War as much more complex and more thoroughly networked among national and other agents than the triumphant Western narrative of two warring empires has long suggested. On the other hand, I also expect that the comparison between Cold War and contemporary manifestations of spies and spying, particularly in television, will guide us to understand significant transformations in the nature, effects, and experience of surveillance. These transformations involve the global political and affective impact of populism and authoritarianism, stark economic inequality, widespread digital state and corporate surveillance, a conservative backlash against the rights of women, minorities, and immigrants, the decline of democratic institutions, and the impact of fake news delivered by algorithms.

Equally important, the comparison between Cold War and contemporary spy TV turns the spotlight on a radical transformation of technological and media networks themselves, from nation-based broadcast networks to streaming and content-provider platforms that actively facilitate a more widespread, insidious, and inescapable sense of surveillance. In particular, I argue that there is a synergy between the structures of broadcast television and Cold War representations of spying on the one side and contemporary, digital, SVOD (subscription video on demand) television and the spying- and surveillance-related content offered by streaming services on the other. During the Cold War, which coincided almost exactly with the broadcast era, particularly in Europe, television was largely under the control and regulation of nation-states and networked internationally by institutions such as the European Broadcasting Union (EBU), Organisation Internationale de Radiodiffusion et de Télévision (OIRT), and International Telecommunication Union (ITU). As the editors of a recent book on European broadcasting during the Cold War put it, these organizations "functioned as crucial gateways for transnational interaction, both on the technical and juridical level as well as on the level of intercultural communication," and acted as mediators and agents of cultural and political change.[2] The central role of these international institutions has significantly declined since the end of national broadcast monopolies and the dominance of linear, over-the-air broadcasting.

Of course, a proper comparison between Cold War and contemporary manifestations of the spy genre would require a much more extensive study. Given this volume's focus, I channel this comparison through the more specific question of how recent spy-related media content revisits and revises the received, Western-centric history of the Cold War. Accordingly, my emphasis falls on the far less known socialist versions of the spy drama, which already imply a critical revisionist perspective that offsets the dominant view of the conflict. Juxtaposing these with representations of the popular Western repertoire of the genre foregrounds how and why the Cold War remains an indispensable historical, philosophical, and affective reference point for understanding the widespread melancholia and anxiety produced by neoliberal capitalism.

I compare the significance of spying in these programs—which were produced by national broadcasters and circulated within international broadcast networks that had control and regulation over the production, marketing, and distribution of content—with current, globally traveling spying-related content. The latter emerges from a media industry whose primary actors have shifted from national industries and international organizations with more or less visible, transparent, embodied, human agents at their heads to integrated technological and media companies whose digitally networked operations are increasingly underscored by big-data-based content production and consumer surveillance. Netflix, most prominently, functions as a surveillance empire that promises a great deal of individual agency grounded in infinite choices. Yet each choice leaves a digital trace of information that allows the company's algorithmic gaze to capture and ultimately shape our images in ways that leave us in a state of anxiety over our loss of control. This state of disembodied paranoia over ubiquitous, inescapable surveillance is, in turn, reproduced as represented content in a large number of contemporary television dramas distributed by streaming platforms. I end by underscoring the importance of recognizing this feedback loop between spying as content and spying by technology and thinking seriously about how to turn it into creative methods of understanding and pedagogies of interruption.

## Cold War TV Spies

Beyond the enduring prototype of James Bond, fictional TV series that revolved around spying were a universally loved genre of the Cold War. This was a loose generic bag that mixed detective and spy dramas, historical adventure shows, and comedy; the shows traveled widely and were also adapted to produce local variants. In fact, as Jonathan Bignell shows, they could be seen as transnational formats before formats were officially codified as such. Bignell examines the interchange between Hollywood and the British Elstree Studios, which swapped a number of long-running detective and adventure drama serials in the 1960s and '70s, including *Rawhide* and *Gunsmoke*, crime dramas such as *77 Sunset Strip* and *M Squad*, and spy series such as *The Man from UNCLE, I Spy*, and *Mission Impossible*. British companies ABC and ITC sold their own similar series back to the US. *The Saint*, the first one-hour British spy series popular on the US market, and *The Avengers* used British vocabulary, costume, and décor, but their story lines were similar to those of American spy shows.[3]

This international genre family blended elements of crime, espionage, and costume adventure. It developed a "distinctive spatial aesthetic that is a national and international hybrid."[4] Bignell calls such shows' generic style "telefantasy." Narratively, the British programs tended to feature international adventurers and spies who traverse, police, and manage the bipolar spatial organization of the Cold War. Politically, they were about a world system that needed to be stabilized and controlled by elite nations (Britain and other major European countries) and their institutional representatives, working together with the US. The hybrid genre also prefigured a cross-fertilization between TV and film technology that is now a routine aspect of media convergence.

These telefantasy hits were also popular in the East. They translated well into socialism's dualistic worldview, which allowed little ambivalence between (male) heroism and cowardice. *The Saint* and *The Adventures of Robin Hood* were wildly popular events on socialist screens.[5] The NBC crime show *Columbo* (1971–2003) was sold to forty-four countries and swept Eastern European nations in the 1970s and '80s, when the atmosphere in the east and west of Europe became more welcoming to American imports. West German police dramas also remained popular in Eastern Europe throughout the socialist period. *Derrick* (1974–1998), *Crime Scene (Tatort*, 1970–), and their kin were a good fit for the paternalistic ethos of socialist TV by virtue of their older, more respectable or authoritative detectives and their more subdued dialogue-based styles.

But socialist TV industries also produced their own homegrown spy and crime dramas. East German television was under particular pressure to answer the competition presented by the West German series, which most households in the GDR were able to receive. One of the GDR's most successful responses was *Police Call* (*Polizeiruf 110*, 1971–), a detective show launched as a rival to *Tatort*.⁶ It was later picked up by ARD (Arbeitsgemeinschaft der öffentlich-rechtlichen Rundfunkanstalten der Bundesrepublik Deutschland, a West German broadcaster association at the time) and was so popular that it survived the GDR's demise. The show's longevity is due to the balance it struck between telefantasy, or the fictionalization and dramatization of crimes, and the pedagogical drive and reality-based aesthetic at the center of socialist TV. Unlike the West German *Tatort*, which focused on the protagonists' private lives, *Polizeiruf* foregrounded and exalted the shared public investment in police activities addressing frequent crimes such as fraud, theft, juvenile delinquency, alcoholism, child abuse, rape, and domestic violence. The scripts were keen to model appropriate socialist behaviors and reject inappropriate ones. As the socialist order declined, *Polizeiruf* also shifted toward more serious crimes, the psychological motivations of the people involved, and a more sensationalized presentation—essentially replicating *Tatort*'s aesthetic and moral universe. Post-unification episodes only differ from *Tatort* in their preference for former East German settings. *Polizeiruf 110* was a prime example of how socialist television tried to navigate between the educational imperative that it had to privilege, the ideological expectation that it would support the authority of socialist parties, and viewers' yearning for telefantasy.

The Czechoslovak series *The 30 Cases of Major Zeman* (*30 případů majora Zemana*, 1976–1980) was an especially high-profile production. Originally planned as a tribute to the thirty-year anniversary of the Czechoslovak National Security Police in 1975, it was made by Czechoslovak Television's Army and Security Department, rather than by its Department of Entertainment (which was in charge of other serials), and was sponsored by the Ministry of the Interior, whose officials closely supervised the production.⁷ Each of the thirty episodes (as opposed to the standard seven to ten) cost a million and a half Czechoslovak crowns, almost as much as a feature film.⁸ The show follows young communist Jan Zeman for thirty years of his life, from the time he joined the police force until his retirement. Each episode is dedicated to one year of socialist history from 1945 onward. Petr Bílek calls the serial "propagandistic entertainment" that blended the detective or crime genre with features of the adventure drama and spy thriller.⁹ While Zeman was responsible for solving criminal cases, the episodes also emphasized his harmonious collaboration with the secret police.

Although it was never officially acknowledged, Zeman's character was conceived as a kind of socialist James Bond. Bílek claims that this influence was mediated by other socialist serials that carried the impact of James Bond more explicitly, such as the Polish serial *More than a Life at Stake* (*Stawka większa niż życie*, 1967–1968). The Polish James Bond of that show, Hans Kloss, is a double agent during the war—a Pole who is captured by Soviet intelligence, impersonates a German spy, and pretends to work for the Nazi Abwehr. The question of whom Kloss ultimately worked for was left obscure, other than that he was serving the socialist cause.[10]

Kloss's persona, in turn, evokes the legendary Max Otto von Stierlitz, the spy hero of the Soviet serial *Seventeen Moments of Spring* (*Semnadtsat mgnoveniy vesny*, 1973), another important influence on *Major Zeman*. Stierlitz is a double agent, a Soviet spy originally named Maxim Maximovich Isaev, who operates in Nazi Germany to gather intelligence on secret negotiations between Nazi leaders and Western allies.[11] This twelve-episode drama, created by Tatiana Lioznova at the Gorky Studio for Children's and Youth Films, was one of the first attempts by Soviet Central Television to use the miniserial format to create an ideologically manageable hybrid between propaganda content and the serial form's "Western" pleasures. As in *Major Zeman*, this navigation between the two was essential for reforging the relationship between state authority and the public.[12]

Besides these ideological gains, Soviet television also embraced the miniserial for its economic benefits. As Christine Evans notes, Soviet cultural producers were quite willing to compromise their ideological principles to get access to foreign markets.[13] *Seventeen Moments* proved to be an effective vehicle for reaching audiences within and beyond the bloc. Like *Major Zeman* and similar serials that circulated within Europe in the 1960s and 1970s, it mixed crime and detective drama with the spy and adventure format and that of partisan films set in wartime. It was based on a spy novel by Iulian Semenov, which was also turned into a "genuine political film" promoted "from above," mixing in the features and goals of a serious documentary.[14] The miniseries adaptation was popular not simply for its fictional pleasures, but also for its accidental campiness; it generated a large collection of jokes due to its extreme long takes, nostalgic and slow movements, and relentless pathos.[15]

The hybrid global spy genre not only linked the Soviet-controlled world with the European television market, but also shifted socialist television's didactic thrust from straightforward news and educational programming to more popular fictional formats. The way socialist television filled this generic template varied in significant ways, however. While Major Zeman solved his thirty cases with the help of national and international intelligence and crime networks, showcasing the principle of collaboration, Stierlitz acted as a lone wolf with personal command over his helpers. While Zeman was a dedicated family man, Stierlitz only managed to cobble together a temporary, symbolic family during one of his missions. And in Evans's words, *Seventeen Moments* "entirely excludes everyday life, romantic love, and family dynamics," the essential ingredients of Czechoslovak serials, and revolves around "a kind of sexless, imperial nuclear family."[16]

Like Bond, both Zeman and Stierlitz continue to thrive in reruns and nostalgic recollections, generating countless intertextual references, parodies, and political discussions. They continue to bind together the politics of everyday life and the politics of the state. This is particularly relevant in the case of Vladimir Putin's reliance on socialist television in boosting Russian imperial nationalism. The imperial legacy of *Seventeen Moments* and other Soviet spy and war dramas has merged with the international Cold War legacy of the Bond-type spy figure to rebrand the stale KGB persona of Putin himself. As a recent article summarizes, "Gifted a virtually blank canvas to work on, the Kremlin propaganda machine created Project Putin to fill the void, modelling the future leader as a modern day Stierlitz, a fictional World War II spy popular in dozens of Soviet-era novels and movies."[17]

## Twenty-First-Century TV Spies

It is hard to ignore the preponderance of spying and surveillance—frequently embedded in the thematic cluster of crime, corruption, anxiety, and paranoia—in television and popular films of the past decade. The Cold War provides ready narrative and aesthetic furnishings for addressing these themes. In some cases, the template is resurrected as a set of clichés, as in the summer comedy spoof *The Spy Who Dumped Me*, a romp across Europe in the service of a highly unoriginal mission to deliver a flash drive to the right agent. Most of the film was shot in Budapest, a post–Cold War center of global runaway production, whose versatile settings have provided a heavily tax-incentivized backdrop to more expensive urban locations for a number of Cold War–inspired recent spy and science fiction productions.[18] As a spy spoof, the film unabashedly enlists double and triple crossings, misunderstandings, hints of romance, car chases, violent battles, cartoonish antagonists such as a Russian Olympic gymnast turned soulless torturer, and protagonists such as a handsome British spy working for the good agency. It also sprinkles cosmetic changes on top of the formula, such as two bumbling women BFFs who become accidental spies, as well as extended, graphic, and gratuitous scenes of violence.

These two ingredients—extreme violence and the replacement of dashing male heroes with gorgeous female ones—are recurring superficial ways to update the spy genre. They are present in *Red Sparrow* (dir. Francis

Lawrence, 2017, and also mostly shot in Budapest), featuring Jennifer Lawrence as a Russian spy who is trained to use seduction to get information, and in the more suspenseful action thriller *Atomic Blonde* (dir. John Leitch, 2017), a vehicle for an icy-cool Charlize Theron coming off a similarly eroticized and fierce persona in *Mad Max: Fury Road*. Theron literally emerges from an ice bath at the film's outset, recharged and ready for action as an MI6 agent dispatched to Berlin on the eve of the Wall's collapse in order to recover a microfilm and save the world. The recreation of 1988 Berlin is as stylized as Theron's outfits, stilettos, and manicure, and as choreographed as the violence she unleashes in prolonged fights against impossible odds, against a soundtrack dripping with nostalgia, featuring Queen, David Bowie, George Michael, and, of course, Nena's "99 Red Balloons."

Similar to other filmic fictions that capitalize on a revival of Cold War nostalgia triggered by a serious reckoning with postwar history amid the reemergence of global populism and authoritarianism, *Atomic Blonde* is set against a familiar superpower arrangement in which spies working for the Soviet Union, the US, and Western Europe (Britain) act as the chief agents. This attempt to recall the ghost of the Cold War from the last minutes before it expired, expressed in self-reflexive aestheticization and through a burnt-out, cynical agent based in Berlin (played by James McAvoy), strikes one as a perhaps unintentionally pure deployment of nostalgia for the world of Western tropes through which the Cold War has been imagined. Indeed, the film evokes not so much the Cold War but its cinematically encoded memory, sound, and feel, thereby acknowledging that the Cold War of the movies was, to begin with, primarily an aesthetic construction. This, in turn, is all we are left with now that the conflict has lost its power to provide a rational epistemological road map for the future.

The marketability of Cold War spy-show settings has also been recognized by television executives in a somewhat different set of productions, which self-consciously hover between homage and parody. The French series *A Very Secret Service* (2015–2018), originally produced for Arte and released in the US as a Netflix original, is a workplace comedy set in 1960 in a secret intelligence agency. While there is some light, humorous self-criticism targeting blatant office sexism as well French nationalism and xenophobia (manifest in the agency's attitudes toward former colonies), much of the plot revolves around office intrigue and romance, dwarfing the importance of the various intelligence missions.

The Amazon Prime original *Comrade Detective* (2017) is another twist on the reflexive-nostalgic approach to the Cold War. It merges the timeworn buddy cop genre with executive producer Channing Tatum's idea to create a simulation of a 1980s Romanian propaganda-fiction series. The show was inspired by writer-creator duo Brian Gatewood and Alessandro Tanaka's discovery of late-Soviet propaganda television and—wait for it—*Major Zeman* and *Polizeiruf 110*. The resulting fake Romanian propaganda series—allegedly lost, then found and restored—was shot in Bucharest featuring Romanian actors, then dubbed into English by American A-listers, underscoring the Cold War's resurgent popularity as a theme. *Comrade Detective* is an innovative attempt at historical revision in that it intends to draw parallels between (anticommunist) propaganda in the US and anti-capitalist propaganda in an Eastern Bloc represented by Romania. However, the attempt is thwarted because the show remains lodged in Western perspectives on the Cold War and presents (its idea of) Eastern propaganda in a sweeping and exaggerated fashion. For instance, the second episode of the single season produced centers on Romanians' inability to understand the point of the board game Monopoly, which they come across in a confiscated car, since they have no idea what individual property means. This casts communist propaganda as less sophisticated and more heavy-handed but also highly effective, mapping it onto an even more retrograde hierarchy between the enlightened civilizing West and primitive natives not unlike Dracula—another, older Western invention planted into a mystical Romania.[19]

Much more fruitful for our investigative purposes are contemporary television dramas that "raise the curtain" of the Cold War, to borrow from one of the recent books that set out to expose "the many forms of interaction and cooperation between the two 'blocs,' demonstrating that earlier concepts and histories of the Cold War reflected ideological presuppositions rather than historical reality."[20] These series take on spying as a mode of reordering the contemporary world—as a way of seeing, an epistemological matrix, and a representation of a major global affective condition. While most of these programs draw on the Cold War as a representational resource, they also return to it to create a widely accessible historical template. Against this, they conceptualize and assess the universal threat of surveillance and power inequality that most of the world's inhabitants find themselves facing today in the wake of a major shift to right-wing populism, propaganda, and inescapable surveillance that is enabled, if not controlled, by an entirely new set of social networks powered by digital technology.

The Cold War networks of spying were embodied by swell, desirable, or, in the East, at least witty or smart male agents who represented powerful nation-states in a good-versus-evil battle (or their parodic doubles). Conversely, the spies in these recent allegorical dramas about surveillance have good hunches but routinely turn out to be tragically underinformed as they try to understand and battle forces whose agencies and power they misrecognize and underestimate. They find themselves embroiled in networks that are almost supernaturally inscrutable. These networks no longer map onto nation-states. They are transnational, involving political representatives, corporate executives, social media influencers, grassroots organizers, lone operators, various representatives of the media, and, most menacingly, rogue bots and autonomous data. Quality dramas made or carried by transnational streaming platforms have become synonymous with a formula that mixes the spy, political, sci-fi, and crime drama genres—a blend that has resonated well with a global population united by Netflix, Amazon Prime, HBO, Hulu, and others, but that also carries local inflections that specifically address particular national or regional populations.

*The Americans*, cable network FX's popular and universally acclaimed spy drama (2013–2018) created by former CIA officer Joe Weisberg and carried by Amazon Prime, follows a married couple who are Russian spies posing as ordinary Americans raising two children in a Washington, DC, suburb in the early 1980s. The very situation of Russians successfully passing as a pair of likable Americans under the nose of their CIA-agent neighbor muddles the Cold War's foundational construct of two essentially incompatible cultures, peoples, and value systems. And much of the suspenseful series' dramatic depth comes from Elizabeth and Philip's moral and emotional ambivalence about carrying out missions grounded in the assumption of a relentless and dogmatic battle between two countries. This ambivalence escalates to the point at which, by the sixth and final season, Philip retires from his spy work to devote himself to his former front job as a travel agent and Elizabeth disobeys her order to assassinate a reform-friendly pro-Gorbachev envoy, allowing the series to wrap up along with the Soviet Union and the Cold War.

The sci-fi alternative-history thriller *Counterpart*, created for American cable network Starz (2017–2018), was filmed in Berlin, where the plot is set in the not-too-distant future. The show's premise is that, in 1987, East German scientists accidentally opened a portal to a parallel reality, and thus everything and everyone in the contemporary world has a counterpart in this other sphere. Agent Howard Silk, living a Kafkaesque life of routine and predictability working for a UN agency, gets a visit from alternate Berlin by his doppelgänger (both played by J. K. Simmons), who is much closer to the archetype of the confident, resourceful, smooth-talking spy than our humble Howard. The ensuing crossings between the two worlds evoke the Cold War's good-evil binary only to question its usefulness as a way of navigating history in light of the present and of prospects for the future.

It is no coincidence that the doppelgänger motif of double or multiple identities and lives, which crystallizes in the spy figure (see *The Americans*), has proliferated in recent popular American TV and film, from *The Leftovers*, *The Deuce*, *Fargo*, and *The Good Place* through *Logan*, *Alien: Covenant*, *Twin Peaks*, and, of course, *Us*. Some critics link this multiplying of identities and places to the surrealism and absurdity of a political reality that fundamentally undermines the moral compass of a good-evil dynamic, arguing that "the doppelgänger trend seems perfectly right for a political moment when, on a daily basis, it feels appropriate to question whether our eyes are actually seeing what they're seeing."[21]

The divided city of Berlin, a microcosm of the global Cold War divide within a contained and manageable allegorical space, is also a recurrent element in recent TV, such as in the popular drama series *Deutschland 83* (2015), where East German border guard Martin Rauch is blackmailed into moving to the West to spy on military operations in the titular year. Another hapless, accidental hero, Martin finds himself in a key position to prevent war between East and West. The follow-up season, *Deutschland 86* (2018), expands the show's Cold War historical purview beyond Europe, placing Martin in the midst of an international arms deal in South Africa.

Netflix also recruited venerable Polish filmmaker Agnieszka Holland, who had previously worked on the Czech HBO original political-historical miniseries *Burning Bush*, to direct the first Polish Netflix original. Simply titled *1983*, and thus joining a growing list of original drama productions evoking the late Cold War, this is yet another dystopian alternative-history series—set not in the 1980s, but in 2003, in a Poland isolated from the rest of the world (where the Iron Curtain has fallen) and where communist authoritarianism has remained frozen since 1983. While not nearly as seamless and successful a blend between Netflix's traveling quality aesthetic and local contributions as *Deutschland 83*, it is clearly an allegory for Poland's ruling Law and Justice Party's (PiS) attempts at nationalistic ideological isolation, where the power of (online) propaganda insulates from reality.

This is just a small sample of the international array of quality dramas that feature contemporary descendants of Cold War spies and detectives: rather than suave superheroes or their bumbling parodic doubles, contemporary spies tend to be isolated truth-seekers of great instinct, stubborn determination, and with limited support, who find themselves up against conspiracies and insurmountable, unforeseen, and often invisible opponents.[22] The spies, journalists, and other truth-seekers of recent shows don't necessarily get the job done for us. Instead, they become increasingly mired in folds of conspiracy, which lessens their knowledge and weakens their authority.

Their struggles are magnified versions of the viewers' sense of entanglement in digital networks that spy on and shape us.

## Agents without Agency?

Why does the formula of the Cold War–inflected traveling drama about digital surveillance, international corruption, conspiracy, and crime appeal so broadly around the world? One reason is certainly the global threat of creeping authoritarianism, right-wing nationalism, and isolationism, and their attendant xenophobia, racism, and patriarchal control—themselves responses to the failure of free-market capitalism, which the demise of communism unleashed and subsequent global crises (most prominently the 2008 recession) have deepened. In other words, while memories and images of the Cold War provide a template for representing these structures of feeling, the current global spread of anxiety is the product of unbridled, digitally enhanced capitalism. In turn, this calls for a historical revision of our entire understanding of the Cold War and for critical approaches that are not limited to the analysis of representations, but also take into account media platforms, technologies, and industries.

We are clearly long past the immediate post–Cold War optimism about the digital revolution's potential to lend consumers agency through the promise of interactivity, picking up the mantle of revolution after socialism ran out of steam. Instead, in the twenty-first century, the internet and big data seem to have grown into untraceable, mysterious empires that keep people in their own digital enclosures—a term Mark Andrejevic uses in his influential book, *iSpy: Surveillance and Power in the Interactive Era*, to describe Google's extension of free internet to San Francisco in 2006 in exchange for tracking and mining users' digital footsteps.[23] Rather than government intelligence agencies led by human spies, digital networks work through dehumanized, depersonalized algorithmic apparatuses that may be deployed by Russian bots posing as citizens of other countries, Silicon Valley tech giants, or, most important to this argument, the very media companies that have consolidated control over the streaming revolution that, they claim, finally extends the freedom of access and abundance to consumers.

As a "pioneer straddling the intersection where Big Data and entertainment media intersect," Netflix generally stands as shorthand for the content-provider and streaming-platform companies that have been vying for domination over media markets in recent years.[24] In a recent *Saturday Night Live* mock commercial, Netflix is likened to an all-encompassing empire with limitless funds to invest in new content: "We're spending billions of dollars in making every show in the world. Our goal is the endless scroll," announces a sensationalizing male voice over an image of the spinning globe imprinted with the familiar Netflix catalogue. "Even we haven't seen them all," the voice-over adds, sending up Netflix's famous algorithm-based model of developing new shows based on the consumer data collected through interaction with the catalogue.[25]

Netflix famously disrupted television's traditional content development and marketing model when it remade the 1990s BBC series *House of Cards* following the recommendations of a proprietary "collaborative filtering" algorithm that analyzed trillions of Netflix data points, using viewer ratings, history, and behavior related to content that already existed on the service.[26] The algorithm suggested, among other things, a concentrated viewer interest in surveillance-themed drama.[27] In other words, in an eerie feedback loop, Netflix gives us content that represents our reality of algorithmic surveillance by deploying the very algorithmic surveillance that increasingly envelops and shapes our lives and identities in the first place. Far from being a neutral platform of infinite choices available to autonomous consumer agents, Netflix creates publics held together by data: they are "streamed-to," "data-driven," "data-drawn" publics "that are mobilised for, and disciplined into, sustained personal data production" as "data-breeding publics."[28] As Rocco Bellanova and Gloria González Fuster write, "Every move our fingers make on the platform is a trace for an archive about users' behaviours, and these data, once properly mined, will 'feed back' into what we (and others) will be suggested to watch."[29]

Are Netflix and its peer streaming companies even more insidious versions of Big Brother, the allegory of the authoritarian state associated with communism? Dan McQuillan usefully compares George Orwell's parable of surveillance and propaganda with what he calls "algorithmic seeing," connecting the history of data with the histories of other audiovisual media.[30] However, he also points out crucial differences between algorithmic seeing and Big Brother: "Whereas the power of surveillance in Orwell's vision depended on human watching facilitated by the transparent portal of the vision screen, big data is processed into meaning by machines; specifically by datamining and machine learning algorithms."[31] While big data has immense potential to reveal otherwise invisible connections, its operations remain opaque by virtue of its very size: "It is not possible to directly apprehend how a machine learning algorithm has traversed the data because of the number of variables involved and the complexity of the function that the algorithm has derived to map inputs on to output."[32] Furthermore, unlike surveillance and seeing technologies associated with earlier media, the algorithmic eye is "oracular," rather than "ocular." That is, because big data algorithms substitute correlation for causation or relate past observation to predicting future ones, the temporality of big data is future-oriented and predictive.[33]

It is in the political implications of a data-based apparatus that operates through algorithmic seeing that we discover perhaps unexpected convergences between Big Brother and big data. McQuillan argues that algorithmic vision lends itself to authoritarianism because its actions and consequences are not legible to and thus not easily understood and challenged by traditional social actors. It evades a democratic oversight that would challenge its taken-for-granted, scientific teleology. There is a correlation between the worship of "scientific" big data and the neoliberal surveillance state's worship of economic growth, progress, and numbers. This investment in linear progress—measurable in terms of numerical output and in the service of an unquestioned teleology—also connects the underlying rationality of late capitalist neoliberalism with that of communism's ideological underpinning of ongoing revolution with a permanently-deferred end point. Both ideologies call for individuals who are devoted to constant self-improvement and readiness for competition.

Both also logically produce uncertainty, anxiety, and a loss of agency. But while communist authoritarianism asserted its control through national and international institutions headed by actual human agents who could be resisted and even overthrown, political power that justifies itself in relation to the algorithmic logic of machine learning is derived from patterns of coincidence. It is ultimately irrational, disconnected from human reasoning. The affective response to this contradiction is paranoia, a thought process driven by a sense of constant threat and anxiety—the pandemic of neoliberalism.[34] Big data's algorithmic seeing encases its data-breeding publics in a performative feedback loop: instead of discovering stable taxonomies, predictive algorithms may and do change people's behaviors.[35] Algorithm-empowered streaming services such as Netflix help perpetuate the very paranoiac sensibility that their surveillance-related content narrativizes for anxious viewers. They present in dramatized serial form a habitus epitomized by Franz Kafka's *The Trial*, in Joseph K's sadomasochistic internalization of how his surreal trial reshapes his social status and relationships. Netflix and its peers are underscored by a mode of governance that, McQuillan writes, rather than "seeing like a state," sees "like a secret state."[36]

Beyond formal similarities, we find in the end a convergence between communist, state-led authoritarianism under human dictators and neoliberal authoritarianism underscored by big data. Although both versions are primed to produce dictators, the structure of domination is more impenetrable and insidious in the case of the neoliberal surveillance society of competitive authoritarianism because its scientific technological base supports blind faith in the inherent progress of the market.

The assemblage of films and TV programs I have discussed relate these two forms of authoritarianism and surveillance to each other with varying levels of critical intentionality. A representational/ideological analysis suggests that these products respond to a shared need to manage the fundamental insecurity and paranoia induced by algorithmic surveillance by resurrecting agents from earlier spy drama conventions. A further, more complicated but possibly more important question concerns the double role of the very technological and economic apparatus that represents our structures of feeling but is also enabled by and actively participates in producing them. Is there perhaps any agency to be gained from recognizing Netflix's double role, from its exposure of data-based mechanisms of surveillance through our favored narratives? Bellanova and González Fuster take up this very question in their essay "No (Big) Data, No Fiction?" They leave some room for optimism in answering the question, arguing that algorithms may produce new kinds of user networks that are able to "think surveillance with and against Netflix, through and besides its fiction."[37] When we watch the surveillance practices depicted by a given story line, we may understand better how we are tracked by, and trapped in, multiple public and private high-tech surveillance systems. As they write, "When we realize how Netflix actually works, we may come to finally visualize algorithmic surveillance as an 'embodied' practice, a perception overall too rare in many other social settings."[38]

Perhaps the most educating object of study with which to begin to conclude this chapter would be Netflix's documentary *The Great Hack* (2019), which its creators, Karim Amer and Jehane Noujaim, call a "modern horror story" about Cambridge Analytica's practices of data tracking, harvesting, and targeting to help antidemocratic political causes such as Brexit in the UK and the election of Donald Trump in the US.[39] The directors' explicit aim was to capture algorithmic vision, the way "the algorithm sees us," through the visual language of the documentary, in order to "help people understand our own fragility and the superstructure that exists around us, and how it's constantly sucking and collecting your behavior."[40]

While the film identifies Cambridge Analytica as the main villain for misusing its big data to change collective behavior, it is hard to miss the irony that SVOD streaming platforms such as Netflix, which produced the film, operate in the same way. This irony then alerts us to the need to update our approach to spying content produced and delivered by spying platforms. More precisely, this collision of content and platform necessitates that we fuse the textual and representational approaches that enable us to analyze older content with analysis of recent, fundamental changes in the very nature of the media. As Andrejevic, Hearn, and Kennedy write, television has shifted from broadcasting and its national and international institutions to "logistical media ... whose content is not so much narrative or representational but organizational."[41] In other words, according to Ramon Lobato, "The way platforms present and filter content is fundamentally distinct from the flow of linear broadcasting. Television is acquiring—unevenly, but substantively—a database form."[42] Netflix and its rivals are, of course, both representational and logistical media, and this hybridity invites hybrid methodologies at the interfaces of algorithmic and human vision, neither ignoring streaming platforms' big-data-based operations in favor of representational analysis nor exempting them from ideological analysis on the grounds of big data's association with scientific objectivity. Clusters of representation produced by data-based television that evoke Cold War spying to comment on contemporary surveillance are logical starting points for such an inquiry.

## Notes

1. One of the best of the many histories of the relationship between the Cold War and the spy genre in American television is Kackman, *Citizen Spy*.
2. Badenoch et al., "Airy Curtains in the European Ether," 17.
3. Bignell, "Transatlantic Spaces," 56.
4. Ibid., 55.
5. Roger Moore, star of *The Saint*, visited Budapest and was interviewed on the nightly news in 1971. See Dunavölgyi, "A magyar televíziózás története a hatvanas években: 1971."
6. Breitenborn, "'Memphis Tennessee,'" 394.
7. Garai, "Milyen sorozatokat lathatunk a TV-ben?"
8. Bílek, "The 30 Cases of Major Zeman," 49. See also Bren's important work on Czechoslovak serials in *The Greengrocer and His TV*.
9. Ibid., 50.
10. Ibid., 52.
11. Ibid.
12. See Evans, *Between* Truth *and* Time, 150–182. On the relationship between *Seventeen Moments* and the Bond phenomenon, see Amar, "Between James Bond and Iosif Stalin."
13. Ibid.
14. Ibid., 158.
15. Ibid.
16. Ibid., 164.
17. Wray, "Vladimir Putin's Control."
18. For instance, *Blade Runner 2049*, *Red Sparrow*, *Inferno*, *Spy*, *Atomic Blonde*, *Tinker Tailor Soldier Spy*, *The Terror*, *Read Heat*, *Spy Game*, *A Good Day to Die Hard*, and *The Martian*.
19. To compound the blunder, the show ignores the fact that socialist countries placed a great deal of emphasis on cultivating the pedagogy of persuasion through playful and enjoyable forms of socialization, including socialist versions of Monopoly, a board game that trains players to navigate a state-controlled economy in a competitive fashion.

20. Badenoch et al., "Airy Curtains in the European Ether," 11.
21. Chaney, "Why Are There So Many Doppelgängers." See also Epstein, "Watch This."
22. To appreciate the scale and impact of the phenomenon, consider some other versions of the locally produced, globally streaming versions of the quality spy/conspiracy crime drama: The Australian Netflix series *Secret City* (Showcase, 2016, followed by Netflix release in 2018) features investigative journalist Harriet Dunkley, who is trying to uncover a vast, international military conspiracy that involves the Australian political leadership's role in the midst of heightening tension between China and America. Nordic noir crime/conspiracy drama *Mammon*, originally produced for Norwegian public broadcaster NRK (2014, 2016), follows the increasingly desperate attempts of an investigative journalist to expose corruption in a company run by his brother. *Mammon* was adapted by HBO for its Czech and Polish versions, which also featured journalists in a hopeless struggle to expose a tangle of corrupt business arrangements among financial elites whose alliance goes back to the immediate post-Wall years. HBO Europe's first-ever coproduction, with the German pay TV channel TNT Serie, is entitled *Hackerville* (2018). Cocreated by Jörg Winger and Ralph Martin, who were also behind *Deutschland 83* and *Deutschland 86*, *Hackerville*'s six episodes revolve around spying as a theme that draws into its narrative and historical arc contemporary cybercrime and Cold War surveillance by the Romanian secret police agency Securitate. The series sends Romanian-born German cyber cop Lisa Metz to uncover a hacking operation in Timișoara, where in the course of her investigation she also uncovers her own family history, including her father's shady involvement with the secret police during late Communism.
23. Andrejevic, *iSpy*, 1.
24. Leonard, "How Netflix Is Turning Viewers into Puppets."
25. YouTube, *Netflix Commercial*.
26. Havens, "Media Programming in an Era of Big Data."
27. Bellanova and González-Fuster, "No (Big) Data, No Fiction?," 2–3.
28. Ibid., 19.
29. Ibid., 5.
30. McQuillan, "Algorithmic Paranoia."
31. Ibid., 2.
32. Ibid., 3.
33. Ibid.
34. Wilson, *Neoliberalism*.
35. Predictions change the conditions for the learning of machine learning. The situation has the potential for "a machinic form of paranoiac self-justification, an algorithmic attribution bias that generates systematic errors in evaluating the reasons for observed behaviours. Under these conditions, algorithmic seeing tends towards paranoia." McQuillen, "Algorithmic Paranoia," 6.
36. Ibid.
37. Bellanova and González-Fuster, "No (Big) Data, No Fiction?," 233.
38. Ibid.
39. Dreyfuss, "Netflix's *The Great Hack* Brings Our Data Nightmare to Life."
40. Ibid.
41. Andrejevic et al., "Cultural Studies of Data Mining," 40.
42. Lobato, "Rethinking International TV Flows Research."

## Bibliography

Amar, Tarik Cyril. "Between James Bond and Iosif Stalin: Seventeen Moments of Spring, a Soviet Cultural Event of the Cold War and the Post-Thaw." *Kritika: Explorations in Russian and Eurasian History* 21, no. 3 (2020): 624–658.

Andrejevic, Mark. *iSpy: Surveillance and Power in the Interactive Era*. Lawrence: University of Kansas Press, 2007.

Andrejevic, Mark, Alison Hearn, and Helen Kennedy. "Cultural Studies of Data Mining: Introduction." *European Journal of Cultural Studies* 18, no. 4–5 (2015): 379–394.

Badenoch, Alexander, Andreas Fickers, and Christian Henrich-Franke. "Airy Curtains in the European Ether." In *Airy Curtains in the European Ether: Broadcasting and the Cold War*, edited by Alexander Badenoch, Andreas Fickers, and Christian Henrich-Franke, 9–26. Baden-Baden: Nomos, 2013.

Bellanova, Rocco, and Gloria González-Fuster. "No (Big) Data, No Fiction? Thinking Surveillance with/against Netflix." In *The Politics and Policies of Big Data: Big Data, Big Brother?*, edited by Ann Rudonow Sætnan, Ingrid Schneider, and Nicola Green, 227–246. London: Routledge, 2018.

Bignell, Jonathan. "Transatlantic Spaces: Production, Location and Style in 1960s–1970s Action-Adventure TV Series." *Media History* 16, no. 1 (2010): 53–65.

Bílek, Petr A. "The 30 Cases of Major Zeman: Domestication and Ideological Conversion of a James Bond Narrative in the Czech TV Serial Context of the 1970s." In *National Mythologies in Central European TV Series: How J.R. Won the Cold War*, edited by Jan Čulík, 45–59. Brighton: Sussex Academic Press, 2013.

Breitenborn, Uwe. "'Memphis Tennessee' in Borstendorf: Boundaries Set and Transcended in East German Television Entertainment." *Historical Journal of Film, Radio and Television* 24, no. 3 (2004): 391–402.

Bren, Paulina. *The Greengrocer and His TV: The Culture of Communism after the 1968 Prague Spring*. Ithaca, NY: Cornell University Press, 2010.

Chaney, Jen. "Why Are There So Many Doppelgängers in Pop Culture Right Now?" *Vulture*, June 2, 2017. https://www.vulture.com/2017/06/doppelgngers-are-all-over-pop-culture-right-now.html.

Dreyfuss, Emily. "Netflix's *The Great Hack* Brings Our Data Nightmare to Life." *Wired*, June 24, 2019. https://www.wired.com/story/the-great-hack-documentary/.

Dunavölgyi, Péter. "A magyar televíziózás története a hatvanas években: 1971." Accessed September 18, 2021. http://dunavolgyipeter.hu/televizio_tortenet/a_magyar_televiziozas_tortenete_az_1970-as_evekben/1971.

Epstein, Adam. "Watch This: *Counterpart*, a Kafkaesque Sci Fi/Spy Show about The Roads Not Taken." *Quartzy*, January 21, 2018. https://qz.com/quartzy/1184297/watch-this-counterpart-a-kafkaesque-sci-fi-spy-show-about-the-roads-not-taken/.

Evans, Christine. *Between Truth and Time: A History of Soviet Central Television*. New Haven: Yale University Press, 2016.

Garai, Tamas. "Milyen sorozatokat lathatunk a TV-ben?" *Fejér Megyei Hírlap*, January 24, 1985.

Havens, Timothy. "Media Programming in an Era of Big Data." *Media Industries Journal* 1, no. 2 (2014). Accessed September 18, 2021. https://quod.lib.umich.edu/m/mij/15031809.0001.202/--media-programming-in-an-era-of-big-data?rgn=main;view=fulltext.

Kackman, Michael. *Citizen Spy: Television, Espionage and Cold War Culture*. Minneapolis: University of Minnesota Press, 2005.

Leonard, Andrew. "How Netflix Is Turning Viewers into Puppets." *Salon*, February 1, 2013. https://www.salon.com/abtest1/2013/02/01/how_netflix_is_turning_viewers_into_puppets/.

Lobato, Ramon. "Rethinking International TV Flows Research in the Age of Netflix." *Television and New Media* 19, no. 3 (2018): 241–256.

McQuillan, Dan. "Algorithmic Paranoia and the Convivial Alternative." *Big Data and Society* 3, no. 2 (2016): 1–12.

Rigby, Elizabeth. "Nordic Noir Left in Shade by Cold War Spy Drama." *The Times*, January 13, 2016.

Tate, Gabriel. "*Deutschland 86* Takes Cold War Spies to Cape Town." *The Times*, March 5, 2019. https://www.thetimes.co.uk/article/deutschland-86-takes-cold-war-spies-to-cape-town-q9ggkowr2.

Wilson, Julie. *Neoliberalism*. New York: Routledge, 2017.

Wray, Michael. "Vladimir Putin's Control of Russia is Built on Controlling the Media." *The Courier-Mail*, February 3, 2017. http://www.couriermail.com.au/news/queensland/vladimir-putins-control-of-russia-is-built-on-controlling-the-media/news-story/65f6ff89632c21de7030fd4e28677691.

YouTube. *Netflix Commercial—SNL*. December 2, 2018. https://www.youtube.com/watch?v=lqRQ5Y6OYi4.

ANIKÓ IMRE is Professor of Cinematic Arts at the University of Southern California. She is author of *Identity Games: Globalization and the Transformation of Media Cultures in the New Europe* and of *TV Socialism*. She is editor (with Timothy Havens and Katalin Lustyik) of *Popular Television in Eastern Europe During and Since Socialism* and (with Katarzyna Marciniak and Áine O'Healy) of *Transnational Feminism in Film and Media*.

# INDEX

Note: Page numbers in *italics* refer to figures.

*Accattone* (film, dir. Pasolini, 1961), 90
Aczél, György, 105
Adorno, Theodor, 181
*Adrift* (film, dir. Kadár, 1969), 231
*Adventures of Robin Hood, The* (television series), 280
Afghanistan, 26
Africa, 5, 8, 93, 123, 144; as allegory for Eastern Europe, 203; anticolonial movements in, 82; decolonization in, 195; GDR radio broadcasts to, 140; international film festivals and, 159; Kapuściński's reportage from, 199
agency, loss of, 288–92
Aitmatov, Chinghiz, 68
Albania, 170
Albee, Edward, 178
*Alexander Nevsky* [*Aleksandr Nevskiy*] (film, dir. Eisenstein, 1938), 80, 84
Alfredson, Tomas, 277
Algeria, anticolonial movement in, 82
Ali, Tariq, 202
*Alias Gardelito* (film, dir. Murúa, 1961), 90
allegoresis, 199, 200, 202
Allende, Isabel, 177
*All Quiet on the Western Front* (film, dir. Mann, 1979), 237
Almendros, Nestor, 86–87
Almgren, Birgitta, 142
*Alphaville* (film, dir. Godard, 1965), 168
Álvarez, Santiago, 81–82, 88
*Amadeus* (film, dir. Forman, 1984), 237
Amazon Prime, 286
Amer, Karim, 291
American Forces Network radio, 50
*American Postcard* [*Amerikai anzix*] (film, dir. Bódy, 1975), 6, 99, 101, *107*; American Civil War setting of, 106; BBS film distribution and, 104; at Mannheim Film Festival, 106–9

*Americans, The* (FX television spy drama, 2013–2018), 277, 286, 287
Andrejevic, Mark, 288, 292
Andrews Sisters, 47
*Angélique, the Marquise of the Angels* [*Angélique, marquise des anges*] (film, dir. Borderie, 1964), 167
Angola, 245, 254
Anouilh, Jean, 67
anticommunism, 54, 95n50, 199, 204, 206, 285; anglophone translation of East European literature and, 194, 206; collapse of Soviet Union and, 205; geopolitics of film markets and, 251; liberal anticommunist intellectuals, 90; US support for movements in Socialist bloc, 203
anti-imperialist movements, 7, 195, 196, 205, 207n8, 208n10
antisemitism, 48, 51, 52
Antonioni, Michelangelo, 164, 168, 169
Apor, Balázs, 53
Applebaum, Rachel, 53
Arabsat (Arab League satellite network), 270–71
Arbuzov, Aleksei, 68
*Arcades Project* (Benjamin), 19
*Architects, The* [*Die Architekten*] (Heym novel, 1963), 20–21, 26
Argentina, film criticism in, 81, 84
*Arsenal* (film, dir. Dovzhenko, 1929), 80
Asher, Robert, 157
Asia, 5, 93, 144; GDR radio broadcasts to, 140; international film festivals and, 159; rebuilding of war-destroyed cities in, 27
Atget, Eugène, 31, 32, 38n40
*Atomic Blonde* (film, dir. Leitch, 2017), 277, 284
*Attack and Retreat* [*Italiani brava gente / Oni shli na vostok*] (De Santis, 1964), 247, 250
Australia, 177, 183, 188n25

Austria, 142
*Avengers, The* (British television spy series), 280

Babel, Isaac, 69
Babiracki, Patryk, 48, 53, 56n36
Baldwin, James, 182, 186
Bammer, Angelika, 185
"Bandersnatch" (episode of *Black Mirror* TV series, 2018), 121, 135n24
Bańkowicz, Ryszard, 196
Barrandov Studios, 227, 228, 237, 240n2; *The Bridge at Remagen* (film) and, 236; as East European hub of Western film productions, 230–34
Baskakov, Vladimir, 249
Bathrick, David, 184, 185, 187
Batista, Fulgencio, 78
*Battleship Potemkin [Bronenosets Potemkin]* (film, dir. Eisenstein, 1925), 79, 80
Bauschinger, Sigrid, 185–86
BBC (British Broadcasting Corporation), 141, 150, 289
BBS (Balázs Béla Stúdió), 94, 99, 103, 111; *American Postcard* and, 106, 108–9; as "antechamber" of film industry, 101, 113n4; Community Culture Group (*Közművelődési Csoport*), 110; documentary branch, 109–11; film distribution and, 104–6; shifting membership structures at, 100–101, 113n5
Becher, Johannes R., 177
Becker, Jureck, 179
Belarus, Kekkonen's state visit to, 212, 215, 222n7
Bellanova, Rocco, 289, 291
Benjamin, Walter, 19, 27, 31, 35, 200
Benvenuto, Sergio, 89
Berendse, Gerrit-Jan, 179
Berg, Jerome S., 144–45, 149
*Berlin* (documentary film, dir. Raizman and Svilova, 1946), 161
Berlin, Irving, 45, 47
Berlinale film festival, 103, 108
*Berlin Alexanderplatz* (Döblin novel, 1929), 29
Berlin International Film Festival, 170
Berlin Wall, 7, 25, 144, 148, 149, 284
Beumers, Birgit, 248
Bezdíček, Josef, 45, 48, 52, 53, 54, 55
Bignell, Jonathan, 280
Bílek, Petr, 281
"Bit of Ethiopia, A" ["Trochę Etiopii"] (Kapuściński, 1978), 197–201

Blackbourn, David, 20
*Black Stars [Czarne gwiady]* (Kapuściński, 1963), 193, 197
*Black Tulip [La Tulipe noire]* (film, dir. Christian-Jaque, 1964), 167
Black Wave films (Yugoslavia), 102
Blas Roca Calderio, 90–91
*Boccaccio-70* (film, dir. Monicelli, Fellini, Visconti, and De Sica, 1962), 165
Bódy, Gábor, 6, 99–100, 111, 112, 113; on BBS as "antechamber" of Hungarian film industry, 101, 113n4; departure from the BBS, 109, 114n33; international circulation of *American Postcard* and, 107, 108; Mannheim Film Festival and, 103, 104; materiality of film and, 106
Boillat, Alain, 158
Bokarev, Gennady, 69
Bolshakov, Ivan, 160
Bond, James (fictional character), 277, 279, 281–82, 283
Bondarchuk, Sergei, 240n1, 250
Bondarev, Aleksandr, 166–67
Borderie, Bernard, 167
boulevard, as resurrected form, 17, 18–22, 28
*Boulevard du Temple* (Daguerre photograph, 1838 or 1839), 18
Brand, William R., 201
Brazil, 27, 81, 84
Brecht, Bertolt, 69, 84, 183
Bren, Paulina, 122
Brennan, Timothy, 205
Brezhnev, Leonid, 92, 166, 271
*bricolage*, 118, 134
*Bridge at Remagen, The* (film, dir. Guillermin, 1969), 8, 33, 227, 237, 238; film history overtaken by political history in making of, 234–36, 239–40; Wolper as producer of, 229, 234
*Bridge on the River Kwai, The* (film, dir. Lean, 1957), 167
*Brooklyn Bridge* (Rose, ca. 1953), 35
Budaev, Sergei, 160, 161
Bug-Byte Software, 119, 125
Bulgakov, Mikhail, 67, 69
Bulgaria, 170, 265, 267
Buñuel, Luis, 90

Cabrera Infante, Guillermo, 86, 88
Cabrera Infante, Sabá, 87, 88
Calvino, Italo, 201, 202

298  INDEX

Cambridge Analytica, 291
Caminito, Augusto, 254
Cannes Film Festival, 106, 113, 160, 161, 162, 167
capitalism, 134, 205, 207, 255, 279; digital technology and, 288; post-Fordist, 228; urban alienation and, 35
Caputo, Antonio, 250
Cardiff, David, 150
Casanova, Pascale, 185, 194
*Cassandra* [*Kassandra*] (Wolf novel, 1973), 186
Cassavetes, John, 162
Castro, Fidel, 77, 80, 81, 91; Cuban film directors and, 82; Western leftists' rift with, 92; "Words to the Intellectuals" address, 88, 93
Caute, David, 47
Čech, Vladimír, 82
*Cement* (Gladkov novel, 1925), 25
censorship, 122, 123, 164; in Czechoslovakia, 229; of Hungarian films, 105; loosening of, 5; in Poland, 199; self-censorship, 63, 229
*Chapayev* (film, dir. Georgy and Sergei Vasiliev, 1934), 86, 161
Chekhov, Anton, 67, 69
Chiaureli, Mikhail, 161
China, Nixon's visit to, 212
*Chinoise, La* (Godard, 1967), 165
Chkheidze, Rezo, 162
Christian-Jaque, 167
*Christ with a Rifle on His Shoulder* [*Chrystus z karabinem na ramieniu*] (Kapuściński, 1975), 193
Chukhrai, Grigory, 246, 250, 252, 253, 255
Chytilová, Věra, 104
cinema, 6–7, 35; British direct cinema, 85; cinema verité, 218; Czechoslovak New Wave, 231; French New Wave, 85; live translation and, 160–70; "runaway productions" of Hollywood in East Europe, 230, 237, 238–40, 240n2, 241n9; Soviet montage, 80; "spoken cinema," 158–59, 163, 165, 166, 170–71, 172n56. *See also* Cuba, Soviet cinema in; film festivals
Clarke, Arthur C., 262
Claus, Carlfried, 181
Clerici, Gianfranco, 250, 254, 257n41
*Closely Watched Trains* [*Ostře sledované vlaky*] (film, dir. Menzel, 1966), 238
CNC [National Council of Culture] (Cuba), 85, 91
Cold War, 47, 51, 55, 69, 211; East–West literary exchange visits during, 177–79; end of, 207; Eurocentric framing of, 102; film festivals and, 102–4, 160, 161–62; final years of, 193, 194; Finnish neutrality in, 63, 65; geopolitical order of, 52; international East German radio broadcasting during, 140–42; satellite networks and, 261, 262, 265, 271; Second–Third World relationships, 5, 196; shortwave radio and, 150; state visits during, 212, 215; technology race and, 261; televised art as site of foreign policy and, 62, 70; transnational socialist cultures of, 78; "worldmaking" projects of, 4. *See also* spies, in Cold War media
Cold War media, 2, 6, 9, 94
colonialism/colonial world, 19, 22, 26–27
*Columbo* (NBC crime show, 1971–2003), 280
COMECON (Council for Mutual Economic Assistance), 92
Comintern (Communist International), 4, 207n8
Communist Party, Cuban, 92
Communist Party, Czechoslovak, 43, 45, 51, 117, 122
Communist Party, Finnish, 64
Communist Party, French, 161
Communist Party, Hungarian, 109
Communist Party, Italian, 247
Communist Party, Polish, 197, 201, 207n9
Communist Party, Soviet, 87, 92, 158, 164, 165, 166
Communist Party, US, 181
computer games, 3, 5, 132–34; "British surrealist" game design, 120, 135n24; clones (imitations) of, 132; conversions of, 126, 127–29, *128*, *129*; microcomputer hobbyists in Czechoslovakia, 7; as niche entertainment, 118; ports of, 126, 127, 128; software piracy and, 124
*Comrade Detective* (Amazon Prime television spy drama, 2017), 277, 284–85, 292n19
comsat (communications satellite) industry, 261
Comsat corporation, 263–64
Connery, Sean, 250
Constantin Film (Germany), 229, 232
contact zones, 159
copyright, 5, 123, 126, 129, 183
Cortez, Stanley, 235
cosmopolitanism, 52, 55; anticosmopolitanism, 43, 51, 57n40; of Cuban cinema, 93

INDEX 299

*Counterpart* (Starz Network television spy drama, 2017–), 277, 286
*Cranes Are Flying, The* [*Letiat zhuravli*] (Kalatozov, 1957), 86
*Crime Scene* [*Tatort*] (West German TV police drama, 1970–), 280, 281
Cristaldi, Vides di Franco, 249
*Cristobal Colón* [*Christopher Columbus*] (Kožik and Bezdíček, radio play, 1934), 45
Crosby, Bing, 47
Cuba: Intersputnik network and, 265; intervention in Angolan civil war, 254
Cuba, Soviet cinema in, 6, 77–83, 93–94; Cuban film culture and, 78; cultural polemics of 1960s and, 86–93; Socialist Bloc coproductions, 82–83; Soviet cinema in prerevolutionary Cuba, 83–85. *See also* ICAIC
Cuban Missile Crisis, 77, 81
Cukor, George, 167
cybernetics, 7, 122
Czechoslovak Filmexport (Československý filmexport), 232, 234, 236, 239
Czechoslovakia, 4, 22, 79, 170; American / Western films shot in, 229–40; debates on socialist realism in, 47–48; ethnic Germans in, 29; experimental modernist architecture in, 27–28; Intersputnik network and, 265, 267; Karlovy Vary Film Festival, 80, 82, 160, 167; Koliba studios (Bratislava), 238; Normalization period (post-1969), 236; Sovietization in, 48, 55; television detective shows in, 281–82; Western radio broadcasts received in, 52, 57n68. *See also* Prague, city of
Czechoslovakia, computer gaming in, 118, 121–22, 132–34; copyright and, 123–24, 138n32; *Manic Miner* as game to program with, 124–26; *Manic Miner*'s arrival in, 123–24; modifications to *Manic Miner*, 126–29, *128*, *129*; Svazarm (Union for Cooperation with the Army) clubs, 122, 127; "*vnye*" milieus and, 122
Czechoslovakia, Warsaw Pact invasion of (1968), 81, 91, 165, 227, 238; international shock and revulsion at, 25; making of *The Bridge at Remagen* interrupted by, 8, 235–36, 239–40
Czechoslovak Radio, 6, 43, 44, 48, 54; "golden age" of, 45, 56n9; show trials broadcast by, 51, 52, 57n57; socialist-realist jazz at, 48–51, 55
Czechoslovak State Film (Československý státní film), 227–28, 231, 234, 241n31

Daguerre, Louis, 18
Damrosch, David, 177, 184, 185, 186, 187, 194
Dárday, István, 99, 109, 111
Davis, Angela, 181, *182*, 186
De Laurentiis, Dino, 229, 240n1, 249
Denning, Michael, 177
*Derrick* (West German TV police drama, 1974–1998), 280
De Santis, Giuseppe, 164, 247
De Sica, Vittorio, 165, 250
*Deutschland 83, 86,* and *89* (AMC Networks and RTL television drama, 2015–), 278, 287, 293n22
Dietch, Gene, 231–32, 241n26
digital technology, 8, 285, 288
*Divided Heaven* [*Der geteilte Himmel*] (Wolf novel), 184, 189n69
Dixon, Christa, 180, 181
Djagalov, Rossen, 53, 102, 159, 177, 188n15
Döblin, Alfred, 29
Doctorow, E. L., 178
*Dolce vita, La* (film, dir. Fellini, 1960), 90
Domosławski, Artur, 193, 201–2, 207n1
*Donkey Kong* (computer game, 1981), 120
*Don Quijote* [*Don Kikhot*] (film, dir. Kozintsev, 1957), 86
doppelgänger motif, 286–87
Dorůžka, Lubomir, 49–50
Dósai, István, 105
Dostoyevsky, Fyodor, 67
*Dragon, The* (Shvarts play, 1944), 61
Drutse, Ion, 61
Dubček, Alexander, 235
Du Bocage, Francisco, 27, 35
Ducháč, Miloslav, 49, 50
Dürrenmatt, Friedrich, 178
Duvivier, Julien, 230
Dvořák, Antonín, 45, 56n30
DXers (shortwave radio enthusiasts), 144
*Dynamite Dan* (computer game), 129–30

East Berlin, 20, 23, 28, 37n27; Davis (Angela) in, 181, *182*; rebuilding of Alexanderplatz, 29–30. *See also* Stalinallee [Stalin Boulevard]
EBU (European Broadcasting Union), 64–65, 278
Eisenstein, Sergei, 79–81, 83, 84, 89–90, 95n29, 170
Eixample District (Barcelona), 19
Elek, Judit, 99

Elstree Studios (Britain), 280
Emmerich, Wolfgang, 183
*Emperor, The: Downfall of an Autocrat [Cesarz]* (Kapuściński, 1978/1983), 7, 194–95, 207n1, 208n26; as allegory in Poland, 197–201; anglophone reception of allegory, 201–6
Engels, Friedrich, 19, 28
Erdman, Nikolai, 69
Ergas, Moris, 229, 231
Ermash, Filipp, 253, 255
Estonian Soviet Socialist Republic, 1
Ethiopia, 26, 197–98, 203, 206
ETV (Estonian television), 1, 3
Europe, Eastern, 4, 33, 203, 206; film festivals in, 80; Hollywood movies shot in, 227–40; Intervision TV network, 263; monumental aesthetic in, 29; panoramic boulevards in socialist cities, 19–20; popularity of West German television police dramas in, 280; rebuilding of war-destroyed cities in, 27; urban space in, 6
Europe, Western, 2, 5; Czechoslovak computer enthusiasts in, 123; Eurovision TV network, 263; satellite networks and, 264, 267; Socialist Bloc films screened in, 100
European Concerts (1930s), 4
Eurovision (West European TV network), 263
Eurovision Song Contest, 4
Eutelsat (European satellite network), 271
Evans, Christine, 8, 282, 283
*Every Day War [Co dzień wojna]* (Passent, 1968), 195
Evtushenko, Evgeny, 88
*Experimental Cinema* (US journal), 83
*Exterminating Angel* (film, dir. Buñuel, 1962), 90
*Eyes on Mexico [Oczy na Meksyk]* (Bańkowicz and Ziemny, 1968), 196

Fábera, Miloslav, 237
*Faces* (film, dir. Cassavetes, 1968), 162
*Family Nest [Családi tűzfészek]* (film, dir. Tarr, 1977), 6, 100, 101; docu-fiction film opportunities and, 109–11, *110*; Hungarian victories at Mannheim Film Festival and, 111–12
fascism, 21, 28–29
Fassone, Riccardo, 118
Fehervary, Helen, 186–87
Feinberg, Melissa, 45–46, 51

Feldman, Milton, 235
Fellini, Federico, 90, 164, 165
feminism, 7, 185, 187, 190n77
Ferrez, Marc, 27
Fídler, Miroslav, 123, 132
film festivals, 3, 6–7; Soviet and Eastern European, 80, 82, 102, 159; Soviet film translation at European festivals, 160–63; Western, 108. *See also* Mannheim Film Festival
*Filmkultúra* (Hungarian film magazine), 108, 112, 113n5
Film Language Series [Filmnyelvi sorozat] (Hungary), 101
Finland, 1, 7–8, 66, 142; Civil War (1918), 69; neutrality of, 2, 9n3, 63, 64, 71; political parties, 64. *See also* MTV [Mainos-TV, Finland]; YLE [Yleisradio]
Finlandization, 62, 71
Finnish-Soviet relations, 2, 9n3, 61, 62, 70–71; computer games and, 118; doublespeak and, 65, 71; Finland's independence linked to October Revolution, 61, 66; Finland-Soviet Society, 69; neutrality as balancing act, 64–65; nuclear energy technology and, 218, 219; sauna diplomacy, 219; "Soviet Literature" ("Neuvostokirjallisuutta") series, 70; televised repertory theater and, 67–70; televisuality of state visits, 211–21; Treaty of Friendship, Cooperation, and Mutual Assistance (1948), 63; World War II and, 215, 217
FIPRESCI (International Federation of Film Critics), 170
Fitzgerald, Ella, 50
*Five Days in June* (Heym novel, 1959), 26
Flakierski, Henryk, 204
*flânerie* (urban strolling), 19
Flo, Juan J., 89, 90
Fogel, Susanna, 277
formalism, 47, 87
Forman, Miloš, 237
*For Whom Havana Dances [Para quién baila La Habana]* (film, dir. Čech, 1962), 82
Foundation for European Intellectual Cooperation, 178
*Foundation Pit, The [Kotlovan]* (Platonov novel, 1930), 25
Fraga, Jorge, 89
France, 178, 229, 266
Franco London Films, 229

INDEX 301

Frank, Karl Hermann, 29
"Freedom Train, The" (Berlin), 45
"Freedom Train, The" (United States, 1947–1949), 46–47
*French Lessons [Ranskantunnit]* (TV drama, dir. Tashkov, 1980), 68
FRG [Federal Republic of Germany] (West Germany), 145, 176, 180; film festivals in, 103, 113; GDR literature in, 183, 185; Goethe Institute funded by, 182; Hallstein Doctrine, 178–79, 188n24; Independent Film company, 232; Mannheim Film Festival, 6; Ostpolitik (Eastern policy), 103; tabletop games from, 134; television police dramas from, 280
Friedlaender, Jan, 50
Frisch, Max, 178, 201
*From Evening to Midday* (Rozov play, 1970), 61, 67
"From Warsaw, 1982" ["Z Warszawy, 1982"] (Kapuściński), 199
*Fuera del juego [Out of the Game]* (Padilla, poetry collection, 1968), 91
Fuka, František, 117
Furman, Roman, 68

Gagarin, Yuri, 263
Galatea Spa (Italian film company), 247
Garcia Buchaca, Edith, 89
García Espinosa, Julio, 84, 89
García Lorca, Federico, 67
García Márquez, Gabriel, 177
Gatewood, Brian, 285
Gazzara, Ben, 235
GDR [German Democratic Republic] (East Germany), 4, 17, 170, 177, 187, 232; Aufbau Verlag (Press of the Rebuilding), 20; demise of, 26, 149, 281; diplomatic recognition of, 142, 178–79, 188n24; disintegration of communist authority in, 147–49; international isolation of, 186; Intersputnik network and, 265, 267; Leipzig film festival, 103; literary exchange visits and, 177, 178–79; making of *The Bridge at Remagen* and, 235; national anthem, 20, 36n11, 139; reconstruction projects in, 20; Stalinism in, 25; Stasi surveillance of literary scene, 179, 182–83, 187n3, 188n32; Swedish-language radio broadcasts from, 7, 139; television detective shows in, 280–81; US academics' visits to, 184; Writers' Union, 182–83,

188n32. *See also* Berlin Wall; East Berlin; RBI (Radio Berlin International); SED [Sozialistische Enheitspartei Deutschlands]
Geithner, Michael, 134
Gelman, Aleksandr, 61, 68, 69
General Directorate of Film [Filmfőigazgatóság] (Hungary), 101, 113n3
geopolitics, 2, 8, 77, 78, 102, 206; of film markets, 251–52; undermined by "hidden integration," 272n10
Germany, East. *See* GDR
Germany, Nazi. *See* Nazism
Germany, West. *See* FRG
Gershwin, George, 50
Getino, Octavio, 82
Gielżyński, Wojciech, 196
Gierek, Edward, 197, 199
GIK [later, VGIK] (Moscow film school), 83
Gilbert, Lewis, 237
Gladkov, Fyodor, 25
Glinka, Mikhail, 48
globalization, 177, 194, 201, 240, 261, 271
Global North, 194
Global South, 3, 104, 112, 194, 208n10
Godard, Jean-Luc, 165, 168
Gogol, Nikolai, 67, 69
*Golem* (film, dir. Duvivier), 230
González Fuster, Gloria, 289, 291
Gorky, Maksim, 61, 67, 68, 69, 177
Gorky Studio for Children's and Youth Films (Soviet Central Television), 282
Gosfil'mofond (Soviet State Film Repository), 163, 165, 168
Grade, Lew, 250
*Granta* magazine / Granta Books, 194
Grass, Günter, 201
*Great Hack, The* (Netflix documentary, 2019), 291
Gregor, Ulrich, 108, 170
Guevara, Alfredo, 80, 82–85, 90, 93
Guevara, Che, 81, 91
Guillermin, John, 8, 33, 235, 236, 239
Gunning, Tom, 159
Gutiérrez Alea, Tomás, 84, 89, 90

*Hackerville* (TNT Serie/HBO Europe, 2018), 293n22
Haile Selassie I, 194, 197, 198, 199, 201
*Handmaid's Tale, The* (Hulu television drama, 2017–), 277–78
Harcourt Brace Jovanovich, 194, 201, 205

Haussmann, Baron, 18–19, 28
Havana Cultural Congress (1968), 78
Havel, Miloš, 230
HBO (Home Box Office), 286, 287, 293n22
Henninger, Gerhard, 182
Hermlin, Stephan, 181, 183
"heterolingual address," 159, 170
Heym, Stefan, 20–21, 26, 179
Hill, George Roy, 236, 237
Hine, Lewis, 24
Hitchens, Gordon, 169
Hoffman, Jerzy, 169
Hoffmann, Kurt, 232
*Holiday in Britain* [*Jutalomutazás*] (film, dir. Dárday, 1974), 111
Holland, Agnieszka, 287
*Homeland* (Showtime television drama, 2011–), 277
"homolingual address," 159, 162, 170
Honecker, Erich, 142, 182
*House in Karp Lane, The* [*Das Haus in der Karpfengasse*] (TV film, dir. Hoffmann, 1963), 232
*House of Cards* (BBC television series, 1990s), 289
"Housing Question, The" (Engels, 1872), 19
*Howling II: Stirba—Werewolf Bitch* (film, dir. Mora, 1985), 237
Hulu, 277, 286
Hungarofilm, 104, 114n17
Hungary, 4, 229, 233; Academy of Theater and Film Arts (Színház-és Filmművészeti Főiskola), 99; Budapest School (Budapesti Iskola) of filmmaking, 109, 111; film studio system in, 99; Film Week, 104, 107, 108, 114n30; General Directorate of Film (Filmfőigazgatóság), 101, 113n3; Hungarian Uprising (1956), 25, 85, 100; Intersputnik network and, 265; Petöf Circle, 88; social distribution (*társadalmi forgalmazás*), 110, 114n40. *See also* BBS (Balázs Béla Stúdió)

*I Am Cuba* [*Ia Kuba / Soy Cuba*] (film, dir. Kalatozov, 1964), 82, 83
*I Am Twenty* [*Mne dvadtsat' let*] (film, dir. Khutsiev, 1965), 162
Iarmatov, Kamil, 169
ICAIC (Cuban Institute of Cinematic Art and Industry), 78, 80, 81, 83, 93; *Cine Cubano* magazine, 80, 84, 88, 90; cultural polemics of 1960s and, 87–92; Declaration of the Cuban Filmmakers (1971), 92; dogmatist, revolutionary, and liberal camps, 85–86, 92; La Rampa movie theater, 79; Socialist Bloc coproductions and, 82; socialist realism and, 88–89; Valdés-Rodríguez and, 84; "What Is Modern in Art?" roundtable (1962), 88
*Idiot, The* [*Idiot*] (film, dir. Pyryev, 1958), 79
*If All of Africa* [*Gdyby cala Afryka*] (Kapuściński, 1969), 193
Ikenberry, John J., 150
*Imperium* (Kapuściński, 1993), 206
Imre, Anikó, 8, 64
Independent Film company (Germany), 232
India, 37n22, 183, 266, 273n33
Indonesia, 177
*Indonesia, Archipelago of Unrest* [*Indonezja, archipelag niepokojów*] (Gielżyński, 1966), 196
infrastructure, 3, 30; of computer gaming, 133–34; European-style colonial capitals, 27; global satellite communications, 8, 261, 262, 265, 271, 272n10; media, 2, 5, 58n69
Ingawanij, May Adadol, 158
Innis, Harold, 52
intellectual property, 92, 134, 273n42
INTELSTAT (US-led satellite network), 260–62; negotiations to integrate with Soviet bloc, 268–70; overtures to Soviet bloc, 263–65; Soviets' proposal of Intersputnik as alternative to, 265–68, 273n32
Interkosmos, 265, 267, 269, 274n54
International Broadcasting Union, 4
International Union of Architects (Moscow, 1958), 17, 29, 30
Intersputnik (Soviet-led satellite network), 260–62, 265–68, 269, 270, 271, 273n32
Intervision (East European TV network), 263
Iosseliani, Otar, 170
Iowa Writer's Workshop, 178
IREX (International Research and Exchange Board), 184, 189n63
Iron Curtain, 4, 8, 47, 255; circulation of Western film and music behind, 117; collapse of, 177; film coproductions across, 247; Hollywood movies shot behind, 227, 229
*Iskusstvo kino* [*Cinema Art*] (Soviet journal), 164
*Island of Swans* [*Insel der Schwäne*] (Pludra novel, 1980; Zschoche film, 1983), 37n20
*I Spy* (television spy series), 280

Italy, 79, 179, 229; armed struggles and terrorism in, 246; history of Italian-Soviet film coproductions, 246–49; State Central Archive [ACS] (Rome), 246; *strategia della tensione* (tension strategy) in, 253; Union of Italian Film Producers (ANICA), 248

*Itemiada* (Fídler, computer game, 1985), 132

*It's a Mad, Mad, Mad, Mad World* (film, dir. Kramer, 1963), 167

ITU (International Telecommunication Union), 278

*Ivan the Terrible*, Part II [*Ivan Grozny*] (film, dir. Eisenstein, 1958), 89–90

*Ivan the Terrible* [*Ivan Grozny*] (film, dir. Eisenstein, 1944), 86

Jameson, Frederic, 202
jamming, of Western radio broadcasts, 5, 51
Jandera, Miloslav, 235
Japan, 251, 252; *benshi* commentators for silent film, 158; computer games in, 119, 120; nationalist imperialism in, 177
Jaruzelski, General Wojciech, 201
jazz, socialist-realist, 6, 43, 48–51, 55
Jelenković, Dunja, 102
Jenne, Daniel, 128, 130
Jeschke, Felix, 53
*Jet Set Willy* (Smith, computer game), 117, 118, 120–21, 130; copyright and, 129, 138n32; *Itemiada* imitation of (1985), 132; modifications to, 126; UK modifications of, 133; VBG Software conversion and, 131
Ježek, Jaroslav, 50
Johnson, Lyndon B., 263, 264, 269, 270
Judt, Tony, 51
Julius Fučík choir, 44, 56n6

Kadár, Ján, 231, 238
Kafka, Franz, 290
Kalatozov, Mikhail, 82, 86, 89, 161
Kant, Hermann, *180*
Kapuściński, Ryszard, 7, 193–95; anglophone reception of, 201–6; dissolution of Socialist Bloc and, 206–7; *The Emperor* as allegorical work, 197–201; socialist reportage as world literature and, 195–97
Karaganov, Aleksandr, 166
Karmen, Roman, 79
Kataev, Valentin, 69
Kazakov, Yuri, 68

"Kde domov můj?" ["Where is my home?"] (Czech national anthem), 45, 56n30
Kekkonen, Urho, 212, 213, 214, 216, 222n25; Kosygin's state visit to Finland and, 216–19; resignation from office, 220
Kennedy, Helen, 292
Kęplicz, Klemens, 196
Khaldei, Yevgeny, 24
Khruschchev, Nikita, 212, 216; Cuba and, 90; "secret speech" of (1956), 25, 30
Khutsiev, Marlen, 162
Kiev, city of, 163
*Kindheitsmuster* [*A Model Childhood / Patterns of Childhood*] (Wolf novel), 181, 189n38
Kiš, Danilo, 205
Kleiman, Naum, 164, 170
Klement, Jan, 237
Klos, Elmar, 231, 238
Koliba studios (Czechoslovakia), 238
Kopecký, Václav, 47, 48, 52
Korean War, 17
Korhonen, Keijo, 70
Kosygin, Aleksei, 212, 216–19, 222n32
Kovács, András Bálint, 111
Kovály, Heda Margolius, 51
Kožík, František, 48, 52, 53, 55, 55n1; as Esperantist, 54; as theorist of radio, 45
Kozintsev, Grigoriy, 86
Kraków film festival, 101
Kramer, Stanley, 167
Kronick, William, 236
Kuleshov, Lev, 81, 84, 95n29
Kulič, Bohuslav, 235
Kumar, Devendra, 162
Kundera, Milan, 205
Kurosawa, Akira, 168
Kyrgyzstan (Kirghiz Soviet Socialist Republic), 212, 213–14, 222n7

Langer, Jo, 50
Länsipuro, Yrjö, 212, 219, 222n32
Larkin, Brian, 118
*Last Ones, The* (Gorky play, 1908), 61, 67, 68
Latin America, 83, 93, 159, 252
Lawrence, D. H., 67
Lawrence, Francis, 277, 283–84
League of Nations, 4
Leal, Orlando Jiménez, 87–88
Lean, David, 167
Leander, Zarah, 149

Le Corbusier, 28
Leitch, David, 277, 284
Lenin, Vladimir, 84
Leningrad, 38n36, 163; film schools in, 164; Moskovsky Prospect, 28; World War II memorials in, 215
Letfus, Oldřich, 44, 45, 50, 52, 55, 56n30
*Letterbox, The* [*Briefkasten / Brevlådan*] (RBI program), 140, 142–44, 145, 146, 150
Levine, Joseph, 250
Lévi-Strauss, Claude, 118
Lewis, Alison, 179
Leyda, Jay, 169–70
Libovický, Vit, 128, 130, 136n51
Lieber, Heinz, 29–30
*Life Is Beautiful* [*La vita è bella / Zhizn' prekrasna*] (film, dir. Chukhrai, 1979), 8, 246, 255–56; geopolitics of film markets and, 251–52; plot summary, 245; political / artistic difficulties in project conception, 249–50; terrorism in southern Europe censored in, 252–55
"linear city," 23
linguistics, 159
Lioznova, Tatiana, 282
*littérisation* process, 194, 205
"Living Under the Rain" (García Espinosa, 1963), 89
Livshits, M. U., 157–58
Lobato, Ramon, 118, 292
Lombardo, Goffredo, 249
*Lone Man in Revolt*. See *Life Is Beautiful* [*La vita è bella / Zhizn' prekrasna*]
Lonská, Zuzka, 50
Löwenthal, Richard, 62
Lunacharskii, Anatoly, 84
*Lunes de Revolución* (Cuban film journal), 86, 88, 92
Lu Xun, 177

Maár, Gyula, 99
MacDermott, Kevin, 51
machine learning algorithms, 289–90, 293n35
Maetzig, Kurt, 22, 82
magical realism, 194, 198, 201
*Maglaxians* (Fídler, computer game, 1985), 132
Magnitogorsk, city of, 31, 38n36
*Magyar Filmszemle* (Hungarian film review), 104
Malý, Martin, 125–26
Mamoulian, Ruben, 64

*Man from UNCLE, The* (television spy series), 280
*Manic Miner* (Smith, computer game), 117, 118–19; copyright and, 138n32; Czechoslovak clones and modifications of, 123, 126–32, 128–32, 133–34, 136n51; early development of, 119–21; Libovický / Jenne PMD 85 conversion, 127–28, 129; *Maglaxians* imitation of (1985), 132; Martiník ZX81 conversion, 127, 128, 134; opening screen of original version, 121; reception in UK and Czechoslovakia, 119, 120, 124–25, 133; Sharp MZ-800 porting of, 128; UK modifications of, 133; variantology of, 118; VBG Software conversion (1987), 131; *Willy Walker* (Šuhajda) inspired by, 130–31
*Manic Miner 2* (Schultze, computer game), 133
Mann, Delbert, 237
Mann, Thomas, 183
Mannheim Film Festival (West Germany), 6, 100, 113, 191; awards for Hungarian films at, 111–12; Eastern European cinemas and, 102–4
Marcus, Harold G., 200, 202
Markvartová, Jitka, 237
Maron, Monika, 179
Martin, Paul, 232
Martiník, Aleš, 127, 134
Marx, Karl, 19
*Mary Poppins* (film, dir. Stevenson, 1964), 167
Maselli, Francesco, 157
*Massacre at Marble City* [*Die Goldsucher von Arkansas*] (film, dir. Martin, 1964), 232
May, Gisela, 179
Mayakovsky, Vladimir, 17
McAvoy, James, 284
McDonald, Peter D., 183
McQuillan, Dan, 289, 290
Meiselas, Nancy, 181–82
*Men at Work* (Hine photograph, 1932), 24
Menzel, Jiří, 238
Mexico, films from, 79, 81
Meyerhold, Vsevolod, 69
MGM film studio, 231, 240n1
Mifune, Tpshiro, 168
Mikhalev, Aleksei, 166
Mikoyan, Anastas, 79
Miller, Arthur, 178
Minsk, city of: Sovetskaia Street, 28; Victory Square, 38n36
*Minutes of a Meeting* (Gelman play, 1974), 61

*Mirror, The [Zerkalo]* (film, dir. Tarkovsky, 1975), 169
*Mission Impossible* (television spy series), 280
modernization, 22, 27, 77
Molniia (Soviet domestic satellite system), 264, 268, 274n54
Monaco, Eitel, 247–48
Mongolia, 265
Monicelli, Mario, 165
*Monty Mole* (computer game), 129–30
Moore, Christine, 177
Mora, Philippe, 237
*More than a Life at Stake [Stawka większa niż życie]* (Polish television spy drama, 1967–1968), 282
Moro, Aldo, 253, 255
Moscow, city of: GIK (later, VGIK) film school, 83; Kutuzov Prospect, 30; Mira Avenue, 38n36; movie theaters in, 163; Red Square, 28; Tverskaya, 37n26
Moscow International Film Festival, 159, 162–63, 166, 167, 168, 169
*Moscow Under Reconstruction* (Rodchenko and Varvara photobook, 1938), 22–23, 30
Most (Czechoslovakia), city of, 33–34, 35, 227, 235
*Mother [Mat]* (film, dir. Pudovkin, 1926), 80
Mowitt, John, 158
Mroczkowska-Brand, Katarzyna, 201
MTV (Mainos-TV, Finland), 1, 2, 6, 61, 70–71; cultural doublespeak of, 71; media policy as striving for cultural legitimacy, 65–67; MTV-Theater, 66, 67–69; relation to YLE, 221n1; Soviet dramas televised by, 62, 63
Müller, Heiner, 179
Murúa, Lautaro, 90
music, 1, 5; pop music on East German radio, 140–41, 145, 149; Soviet campaign against popular music, 48–49; Western music behind the Iron Curtain, 117, 134
Mussolini, Benito, 28, 160, 204
Muybridge, Eadweard, 27
*My Fair Lady* (film, dir. Cukor, 1964), 167–68

Napolitano, Gian Gaspare, 249
*Narcissus and Psyche [Nárcisz és Psyché]* (Bódy, 1980), 109
nationalism, 3, 4, 207, 288
national liberation, 77, 81, 204
NATO (North Atlantic Treaty Organization), 248, 254

Nazism, 26, 29, 167, 182, 237; colonizing plans for Eastern Europe, 20; in Socialist bloc television spy dramas, 282; Third Reich film industry, 230
*Neighbor Quiz / Friendship Match [Naapurivisa / Sõprusvõistlus]* (Finnish-Estonian TV show, 1966), 1–3
Nejedlý, Zdeněk, 48, 56n30, 57n40
Netflix, 286, 287, 288–89, 291, 292
New Latin American Cinema, 80, 81
New Left, 81, 183
New Objectivity, 33
New Photography, 33
*New World Symphony* (Dvořák), 45
New York City, 35
*Night of the Generals, The* (film, dir. Litvak, 1967), 240n1
Nikkilä, Reijo, 212
*1983* (Netflix television drama, 2018–), 278, 287
*Ninety Degrees in the Shade* (film, dir. Weiss, 1965), 231, 235
Nintendo, 120
Nixon, Richard, 212, 271
Nonaligned movement (NAM), 78, 208n10
Nornes, Abé Mark, 158
nostalgia (*Ostalgie*), 8, 283
*Noticiero ICAIC Latinoamericano* (documentary newsreels), 88
Noujaim, Jehane, 291
Novak, Helga, 180
Nuestro Tiempo (cultural society in Cuba), 81, 84, 85

Oberhausen film festival, 102, 103–4, 105, 106
*October* (film, dir. Aleksandrov and Eisenstein, 1927), 80
Odermann, Heinz, 143
OIRT (Organisation Internationale de Radiodiffusion et de Télévision), 64–65, 278
*Old India in a New World [Stare Indie w nowym świecie]* (Kęplicz, 1964), 196
Ondříček, Miroslav, 237
"One Day in the Life of Ivan Denisovich" (Solzhenitsyn), 90
*Operation: Daybreak* (film, dir. Gilbert, 1979), 237
"Order to the Army of Art, An" (Mayakovsky, 1918), 17
*Origin of German Tragic Drama, The* (Benjamin), 200

ORM (Czechoslovak electronic music duo), 134
Orwell, George, 289
Ostrovsky, Aleksandr, 69
*Othello* [*Otello*] (film, dir. Yutkevich, 1956), 79
*Our World* broadcast (1967), 264
*Outsider, The* [*Szabadgyalog*] (film, dir. Tarr, 1990), 111

Pabst, G. W., 86
Padilla, Heberto, 88, 91–92
Pakistan, 266, 273n33
Palme, Olof, 142
*Pandora's Box* [*Puszka Pandory*] (Polish computer game, 1986), 134
*Panoramic Prague* [*Praha panoramatická*] (Sudek photobook, 1959), 22, 31; Karlín district, 32; "Near Invalidovna in the Karlin District," 33, 34; "Pankrác," 32–33
Papuc, Viorela Dana, 212
Paramount Pictures, 240n1
Paris, 18, 28, 162; Atget's photographs of, 31; Champs Elysées, 29; Haussmann's reconstruction of, 19, 30
Parks, Lisa, 261
Pasolini, Pier Paolo, 90
Passent, Daniel, 195
Pasternak, Boris, 88, 201
*Pastorale* [*Pastorali*] (film, dir. Iosseliani, 1975), 170
Patalas, Enno, 103
*Peace Train, The* [*Vlak míru*] (radio cantata, Czechoslovak Radio, 1950), 6, 43–44, 54–55; as cosmopolitan piece, 51, 52; influences on, 45–48; socialist internationalism of, 53–54; socialist-realist jazz and, 49, 50; structure and sound of, 44–45
Penguin Books, 194, 205
Peroutka, Ferdinand, 52
Petelski, Czesław, 169
Petőfi Circle (Hungary), 88
Petrov, B. N., 265
photography, 3, 18, 23, 26
photopanoramas, 6, 17, 172n56; American dream and, 35; critiqued through its own formal qualities, 31–35; crowds and social distance in, 28–31; as experimental and revolutionary form, 22; mass rallies evoked in, 28; between modernization and colonialism, 26–28; as resurrected form, 17, 18–22; Stalinist reconstruction projects and, 31
*Physicists, The* [*Die Physiker*] (Dürrenmatt play), 178
Platonov, Andrei, 25
Plenzdorf, Ulrich, 179
*PM (Pasado meridiano)* (film, dir. Leal and Cabrera Infante, 1961), 87–88
Poland, 4, 48, 193, 194; American films shot in, 240n1; Intersputnik network and, 265; Kapuściński's *The Emperor* as allegory of, 197–201; KOR [Komitet Obrony Robotników] (Worker' Defense Committee), 204; Law and Justice Party (PiS), 287; martial law regime (1981–1983), 201; socialist internationalism reportage from, 195–97; Solidarność (Solidarity) movement, 195, 201, 204–5
Polanski, Roman, 171
Poledňák, Alois, 235
*Police Call* [*Polizeiruf 110*] (GDR TV police drama, 1971–), 281, 285
Polish Press Agency (PAP), 197
*Polityka* (Polish newsmagazine), 193, 195
Ponti, Carlo, 229, 231, 250
populism, 278, 285
Porter, Cole, 50
Portugal, 246, 249, 252; African colonies of, 254; Carnation Revolution (1974), 246, 254, 255
Prague, city of, 31, 38n43, 46, 230, 236; Nazi occupation of, 32; Pařížská street, 19; SS General Heydrich assassinated in, 237; Station of Young Technicians, 122, 123
Pratt, Mary Louise, 159
*Preludio 11* (film, dir. Maetzig, 1964), 82
Prescott, Peter, 203
Proshkin, Aleksandr, 68
Pudovkin, Vsevolod, 80, 81, 84
Puhlmann, Gerhard, 17, 23–24, 30
Purš, Jiří, 236
Putin, Vladimir, 283
Pyonyang (North Korea), city of, 17, 28
Pyryev, Ivan, 79

Quattro Cavalli Cinematografica, 246, 250, 252, 253
*Quest for Christa T (Christa T), The* [*Nachdenken über Christa T*] (Wolf novel, 1968), 176, 184, 185, 187n3, 187n4

Racheev, V. A., 266
radio, 3, 5; as (anti)cosmopolitan medium, 43–44, 51–53; BBC (British Broadcasting Corporation), 141, 150; Deutsche Welle (DW), 149; one-to-one personal address of, 145–46; Radio Free Europe, 50, 52, 57n68, 141; Radio Moscow, 48, 141; Radio Prague, 141; shortwave, 7, 144, 150; Sovietization and, 43; Voice of America, 50, 141; Western stations, 141, 150n5. *See also* Czechoslovak Radio; RBI (Radio Berlin International)
*Radio Art* [*Rozhlasové umění*] (Kožík, 1940), 45
Radio Berlin International. *See* RBI
*Raid Over Moscow* (computer game), 118
railroads, 53, 58n69
Raizman, Yuli, 161
Rakowski, Mieczysław, 195, 207n9
Rand, Max, 220
Rappoport, Gerald J., 231, 237
RBI (Radio Berlin International), 7, 139; Danish-language broadcasts, 151n12; emergence of alternative script (1989), 146–49; end of, 149–50; international broadcasting during Cold War, 140–42; *The Letterbox* (*Briefkasten* / *Brevlådan*), 140, 142–44, 145, 146, 150; Swedish-language broadcasts, 142; Swedish listeners of, 144–46, 150, 151n20
Recife (Brazil), dismantling and rebuilding of, 27, 35
Rectanus, Mark, 184
*Red Beard* [*Akahige*] (film, dir. Kurosawa, 1965), 168
*Red Desert* [*Il deserto rosso*] (film, dir. Antonioni, 1964), 168
*Red Sparrow* (film, dir. Lawrence, 2018), 277, 283–84
*Red Tent, The* [*La tenda rossa* / *Krasnaia palatka*] (film, dir. Kalatozov, 1968), 249, 250
regionalism, 4
Riazanov, Eldar, 250
*Riders of Revolution* [*Vsadniki revolutsii*] (film, dir. Iarmatov, 1968), 169
Ringstrasse (Vienna), 19, 37n26
Ritman, Colin, 121, 135n23
Roberts, Geoffrey, 46
Robeson, Paul, 46
Rodchenko, Alexander, 22–23, 30, 36n16
Romania, 170, 229, 233, 265, 285, 293n22

Rose, Ben, 35
Roth, Philip, 205
Rozov, Viktor, 61, 67, 68
Rushdie, Salman, 202
Rusk, Dean, 270
Russian State Archive for Literature and Art (RGAI), 246
Ruttmann, Walter, 86
Rylek, Tomáš, 123, 132
*Ryszard Kapuściński: A Life* (Domosławski, 2013), 193

*Sad Landscape* [*Smutná krajina*] (Sudek, 1959–1962), 33, 34
*Saint, The* (British television spy series), 280, 292n5
Sakai, Naoki, 159, 162
Salazkina, Masha, 6, 102, 159
Santi, Nello, 247, 249, 251, 255
*Saplings, The* [*Nergebi*] (film, dir. Chkheidze, 1972), 162
Sarnoff, David, 262
satellite television/telephone networks, 3, 260, 262–63
sauna diplomacy, 219, 222n30
Scannell, Paddy, 145–46, 150
Schinkel, Karl Friedrich, 21
Schnapp, Jeffrey, 28
Schütz, Helga, 179
Schwartz, Evgeny, 67
Schwoch, James, 261, 263
Second World, 7, 158, 187n8, 195, 196, 207
SED [Sozialistische Enheitspartei Deutschlands] (Socialist Unity Party), 139, 140, 143–44, 147, 149. *See also* GDR [German Democratic Republic]
Segal, George, 235
Semenov, Iulian, 282
Seven Seas (GDR publishing house), 183, 189n55, 189n69
*Seventeen Moments of Spring* [*Semnadtsat mgnoveniy vesny*] (Soviet television spy drama, 1973), 282–83
*Shadow of the Sun, The* [*Heban*] (Kapuściński, 1998 / 2001), 202, 206
Shakespeare, William, 67
Shapiro, Alan, 229
Shaw, George Bernard, 67
Shohat, Ella, 158
*Shop on Main Street, The* [*Obchod na korze*] (film, dir. Kadár and Klos, 1965), 238

*Short Story from Autumn in the Oak Woods [Jonninjoutavaa]* (TV drama, dir. Virtanen, 1978), 68
Shukshin, Vasily, 69
Shvarts, Evgeny, 61, 69
Siddiqi, Asif, 262
Siefert, Marsha, 240n4, 247
Silicon Valley, 288
*Silk Stockings* (film, dir. Mamoulian, 1957), 64
Silverstein, Bob, 235
Simmons, J. K., 286
Sinclair Research, 119
*Sinn und Form* (GDR literary journal), 181
Siodmak, Kurt, 233
Sizov, Nikolai, 249, 251
*Ski Fever* (film, dir. Siodmak, 1966), 233
Skórzewski, Edward, 169
Škvorecký, Josef, 49, 57n43
Slánský, Rudolf, show trial of, 51, 52
*Slaughterhouse-Five* (film, dir. Hill, 1972), 236–37
Smetana, Bedřich, 48
Smith, Matthew, 117, 124–25, 128, 130, 134n3; American game designers as influence on, 133; as bedroom coder, 119; development of *Manic Miner*, 119–20; as "merchant of mayhem," 121, 126, 135n23; reaction to Martiník's ZX81 version, 134, 136n61
Snyder, William L., 231
*Soccer War, The [Wojna futbolowa]* (Kapuściński, 1978), 193, 206
socialism, 33, 69, 102, 112; architecture and, 20, 21, 37n20; collapse of, 201; failure of, 197; GDR citizens' distrust of, 143; role in economic and media globalization, 262; shortcomings of really existing socialism, 110–11; state-socialist mode of production, 229, 233; successes of, 5, 10n17
Socialist Bloc, 79, 201, 204; anti-imperialism and, 195; capitalist victory over, 207; Cuba and, 80, 82; dissolution of, 206; Hollywood filmmakers and, 230; satellite networks and, 268, 269, 270; solidarity with Third World, 196
Socialist Party of Cuba (PSP), 85, 89, 90
socialist realism: campaign against "formalism" and, 87; in cinema, 79, 81, 85, 86, 87, 89; in literature, 21, 25, 177, 189n69; in music, 45, 47; rejection of, 88, 91
Software Projects company, 120, 121, 125
Solanas, Fernando, 82
Solomon, Anthony, 270

Solzhenitsyn, Aleksandr, 90
South Africa, 177, 183
South America, 5
*Sovetskii ekran* [*Soviet screen*] (journal), 164–65, 170
Sovietization, 43, 48, 55, 82, 93
Soviet Union (USSR), 4, 46, 48, 118, 246; anniversary of October Revolution, 61, 62; APN (Novosti Press Agency), 66, 72n29; architecture in, 23, 28, 36n7, 36n14; collapse of, 205, 261; Czechoslovakia's relationship to, 53–54; Dergue in Ethiopia supported by, 203; geopolitical interests of, 93; literary exchange visits and, 178, 188nn15–16; literary relationships with Third World, 177; Polish socialist internationalist reportage and, 196; satellite networks and, 260–71; Soviet Writers' Congress (1934), 83; sphere of influence of, 3–4; State Committee for Television and Radio Broadcasting, 66; Television and Radio Committee, 62; Thaw period (mid-1950s), 87, 89; xenophobia and antisemitism in, 48. *See also* Finnish-Soviet relations
Soviet Union, cinema and: alternative distribution circuit for foreign films, 7, 158, 165–66; cinema in live translation, 163–66; coproductions with Italy, 240n1, 246–49 (see also *Life Is Beautiful*); film festivals in, 159; geopolitics of film markets, 251–52; Goskino, 246, 249, 251; live translation at European and Soviet film festivals, 160–71; Mosfilm, 247, 249, 253; Sovexport Film, 158, 165, 166, 232; Soviet Union as Hollywood production locale, 229. *See also* Cuba, Soviet cinema in
Spectrum computers, 117, 119–20, 123, 126
Speer, Albert, 26
spies, in Cold War media, 277–79; loss of agency and, 288–92; Socialist bloc television spies, 279–83; in twenty-first-century television, 283–88
Spittel, Christina, 177
*Spy, The* (Netflix television drama, 2019–), 278
*Spy Who Dumped Me, The* (film, dir. Fogel, 2018), 277, 283
Stalin, Joseph, 20–21, 23, 49; death of, 25, 30, 56n37; foreign films viewed by, 160; socialist internationalism and image of, 53; statues of, 25; translated speech in biopic film, 161, 162

INDEX    309

Stalinallee: National Reconstruction Program [*Die Stalinallee: Nationales Aufbauprogramm*] (Puhlmann, 1953), 17, 18, 20, 24, 30; bricks salvaged from ruined buildings, 22; building of the boulevard, 24; panoramic photography in, 21–22

Stalinallee [Stalin Boulevard] (East Berlin), 17, 20; critics of, 26, 36n15; design based on "linear city," 23; workers' uprising in (1953), 25, 26

Stalinism, 26, 45, 86, 91, 92; architectural order of, 30; cinema and, 81, 160; Cuban cinema's rejection of, 89; radio and, 43; socialist-realist jazz and, 49; urban reconstruction and, 6, 22, 26, 36n14, 37n26; xenophobia under, 46

Stalinstadt [later, Eisenhüttenstadt] (GDR), city of, 17

Stálinváros (Hungary), city of, 17

Stam, Robert, 158

Stanek, Łukasz, 4

Stangl, Paul, 20

Stanislavsky, Konstantin, 69

*Star Wars* (film, 1977), 129

Steinbeck, John, 178

Steiner, Reinhold, 266

Steinhart, Daniel, 239

Stepanova, Varvara, 22–23, 30, 36n16

Stevenson, Robert, 167

Stierlitz, Max Otto von (fictional character), 282–83

*Stitch in Time, A* (film, dir. Asher, 1963), 157

*Storm over Asia* [*Potomok Chingis-khana*] (film, dir. Pudovkin, 1928), 80

*Story of a Love Affair* [*Cronaca di un amore*] (film, dir. Antonioni, 1950), 168

*Story of a Young Marriage* [*Roman einer jungen Ehe*] (film, dir. Maetzig, 1952), 21

Straus, Roger W., 184

Streisand, Barbra, 237

*Strike* [*Stachka*] (film, dir. Eisenstein, 1925), 80

Strindberg, August, 67

*Styx* (Smith, computer game, 1983), 120

Sudek, Josef, 6, 22, 31–35, 38n40, 38nn42–43

*Sudeten Germanhood in Struggle and Crisis* [*Sudetendeutschtum in Kampf und Not: Ein Bildbericht*] (Frank, 1936), 29

Šuhajda, Karel, 130–31

Summers, Caroline, 186

*Sunflower* [*I girasoli / Podsolnukhi*] (film, fir. De Sica, 1970), 250, 256n16

Surikov, Aleksandr, 254

surrealism, 33, 287

surveillance technologies, 278, 288, 289–90, 292

Svilova, Elizaveta, 161

SVOD (subscription video on demand), 278, 291

Swank, Emory, 267

Sweden, 142

Sweeney, Alfred, 234, 235

Switzerland, 178

Szabó, István, 104, 105, 114n21

Szabó, István B., 105

Tanaka, Alessandro, 285

Tandy/Radioshack company, 119, 133, 135n10

Taras, Raymond, 204–5

Tarkovsky, Andrei, 169

Tarr, Béla, 6, 100, 113, 113n1; Mannheim Film Festival and, 103; outsider status of, 111

Tashkent Film Festival, 102, 159, 162–63, 166, 168, 169

Tashkov, Evgeniy, 68

Tatum, Channing, 284–85

Tchaikovsky, Pyotr, 48

Tejchma, Józef, 198–99

television, 3, 145; documentaries of Finnish-Soviet state visits, 7–8, 211–21; East-West diplomatic interactions framed by, 211; "era of scarcity," 65; Finnish TV listings as foreign policy, 63; in the GDR (East Germany), 141; internet and, 8; repertory theater and, 6, 65–66, 67–70; spy dramas, 277–78; transatlantic crossing as "holy grail," 263. *See also* satellite television/telephone networks

Telstar, 263

Tendriakov, Vladimir, 69

Teneishvili, Otar, 249, 251

terrorism, 246, 252–55, 257n31, 257n35

*Tessa* (film, dir. Polanski, 1979), 171

*That Sweet Word: Liberty!* [*Eto sladkoe slovo—svoboda!*] (film, dir. Žalakevičius, 1973), 162

theater, repertory, 6, 62, 63, 68, 70

Theron, Charlize, 284

Thiele, Martin, 134

Third World, 7, 102, 158, 177, 187n8, 206; as allegorical space, 200; decolonization in, 195; national liberation movements in, 193; political and economic failures of, 195; postcolonial governance in, 199

Thirdworldist movement, 78, 93, 197, 201
*30 Cases of Major Zeman, The* [*30 případů majora Zemana*] (Czechoslovak TV police drama, 1976–1980), 281–82, 285
*Three Steps on Earth* [*Trzy kroki po ziemi*] (film, dir. Hoffman and Skórzewski, 1965), 169
Tiananmen Square massacre (Beijing, 1989), 25
Tiidus, Hardi, 1
*Time of Indifference* [*Gli indifferenti*] (film, dir. Maselli, 1964), 157
*Tinker Tailor Soldier Spy* (film, dir. Alfredson, 2011), 277
Tito, Josip Broz, 102, 229
*Tom and Jerry* animated cartoon series (1961–1962), 231
Tomoff, Kiril, 48
totalitarianism, 43, 55, 55n2, 206, 207
"transediting" (combined work of translation and editing), 194, 207n3
*Trial, The* (Kafka), 290
Tricontinental Congress (1966), 78, 208n10
Tricontinentalism, 196
Tulloch, John, 65
Turski, Marian, 195
Twentieth Century-Fox film studio, 240n1

UK (United Kingdom), 119, 120, 124–26, 183, 188n25, 291
Ukrainian Soviet Socialist Republic, 157
Ulbricht, Walter, 181
Ultrafax (Sarnoff, 1948), 262–63
*Unbelievable Adventures of Italians in Russia* [*Una matta, matta, matta corsa in Russia / Neveroiatnye prikliucheniia ital'iantsev v Rossii*] (film, dir. Riazanov, 1974), 250
UNEAC (Cuban Union of Writers), 88, 89, 92
United Artists, 227, 234–35, 237
United Nations (UN), 3, 265, 266, 273n32
United States, 54, 119, 203; Christa Wolf's visit to, 179–87; civil rights in, 46, 195; diplomatic recognition of GDR and, 179; GDR literature and, 176, 183–86, 187n7, 190n77; international film festivals and, 161–62; New Left, 183; racial division in, 181; satellite networks and, 260–71; US films screened in Cuba, 79; US musical idiom on Czechoslovak Radio, 45; Vietnam War and, 182, 223n36, 263
UNITEL (global microwave TV network, early 1950s), 262–63
Universal Pictures, 236–37, 240n1

Updike, John, 202
Uruguay, film criticism in, 84, 95n29

Vakhtangov, Yevgeny, 69
Valdés-Rodríguez, José Manuel, 83–85
Vampilov, Aleksandr, 68
Varga, Balázs, 104
Vasiliev, Boris, 69
Vasiliev, Georgy, 86, 161
Vasiliev, Sergei, 86, 161
Vaughn, Robert, 235
VBG Software, 131
Venice Film Festival, 160–62, 167, 168
Vepkhvadze, Giovanni, 163
*Verda Stacio* [*The Green Station*] (Kožíc and Bezdíček, radio program, 1933–1940), 54
Vertov, Dziga, 81
*Very Secret Service, A* (Arte/Netflix television spy drama, 2015–2018), 278, 284
VGIK [All-Union State Film School] (USSR), 164, 167
video translation, pirate, 170
Vienna, socialist government in (1918–1934), 28, 37n26
Vietnam, 82
Vietnam War, 182, 195, 223n36, 263
*View of the Yellow River* [*Widok Żółtej Rzeki*] (Zalewski, 1960), 196
Ville Radieuse (Le Corbusier), 28
*Viridiana* (film, dir. Buñuel, 1961), 90
Visconti, Luchino, 164, 165
*Visit from a Friend* [*Tasavallassa tapahtuu: Ystävä kylässä*] (Finnish state-visit documentary, 1977), 212, 216–20
Vlach, Karel, 49, 50
Vláčil, František, 86–87
Voice of America radio, 50, 141
"Volume and Line: Notes on Panoramic Shooting" (Svidel, 1934), 38n34
*Vow, The* [*Kliatva*] (film, dir. Chiaureli, 1946), 161

Wajda, Andrzej, 89
Warner Bros., 237
Warsaw, city of: Marszałkowska Street, 28; Second World Peace Conference (1950), 46
*Waterloo* (film, dir. Bondarchuk, 1970), 240n1, 249–50
Watkins, Carleton, 27
Weimar Republic (Germany): Alexanderplatz as business and traffic hub during, 29; social housing in, 28

Weisberg, Joe, 286
Weiss, Jiří, 231
Weiss, Peter, 180
Welles, Orson, 86
*What Remains* [*Was bleibt*] (Wolf novella, 1990), 187n3
*What UKK Saw in the Soviet Union* [*Mitä UKK näki Neuvostoliitossa?*] (Finnish state-visit documentary, 1977), 212, 213–16, 220, 222n7
White, Anne, 109–10
*White Dove, The* [*Bílá holubice*] (film, dir. Vláčil, 1960), 86–87
Wierzbicki, Piotr, 204
*Willy Walker* (Šuhajda, computer game), 130–31
Wolf, Christa, 7, *180*, 186–87; mixed feelings toward the United States, 181–82; Oberlin visit (1974), 176–77, 179–83, 189n38; reception in the United States, 183–86, 190n77; recognition in English-speaking world, 176; relationship to GDR state, 182–83, 187n3
Wolf, Gerhard, 179, *180*
Wolff, Helen, 201
Wolff, Kurt, 201
Wolper, David, 229, 234, 235–36, 238–39
Wood, James, 141
World War I, 31, 277
World War II, 20, 21, 29, 215; *The Bridge at Remagen* (film) and, 234; Finland and, 69; Finnish-Soviet relations and, 215, 217; shortages associated with, 3; *Slaughterhouse-Five* (film) and, 236–37; Soviet documentary film of, 161

Yalta Conference (1945), 4
*Yentl* (film, dir. Streisand, 1983), 237
Yerevan (Armenia), Lenin Square in, 30
*Yesterday, Today, and Tomorrow* (film, dir. De Sica, 1963), 165
YLE [Yleisradio] (Finnish Broadcasting Company), 8, 61, 62, 63, 70, 221n1; critics of, 220; Drama Department, 66; journalists of, 212; political diversity on editorial staff of, 216; Program Council and, 64; state visits televised by, 211, 213, 221; Swedish-language broadcasting, 66; Television Theater, 66
Yugoslavia, 102, 208n10, 232; American/Western films shot in, 229, 230, 233, 240n1; film festivals in, 170
Yurchak, Alexei, 122
Yurenev, Rostislav, 162
Yutkevich, Sergei, 79

Zagorsky, A. V., 165–66
Zakhoder, Boris, 178
Žalakevičius, Vytautas, 162
Zalán, Vince, 104, 106, 112
Zalewski, Witold, 196
Zanussi, Krzysztof, 104
Zarecor, Kimberly Elman, 27–28, 47, 48
Zeman, Major Jan (fictional character), 281–83, 285
*Ze země polek* (*From the Land of Polkas*), 51
Zhdanov, Andrei, 47, 56n30
*Zhdanovshchina*, 47, 48, 56n37
Zíb, Antonín, 44, 46, 56n12
Ziemny, Aleksander, 196
Zipser, Richard, 182–83, 188n32, 189n63
ZX Spectrum computer, 117, 119, 127

www.ingramcontent.com/pod-product-compliance
Lightning Source LLC
Chambersburg PA
CBHW031901220426
43663CB00006B/715